D1539068

Neighborhood and Community Environments

Human Behavior and Environment

ADVANCES IN THEORY AND RESEARCH

Neighborhood and Community Environments

EDITED BY

IRWIN ALTMAN
University of Utah
Salt Lake City, Utah

AND

ABRAHAM WANDERSMAN
University of South Carolina
Columbia, South Carolina

PLENUM PRESS • NEW YORK AND LONDON

Library of Congress Cataloging in Publication Data

Neighborhood and community environments.

(Human behavior and environment: advances in theory and research; v. 9)
Includes bibliographical references and index.
1. Community. 2. Community development—Citizen participation. 3.
Neighborhood. 4. Human ecology. I. Altman, Irwin. II. Wandersman, Abraham. III.
Series: Human behavior and environment; v. 9.
HT65.N44   1987   307.3'362   87-11276
ISBN 0-306-42513-0

© 1987 Plenum Press, New York
A Division of Plenum Publishing Corporation
233 Spring Street, New York, N.Y. 10013

Printed in the United States of America

Contributors

DAVID BARTELT • Institute for Public Policy Studies, Temple University, Philadelphia, Pennsylvania

JACK BURGERS • Department of Sociology, Tilburg University, Tilburg, The Netherlands

ARZA CHURCHMAN • Faculty of Architecture and Town Planning, Technion—Israel Institute of Technology, Haifa, Israel

MICHAEL R. EDELSTEIN • School of Social Science and Human Services, Ramapo College of New Jersey, Mahwah, New Jersey

DAVID ELESH • Institute for Public Policy Studies, Temple University, Philadelphia, Pennsylvania

DAVID R. GOLDFIELD • Department of History, The University of North Carolina at Charlotte, Charlotte, North Carolina

IRA GOLDSTEIN • Institute for Public Policy Studies, Temple University, Philadelphia, Pennsylvania

ALBERT HUNTER • Department of Sociology, Northwestern University, Evanston, Illinois

GEORGE LEON • Institute for Public Policy Studies, Temple University, Philadelphia, Pennsylvania

SALLY ENGLE MERRY • Department of Anthropology, Wellesley College, Wellesley, Massachusetts

LEANNE G. RIVLIN • Environmental Psychology, City University of New York Graduate School, New York, New York

WILLEM VAN VLIET-- • Pennsylvania State University, University Park, Pennsylvania

ABRAHAM WANDERSMAN • Department of Psychology, University of South Carolina, Columbia, South Carolina

WILLIAM YANCEY • Institute for Public Policy Studies, Temple University, Philadelphia, Pennsylvania

Preface

This ninth volume in the series deals with a fascinating and complex topic in the environment and behavior field. Neighborhoods and communities are in various stages of formation and transition in almost every society, nation, and culture. A variety of political, economic, and social factors have resulted in the formation of new communities and the transformation of older communities. Thus we see nomadic people settling into stable communities, new towns sprouting up around the world, continuing suburban sprawl, simultaneous deterioration, renewal and gentrification of urban areas, demographic changes in communities, and so on.

As in previous volumes, the range of content, theory, and methods represented in the various chapters is intended to be broadly based, with perspectives rooted in several disciplines—anthropology, history, psychology, sociology, urban studies. Although many other disciplines also play an important role in the study and understanding of neighborhoods and community environments, we hope that the contributions to this volume will at least present readers with a broad sampling—if not a comprehensive treatment—of the topic.

The previous volume in the series, Volume 8, *Home Environments*, and the present volume may be treated as a set. The chapters in the volume on home environments frequently examined residences in relation to the neighborhoods and communities within which they are embedded; it is, in many cases, almost impossible to do otherwise. In the same way, an understanding of neighborhoods and communities frequently requires consideration of the homes and residences in them. As a result, readers may find it useful to treat *Home Environments* and the present volume *Neighborhood and Community Environments* as an integrated pair.

Volume 10 in the series, *Public Places and Spaces,* now in preparation, will complement the volumes focusing on homes, neighborhoods, and communities, yielding a trio of volumes on closely related topics. Ervin H. Zube of the University of Arizona will join me in editing this next volume in the Human Behavior and Environment series.

IRWIN ALTMAN

Contents

CHAPTER 3

COMMUNITY DYNAMICS IN COPING WITH TOXIC
CONTAMINANTS

MICHAEL R. EDELSTEIN
ABRAHAM WANDERSMAN

CHAPTER 4

CAN RESIDENT PARTICIPATION IN NEIGHBORHOOD
REHABILITATION PROGRAMS SUCCEED? ISRAEL'S PROJECT
RENEWAL THROUGH A COMPARATIVE PERSPECTIVE

ARZA CHURCHMAN

CHAPTER 5

ISLANDS IN THE STREAM: NEIGHBORHOODS AND THE POLITICAL ECONOMY OF THE CITY

DAVID BARTELT, DAVID ELESH, IRA GOLDSTEIN, GEORGE LEON, WILLIAM YANCEY

CHAPTER 6

THE SYMBOLIC ECOLOGY OF SUBURBIA

ALBERT HUNTER

CHAPTER 7

NEIGHBORHOOD PRESERVATION AND COMMUNITY VALUES IN
HISTORICAL PERSPECTIVE

DAVID R. GOLDFIELD

CHAPTER 8

COMMUNITIES IN TRANSITION: FROM THE INDUSTRIAL TO THE POSTINDUSTRIAL ERA

WILLEM VAN VLIET--
JACK BURGERS

Introduction

The term *community* is widely used in the social sciences. Yet there is a certain ambiguity associated with its usage because its several meanings are not always precisely differentiated. There are two major ways for describing community—as a geographical place, for example, neighborhoods, and as a set of relationships and resources, for example, social networks (see Heller, Price, Reinharz, Riger, & Wandersman, 1984). In addition, there is some controversy and debate about the importance or lack of importance of the geographical neighborhood; that is, the idea of community as place (Wandersman & Unger, 1985). Some writers believe that the significance of neighborhoods as geographical settings is lessening, as people develop extensive social networks in the wider community beyond the neighborhood. Because technology, communication, transportation, and life-styles have made the city "smaller," neighborhoods may be losing some of the importance they once had (Wellman & Leighton, 1979). Relatives, friends, work settings, and voluntary associations are often located outside one's immediate geographical neighborhood. In summarizing this idea, Keller stated: "There may be a shift from a neighboring of *place* to a neighboring of *taste*" (Keller, 1968, p. 61).

In spite of data and theory supporting the conception of community as extending beyond a geographical locale, Unger & Wandersman (1985) concluded from a review of the literature that neighbors and neighborhoods still have a very important place in many people's lives. The close spatial location of neighbors enables them to perform functions that more distant network members might find difficult to accomplish, such as watching one anothers' homes for intruders, helping with a snowbound car, watching children in an emergency, and providing other forms of support. Immediately proximal neighbors also often serve as support systems by providing emotional and material aid. In addition, they may foster a sense of identification and be a buffer from the feelings of isolation often associated with large-scale urban and suburban communities. Neighbors may also join together to improve the quality of a neighborhood and its services. For example, in a large-scale survey, Fried (1984) found that community satisfaction was an important influence on general life satisfaction for people from many socioeconomic levels. In fact, local residential satisfaction was the second highest predictor of life satisfaction and was second in importance only to marital satisfaction. For purposes of this volume, therefore, the concepts of *neighborhood* and *community* as geographical places *and* as sets of social relationships and resources are theoretically valid and practically useful.

The immediately preceding volume in the series (Volume 8) focused on home and residential environments. A number of chapters in that volume recognized that the home is not always separable from the neighborhood and the community within which it is embedded. Indeed, there are several levels of analysis of homes and neighborhoods and communities. Warren (1981) stated:

> The micro-neighborhood is operationally defined as the next-door neighborhood, the person in the next apartment, or the most immediate set of adjacent households. It is defined when a mother yells out the window to young people playing in the street, "go play in your own neighborhood." That notion in turn leads us quickly into the notion of the residential block. Beyond the residential block beings the walking-distance neighborhood. The administrative definition of a walking-distance neighborhood is usually the elementary school district. In our own research on neighborhoods, the elementary school district has been utilized because it is a compromise between the notions of the very small micro-neighborhood and larger definitions such as "the west side," "the black community," "my part of town," and so forth. (p. 63)

The contributors to the present volume offer a broad range of topics, themes and perspectives on communities and neighborhoods.

First, the backgrounds and approaches of our contributors reflect a strong interdisciplinary interest in neighborhoods and communities. Thus Merry is an anthropologist, Goldfield is a historian, Churchman has a background in planning and environmental psychology, Rivlin is an environmental psychologist, Edelstein and Wandersman are environmental and community psychologists, and Bartelt and his colleagues, Hunter, Van Vliet--, and Burgers are sociologists.

Second, several chapters emphasize the idea of change in communities and neighborhoods. Thus Goldfield (Chapter 7) adopts a historical perspective to describe neighborhood preservation and community values in the 20th century. Many of the movements in city life discussed by

Goldfield play a role in other chapters: City Beautiful, community center, modern city (technology), regional and urban renewal, resident participation, historic preservation, and the like. And, Van Vliet-- and Burgers (Chapter 8) use a cross-cultural perspective to trace the transition of communities from the industrial to the postindustrial era (18th century to the present). They provide a broad conceptual framework to study changes in community functioning in relation to economic, social, cultural, and political factors, and consequences of changes for the spatial qualities of communities. In Chapter 5, Bartelt and his associates also consider the transition of communities and cities from industrial to postindustrial stages. They compare classical ecology, historical ecology, and political economy approaches to understanding community change. In particular, they emphasize the importance of a political economy perspective and treat neighborhoods as islands in the stream of political and economic forces. Their approach is an important contrast to much of the literature on neighborhoods and communities, which typically emphasizes social and physical characteristics of neighborhoods, for example, demographics, neighborhood planning, neighborhood organizations, type of housing, and the like. Within this milieu of economics and ecology, Hunter (Chapter 6) proposes a symbolic ecology perspective to examine suburban and regional development. This approach adds social and symbolic ecology to a political and economic perspective and provides interesting insights into regional development and identity.

Third, a number of chapters examine the role of neighborhood and community members in social change, particularly in relation to emergent and organized citizen participation. For example, Churchman (Chapter 4) emphasizes the proactive role that neighbors can take in revitalizing neighborhoods through citizen participation and citizen partnerships with government. Churchman first proposes a comprehensive framework of resident participation and neighborhood rehabilitation. She then describes results from Israel's Project Renewal program, in the context of results from other countries, and explores the benefits and costs of citizen participation in neighborhood renewal. Other chapters also examine the role of citizen participation in neighborhood change, including Goldfield (Chapter 7) and Edelstein and Wandersman (Chapter 3). Edelstein and Wandersman use a framework of citizen participation in community organizations to explore how residents join forces to cope with an environmental stressor—toxic wastes. On the other side of the coin, several chapters examine the role of large-scale social, political, and economic forces in community change. For example, Van Vliet-- and Burgers (Chapter 8) and Bartelt and his associates (Chapter 5) adopt a broad historical view of community and change and describe how community and neighborhood residents react to changes imposed by external social forces.

A fourth set of issues concerns affiliation and bonding of community members with one another and the conflict, disruption and disharmony that often arise in communities and neighborhoods. For example, Rivlin (Chapter 1) examines personal identity and group affiliation in neighborhoods. She contrasts people's relationships to settings, that is, place attachment, in two very different groups—the homeless and a Hasidic community in Crown Heights, Brooklyn. The chapter provides a comprehensive description of how and why neighborhoods provide important sources of social support. However, interpersonal conflicts are also prevalent in communities. Merry (Chapter 2) uses a neighborhood regulation perspective to examine everyday conflict between neighbors. Much of the literature on neighbor relationships emphasizes positive features of helping, cohesion, and sense of community, whereas relatively little literature focuses on conflict. Merry describes the spatial and social reasons for conflict and its resolution in four neighborhoods in relation to privacy, proximity, and informal and formal means for regulating conflict. In Chapter 3, Edelstein and Wandersman examine a different type of conflict in neighborhood life—that between the neighborhood or community and outside business and government agents. Their analysis of neighborhood conflict and organization is in the context of attempts by communities to cope with toxic contaminants that threaten the viability of communities and their neighborhoods.

The chapters in this volume are ordered roughly in terms of the size or scale of treatment of neighborhoods and communities. The first two chapters illustrate the microscale or interpersonal level of neighborhoods and communities. Thus Rivlin examines personal identity and group affiliation in neighborhoods, and Merry explores conflict between neighbors in several communities.

At a somewhat larger scale, Chapters 3 and 4 discuss the role of neighborhood organizations in community development and change. Edelstein and Wandersman provide a framework for examining the response of communities to the presence of hazardous wastes in the environment. Churchman provides a framework and results on the role of government-mandated neighborhood organizations in community rehabilitation.

Chapters 5 and 6 address larger community units, including the ecology of the city and region in relation to smaller scale communities and neighborhoods. Bartelt and his associates provide a perspective for understanding neighborhood change in relation to the ecology and political economy of the city. Hunter views urban and suburban development through a symbolic ecology perspective.

The last two chapters offer broad-ranging historical perspectives on neighborhood and community development. Goldfield examines changes in neighborhood and city life in the 20th century, and Van Vliet-- and Burgers trace changes in community life from the 18th century to the present.

Each chapter provides insights into the daily lives of people in a variety of communities and neighborhoods and analyzes the visible and not-so-visible forces that have shaped communities. And, importantly, the perspectives, theories, and empirical results presented in the chapters of this volume may not only help us understand neighborhoods and communities but may assist in anticipating and coping in a productive way with the inevitable changes that are likely to occur in these settings. The potential for citizen participation, in particular, offers hope that residents can be more than passive responders and reactors to external influences. Instead, neighborhoods and communities can be proactively changed to become places where people want to live and where they can prosper physically, psychologically, and socially. In many respects, the quality of life in neighborhoods and communities is and can be heavily influenced by how residents relate to one another as neighbors, how they deal with the larger society of which they are part, and how they care for the physical environment.

The editors express their appreciation to the authors for their fine contributions to this volume. We also thank Richard Rich and Ralph Taylor for their comments on several chapters in the volume.

IRWIN ALTMAN
ABRAHAM WANDERSMAN

REFERENCES

Fried, M. (1984). The structure and significance of community satisfaction. *Population and Environment, 7,* 61–86.

Heller, K., Price, R. H., Reinharz, S., Riger, S., & Wandersman, A. (Eds.). (1984). *Psychology and community change: Challenges of the future* (2nd ed.). Homewood, IL: Dorsey Press.

Keller, S. (1968). *The urban neighborhood: A sociological perspective.* New York: Random House.

Unger, D. G., & Wandersman, A. (1985). The importance of neighboring: The social, cognitive and affective aspects of neighboring. *American Journal of Community Psychology*, *13*, 139–169.

Warren, D. I. (1981). *Helping networks: How people cope with problems in the urban community.* Notre Dame, IN: University of Notre Dame Press.

Wellman, B., & Leighton, B. (1979). Networks, neighborhoods and communities: Approaches to the study of the community question. *Urban Affairs Quarterly, 14*, 363–390.

1

The Neighborhood, Personal Identity, and Group Affiliations

LEANNE G. RIVLIN

THE NATURE OF COMMUNAL LIFE

People have lived in communities since prehistoric times. Whether in caves or clustered settlements, congregate shelter has had the same survival qualities found in the flocks, prides, schools, gaggles, and herds of animal species. The survival functions of communities in contemporary times is much more complex than in the past and in many ways is less well understood. This chapter deals with affiliations with others and the role they play in neighborhood life. It will consider the variety of neighborhood types and their functions from a perspective that includes the physical surroundings, individual development, and social group identity. By looking at the lives of two kinds of people that depart from conventional life-styles, neighboring will be examined in light of the profound social and cultural diversity that marks the fabric of the urban experience.

LEANNE G. RIVLIN • Environmental Psychology, City University of New York Graduate School, 33 West 42nd Street, New York, NY 10036-8099.

Neighborhood and Community Concepts

In the wake of the soccer riot in Belgium, a newspaper article quoted a sociologist who had been studying this phenomenon (Thomas, 1985). Eric Dunning of the University of Leicester found that the British soccer (or football) fans are largely drawn from "the rough sections of the working class." Dunning and his colleagues suggest that fighting gives them status, excitement, and meaning.

> It goes hand in hand with close identification with the local community. They fight on behalf of their community against other comparable communities. There is a sense of ownership of the territory even though it's temporary. The Liverpool fans found Juventus fans in what they felt was their territory. (Thomas, 1985, p. 10)

This story reflects one kind of community, the community of like interests and localism, and the extremes to which affiliation may lead group members. There are many other needs served by communities and neighborhoods, and a discussion of their purposes is an essential starting point.

The focus in this chapter is on neighborhoods—one context for community life. The criterion for a neighborhood is the acknowledgment by residents, merchants, and regular users of an area that a locality exists. It presumes some agreement on boundaries and a name and the recognition of distinguishing characteristics of the setting. The naming of a neighborhood has been identified as a signifier of attachment to place (Taylor, Gottfredson, & Brower, 1984), an issue that we will address later. This broadly based conception centers on the views of users although other definitions may exist. Planners may attach neighborhood names to areas, but unless there is evidence of acknowledgment by the local residents, the labels may be of limited use. This does not mean that all locals will agree on boundaries or names. In fact, as this chapter will illustrate, neighborhood identification can vary with group affiliation. However, the recognition by people of a bounded territory as having an integrity and a personal meaning is, in my view, the necessary requirement of a neighborhood. A neighborhood is more than a name applied by outsiders. When a name is used by those living or working within the area, it contributes to the area's identity and becomes a referent for what might be a collection of shops and houses.

The Ecology of Contemporary Neighborhoods

Neighborhoods today serve many of the functions of communal groupings in the past, although they do not necessarily house closely knit communal groups. Although the Stone Age family depended on others around them for survival—hunting large animals had to be a shared task—this level of explicit group cooperation rarely is found today. However, in many neighborhoods, especially poor ones, reliance on neighbors may be essential in times of need, which for some is a daily demand. One might argue that the urban homesteading and "sweat equity" renovation of deteriorated buildings approaches the levels seen in the past because the enormous investment of time and effort depends on the consistent cooperation of others.

For the most part, the resources of contemporary neighborhoods are limited to providing shelter and essential commodities for residents. Although shopping patterns have been changing in the direction of centralized malls and markets and although increasing numbers of people must travel to shop, in many areas the home neighborhood still provides residents with the most essential goods, especially nurturing ones—milk, eggs, bread. This combination of shelter and shopping endows a neighborhood with life-sustaining functions and in the process lays down patterns of social activity that become important parts of people's lives. Even the casual purchase of a carton of milk or a daily newspaper, when it becomes habitual, sets in motion a series of personal contacts that connect people to a place and its occupants. We know the importance of these contacts when they are threatened, for example, when gentrification of a neighborhood forces the owner of a local grocery store or a shoemaker to vacate a shop he or she long has operated. The uproar from residents and the sense of loss, even for people who neighbor in limited ways, is testimony to the significance of these places.

When we speak of contemporary neighborhoods, we are talking about a very heterogeneous unit based on the nature of the geography, the numbers and kinds of people there, the socioeconomic status of these people, their ages, cultural background, and housing form. There also may be internal social qualities that differentiate neighborhoods.

Warren (1971, 1978) has analyzed the social organization of residents and has extracted three dimensions that characterize neighborhoods: interaction, identity, and connections. Warren described six patterns of neighborhoods based on the varying degrees of the three dimensions. The *integral* neighborhood is an area with high levels of face-to-face contacts with norms and values supportive of the larger community. This is a cohesive, high-membership area of block associations and participation in local groups as well as in organizations outside the neighborhood. Warren sees this kind of neighborhood as both "cosmopolitan" and a "local center" (Warren, 1978, p. 316).

The *parochial* neighborhood is high in interaction but low in connections to the larger community. It is protective of its own values and, in Warren's terms, "filters out" values that conflict with its own.

The *diffuse* neighborhood lacks informal social participation and although formal local organizations exist, the leadership, which is indigenous, does not represent the values of local residents.

The *stepping-stone* neighborhood is one made up of residents with little commitment to the area and with strong connections outside. The interaction within is of a formal kind, but residents are attracted more to outside groups than to local ones.

The *transitory* neighborhood is low in interaction, participation, and identity. This is an area of high population turnover providing a typical model for "urban anonymity."

The *anomic* neighborhood lacks participation and identification either with the local community or the larger one. It is seen as "a completely disorganized and atomized residential area" (Warren. 1971, p. 878).

Warren's formulation underlines the variety that can be found in neighborhood types and the subtle interplay of internal and external connections that characterize neighborhood life. However, the typology is lacking in two major respects. First, it does not consider the specific environmental qualities of settings and the ways they affect people's relationships to each other and their neighborhoods. In addition, it does not stress sufficiently the consequences of diversity and leaves the impression that neighborhoods are largely culturally and socially homogeneous, with the possible exception of the transitory one. In fact, several of the neighborhood types can coexist within one neighborhood in the complex ecology of urban life, and in many communities these areas may contain culturally and socially diverse populations, including marginal groups.

At the core, we are dealing with the dual phenomena of neighborhood and neighbors, based, in whatever time in history, on a social foundation, on the interchanges across individuals and groups that constitute the commerce of neighborhood life. Although most definitions of neighbors are based on proximity "the people who live next door, the people who live on the block" (Heller, Price, Reinharz, Riger, & Wandersman, 1984, p. 133), it is possible to consider neighbors as more than residents of a defined locale. They also can include regular participants in the interchange of neighborhood life, people who may reside outside the borders but are central to the functioning and the familiar image of the area. They are the mail deliverers, shopkeepers, service providers such as police, and assortments of people who "hang out" in an area, even the homeless. The regularity of their presence and their roles in local life give them places and status within an area. In turn, they help to define the neighborhood's borders by their presence and their participation in the routine of neighborhood activity and interchange with local residents. This interchange will be flavored by the distance between neighbors, the availability of essential foods and services, and the degree to which individual paths cross in the process of acquiring these essential elements of life. Celebration and relaxation also can lay down a series of social contacts important to the residents. Again, the pattern of local and distant contacts may vary for different individuals, families, and cultural groups.

For some, the area of residence covers all aspects of life—shopping, nurturing of children, acquisition of social services, recreation, celebration of holidays and events, recuperation from illness and tragedy. But this is not the most prevalent experience in neighborhoods today. For many, the neighborhood seems a traditional, old-fashioned image that has vanished along with the trolley car and the organ grinder. Today we think of few local contacts, the "community of limited liability" that Janowitz (1967) has described, the loose connections of people to their neighborhoods (see, for example, Webber, 1963). It would be useful to examine these changes in light of the realities of modern urban life and question the stereotypes of neighborhoods that exist.

One of the stereotypes that has been challenged is the idea of an all-encompassing, nurturing neighborhood that sustains people over their lives. Goering and Rogowsky (1978) have characterized as myth much of the view that neighborhoods are "natural sources" of security, stability, and orientation.

> There have indeed been very few neighborhoods that were anything more than temporary staging grounds for the upward and outward mobility of their residents and there has, in fact, never been a neighborhood that has kept all, or even most, of its population for more than a few years. (pp. 83, 89)

Out-migration has become a familiar pattern of life with displacement and turnover commonplace.

Even for those remaining, the degree of neighboring varies across people and area. Residents of a high-rise building in a large metropolitan area were quite satisfied with limited contacts with neighbors, not because of any hostility, but because of time and work constraints (Degnore, Feldman, Hilton, Love, & Schearer, 1980). Fava (1958) has contrasted neighboring in suburban and urban areas and found that not only is neighboring (based on a neighboring scale) greater in suburban areas than in urban ones, but it increases as the distance from the city center increases. McGahan's (1972) research on urban neighboring found that "not all residents of an area are equally accessible to the structure of opportunities of neighboring" (p. 407). Contrary to the findings of others, McGahan identified more neighboring among single tenants (most of them widowed or divorced) than among married tenants. There is a danger in overgeneralizing concerning neighborhood life and failing to recognize the tremendous heterogeneity that is observable when one looks beneath the surface. Local areas do not serve people in identical ways, and research has documented many of these differing patterns (Rivlin, 1982; Warren, 1971, 1978).

Changes in family structure and residential patterns have altered the functions of local areas. First, the extended family no longer is the rule, except in the most traditional societies. In urban areas the nuclear family is almost a given. In addition, increasing numbers of people are living alone (Horwitz & Tognoli, 1982), and many of these are older people (Riche, 1986). Members of families are spatially dispersed, although some adults are involved in regular caretaking of elderly parents. In a large corporation, a recent survey of employees found 28% of them offering regular help to relatives, 77% of these people at least three times a week (Collins, 1986, January 6). This caretaking may involve travel across considerable distances as adults provide essential services for their families, preparing meals and taking care of financial and household chores.

With the extension of the life cycle and increasing numbers of elderly persons, especially those over 80, the most fragile both physically and economically, the multigenerational household may become more common. There also is evidence of the return of adult children to the family fold, a reaction to unemployment, shortage of low-cost housing, and other economic pressures. In other cases, young children may share their week with two parents, in two different homes. These examples are not the traditional extended family but represent responses to changing conditions and crises that have led to increases in household size or family responsibilities, nonetheless. It is not possible to determine, as yet, how prevalent these patterns are or what demands they make of neighborhoods, but they offer new demographic profiles, at the very least.

Other neighborhood changes have come from the mobility evident in society, especially in Western society. On one level, the automobile has extended horizons for people beyond their immediate areas, providing a wide range for shopping, visiting, and recreation. This 20th-century phenomenon has altered the landscape, connecting remote areas and introducing a new kind of centralized shopping setting—the mall.

A stimulus to recreational shopping, the mall contrasts sharply with the open markets of the past or neighborhood-based stores. It lacks the opportunities for casual social contacts possible in local areas, although it has provided a social gathering place, especially for teenagers. Robert Sommer (1981) has criticized another form of centralized shopping, the use of supermarkets, contrasting them with the more sociable farmer's market that is reappearing in many areas.

The automobile has moved people into domains unavailable in the past. With the development of suburbs and satellite towns, family members move in different directions, no longer held together by the economic imperatives or localism of the past. There is much evidence of this mobility and a valuing of it.

It frequently is cited that in the United States people move on the average of every 5 years. Homeownership changes, on the average, every 7 years (Goering & Rogowsky, 1978). Neither the ancestral home nor the "old neighborhood" is a permanent feature of a person's life. In many cases, the move is voluntary, the result of new job possibilities or improved housing, and signals upward mobility although not necessarily without stress (Rossi, 1981). Toffler (1970) has described a new nomadic class that includes "corporate gypsies," high-level executives on the move to increasingly more powerful positions. For others, residential mobility is a response to stress (Shumaker & Stokols, 1982) and may be a source of considerable grief (Fried, 1963). In many areas, urban renewal projects uprooted people from familiar neighborhoods that were viewed as slums by urban planners and city officials, destroying social ties that had sustained peoples' lives. We have examples ranging from the West End of Boston (Fried, 1963) to the East End of London (Young & Willmott, 1957).

Families have been dispersed for many centuries, certainly from Classical times to the colonial and immigration years in the United States. However, the fluidity today has particular values embedded within it making some forms respectable and envied, other forms pitied or despised. The British writer, Kenneth Allsop, has examined this ambivalence toward mobility in his study of hoboes:

> Mobility is unarguably an indispensible component in an economy of the American character and in a nation of America's size, and so is justifiably prized and commended. But the idea itself has come to be qualified by a cluster of subordinate clauses. Mobility with money is, of course, laudable and desirable—you are then a tourist or an envoy of business. Mobility between firms and cities is proof of a professional man's initiative and ambition. Mobility is also proof of a workless working man's grit, of his determination to hunt down the breach in the wall and find readmission to the commonwealth. (Allsop, 1967, p. 436)

Other forms of mobility are neither appreciated nor tolerated and sometimes are viewed as threats to the American system—the mobility of hoboes or migrants or the homeless. Both voluntary and involuntary mobility as well as the "acceptable" and "unacceptable" forms have altered the national landscape and family and neighborhood structures. It would be useful to examine their impacts in some detail.

THE STRUCTURE OF CONTEMPORARY LIFE

The nature of contemporary life has been the subject of discussions by philosophers, historians, social scientists and planners, and probably most of all, by concerned people of all kinds. With the changes in family structure and increasing urbanism and suburbanism, new forms and new opportunities have appeared. When we examine life today we find a broadened range of movement. The local area no longer is the focus, for most people, as they move across expanses to work, seek entertainment, visit families, shop, and obtain needed services. It is commonplace for social contacts to extend beyond the neighborhood. However, it is interesting to note that with all these changes, the neighborhood remains a model for urban planning, forming the basis for new towns, both in the United States and abroad (Banerjee & Baer, 1984; Keller, 1968).

One generalization frequently made is that contemporary life has turned inward, inside the home, with families in neighborhoods less dependent upon each other for social contacts and entertainment. At the same time life is turned outward, moved by media and public and private transportation to geographies that reach far beyond the neighborhood boundaries. This interesting duality of inward and outward propulsion describes much of the middle-class life-style today.

In his book, *The Fall of Public Man,* Richard Sennett (1978) analyzed the social, political, and economic basis of the "end of public culture," the progression toward an "intimate society," and the increasing privatization of life. This privatization can be seen in many spheres from the tremendous amount of time people are focused on television inside their homes, to the proliferation of home computers among a group that can afford them, creating a domestic source of work interest and entertainment that may make direct contacts with the outside unnecessary. It could be argued that computers have the potential for electronic contacts of a widely ranging sort from those engaged in homework, teenagers dipping into unknown realms, to the acquisition of various services such as banking, purchasing, and paying bills. The potential of computers to reshape family and work relationships seems inevitable, but we must recognize that they now are largely restricted to middle and upper economic classes. Whether they will affect community and neighborhood life is a matter for speculation and future research. However, if electronic contacts ultimately replace many human ones, if shopping that was removed one level from human contact by supermarkets and the telephone now eliminates voice contacts, if computer games replace neighborhood-based activities for children drawing them inward, one can project major alterations in people's relationships to the area around their homes.

THE ROLE OF NEIGHBORHOODS IN PEOPLE'S LIVES

An understanding of the role that the local area plays in people's lives requires a developmental perspective that examines the impact of place over the life cycle. This includes reflecting on the meaning of attachments both to people and to setting.

Place and Development

In books on human development, it is commonplace to find a discussion of the impacts of various persons on an individual's life and personality, the role of parents, siblings, friends, and others. Only recently have the contexts of those relationships been given serious consideration (see, for example, Rivlin & Wolfe, 1985). Yet every relationship is inextricably a component of a complex environmental system in which the human process and the setting define the meaning of the experience to the person. Parenting in a middle class home or in a shelter for the homeless reflects both place and persons, providing very different experiences for the children and adults involved. On the most superficial level, these two settings communicate contrasting messages to those within, messages about their worthiness, their place in the world, their ability to control their present and their future. They also contain different resources and services enabling occupants to play very different kinds of roles with different degrees of power.

Thus physical settings contribute to development in direct and pervasive ways. The term *place-identity* has been used by Proshansky and his associates to describe that contribution (Proshansky, Fabian, & Kaminoff, 1983) Place-identity is seen as a "substructure" of self-identity consisting of "cognitions about the physical world in which the individual lives" (p. 59). The authors delineate the components of the cognitions as "memories, ideas, feelings, attitudes, values, preferences, meanings, and conceptions of behavior and experience" (p. 59). Place-identity is described as both "enduring" and "changing" over the course of life. Although home and its surroundings are part of the process of self-definition, the authors stress the contribution of a broad set of experiences and relationships in a number of different physical settings over the life span.

The notion of place-identity and similar views expressed by Fried (1963), who has used the term *spatial identity*, Tuan (1980), and Relph (1976) underline the significance of the enduring, albeit changing contributions of place to self. Recognition of this environmental contribution to personal development emphasizes an aspect of life easily trivialized or ignored. We can ask how the neighborhood fits into this formulation.

If we begin with children, it is fair to say that the home and the range around it serve as the first and most powerful contexts for place-identity development. Children's immediate settings help to define both the world and themselves within it. For most children up to the age of 6 the home neighborhood is the major arena of socialization. Independent movement and geographic exploration are possible later, perhaps by middle childhood. The eagerness and delight of exploration is described in Roger Hart's study of a Vermont town (Hart, 1979), but for most young children there are constraints on the distances they can go. Thus the two immediate environments, the home and the neighborhood, form the most repeated and powerful contexts for socialization and development providing images that personally contribute to the child's sense of himself or herself. If the first major developmental stage in the formation of the sense of self involves the separation of the child from the world, the next stages involve the development of a sense of identity in which the world plays a significant part. We can describe many different realities that must produce different effects—life in a quiet rural area, in a shelter for the homeless, on a busy urban street, in a suburban area—or life that is unchanging or quickly changing. Each reality deposits powerful experiences that become incorporated into children's conceptions of themselves and those around them.

The neighborhood, thus, is a part of the social, emotional, and cognitive experiences of the child (Unger & Wandersman, 1985). The result, in the long run, is a sense of connection to a place, primarily the home, but also the neighborhood range that forms the geography of the child's *lifeworld*, a term from the phenomenological tradition (Seamon, 1979). The formation of a sense of self and the contribution of places to that process clearly do not end in childhood. The connections laid down to both people and place bond both child and adult to an area that becomes more than just a place or just people but a community in which both are molded into a whole. The process is a continuous one, even as the person moves across geographies. Each set of experiences contributes to persons' sense of themselves, although clearly some kinds of neighborhoods have more enduring or pervasive effects than others (Warren, 1978).

On the most superficial level, the selection of a place to live in adulthood makes a statement of one status or values, or both. Financial limitations and the housing shortage pressing today, especially in the low-cost sphere, constrain choices drastically. Nonetheless, whatever the choices and however little time is spent at home or in the home neighborhood, the setting and structure contribute to the person's sense of self, if only as a place from which the person aspires to escape.

There is evidence that some adults do not consider their housing to be home, in the deepest sense of that word, but rather as a temporary stopping place that neither replaces the parental home nor creates the self-made one that is an expectation for the future. In their interviews with men and women living alone, Horwitz and Tognoli (1982) have identified a sequence of psychological and environmental changes after leaving the parental home. These included an initial phase of living in places that were not felt to be home, followed by awareness of the need for a home, and finally the "psychological and physical arrival at a place that felt like home" (Horwitz & Tognoli, 1982, p. 134). The authors view these phases in the construction of home as "deeply related to people's sense of personal growth and change" (p. 138), underlining the continuity of locating and making one's own home across the life cycle.

However, there is limited empirical documentation of this process, for adults. With the exception of Erikson's (1950) landmark contributions, there has been little research or conceptualization on the adult development process. Levinson (1986) has pointed this out and has begun to remedy the gap. In his work on the "life course," he has articulated the "major seasons in the life cycle" (p. 4), describing a series of "eras." Although the environmental components are not central to the theorization, they nonetheless are included. In examining components of the person's world that are of significance, relationships with others are primary. However, "others" are broadly viewed:

> The other might not be an individual but might be a collective entity such as a group, institution or social movement; nature as a whole, or a part of nature such as the ocean, mountains, wildlife, whales in general, or Moby Dick in particular; or an object or place such as a farm, a city or county, "a room of one's own," or a book or painting. (Levinson, 1986, p. 6)

The "other" can also be the neighborhood. In fact, all relationships have an environmental context. Whether acknowledged or not, the setting is a component of all interactions, of all behavior. In adulthood, creation of a way of life, the movement toward a career, and relationships with others (including family) are place-bound. Moreover, each of these contributes to the formation of self, which continues throughout the life cycle. In this light, it is reasonable to view home building and neighborhood relationships as an ongoing process, one that may differ in content but not in importance as the person matures. This clearly is an area requiring further study because it has been childhood and now the later years that have had the most attention.

Issues of housing have become prime concerns for the elderly, and there is a growing literature on these problems (see, for example, Altman, Lawton & Wohlwill, 1984; Carp, 1976; Day-Lower, West, & Zimmers, 1985). Although few researchers have examined the specific role of the neighborhood in the housing experiences of older people (see Carp & Carp, 1982, as an exception), there is some evidence that ties to a neighborhood may outlive the presence of familiar neighbors. In a study of a changing area in New York City, Stone (1980) found many elderly residents forced by economics and sentiment to remain in a neighborhood now largely occupied by people from a different cultural group. Physical changes to the neighborhood had rendered unfamiliar places that were associated with raising children, friendships, and frequently traveled paths. There was a sadness and a sense of loss in their recollections.

Rowles's studies of older people residing in inner-city areas (Rowles, 1978, 1980) have identified qualities of his residents' geographic experiences that "expressed a subtle meshing of space and time, embracing not only physical and cognitive involvement within their contemporary neighborhood, but also vicarious participation in an array of displaced environments" (Rowles, 1980, p. 57). Among the geographic experiences were strong feelings that were reinforced by interaction with elderly peers, reflecting "a mutual sense of belonging and continuity with a community of a more auspicious past" (p. 60).

Thus, with repeated use and the establishment of social networks, the familiarity of an area can set in place deep roots that connect people to settings, creating powerful sentiment for a place as well as its inhabitants. Even when conditions change, these ties are difficult to break because, for the elderly, the setting has become a part of their own lives and identity.

Place Attachments

Attachment to place has become a recent concern in the neighborhood/community literature, focusing on people's connections to places. Shumaker and Taylor (1983) have defined attachment as "a positive affective bond or association between individuals and their residential environment" (p. 233). Their model of place attachment has five factors that can influence the relationship of people to places. These are local social ties, physical amenities, individual/household characteristics, perceived choice of location of residence, and the perceived rewards outweighing costs of remaining in the neighborhood compared to living elsewhere. One more component seems essential—the symbolic connections and feelings people have for places—the sentiment that Firey described for landmarks in Boston (Firey, 1945) that can exist in many neighborhoods, including transformed ones.

Attachment to place involves the development of roots, connections that stabilize and create a feeling of comfort and security, words that people have used to describe their local areas (Rivlin, 1982). Yi-Fu Tuan has characterized rootedness as "an unreflective state of being in which the human personality merges with the milieu" (Tuan, 1980, p. 6). He considers this ideal state an "irretrievable Eden" for most Americans. People's ability to form attachments and maintain relationships with places depends on the survival of the settings, which is largely a matter of economic conditions. The availability of local public spaces that can be grounds for establishing connections adds another dimension to the qualities that can enhance the formation of roots.

There is considerable debate concerning the degree of alienation from people and places (Sennett, 1978), but the pessimistic views are finding opposing voices. For example, Lofland (1983) has challenged the "conventional wisdom" that urban dwellers are alienated, pointing to new kinds of connectedness in the city, including spatially dispersed forms, forms that may not depend totally on primary relationships. She described Peggy Wireman's "intimate/secondary relationships" where "two persons whose interactions with one another are highly circumscribed may nonetheless define their connections as 'close'" (p. 3). Lofland sees the need for a "rich vocabulary of relationships" that will enable us to describe with accuracy the different ways people relate to others, to places, or to various forms of social organizations. Sociologists, geographers, and environmental psychologists have begun to articulate this vocabulary, but there is much to be done.

One way of viewing place meanings that I have found to be useful is to question the ways style of life encourages connections to place. If a neighborhood serves a range of needs and if these needs are concentrated within an area and are served in ways that are anchored both by time and group membership or group identity, roots to that area are likely to be deep. This formulation of attachments thus isolates four significant neighborhood domains: *the ways personal needs are met, their location and distribution over space, the role of affiliations to others* in the area, and the *temporal patterns* of each one. All of these contribute to the formation of an ecological niche, a safe haven within a place. How this occurs is important to understanding connection to places.

The *servicing of needs* covers a wide range that includes shopping, socializing, work, recreation, community work, and religious or ethical affiliations. These activities can be distributed broadly across a geography or concentrated within the neighborhood. When they are *concentrated* and a local area becomes the context for servicing the major domains of life, that area will assume a particular importance to residents, in contrast to instances where people go all over a city to fulfill their needs. If the concentrated servicing of needs occurs in an area in which strong *affiliations to individuals and groups* exist, which can be familial, religious, ethnic, cultural, or interest affiliations, that is, where people share with others a strong bond and common concerns, another stimulus to attachments exists. Finally, time must be entered as a factor. The complex nature of the *temporal* dimension in peoples' relationships to settings has been described by Werner, Altman, and Oxley (1985) in their transactional perspective, "Temporal Aspects of Homes." In their analysis, the distinction is made between linear time that addresses past, present, and future, and cyclical time that is represented in the image of a spiraling, recurrent form. For the present view, time must be factored into the domains of satisfying needs, their distribution, and existing social ties in order to understand their relationship to attachment to neighborhood. If an area has been the context for meeting needs over time both in a linear and cyclical manner, and where concentrated use of the neighborhood has built sets of relationships, habits, and memories that have developed, over time, and where group affiliations have existed, over time, the combined power of each domain is likely to have created strong attachments to the place and its people. Much of this can be seen in the descriptions of the elderly offered by Rowles (1978).

The perspective that has been described examines the specific contribution of each of the four domains, although it is not possible to draw any conclusion about their relative importance to attachment or their interactive nature. Rather, building on the work of researchers who have examined attachment to place both empirically (for example, Fried, 1963; Rowles, 1978, 1980; Stone, 1980) and theoretically (Tuan, 1980; Werner, Altman, & Oxley, 1985), we can begin to articulate the significance of places to people and the ways attachment can occur.

Roots can be strengthened in a number of other ways. Acquiring property by purchasing or appropriating it is one way. The presence of influential persons such as spiritual leaders (Rivlin, 1982) can encourage loyalty to a place and the people that live there. Physical landmarks also can act as reminders of a locality's significance as they identify areas and provide distinctive descriptors for them. The converse of the establishment of roots, failure to develop attachments in an area, may threaten health and well-being (Stokols, Shumaker, & Martinez, 1983) and lead to poor mental health (Shumaker & Taylor, 1983). Roots and attachment thus act to strengthen and nurture, although some people apparently do not require propinquity to establish these connections.

A PERSPECTIVE ON PEOPLE'S RELATIONSHIP TO SETTINGS

In conceptualizing the relationships of people to their settings, it is useful to consider the existence of a spectrum of social, political, and economic structures that hold people to places.[1] At one extreme are the least socially bound and geographically structured people who are without stable ties to others or to areas. These are people who lack a geography that is consistently traversed in satisfying their needs, who do not have stable relationships or a predictability in their lives that extends over time. The homeless would fit into this end as would perpetual travelers, people on the move who lack the alternative social structure and supports seen in groups such as tramps or the familiar and repeated routes of nomads and gypsies. The other extreme would be the most highly place-bound persons with structured lives, strong affiliations, powerful group ties, people whose days are lived out in a concentrated area and whose philosophy binds them together within that area over time. I would suggest that among others, some Hasidic sects meet this criterion. This view acknowledges the fact that individual and group life histories and the person/place relationships that have transpired will contribute both in the long- and short-run to an individual's life-style. It analyzes the qualities that are the ingredients of attachment to place along a spectrum of structures that creates degrees of rootedness and uncovers the diversity of human existence. Using two extreme cases, the homeless and the Lubavitcher Hasidim, the significance of context will be examined.

Life with Group Roots: The Lubavitch

The Lubavitch are a group of Orthodox Jews, actually a sect of Hasidic Jews, whose origins stretch back to 18th-century Eastern Europe

[1] I am indebted to Irwin Altman for suggesting this formulation.

when Rabbi Yisroel Baal Shem Tov introduced an alternative to the rationalism and scholasticism of the religious practices of the time (Shaffir, 1974). The new form emphasized joyousness in prayer and mystical communication with God. Individual groups developed, most taking their names from the small towns and villages in which they formed. The Lubavitcher movement began in White Russia in 1773 and has had a long line of influential Rebbes—spiritual leaders respected for their wisdom and piety. After World War I and the Russian Revolution, the movement settled in Poland. With the fall of Warsaw during World War II, the Rebbe, Joseph I. Schneersohn, escaped to the United States, aided by the U.S. Department of State. He arrived in New York on March 19, 1940, and settled in Brooklyn, setting up his headquarters in the Crown Heights area.

The group that clustered around the Rebbe was a small one until the end of the war when they were joined by members emigrating to the United States. Their numbers also were increased by their policy of recruiting among Jews, especially among nonobservant Jews, inviting them to join the community. Outreach programs were established in major cities throughout the United States and in many other countries as well. It is commonplace to find Lubavitcher meeting places near campuses of universities with active programs among the students. The group has become one of the largest Hasidic sects and a very influential one in New York City.

The Hasidim have been studied by social scientists and documented by journalists. The Satmar sect in the Williamsburg section of Brooklyn has been described by Gersh and Miller (1959) and Poll (1962). Mayer's (1979) study of Borough Park and Mintz's (1968) analysis of Hasidic legends have added to the picture of Hasidic life and philosophy. The Lubavitch, in particular, have been the focus of work by Levy (1975) who studied the Crown Heights group, by Shaffir (1974) who examined Montreal's Lubavitch as well as a recent account of family and community life by a staff writer for *The New Yorker* magazine (Harris, 1985). My own interest in the Lubavitch was piqued by two articles by Weiner (1957a, 1957b) and his later book (1969). What most intrigued me was their impact on Crown Heights, a neighborhood in which I had spent most of my childhood. The area had been a largely middle-class Jewish one, but neither Hasidic nor Orthodox. In the late 1950s many families moved out, and it became predominatly black (many from the Caribbean Islands) with an Orthodox, Jewish minority, mainly Lubavitch.

Members of this group, much as a number of other religious sects, live within a sharply defined code of behavior, one that dictates their dress, their diet, their religious practices, their family relationships, their schooling, and their socializing. The life-style emanates from their religious views that have become a canon for their daily existence, defining activities and patterns of social encounters. The Lubavitcher lifestyle also requires a critical mass of others like themselves in order to provide the food, clothing, prayer, education, and friends that are needed. As a result, it is necessary for them to reside in close proximity to people like themselves, people who share common needs, people who would be unable to sustain these requirements in a dispersed community. The additional constraint of Sabbath worship, which prohibits the use of any means of transportation from sundown Friday to sundown Saturday, makes it essential to live within walking distance of a synagogue.

Although there are many Lubavitcher communities in the United States, Canada, Israel, and elsewhere, the major one is in the Crown Heights neighborhood in Brooklyn. Unlike other Hasidic sects that have moved away from changing neighborhoods, the Lubavitch have not left Crown Heights. The explanation rests in a complex combination of factors, but the most important reason revolves around the role of their Rebbe, their spiritual leader. His influence extends to all aspects of the lives of members of this religious community, and no major decision is made without his advice. The Rebbe has taken a particular stand regarding Crown Heights. He has rejected the possibility of relocating, maintaining that doing so would jeopardize those unable to leave, especially the elderly and the poor. Instead, he has urged his members to rebuild the neighborhood and to remain, and he has been successful in keeping them in the area. Available property has been acquired, often with the assistance of a community organization established for that purpose. Although there have been many problems in the community, "an uneasy peace" with black residents has resulted (Oser, 1981; Rule, 1979).

In interviews with the Lubavitch who live in Crown Heights, they described their neighborhood boundaries in ways that were acknowledged by other group members (Rivlin, 1982) despite the fact that official limits as well as those of the black residents in the area have been defined in different ways. The presence of Jews in the area constituted the criterion for setting the boundaries, although the blocks identified were not necessarily exclusively Lubavitch (although many were largely Jewish).

This agreement over boundaries can be explained by what happens in the area. When residents provided an account of their daily activities—shopping for food and clothing, socializing, recreation, children's schooling and play, local self-help groups, study groups for men and women, community volunteer work among their own members, shared festivals and holidays, celebrations of the birth of children, weddings, and most of all, prayers—almost all were centered in their own community. Although some worked in Crown Heights, most had jobs outside the area. If they work in mid-Manhattan, they are able to use a private bus service for transportation. The Lubavitch do go outside their area to shop, and a private bus links them to other Orthodox Jewish areas in Brooklyn.

However, the major portion of their time is spent in Crown Heights, and the neighborhood services their basic needs for kosher food and clothing that meet their religious requirements. Local synagogues are within easy walking distance, enabling them to participate in daily religious services, which are mandatory for males.

Although some children attend Lubavitcher schools outside Crown Heights, most attend local parochial schools run by the group. Some families have moved outside Crown Heights to the middle-class neighborhoods that are nearer to their children's schools, but this may jeopardize their status within the Lubavitcher community (Levy, 1975). Most Lubavitch have remained in Crown Heights, faithful to the Rebbe's commitment to the area and out of reverence to him. "Spiritually, I wouldn't want to live anywhere but near the Rebbe. Without him life would be devoid of meaning." This comment was characteristic of the responses to questions concerning possible relocation. The residents would leave only if they were asked to establish Lubavitcher communities in other places. In this case, they would be "messengers of the Rebbe"—an honor for a family.

The Lubavitch live in a community with considerable propinquity to each other. Paths cross in many directions for life-sustaining as well as social functions. But this occurs out of deep commitment to a belief system and a group, not out of neighborhood affection. The cohesiveness of this group is built on mutual needs and a total life covered by the belief system and joins with the reverence for the Rebbe to create strong roots to the area. Both as individuals and as group members, the attachment is reinforced by their daily activities, their home practices, and in places of worship. It is enhanced by practices that extend over time, repeating themselves in cyclical ways (Werner et al., 1985). The weekly celebration of the Sabbath with its rituals and reading of the Torah, ceremonies for marriages, births, male coming of age (bar mitzvah), deaths, and holidays all reflect the cyclical nature of religious life. These practices reach back to Jews of the past and also project into the distant future as they connect the present generation to their co-religionists in general, and other Lubavitch, in particular.

A dress code that mandates modesty in appearance also distinguishes members of this group. However, their clothing is not as distinctive or unusual as among other Hasidic sects. The Lubavitch men in dark suits and hats and women in long sleeves, skirts (not pants), and heads covered with scarves or wigs mark group members, defining them to themselves and others as distinctive.

Language also is a mechanism for cohesion. Although the Lubavitch do speak English, their daily secular language is largely Yiddish that is used to communicate to each other. Hebrew is the language of prayer. This linguistic pattern establishes another link to people and a distinctiveness when viewed by the larger community.

Stokols and Shumaker (1981) have described two kinds of place dependence, "geographic place dependence" and "generic place dependence." Generic place dependence is the "degree to which occupants perceive themselves to be strongly associated with and dependent on a category of functionally similar places" (p. 481)—concern for a type of place that the person may not even have experienced, that has general meaning to an individual (for example, concern for all Jewish communities that we might expect of observant Jews or concern for all natural areas that a preservationist might feel). Geographic place dependence, the "degree to which occupants perceive themselves to be strongly associated with and dependent on a particular place" (p. 481), seems closer to the Lubavitcher experience. Although other Orthodox communities might supply their need for kosher food and clothing, it is unlikely that their feelings for their group and their Rebbe could be met by other religious groups because membership within their community defines a particular genre of observant life. The attachment to a place and dependence on it interacts with attachments to people and ties believers into the network of others like themselves. Interestingly, Crown Heights serves the entire Lubavitcher movement, wherever people may live, as a center, a focus. Pilgrimages to Crown Heights for the celebration of holidays are commonplace because Lubavitch all over the world identify with the area. They, too, are geographically place dependent upon the world headquarters of their movement, and the area is very much a part of their lives, although we would not expect the same kind of attachment evident in residents.

At times, group members take to the streets for weddings that commonly are performed under the stars, for festival celebrations and holidays, for gatherings to hear the Rebbe speak. But there is little concern with neighborhood beautification, something that one expects to find in suburban neighborhoods or in reviving neighborhoods. Rather, there is another kind of environmental value and ethic, one that seeks to preserve the area as a Jewish community and a commitment to have it continue as a home and center for their group. The neighborhood has assumed symbolic meaning both to residents and other Lubavitch, becoming more than a place to visit or a residence. It is the geographic arena of complex personal and group affiliations. What has developed is an emotional-symbolic place with a respected and influential leader and an all-embracing philosophy of life that offers members a strong sense of their identity and connections that reach out to the past and to the future. These are powerful ingredients for affiliation, and once the acceptance of the code has occurred, either by growing up Lubavitch or by "returning" to the fold (these "converts" or returnees are called *Ba'al T'shuva*, "repentants"), the rootedness to the Lubavitcher community develops. This is not to imply that members do not leave—some do, merely by moving outside Crown Heights. A number of Russian and Iranian Jews have left the fold, even if they have not relocated. But for most, the place, the practices, and the people all nurture the rootedness and attachments.

The neighborhood is covered with indications of the presence of the group—Jewish signs on shops and schools and people in distinctive clothing that share values, language, and practices as well as a history. In fact, there are many signifiers of ethnic neighborhoods such as Crown Heights where the shops, housing, and visible decorations such as murals provide identity cues that may be enhanced by local festivals and celebrations (Brower, 1977). The Chinatowns and Little Italies are among the most conspicuous types, but Hispanic, Middle Eastern, and Oriental neighborhoods have their own specific qualities that signal the fact that a particular group is living there. These public spaces, inscribed with the sounds and smells of ethnic life, offer sharp contrasts to the anonymous malls and bland shopping streets that are found throughout many suburban areas and cities.

The consequence of these images of places has two components, their impact on strangers and their impact on local residents. For strangers, the walk through Crown Heights or Chinatown or Little Italy may be an exotic experience, a form of Sunday recreation that contrasts with their usual routine. For members of the groups living in these areas, there is a totally different experience. There is, in Halbwachs's view, a "collective memory," an experience shared with an "affective community" (Halbwachs, 1950/1980):

> Most groups—not merely those resulting from the physical distribution of members within the boundaries of a city, house, or apartment, but many other types also—engrave their form in some way upon the soil and retrieve their collective remembrances within the spatial framework thus defined. In other words, there are as many ways of representing space as there are

groups. . . . Each group cuts up space in order to compose, either defini-
tively or in accordance with a set method, a fixed framework within which to
enclose and retrieve its remembrances. (pp. 156–157)

Having "engraved their form" in Crown Heights, the Lubavitch maintain a cohesive image within the area and a setting for the collective
remembrances of all group members.

It is interesting to consider the Lubavitch in light of the formulation
of neighborhood meaning and attachment described earlier, based on
the variety of personal needs served in an area and the ways they are
met, their location and distribution over space, the ties to people in an
area, and the time context. The Crown Heights neighborhood serves a
broad range of personal *needs*, covering almost all aspects of the lives of
people involved, expecially, but not exclusively, their spiritual needs.
These occur in a compact geography that contains a total life support
system for them, one that is serviced by members of their own group,
people they feel they can trust. The ties that exist to these members are
strong ones that transcend the geography, although the presence of the
Lubavitch endows the physical area with meanings that blend with the
group's philosophy of life. The setting thus has become a kind of home-
land for all Lubavitch, including those living in Israel. It is to the main
synagogue and headquarters at 770 Eastern Parkway that pilgrims come
to be in the middle of the Lubavitcher community and, most of all, near
the Rebbe. The presence of this influential spiritual leader provides the
strongest tie to the neighborhood, and his headquarters has become a
landmark for the group. *Time* factors also work to establish roots both to
the group as a whole and to the area. The history of the Lubavitch with
its stories, legends, persecutions, and lineage of extraordinary leaders
provides a rich heritage of group membership memorabilia on which to
draw. Thus the group has embroidered its Jewish history and its Hasidic
history onto its own Lubavitcher history. All of these are evoked in daily
life, in special commemorations, and in relationships to the community.
These are enhanced by another aspect of time, the cyclical nature of their
lives, the rituals that define daily and weekly life, creating both continuity to the past but also a reach toward the future. The regular celebration of holidays punctuates their lives with customs that also reach
back and move forward. It may well be that the Jewish use of a lunar
calendar further enhances the time mode and its role in their lives. Its
cycle is keyed to a visible force, and its variance from the secular calendar (which they cannot ignore) also can act to bind the group more
closely together. And this time scheme is conspicuous in the shops, in
the dress of group members, in the signs as significant holidays or the
Sabbath approach.

For the Lubavitch, the neighborhood, its Jewish people, landmarks, and resources act to encourage a form of group place-identity where the setting contributes in distinctive ways to the uniqueness and cohesiveness of the group. The manner in which the ideology is laid out in space and the proximity of others with a similar belief system affect the belongingness, connectedness, and distinctiveness of the group. It results, in Warren's terms, in a "parochial neighborhood" (Warren, 1978) where affiliations enable Lubavitcher residents to be independent of others in the area and focused on their own group members. The creation of a Lubavitcher enclave within a predominantly black neighborhood is a product of a distinctive life-style and a cohesiveness that circumscribes their worlds.

LIFE WITH ROOTS MADE DIFFICULT: THE HOMELESS

Quite a different life-style from that of the Lubavitch can be found in the experiences of the homeless who are outside the parameters of Warren's neighborhood typology. At best, they inhabit "transitory" or "anomic" neighborhoods superimposed over existing ones in which they are treated as outsiders. Homelessness in the United States has become a critical national problem affecting more and more persons each year, although rarely voluntarily. The statistics are difficult to obtain because homelessness, by its very nature, makes accounting near to impossible. The "hidden homeless," people who are able to maintain a fragile grasp on temporary shelter in the homes of friends and family, and the "invisible homeless," who are without shelter but are not recognized as homeless, do not enter the tallies. Unless the homeless person uses a public or voluntary agency that keeps accounts, he or she will slip between the assessment cracks. The figure of 2 to 3 million over the course of a year is mentioned frequently for the United States, but any statistics must be regarded as estimates (Hopper & Hamburg, 1984).

The homeless are not a monolithic group; there are many different kinds of homeless persons, and homelessness exists in a number of different, albeit overlapping forms (Rivlin, 1985). The *chronic* kind, which might be epitomized best by the "Bowery bum" stereotype, is associated with alcoholism and drug abuse. The victims, largely males, may spend the day on the streets associating with others like themselves, but usually there is sufficient money for a "flophouse" bed. There is evidence of informal social support within clusters of men, and occasionally there are signs of a community structure within a specific area.

Periodic homelessness takes a number of forms. One type occurs when people leave their homes because of pressures, with the home still there for a return. Migrant workers are subject to another kind of periodic homelessness, although most have homes somewhere. They may travel with their families and are given temporary housing on their work sites, but the regular uprooting has significant impacts, disrupting family life, as Coles (1970) has documented. Gypsies and nomads might appear to be periodically homeless, but a close examination of their lives reveals that their paths are regular ones, not haphazard, with familiar places and people along the route. In addition, they also may leave stable homes behind, places to which they can return.

Temporary homelessness is the most time-limited form and is a result of a temporary crisis—a fire, flood, hurricane—or a move from one community to another. A hospitalization also fits into this category, as it removes a person from home and community. However, once the crisis is over and new housing located or old housing repaired, or once the person leaves the hospital, he or she is able to resume his or her role and create or re-create a home. We might consider that their roots have been damaged but not destroyed. In many cases, group affiliations, friends, and family still are there and are able to assist. In the case of voluntary relocation, the previous experiences of people and their resources help their integration into a new community, however difficult or stressful this may be. The existence of a cohesive but welcoming neighborhood may facilitate this process as well.

Total homelessness is the most traumatic form. It involves the complete loss of home and contacts with community because of natural disasters, economic upheavals, interpersonal conflicts, and mental illness. In this case, the home-building process has been undermined along with the loss of the home, with the total loss of physical and social supports, including community connections.

Why people are subject to these varying kinds of homelessnesses is a complicated story. In fact, we know that some degree of mobility has been characteristic of the society in the United States, especially in the early years of its history. Allsop (1967) found "a unique kind of mobility" (p. 31) in this country with widespread restlessness and people on the move in their automobiles, campers, and vans. But this is qualified mobility, the movement of people with resources and with community supports. Even the hoboes that Allsop studied were less aimless wanderers than men trying to resettle, to find jobs despite union and local opposition.

Residential mobility levels have remained quite stable, hovering at about 20% from 1947 to 1980 (Rossi & Shlay, 1982). But large numbers do move and are able to connect themselves with the people and resources

they require. In many cases, this is facilitated by preexisting group affiliations, not all of them community-bound. One's age, interests, religious background, and work all can assist the process of establishing
roots in a new place, even if these affiliations are dispersed over a wide
area. But for the homeless, this rarely is possible. If we examine the
people affected by homelessness of the chronic, periodic, temporary and
total form, we may have some explanation of why this is so.

There are many different kinds of persons now homeless: people
who have lost their marginal housing (especially single men and women
and poor elderly), ex-offenders, runaway youths, "throwaway youths"
(young people who are victims of family abuse or abandoned by their
families), young people who have left foster care, single-parent households, women escaping domestic violence, both legal and undocumented immigrants, alcoholics and drug abusers, Native Americans
who have left the reservations after federal cutbacks and unemployment, other victims of unemployment and changes in the job market
who have been identified as the "new poor," and former psychiatric
patients. Natural disasters such as floods and accidental and intentional
fires, the loss of low-cost housing through fires, demolition and upgrading, and pervasive changes in the job market with a reduction in the
number of skilled and unskilled jobs, a rise in the poorly paid service
economy—all affect the people we have been discussing. With fewer
benefits due to federal cutbacks, an unfortunate scenario ensues that
allows the individuals involved to slip out of available supports and onto
the streets.

Within these groups, minorities and children are among the most
affected. Contrary to the assumptions of many, deinstitutionalized mental patients do *not* make up *most* of the homeless. They constitute about
20% to 30% of the total numbers. However, the process of institutionalization, over the years, strips them of the community skills and
contacts that would facilitate reintegration into a neighborhood. They
lack what the Lubavitch possess in abundance, an all-encompassing
family and community structure that contains various kinds of social
supports and self-help mechanisms.

This does not mean that there are no instances of families helping
the homeless or the homeless helping each other. Their stories reveal
the desperate attempts of friends and relatives to take them in, although
the hospitality often erodes, over time, as financial and space constraints
create pressures that become intolerable. There are communities of
homeless persons, some in shelters, some unsheltered, where much
sharing and support can be seen. There are groups of unrelated homeless persons who identify themselves as "families"—who are concerned

about what is happening to members and solicitous of their welfare. But these affiliations occur despite many obstacles—the lack of permanent housing, fragile financial conditions, and authorities who are eager to have the homeless disappear, especially when they are present in groups.

The homeless have not organized on their own behalf, although there are indications that this is changing. Homeless communities are beginning to advocate for their needs as leadership from within and support from outside advocacy groups has emerged.

However, the experience of homelessness saps strength from those affected, and even though there are capable and supportive persons within the group, their energies are diffused by the tremendous efforts needed to survive. It is questionable as to whether the homeless perceive themselves as a unitary group—their lives and problems are so varied. It also is unrealistic to expect that they could address the social, political, and economic bases of their situation—the shortage of jobs, the lack of affordable housing, the cutback in services that have produced the homeless in the numbers we see today. Victims may blame themselves or be blamed by others (Ryan, 1976), and although this is undocumented for the homeless, it may characterize at least some.

The homeless also suffer from considerable discrimination from neighborhoods. They are sharing the experience of former psychiatric patients, the developmentally and physically disabled, and the elderly for whom group homes are difficult to acquire. Resistance is now predictable when the possibility of a shelter or group home arises in a neighborhood, even when residents express concerned and sympathetic views toward the homeless (Rivlin, 1985).

Homelessness is an isolating experience. Although most homeless persons find places for themselves—in shelters or welfare hotels or the street—they do not have the community ties and neighborhood contacts that sustain most of us. They may become familiar faces in an area, and they may find safe refuges that offer protection from the elements, but they are tolerated, at best. There are isolated instances of a neighborhood providing food for its local street person, but rarely is adequate shelter offered. This is not to ignore the work of advocacy groups, but their efforts are limited at best.

Although the public identifies the homeless with one generic term, they are not a homogeneous group. There is danger in applying a generic label to homelessness because it obscures the individual needs that exist. Homeless families with young children require different services and resources than do unemployed young persons or the elderly poor. Neither the welfare hotels nor the public shelters that have been used in many areas as housing for homeless families service the needs of children or parents. Feeding a family of four in a single hotel room with no refrigerator and a single hotplate makes meeting an ordinary need for nourishment into a major obstacle. Life in the vicinity of these hotels has few community resources—they often are located in commercial areas of the city or in deteriorated neighborhoods. The homeless children in New York City share the streets in which they play with prostitutes, pimps, drug dealers, and tourists. Neighborhood life of a sort exists, but it is hardly a nurturing one. The large public shelters are even worse because the family is likely to be moved from one unfamiliar neighborhood to another, placed in huge, barracklike structures that might be armories or gymnasiums. There is no privacy, no familiarity, and no opportunity to develop community ties.

In applying the model of neighborhood meaning and attachment to the homeless, there is a marked contrast to the description of Lubavitcher life. The ways personal needs are met and the range that can be met are sharply limited in the case of the homeless. Although their personal needs are those of other people, their ability to fulfill them is constrained by their realities, whether we are considering people in large public shelters, the welfare hotels, in small voluntary shelters, or the unsheltered. Activities that most of us take for granted—eating, sleeping, toileting, and maintaining personal hygiene—are major obstacles for the homeless. In large shelters there is competition for amenities and necessities that are available on schedule and not on need. Welfare hotels provide a bare minimum for the families that reside there. And for the unsheltered, needs are fulfilled according to the goodwill or tolerance of others.

Where these needs are fulfilled also differs when we compare the lives of homeless with other populations. For most people, the security and amenities of a home and home neighborhood, of work settings, and other domains of the lifeworld are available for meeting various needs. The selection of appropriate settings is a matter of life-style, economic situation, and available resources. However, the options available to the homeless are based more on their ability to negotiate a place in the system of exchange, their ability to locate free or inexpensive nourishment, their ability to find safe refuges for rest or places where they are permitted to clean themselves. In some cases, this requires covering considerable distances over the course of a day. For the young and healthy, this may not be impossible, but for families or the elderly or people who are ill, the ability to travel is sorely constrained. It is true that some homeless persons have created life support systems for themselves in railroad stations or other public areas, but this is neither easy nor commonplace. Others weave together a series of settings and services to sustain themselves. In some rare cases, their presence over time may lead to some tolerance on the part of others in the area, but this, too, is unusual.

For the most part, homeless people have fragile ties to others. The homeless experience is an alienating one for individuals and for families. Communities of homeless persons are not commonplace. More usual are the arbitrary congregations in places where they are herded along with many strangers, hardly the ingredients for the formation of communities or the development of attachments to people or places. If anything, the huge public shelters that are municipalities' solutions to the problem of homelessness work against affiliations and neighborhood roots.

The time dimension enters in ways that are particular to the homeless when contrasted with the Lubavitch and with other individuals and groups. Time often is turned about. Many homeless persons find that sleep is easier and safer by day and in public, where the presence of others assures some degree of protection. In the process, they convert the public arena into a setting for activities that for most of us are private, altering the ordinary patterns of publicness and privateness (Forrest, Grecni, Mesnikoff, & Paxson, 1979). In addition to this time and privacy inversion, filling the hours of the days is a major challenge, especially if the person has considerable belongings and an appearance that distinguishes him or her as homeless. There are many constraints on where a person burdened with overflowing shopping bags or carts can go. Moreover, the cycle of time has degrees of unpredictability embedded within that are threatening rather than reassuring. Whatever attempts that are made to build in some predictability by establishing a routine and regular paths, the lack of control over the public arena and its inhabitants and the loose or absent connections to people all conspire to threaten homeless persons' connections to their settings.

FUTURE DIRECTIONS

Our journey through the lives of the Lubavitch and the homeless provides dramatic contrasts and an opportunity to reflect on many questions raised by two diverse situations. By looking at these cases through the lens of neighborhood meanings and attachment, a number of issues are revealed that require additional thought and research. I will outline four that are especially promising. They deal with the need to (a) uncover the now obscure formation of neighborhood meanings and affiliations;

(b) assess the impact of new technology on public and private life; (c) enhance our vocabulary of spatial and social relationships; and (d) address the restrictiveness of community and neighborhood experiences.

Understanding the formation of neighborhood meanings and affiliations requires a longitudinal view of people's lives, one in which relationships to people and places are viewed as an ongoing process rather than as a cut in time. Yet the literature on neighborhoods has largely neglected the time dimension, with empirical research either examining problems at one point in time or looking at age differences rather than temporal effects. There is every reason to believe that the development of neighborhood meanings and relationships evolves over time, and to neglect temporal factors is to miss this process of growth. Retrospective accounts are easier to obtain than longitudinal ones but are fraught with error, relying as they do on memory. Repeated interviews with panels of informants at all stages in their life cycles could begin to articulate the evolution of neighborhood meanings and the ways relationships with people contribute to them. This does not presume that there is a unitary progression toward attachments. In fact, the homeless situation demonstrates that there are many levels of associations and attachments, with some people in quite isolated situations. The longitudinal view can begin to articulate this complex process of place-bound associations and address questions concerning their role in stabilizing people's lives.

The time-bound factors of neighborhood life also need attention, including the role of rituals and celebrations and the impact they have on the lives of people in an area. If repeated events such as monthly meetings and seasonal block parties act to anchor people in neighborhoods, providing mechanisms for airing concerns or connecting up with others, it would be well to understand their functions and to devise ways of supporting such efforts. Some evidence of these impacts can be found in neighborhood research that has examined local participation (see, for example, Chavis, Hogge, McMillan, & Wandersman, 1986; Unger & Wandersman, 1985).

The ways new technologies are impacting neighborhood life open up an area of concern that is likely to be with us for some time. This is especially relevant to the introduction of microcomputers, which raises many intriguing questions.

On the basis of her research on the use of microcomputers in the home, Horwitz (1986) has proposed some new possibilities that relate to local life. She outlines an area in need of study, one that envisions opportunities for mutual assistance and advice around the microcomputer, communication that can cut across age and rank. Although it is difficult to predict the extent of this new arena for connections because home use of computers is comparatively limited, Horwitz sees the need to explore these alternatives to the potentially isolating effects of computers and computer-based systems.

This reformulation of residential life signals the value of reconceptualizing both the meaning of the neighborhood and the role of public space. We can question whether technology will affect patterns of daily life, reducing the amount of shopping outside the home neighborhood, intensifying uses of local services and local settings. We can see new work patterns resulting from technology (Aronowitz, 1985), and these also are likely to alter the relationship to the home, to the neighborhood, and to the larger community. It would be well to anticipate these impacts and the people they will affect.

A major interdisciplinary effort is required to articulate the complex consequences of these profound changes in our lives. If automobiles and motorized public transportation have expanded our worlds, making the immediate neighborhood less critical to satisfying our basic needs, the computer has the potential of drawing people back to the home and the home range. This raises many questions concerning the profile of neighborhood life, not the least of which is the role that neighborhood public spaces can play in the future as grounds for drawing people together.

Lofland's directive for an enhanced vocabulary of relationships (Lofland, 1983) is especially significant to a future analysis of neighborhood issues. It is clear from the two cases studies that conventional images of neighboring hardly cover the range and repertoire of relationships that are possible in a specific area or for particular people. These can extend from the group associations encouraged by a charismatic and revered leader to the supportive relationship of a homeless community member who provides essential resources for friends. A typology of community affiliations would be a useful goal for this broadened view of neighboring, but this requires extensive empirical documentation and ability to rise above the stereotypic categories of neighborhood roles. It also is necessary to look for hidden members of a neighborhood, people who are present but not in conventional places or relationships. Earlier I suggested viewing shopkeepers and others who regularly provide services to an area as neighbors, as members of the community, but there are many others who are yet to be identified.

Homeless inhabitants of neighborhoods are one such example. Their presence, usually ignored, makes them no less neighbors than the people with more structured and traditional roles. Failure to acknowledge affiliations to others is a denial of connections to people, making it easy to reject shelters in a neighborhood and withhold expressions of concern for those in fragile conditions. Perhaps a broader look at neighborhood people can help to articulate the relationships Lofland (1983) suggested are there, providing a new perspective on neighborhood meaning.

This broadened view also must address the restrictiveness of neighborhood life, the exclusiveness of affiliations and sharing that is evident in the two cases that have been described. If neighborhoods can offer security, satisfaction of needs, stable social relationships, public spaces for consistent events, and a context for affiliations, they also contain mechanisms to exclude, rule out, and reject. Both people and places can be victims of these proscriptions as specific kinds are prohibited in a particular area. Neighborhoods may exclude playgrounds, grocery stores, and public gardens as well as particular ethnic groups, teenagers, and the poor. Sometimes formal, more often informal, these measures make life very difficult for those targeted. Racial and cultural prejudices offer examples of the toll that exclusionary practices take.

An analysis of neighborhoods such as the Lubavitcher community of Crown Heights provides not so much a model—for it has an identity and resources that many other groups do not possess—but rather a picture of how group membership and place affiliations can structure neighborhood life and encourage mutual assistance. We need to examine these affiliations more closely and try to identify how they can be translated into other contexts. Some perplexing questions remain: Can self-help be encouraged in less cohesive groups? A study of the communities of homeless persons could help to clarify this question. Can neighborhood residents learn to accept the presence of diversity, including people with serious afflictions and incorporate them into community life? Studies of neighborhoods that have accommodated diverse persons are required. Does the availability of local public spaces help to facilitate the process of integration? Research on public spaces and neighborhood life can address this issue.

There are many important lessons to be learned from neighborhood case studies of a widely ranging sort, including places where group homes and shelters are accommodated. But it also is essential to deal with homelessness in direct ways. The answer is not increasing the numbers of shelters, however many amenities they possess. Shelters should provide temporary, emergency care. The proliferation of large, permanent shelters will lead to conditions that isolate residents and work against the development of neighborhood roots. It will create a new institutional form that is unhealthy both for the shelter residents and local communities, one that deflects from dealing with root causes. More appropriate are efforts directed toward the reasons for homelessness and efforts to encourage low-cost housing and jobs. In addition, we need to recognize the existence of communities of homeless persons, support these networks, and encourage others, thus expanding self-help efforts. The homeless must be involved in creative planning for their futures, with communities utilizing their skills and experiences, thus growing closer to them. In our search for a contemporary model for neighborhood life and an understanding of its contribution to identity, we might well take to heart the words of the Roman poet Horace (B.C. 65–8) in his letter to Lollius:

> It is your concern when your neighbor's wall is on fire.
> And flames neglected are wont to gather strength.
> —Epistles, I, XVIII, lines 84–85

Acknowledgments

The editors have provided excellent guidance from their reading an earlier draft of this chapter. The generous and perceptive counsel of Jaime Horwitz has touched these pages in many ways, and I am most grateful to her.

REFERENCES

Allsop, K. (1967). *Hard travellin': The hobo and his history*. New York: The New American Library.

Altman, I., Lawton, M. P., & Wohlwill, J. T. (Eds.). (1984). *Elderly people and the environment*. New York: Plenum Press.

Aronowitz, S. (1985, fall). Why work? *Social Text, 12,* 19–42.

Banerjee, T., & Baer, W. C. (1984). *Beyond the neighborhood unit: Residential environments and public policy*. New York: Plenum Press.

Brower, S. (1977). *A year of celebration*. Baltimore, MD: Department of Planning.

Carp, F. M. (1976). Housing and living environments of older people. In B. Binstock & E. Shanas (Eds.), *Handbook of aging and the social sciences* (pp. 244–271). New York: Van Nostrand Reinhold.

Carp, F. M., & Carp, A. (1982). Perceived environmental quality of neighborhoods. *Journal of Environmental Psychology, 2,* 295–312.

Chavis, D. M., Hogge, J. H., McMillan, D. W., & Wandersman, A. (1986). Sense of community through Brunswik's lense: A first look. *Journal of Community Psychology, 14,* 23–40.

Coles, R. (1970). *Uprooted children: The early life of migrant farmworkers*. Pittsburgh: University of Pittsburgh Press.

Collins, G. (1986, January 6). Many in work force care for elderly kin. *New York Times,* p. B5.

Day-Lower, D., West, S. L., & Zimmers, H. (1985). *Designing shared housing for the elderly*. Philadelphia: National Shared Housing Resource Center.

Degnore, R., Feldman, R. M., Hilton, W. J., Jr., Love, K. D., & Schearer, M. (1980). *Phipps*

Plaza West: Evaluation of an urban housing option. New York: City University of New York, Center for Human Environments.

Erikson, E. H. (1950). *Childhood and society.* New York: Norton.

Fava, S. F. (1958). Contrasts in neighboring: New York City and a suburban county. In W. M. Dobriner (Ed.), *The suburban community* (pp. 122–131). New York: G. P. Putnam's Sons.

Firey, W. (1945). Sentiment and symbolism as ecological variables. *American Sociological Review, 10,* 140–148.

Forrest, A., Grecni, J., Mesnikoff, W., & Paxson, L. (1979). *For people's sake: A study in Grand Central Terminal.* In L. G. Rivlin, M. Francis & L. Paxson, (Eds.), *Grand Central Terminal: A human perspective* (pp. 6–18). New York: City University of New York, Center for Human Environments.

Fried, M. (1963). Grieving for a lost home. In L. J. Duhl (Ed.), *The urban condition* (pp. 151–171). New York: Basic Books.

Gersh, H., & Miller, S. (1959). Satmar in Brooklyn, *Commentary, 28,* 389–399.

Goering, J. M., & Rogowsky, E. T. (1978, summer). The myth of neighborhoods. *New York Affairs, 5,* 82–86.

Halbwachs, M. (1980). *The collective memory* (F. J. Ditter, Jr., & V. Y. Ditter, Trans.). New York: Harper & Row. (Original work published 1950).

Harris, L. (1985). *Holy days: The world of a Hasidic family.* New York: Summit Books.

Hart, R. (1979). *Children's experience of place: A developmental study.* New York: Irvington.

Heller, K., Price, R. H., Reinharz, S., Riger, S., & Wandersman, A. (1984). *Psychology and community change* (2nd ed.). Homewood, IL: The Dorsey Press.

Hopper, K., & Hamburg, J. (1984). *The making of America's homeless: From skid row to new poor.* New York: Community Service Society of New York.

Horace (Horatius Flaccus, Quintas). (1911). *Horace's complete works* (J. Marshall, Trans.). New York: E. P. Dutton.

Horwitz, J. (1986). *Working at home and being at home: The interaction of microcomputers and the social life of households.* Unpublished doctoral dissertation, City University of New York.

Horwitz, J., & Tognoli, J. (1982). Role of home in adult development: Women and men living alone describe their residential histories. *Family Relations, 31,* 335–341.

Janowitz, M. (1967). *The community press in an urban setting.* Chicago: University of Chicago Press.

Keller, S. (1968). *The urban neighborhood: A sociological perspective.* New York: Random House.

Levinson, D. J. (1986). A conception of adult development. *American Psychologist, 41,* 3–13.

Levy, S. B. (1975). Shifting patterns of ethnic identification among the Hassidim. In J. W. Bennet (Ed.), *The new ethnicity: Perspectives from ethnology* (pp. 25–50). New York: West Publishing.

Lofland, L. H. (1983, September). *The sociology of communities: Research trends and priorities. Social interaction.* Paper presented at the meeting of the American Sociological Association, Detroit, Michigan.

Mayer, E. (1979). *From suburb to shtetl: The Jews of Boro Park.* Philadelphia: Temple University Press.

McGahan, P. (1972). The neighborly role and neighboring in a highly urban area. *The Sociological Quarterly, 13,* 397–408.

Mintz, J. R. (1968). *Legends of the Hasidim.* Chicago: University of Chicago Press.

Oser, A. S. (1981, May 8). Efforts to rehabilitate Crown Heights apartment houses. *New York Times,* p. B5.

Poll, S. (1962). *The Hasidic community of Williamsburg.* Glencoe, IL: Free Press.

Proshansky, H. M., Fabian, A. K., & Kaminoff, R. (1983). Place-identity: Physical world socialization of the self. *Journal of Environmental Psychology, 3,* 57–83.

Relph, E. (1976). *Place and placelessness.* London: Pion.

Riche, M. F. (1986). Retirement's lifestyle pioneers. *American Demographics, 8*(1), 42–44, 50, 52–54, 56.

Rivlin, L. G. (1982). Group membership and place meanings in an urban neighborhood. *Journal of Social Issues, 38*(3), 75–93.

Rivlin, L. G. (1985, August). *Making a difference: Concern for the homeless.* Paper presented at the meeting of the American Psychological Association, Los Angeles, CA.

Rivlin, L. G., & Wolfe, M. (1985). *Institutional settings in children's lives.* New York: Wiley.

Rossi, P. H. (1981). *Why families move* (2nd ed.). Beverly Hills, CA: Sage Publications.

Rossi, P. H., & Shlay, A. B. (1982). Residential mobility and public policy issues: "Why families move" revisited. *Journal of Social Issues, 38*(3), 21–34.

Rowles, G. D. (1978). *Prisoners of space? Exploring the geographical experience of older people.* Boulder, CO: Westview Press.

Rowles, G. D. (1980). Toward a geography of growing old. In A. Buttimer & D. Seamon (Eds.), *The human experiences of space and place* (pp. 55–72). New York: St. Martin's Press.

Rule, S. (1979, June 18). An air of aloofness covers tensions in Crown Heights. *New York Times,* p. B6.

Ryan, W. (1976). *Blaming the victim* (rev. ed.). New York: Vintage Books.

Seamon, D. (1979). *A geography of the lifeworld.* New York: St. Martin's Press.

Sennett, R. (1978). *The fall of public man.* New York: Vintage.

Shaffir, W. (1974). *Life in a religious community: The Lubavitcher Chassidim in Montreal.* Toronto: Holt, Rinehart & Winston.

Shumaker, S. A., & Stokols, D. (1982). Residential mobility as a social issue and research topic. *Journal of Social Issues, 38*(3), 1–19.

Shumaker, S. A., & Taylor, R. B. (1983). Toward a clarification of people-place relationships: A model of attachment to place. In N. R. Feimer & E. S. Geller (Eds.), *Environmental psychology: Directions and perspectives* (pp. 219–251). New York: Praeger.

Sommer, R. (1981). The behavioral ecology of supermarkets and farmer's markets. *Journal of Environmental Psychology, 1,* 13–19.

Stokols, D., & Shumaker, S. A. (1981). People in places: A transactional view of settings. In J. H. Harvey (Ed.), *Cognition, social behavior, and the environment* (pp. 441–488). Hillsdale, NJ: Lawrence Erlbaum Associates.

Stokols, D., Shumaker, S. A., & Martinez, J. (1983). Residential mobility and well-being. *Journal of Environmental Psychology, 3,* 5–19.

Stone, A. (1980). *Attachment to neighborhood: A case study.* Unpublished manuscript.

Taylor, R. B., Gottfredson, S. D., & Brower, S. (1984). Neighborhood naming as an index of attachment to place. *Population and Environment, 7,* 103–125.

Thomas, J. (1985, May 31). British soccer fan: Why so warlike? *New York Times,* p. 10.

Toffler, A. (1970). *Future shock.* New York: Random House.

Tuan, Yi-Fu. (1980). Rootedness versus sense of place. *Landscape, 24*(1), 3–8.

Unger, D. G., & Wandersman, A. (1985). The importance of neighbors: The social, cognitive and affective components of neighboring. *American Journal of Community Psychology, 13*(2), 139–160.

Warren, D. I. (1971). Neighborhoods in urban areas. In *The encyclopedia of social work* (pp. 772–782). New York: National Association of Social Work.

Warren, D. I. (1978). Exploration in neighborhood differentiation. *Sociological Quarterly, 19,* 310–331.

Webber, M. M. (1963). Order in diversity: Community without propinquity. In L. Wingo, Jr. (Ed.), *Cities and space: The future use of urban land* (pp. 23–54). Baltimore: The Johns Hopkins Press.

Weiner, H. (1957a). The Lubovitcher movement: I. *Commentary, 23,* 231–241.

Weiner, H. (1957b). The Lubovitcher movement: II. *Commentary, 23,* 316–327.

Weiner, H. (1969). *9 1/2 Mystics.* New York: Holt, Rinehart & Winston.

Werner, C., Altman, I., & Oxley, D. (1985). Temporal aspects of homes: A transactional perspective. In I. Altman & C. Werner (Eds.), *Home environments. Human behavior and environment. Advances in theory and research* (Vol. 8, pp. 1–32). New York: Plenum Press.

Young, M., & Willmott, P. (1957). *Family and kinship in East London:* Glencoe, IL: The Free Press.

2

Crowding, Conflict, and Neighborhood Regulation

SALLY ENGLE MERRY

INTRODUCTION

Neighborhoods are physical places. They are geographical locations in which people live side by side in a wide range of physical arrangements. This spatial proximity inevitably produces certain kinds of intrusions or annoyances among the households that share the space. Intrusions may take the form of noises, smells, or visually observable messes. They may be produced by mobile members of households such as dogs and children, or they may result from the social interdependence of people who live together. In American neighborhoods, at least, the appearance and upkeep of one person's house makes a statement about the other houses in that neighborhood and the nature of the neighborhood as a whole. People who live together in neighborhoods must find some way to regulate that part of their lives that they share; they must learn to deal with these inevitable intrusions and annoyances. Most of the time, in most neighborhoods, residents find ways to cooperate, to reciprocate, and to develop shared rules and techniques for managing dogs, noise,

SALLY ENGLE MERRY • Department of Anthropology, Wellesley College, Wellesley, MA 02181.
 The research described in this chapter was supported by a grant from the National Science Foundation and the National Institute of Justice. Additional funding was provided by Wellesley College and the Wellesley College Braitmeyer Foundation Fund.

children, neatness, and so forth. But occasionally these systems of neighborhood regulation fail, and conflicts erupt.

This chapter explores systems of neighborhood regulation and the conditions under which these systems fail. It is an ethnographic study of four small neighborhoods in a northeastern city. I will describe each neighborhood and the nature and frequency with which the residents report problems arising from sharing space. I call such difficulties *proximity problems*. The neighborhoods I will describe vary by social class, by patterns of social life, and by physical design. As the analysis demonstrates, patterns of neighborhood regulation are very complex and depend upon environmental design as well as social organization, culture, politics, economics, the history and future of a neighborhood, and the relationship between a neighborhood and its surrounding town.

An anthropological study of neighborhood life views neighborhoods as miniature social systems that are part of a larger social order and cultural system. Behavior such as calling the police in response to a noisy neighbor is understood in the context of cultural patterns that prescribe rules of neighborhood life and define appropriate and acceptable means of dealing with annoyances of this type. The social organization of the neighborhood creates patterns of authority and channels of communication. The history of a neighborhood defines its social identity, its shared rules of neighborhood life, and its traditional means of dealing with proximity problems. Physical design is an important aspect of neighborhood life, but its effect can only be understood within the total social and cultural context of the neighborhood and the larger society.

The bulk of anthropological and sociological research on systems of neighborhood social regulation has focused on low-income neighborhoods in which the dominant mode of ordering is based on kinship, ethnicity, territory, and the creation of personal and particularistic social ties, as I will discuss later. In more affluent neighborhoods, however, I observed a different system of neighborhood regulation, one based on spacing houses farther apart, placing a high value on privacy, and relying more heavily on government regulation and police intervention. This alternative form of neighborhood regulation depends upon space, privacy, government, and economic forces that insulate the neighborhood from social transformation.

CROWDING AND ENVIRONMENTAL PSYCHOLOGY

As the study of crowding within environmental psychology has matured, the role of regulatory processes—the ways people cope with density—has become increasingly prominent. Early research on crowding of animals showed that high densities produced severe stress, leading to physiological changes and even to massive interference with reproduction and group survival. But studies of humans have consistently revealed far more complex patterns (cf. Baum, 1987). High densities of people do not always produce a sense of crowding or the responses of stress, withdrawal, or aggressiveness observed in animals. Density seems a necessary but not sufficient condition for the experience of crowding. As Baum points out:

> Density refers to physical conditions associated with numbers of people in given amounts of space. Crowding, on the other hand, is an experience—the outcome of appraisal of physical conditions, situational variables, personal characteristics, and coping assets. Under some conditions and for some people, a given level of density in a setting will lead to crowding, while in other conditions or for other people, it may not. In much the same way as people evaluate and interpret stressors (Lazarus, 1966), crowding is an outcome of evaluation of settings. Density is only one of several aspects of settings that appear to determine the outcomes of these appraisals. (1987)

The extensive body of research on crowding summarized in Baum's recent review of the literature indicates that the effect of density, both social and spatial, is highly variable among individuals and situations (1987). Sometimes density produces a feeling of crowding, and sometimes it does not; some people can tolerate more crowding than others, and crowding in some settings is more stressful than in others. In an effort to explain the complex and elusive relationship between density and human behavior, Freedman (1975) developed the density/intensity hypothesis: He argued that density increases the intensity of an individual's feelings about a situation, whether they are pleasant or unpleasant. Loo (1977) points out that there are important individual differences by sex, by experience, by age, and by individual psychological characteristics in response to density. In sum, there seem to be important cultural and social factors affecting the conditions under which density feels like crowding.

Humans clearly develop social and cultural practices and institutions that mitigate the impact of crowding. They cope with density through social strategies: interactional ones, such as avoiding eye contact, physical techniques, such as using chairs as barriers, or cultural ones, such as shared ideas of personal space and interactional distance (Aiello, 1987). A more helpful way to think about the effects of density on human behavior is, therefore, to examine the adequacy of social and cultural mechanisms that humans develop to deal with high-density settings. As Stokols (1977) points out, crowding stress can be avoided or reduced through the enhancement of an individual's perceived control over the environment. Altman's (1975) model of privacy regulation is very useful in conceptualizing the relationship between density and the experience of crowding. He defines crowding as a situation in which privacy-regulation mechanisms do not work adequately, causing more social contact to occur than is desired (1975). Persons or groups use various mechanisms, including social ones, to produce desired levels of interaction. When they achieve the desired level of privacy, the system is successful; when they experience too much interaction, they feel crowded, and when they experience too little, they feel isolated. This model describes a feedback system in which a situation of crowding results in coping mechanisms regulating levels of social interaction that may or may not be successful in reducing stress and the sense of crowding.

But how does this regulation work? Altman's model suggests that the adequacy of regulatory processes is critical to the experience of crowding but does not elucidate the range of coping mechanisms that humans have developed. Furthermore, his model focuses on interpersonal interaction; yet many of these coping mechanisms are parts of the cultural and social orders: building styles, street layouts, clocks as devices to sort out appropriate kinds of behavior by time, class and ethnic boundaries that prohibit intimate exchanges and define limited and superficial patterns of interaction and so on. The cross-cultural literature provides a wealth of evidence about social and cultural mechanisms used to regulate interaction and mitigate the impact of density. This chapter examines regulatory processes that take place in American urban and suburban neighborhoods to manage the effects of density—the inevitable intrusions of people upon those they live nearby. It is a study of coping responses that describes social, cultural, and political processes, including the ways neighborhoods develop shared rules of behavior and patterns of social control.

VARIETIES OF NEIGHBORHOOD SOCIAL CONTROL

Social control is the process by which individuals are induced to conform to the norms of their society (see generally Black, 1984). Social control processes can be roughly divided into formal processes, which depend on the state, such as the police and the courts, and informal processes, which are part of the social fabric of social groups. Informal processes include gossip, scandal, joking, insults, slander of reputation, ostracism, and exile from a group. Except for a few small-scale societies of hunters and gatherers, every society contains both formal and informal mechanisms for achieving social control; it is the mix that is highly variable. A substantial body of theory within sociology and anthropology argues that as societies become larger and more complex, informal social control becomes relatively less effective, and a larger proportion of the regulatory burden is undertaken by the state. Formal and informal control are inversely related to each other (Black, 1976; Schwartz, 1954).

In the early 20th century, urban sociologists of the Chicago School argued that within large, dense, socially heterogeneous, and permanent settlements, informal social control atrophies, and new problems of social order develop (Wirth, 1938). The anonymity and impersonality of the city breed social disorganization, crime, personality disruption, and suicide, among other social ills. Formal systems of social control become central to the maintenance of social order (cf. Hannerz, 1980).

This theory has been much criticized, yet it provides an accurate description of some aspects of urban life. The Chicago sociologists themselves documented many small pockets of intimate and personalistic social life within cities, ordered by informal social control, such as the Jewish ghetto (Wirth, 1928), the taxi-dance-hall girls (Cressey, 1932), and the leisured Chicago elite (Zorbaugh, 1929). The urban ethnic village, in particular, is a settlement whose residents are intertwined by social ties of ethnicity, family, and neighboring (Gans, 1962). In the urban village, the thesis that the city is anonymous, ordered primarily by formal systems of social control, does not apply. Close-knit social networks of intimate social ties link neighbors together and facilitate effective informal social control among residents and adequate surveillance of strangers. Jane Jacobs, for example, described the vibrant street life of the North End of Boston and the safety provided by the continuous informal surveillance of the street in this Italian neighborhood (1961). In Suttles's study (1968) of a multiethnic poor neighborhood in Chicago, he argued that similar processes can unite people who live together across the boundaries of ethnic villages. He described a system of social order based on personal social ties that organized neighborhoods of differing ethnicity within a shared territory. He argued that the residents of this area formed a provincial morality, different from the public morality that regulates relations between individuals in wealthier neighborhoods, by which they could establish relations based on trust. They trusted only those whom they knew personally. Further, they organized themselves into corporate groups that facilitated the indentification and location of strangers in social space, such as teenage gangs. Finally, ties of ethnicity and territory linked residents together into larger groups that coalesced during periods of conflict in a form of political organization Suttles calls *ordered segmentation*. A substantial body of urban sociology and anthropology over the past four decades has continued to document the ways ties of kinship, friendship, and ethnicity create a personalistic social order within stable urban communities (e.g., Gans, 1962; Greenberg, Rohe, & Williams, 1984; Hannerz, 1969; Hunter & Suttles, 1972; Stack, 1974; Suttles, 1972; Unger & Wandersman, 1985; Whyte, 1943; Young & Willmott, 1957).

Newman examined the relationship between informal social control and architectural design, arguing that certain features of building layout, size, and design create the social fabric of community and foster informal surveillance (1973). Through design, architects can create informal social networks and a social system in which people feel responsible for the territory in which they live and will act collectively to defend that space, thus helping to control crime. For architecture to create this sense of territorial responsibility, it must define space clearly by grouping units of housing together, by providing for visual suveillance of public space, and by providing symbolic and physical demarcation of space. His comparison of public housing projects in New York City indicated that crimes occur in areas that are least subject to surveillance and that buildings with better "defensible space" tend to have lower crime rates. In a reexamination of his thesis in a different housing project, however, I argued that design is a necessary but not sufficient condition for producing defended space (1981b). For residents to defend space, they must feel that they are members of a group that has the right and the responsibility to exercise control over that territory (see also Murray, 1983; Wandersman, Andrews, Riddle, & Fancell, 1983).

Thus research on the role of informal social control in cities presented a vision of city life as a mosaic of small communities in which personal social relationships create order. Relations between these small communities are problematic. Informal social processes do not produce order across the boundaries between ethnic and class groups when a territory lacks a dominant ethnic or social group (Merry, 1981a). The anonymity of these relationships requires more formal systems of social control. If a neighborhood, as a physical place, consists of persons linked by webs of personal ties, the management of proximity problems is simply an aspect of the system of informal social control by which the neighborhood is governed. If a neighborhood consists of people who have no other relationship with each other and who belong to different communities, the negotiation of the details of daily life becomes problematic. Formal systems of social control may take on a larger role: Residents may call the police more often and take their neighbors to court. Under these conditions, the anonymity and social disorganization that the Chicago School argued was a characteristic feature of urban life may occur.

This chapter describes two kinds of neighborhoods with minimal informal social networks and weak informal social control. One of these is a transitional neighborhood with frequent conflicts that are symptoms of its lack of an overarching social order. The other represents an alternative system of ordering that depends on formal social control, on a shared normative system guaranteed by the homogeneity of the population, by spacing, and by norms of privacy that diminish the kinds of interaction that might lead to conflict. After describing four different neighborhoods and the patterns of conflict and conflict management in each, I will develop a model of the alternative form of neighborhood regulation and a theory to explain the high level of conflict in the transitional neighborhood.

THE RESEARCH AND THE SETTING

RESEARCH METHODS

The research described in this chapter comes from two separate studies. The first, carried out between 1980 and 1983 in collaboration with Susan S. Silbey, examined the way mediation functions in different kinds of American neighborhoods and focused on the kinds of disputes citizens take to court and to mediation programs. Mediation is one of the forms of alternative dispute resolution developed in the past decade to serve as an alternative to courts for interpersonal disputes. This research suggested that plaintiffs turn to the courts as a last resort, when they are seeking justice rather than reconciliation (Merry & Silbey, 1984). Further, it delineated two styles of mediation adopted by mediators in their efforts to help parties settle cases without imposing a decision (Silbey & Merry, 1986). The mediation study examined the case files of two mediation programs, a total of 868 cases, observed 118 mediation sessions in which the parties discussed their conflicts during a 1- to 4-hour private and informal session, interviewed 124 mediation participants after their sessions concerning their reactions to the process and the course of their conflict, and followed about 30 of these cases back to court when they failed to settle.

In order to determine the relationship between the problems arriving in court and mediation and those occurring within neighborhoods, we designed a questionnaire of 88 items intended to assess the number of problems neighborhood residents had of the sort that had appeared in mediation. This survey also asked about the nature of the social organization of the neighborhood, the extent of informal neighboring, perceptions of the neighborhood, and the ways these residents dealt with the problems they encountered. This questionnaire was administered to 93 individuals in three small neighborhoods: 36 in one, 32 in a second, and 25 in a third. In all three neighborhoods, the interviewer left a letter describing the study; then a few days later knocked on the door and requested an interview. Interviews typically lasted between 45 and 90 minutes. In addition to the formal interviews, we conducted extensive ethnographic research in each neighborhood, talking to five or more residents in each one over a period of about 9 months about their neighborhood, how they felt about it, and how they handled disputes. We also studied specific disputes from these neighborhoods in detail, both those that went to mediation and court and those that did not.

This research suggested that there were significant differences in the frequency of problems and conflicts in neighborhoods of different social composition, class, and physical design. One of the neighborhoods, a suburb of single-family homes, was intriguingly different from the other more urban and working-class neighborhoods. It had less conflict and more pervasive norms of privacy between neighbors. To see if these differences were enhanced when density was even lower and income levels even higher, in the summer of 1985 I studied a fourth neighborhood, a yet more affluent suburb. A research assistant and I replicated the previous survey with the same questionnaire, interviewing 35 residents.[1] As in the case of the other three neighborhoods, we supplemented this formal interviewing with an ethnographic study of the town and discussions with the police and the local court. Because this neighborhood was not served by a mediation program, however, we were unable to collect comparable information on the frequency with

[1]Neighborhoods differed greatly in refusal rates. In the first suburb, Riverdale, refusals were rare, whereas in the three other neighborhoods, at least half of those contacted refused. This variation is not related to social class or frequency of problems, however, because the highest number of refusals came from the most transitional and problem-ridden neighborhood and from the most affluent and stable one. It probably varied with the interviewer. The interviewer in the neighborhood with low refusal rates was a resident of that neighborhood. In the other three neighborhoods, the interviewer was a college student. The students were not complete outsiders, however. One spent 2 months living in the neighborhood where she was working, and another went to college in the town she was studying. Nevertheless, they had less success in persuading people to be interviewed than the mature woman who lived in the neighborhood she was studying. In all four neighborhoods, women were more likely to agree to an interview than men.

which disputes were handled in mediation. Both the police and the local court resisted our efforts to learn more about the nature and frequency with which they handled interpersonal disputes, arguing that this was a town in which residents valued their privacy and that such family and neighbor disputes were the "heartbeat of family life" that people wished to keep private. In fact, their resistance revealed something about the role that the police and the court feel that they play in the town.

THE SETTING

The four neighborhoods differ by social class, physical design, and stability. Each had a population of approximately 1,000 residents. The first three neighborhoods are located in a town that serves as the commercial and industrial center of a larger region of suburban towns. Jackson (a pseudonym)[2] is a predominantly working-class town of about 35,000 inhabitants dominated by a Yankee elite. The majority of the inhabitants are of white ethnic heritage: second- and third-generation immigrants from Ireland, Poland, Portugal, French Canada, Italy, and Greece. They formed the backbone of the working population during the city's florescence as a textile and leather-producing center in the early 20th century. As the economy has diversified into other forms of manufacturing and a substantial service sector, many have moved into lower middle-class technical and clerical jobs. In recent years, a new population of Hispanics from Puerto Rico and the Dominican Republic has arrived and taken the poorest housing from the French Canadian residents, but their numbers are small, and the town remains a fairly homogeneous white, Catholic community whose residents feel insulated from the metropolitan center on its borders. The 1980 census reported that the median family income in Jackson was $19,138 and the town was 97% white. Of those over twenty five, 67% were high school graduates and 14% college graduates. In 1977, the unemployment rate was 9 1/2%.

The three neighborhoods we studied in this town have distinct local identities and histories. Hilltowne is a white, working-class neighborhood of small duplexes and an occasional single-family house. Built early in the 20th century for the more prosperous and upwardly mobile residents of Jackson, predominantly Irish and French, it still has a mixed ethnic identity. The neighborhood has more family linkages than the others. Families often rent an apartment to children as they marry and

---

[2]All the place names used in this paper are pseudonyms in order to protect the privacy of the individuals being described.

establish independent households. For many Hilltowne residents, buying a home is beyond their means and inheriting the family house is the
only way they will be able to own a home. Mobility is relatively low, and
many residents have other family members living on the same street.
According to 1980 census figures, the median family income was
$20,625. Of those over 18, 69% had completed high school, and 9% had
4 years of college or more. Sixty-three percent of the households were
nuclear families, and 52% owned their own homes.

Oldtowne, the second neighborhood, is one in transition. Originally an elite neighborhood during the peak of the town's economic importance at the close of the 18th century, it contains beautiful houses built at
that period plus multifamily structures built in later years. As might be
expected of a neighborhood designed and substantially constructed during the 18th and 19th centuries, the buildings are small and packed
together, the streets are narrow, and parks are few. The houses sit
directly on the sidewalks and are separated from one another by no
more than a few feet. They have backyards of only a few square feet and
generally do not have off-street parking spaces. Some of the houses are
sufficiently set back to carve out a small parking space in the front.
Backyards are generally fenced, and fences are common between houses
that are a little distance apart.

During the first half of the 20th century, this was a Polish ethnic
village housing the recently arrived workers in the textile mills and
leather factories. It boasted an active community life, numerous self-
help associations, two Polish lawyers, and small family stores on every
street corner. With the postwar era, however, a long-term decline began
as the more affluent and upwardly mobile Polish families moved out,
leaving a population of elderly, poor, and single mothers who could not
afford to leave. A few are still trapped in the neighborhood because they
cannot move away. Another group of oldtimers has chosen to remain
because they are attracted by the prospect of preserving and upgrading
the historic neighborhood.

During the 1970s, absentee landlords purchased many of the multifamily dwellings and turned them into apartments for low-income and
welfare tenants. By 1980, low-income white tenants constituted a significant minority in the neighborhood. However, during the 1970s, the city
government decided to invest in upgrading the neighborhood, an area
of considerable historic and tourist interest. A major urban renewal
project on the borders of Oldtowne changed its image and encouraged a
flood of young, moderately wealthy professional people who bought
and renovated the older "period" houses. The small size of the houses
and the lack of open space guaranteed that young professionals would

not remain long after their children were born, however, and they typically stayed only a few years.

The area was extremely transient in the 1970s. A local agency used city poll lists to determine turnover and reported that between 1971 and 1976, 63% of the total housing units in the area changed hands. In the 2-year period between 1974 and 1976, 48% of the units changed hands. By the mid-1980s, Oldtowne was a very heterogeneous neighborhood. People of varying life-styles, class backgrounds, and values found themselves squeezed together around limited parking spaces and tiny yards. According to the 1980 census, the median family income was $20,050 and $14,972 for the two parts of the neighborhood. Of those over 18, 65% had finished high school, and 15% had 4 years of college or more. Only 37% of the households were nuclear families, and only 31% owned their homes.

Riverdale, the third neighborhood in Jackson, is a recent suburban development within the city limits. It is a neighborhood of nuclear families. Built 15 years ago, it is a collection of single-family homes clustered closely together on relatively small lots, usually about 1/5 of an acre. Each has an individual backyard, and the houses are overall quite similar. The houses are separated from each other by about 30 to 40 feet, but this does not provide enough space for plantings to create barriers between the houses. Sidewalks line the streets, and houses have garages and off-street parking spaces. Many people have fenced in their small backyards, but few have built fences between the houses. In contrast to Hilltowne, which looks like an urban neighborhood with rows of small houses close together along straight streets, Riverdale looks like a suburb with its curving streets and single-family homes of similar design. The population is economically homogeneous, although the neighborhood contains a wide range of ethnic backgrounds. It can be characterized as a middle-class suburb. According to the 1980 census, the median family income was $23,951.[3] Seventy-one percent of the households were nuclear families, and 62% owned their houses. Of those over 18, 77% had finished high school, and 12% had 4 years of college or more. Thus, on the average, Riverdale residents are somewhat wealthier and better educated than those in Oldtowne and Hilltowne, although there is a substantial minority of more educated, affluent newcomers in Oldtowne.

The fourth neighborhood is part of Hamilton, an affluent suburb of 27,200 residents that serves as a bedroom community for the nearby

---

[3]Because the census blocks do not precisely follow the boundaries of the Riverdale development, these figures include some families that live outside the neighborhood.

metropolitan center. The neighborhood itself has no special name nor a particular history or identity. It appears to be a typical suburb with houses fairly widely spaced along tree-shaded streets and set well back from the sidewalks. Lot sizes average between a quarter and a third of an acre, somewhat larger than Riverdale lots. Uneven terrain and plantings produce a fair amount of privacy in backyards, but the houses are easily visible to each other along the streets. Almost all the houses have garages or off-street parking. It looks much like Riverdale except that it is less dense and has more lush vegetation. The house styles are more varied, ranging from some 19-century frame houses to more elegant brick houses and modern split-level dwellings built in the 1960s. Eighty-two percent of the units in this neighborhood are owned rather than rented.

Hamilton grew rapidly earlier in the century but is now an established suburb with little room for further development. It has long been known as an elite community, a reputation enhanced by its superior schools and services. It was recently featured as one of the 10 most elite suburbs by the metropolitan newspaper. The established reputation and lack of room for future development suggests little uncertainty concerning the future social class status of this town. Although there is some ethnic, racial, and class mixture in the town, it is considered to be a predominantly WASP, upper middle-class community. According to the 1980 census, it was 97% white and had a median family income of $36,700, almost double the income of the Jackson neighborhoods. Ninety-three percent of the residents over 25 had finished high school, and 56% had 4 years of college or more. Only 3.4% were unemployed. There is virtually no industry and only a small commercial center, no liquor stores because the town has voted to remain dry, and until recently, no flouridation of the drinking water. The town is generally considered to be politically and socially conservative. House prices are high and continue to rise. They are roughly double the prices of houses in the Jackson neighborhoods.[4]

The characteristics of the survey respondents reflect these neighborhood differences. Oldtowne respondents were significantly more recent arrivals in their neighborhood: 44% had lived there less than 3 years, in comparison to 8% of Hilltowne respondents, 11% of Riverdale residents, and 12% of Hamilton respondents.[5] There were significant

[4]According to the 1980 census, the mean value of houses in the Hamilton neighborhood was $94,100 in comparison to $55,400 and $40,400 for two parts of Oltowne, $43,000 in Hilltowne, and $56,800 in Riverdale.

[5]Fewer respondents had lived in Oldtowne for a long time: 34% had lived in the neighborhood over 13 years in contrast to 52% of respondents in Hilltowne, 67% in Riverdale, and 57% in Hamilton.

differences in education and income between the respondents, with Hamilton respondents substantially more educated and affluent than respondents in the other neighborhoods (see Table 1). Fully 68% of Hamilton respondents had completed college in comparison to 29% of Oldtowne respondents, 32% of Hilltowne respondents, and 17% of Riverdale respondents. Clearly, the respondents are more highly educated than the average for the neighborhoods in which they live, particularly in the neighborhoods with relatively high refusal rates. More educated people were more willing to be interviewed.

Hamilton respondents are far more affluent than respondents from other neighborhoods: 74% said they had a family income over $35,000 in comparison to 17% of Oldtowne respondents, 13% of Hilltowne re-

TABLE 1. COMPARISON OF RESPONDENTS IN FOUR NEIGHBORHOODS

	Oldtowne N = 32	Hilltowne N = 25	Riverdale N = 36	Hamilton N = 35	Total N = 128
		Education			
High school diploma or less	32%	42%	37%	9%	29%
Some college	39%	17%	46%	23%	32%
College degree	16%	25%	11%	34%	22%
Advanced education or degree	13%	17%	6%	34%	18%
Significant at $p < .01$ Missing = 3					
		Family income			
0–$16,000	37%	40%	0	4%	18%
$16–35,000	47%	47%	74%	22%	50%
Over $35,000	17%	13%	27%	74%	32%
Significant at $p < .01$ Missing = 26					
		Occupation			
Professional, technical	38%	4%	20%	15%	20%
Managerial	10%	0	6%	15%	8%
Sales	3%	0	3%	6%	3%
Clerical	7%	13%	31%	9%	16%
Craftsmen	3%	0	9%	6%	5%
Operatives	0	0	6%	0	2%
Service workers	0	9%	9%	3%	5%
Retired	21%	35%	0	24%	18%
At home	17%	35%	14%	15%	19%
Student	0	4%	3%	9%	4%
Significant at $p < .01$ Missing = 7					

spondents, and 27% of Riverdale respondents. More poor people were interviewed in Oldtowne and Hilltowne than in the other neighborhoods, whereas the Riverdale respondents include no poor and no very rich individuals (see Table 1). No one interviewed in Hilltowne or Riverdale had a family income over $50,000, whereas 10% of Oldtowne residents and 56% of Hamilton residents had family incomes over this amount.[6] The Oldtowne respondents reflect the mixed social and economic composition of the neighborhood. Somewhat under half are young professionals, about the same proportion are old-timers, and a few are the more recent welfare poor. Although a high proportion of respondents in all the neighborhoods are retired or at home, their occupational distribution suggests that there are more professional and managerial workers in Oldtowne, Riverdale, and Hamilton than in Hilltowne (see Table 1).

The average age of the respondents was 46, with Hamilton residents slightly older than the rest. This is somewhat older than the mean age of adults in the three Jackson neighborhoods, which is about 42. Seventy-one percent of the respondents were women, reflecting those who are available to be interviewed at home and those who were willing to cooperate. There were not significant differences in the sex ratios of respondents between the neighborhoods.

PATTERNS OF NEIGHBORHOOD CONFLICT

I surveyed the residents of these four neighborhoods to determine how often they experienced proximity problems and what they did about them. Each respondent was presented with a list of these problems and asked whether or not he or she had experienced these problems, how long they had gone on, and what he or she did about them. The list was based on problems that commonly appeared in mediation sessions. The 41 problems were divided into four categories: neighborhood problems, family problems, friendship problems, and consumer and services problems. Of the 402 problems mentioned by the 128 respondents, 245 were proximity problems. Most of the rest concerned family conflicts over money, work, and child rearing and problems with consumer goods.

A problem, as identified in the survey, represents the early stages of

---

[6]Income figures might be slightly affected by the fact that the Hamilton survey was conducted 2 to 3 years after the other surveys, but this was a period of relatively low inflation.

a conflict. It is an annoyance that the respondent has been unable to eliminate through tolerance, discussion, or some third-party intervention such as the police. Respondents did not mention annoyances that they had managed successfully, such as the barking dog whose owners always take it in when they call to complain. For three-quarters of all problems (not only neighborhood problems), the respondent had made some effort to resolve the problem.[7] The respondent had called the police for one fifth of the problems, had talked directly to the other person in about one third, and had taken direct action or turned to an intermediary for help in one fifth. These are all problems that resisted easy settlement. Over 60% had persisted for a year or more, and only 30% had been resolved at the time of the interview. Many of these problems have the potential for escalating into court battles, although very few of the problems reported in the survey had actually progressed that far.

The respondents in the changing neighborhood reported many more proximity problems than did the respondents in the other three neighborhoods (see Table 2). Oldtowne residents reported twice as many problems as the average for all four neighborhoods. In Oldtowne, each respondent reported an average of 4.1 problems. In Hilltowne, the stable working-class neighborhood, each reported 2.1 problems; in Riverdale, the middle-class suburb, 1.1; and in Hamilton, the affluent suburb, 0.7. As Table 2 indicates, the most common problems were noise, dogs, vandalism, and children.

The difference between neighborhoods is particularly marked for noise problems. Fully 69% of the Oldtowne respondents complained about noise from neighbors, whereas only 28% of Hilltowne respondents, 17% of Riverdale respondents, and 17% of Hamilton respondents reported noise problems. Oldtowne respondents were also far more likely to report dog problems, problems with children playing in the street, vandalism, and harassment. When respondents were asked if there were serious problems in their neighborhoods, 38% of Oldtowne respondents said yes as did 16% of Hilltowne respondents, but only 6% of both Riverdale and Hamilton respondents felt that way. This difference is statistically significant. It appears that the denser, transitional neighborhood has significantly more problems than the other three. The two suburban neighborhoods have somewhat fewer than the stable working-class neighborhood.

Does Oldtowne have more dogs and children than the other neigh-

---

[7]Unfortunately, I was unable to sort the problems by type of problem in order to describe the responses to proximity problems alone because of the organization of the data file.

TABLE 2. PROXIMITY PROBLEMS BY NEIGHBORHOOD[a]

Problem	Oldtowne N = 32		Hilltowne N = 25		Riverdale N = 36		Hamilton N = 35		Total N = 128	
	n	%	n	%	n	%	n	%	n	%
Noise from neighbors	(22)	69	(7)	28	(6)	17	(6)	17	(41)	32
Dogs making messes	(17)	53	(10)	40	(7)	19	(7)	20	(41)	32
Vandalism	(16)	50	(8)	32	(3)	9	(2)	6	(29)	23
Barking dogs	(14)	44	(3)	12	(8)	22	(4)	11	(29)	23
Children playing in the street	(12)	38	(4)	16	(3)	8	(0)	0	(19)	15
Children harassing adults	(9)	28	(3)	12	(3)	8	(0)	0	(15)	12
Fights over parking spaces	(8)	25	(5)	20	(0)	0	(1)	3	(14)	11
Trespassing, using yard or driveway	(11)	34	(2)	8	(0)	0	(0)	0	(13)	10
City services	(7)	22	(4)	16	(0)	0	(1)	3	(12)	9
Fences	(4)	13	(1)	4	(4)	11	(0)	0	(9)	7
Name calling	(5)	16	(3)	12	(0)	0	(0)	0	(8)	6
Fights between children	(4)	13	(1)	4	(2)	6	(1)	3	(8)	6
Adults bothering children	(3)	9	(1)	4	(2)	6	(1)	3	(7)	5
No problems mentioned	(3)	9	(7)	28	(16)	44	(17)	49	(43)	34
Total number of problems reported	132		52		38		23		245	
Average per respondent	4.1		2.1		1.1		0.7		1.9	

[a]Percentage of respondents reporting each problem.

borhoods? I did not do a census of dogs or children, but I did ask respondents how many dogs and children they thought lived in their neighborhoods. In all four neighborhoods, respondents evaluated the dog population about the same, an average of about five or six dogs. The neighborhoods did differ in the number of children the respondents thought lived there, but the neighborhoods in which the respondents thought there were more children were not those in which children were most often regarded as a problem. Hilltowne respondents reported the most children, with Riverdale close behind. Yet respondents in both of these neighborhoods were much less likely to report a problem with children playing in the street than those who lived in Oldtowne: 12% and 8% reported this problem, in contrast to 38% in Oldtowne. These data suggest that the relatively few children playing in the streets in Oldtowne are more bothersome to the residents than the more numerous children in Riverdale and Hilltowne. Oldtowne residents also seem more sensitive to the same dog population. Clearly, Oldtowne is a much denser neighborhood. It is also far more socially heterogeneous and changing. In this transitional neighborhood, there is uncertainty about the rules for neighborhood life, and behind this a deeper uncertainty about the kind of neighborhood it is, to whom it belongs, and whose rules should apply.

ASPECTS OF NEIGHBORHOOD REGULATION

I will discuss several aspects of the process of neighborhood regulation. Regulation has spatial, political, cultural, and economic aspects. Regulatory processes are human constructions developed to cope with living close together and mitigating the impact of density.

SPACE AND PHYSICAL DESIGN

Greater space between houses is associated with fewer proximity problems. The most common neighborhood problems listed in Table 2 are related to proximity. Off-street parking eliminates battles over parking spaces, particularly the northeast phenomenon of a battle over the parking space laboriously shoveled free of snow. More space between houses decreases the frequency of annoyances and intrusions of noise, dogs, children, cars, and so forth. Spacing houses farther apart is obviously one way to reduce proximity problems.

Another approach is to build physical barriers between houses. If a family can afford it, its first response to conflict with a neighbor is typically to erect a fence. Most of the backyards in Oldtowne and Hill-towne are fenced, and Riverdale residents are beginning to put up fences. They are less common in Hamilton. Residents also close windows to keep out noise or buy locks to put on gates if they have already invested in a fence. Sometimes they will try to create a new parking space in the frontyard to manage a parking conflict. Parks provide an important solution to problems of loud children's play and dog messes. However, whether or not residents can use parks to solve these problems depends on whether or not there is a park nearby.

Creating and maintaining a homogeneous housing stock facilitates the regulation of neighborhood life. A heterogeneous housing stock contributes to proximity problems by housing people of different lifestyles and norms next door to each other. In Oldtowne, for example, small "period" homes, built in the 17th and 18th centuries, are interspersed with larger three-story apartment buildings. These square, unadorned frame buildings were originally built to house the poor mill workers who inhabited the neighborhood in the 19th century and are now divided into several small apartments and typically in poor repair. A transient population of young people, students, and welfare families occupies these buildings. When Oldtowners talk about neighborhood problems, their complaints generally focus on the residents of these buildings. The residents of these buildings feel that their neighbors talk about them all the time. The young professionals moving into the neighborhood prefer the old period houses, whereas the old-timer Polish families typically live in small single-family houses or duplexes of more recent date. Thus the variation in the housing itself has fostered the social diversity of the neighborhood. Similarly, in Hilltowne, the few units that are entirely rented tend to attract people whom the other residents consider troublesome and unwelcome. These houses are not greatly different in design from the other houses, however.

In contrast, the two suburban neighborhoods have highly similar housing stock, consisting largely of single-family detached homes with three or four bedrooms. When these units are rented, as a few are in the Hamilton neighborhood, the residents still worry that they will have a bad impact on the neighborhood, but the character of the buildings guarantees that the rents will be high. Although there is greater turnover in these units, the tenants have not become a source of problems. A homogeneous housing stock contributes to the stability of a neighborhood by communicating consistent messages about its social class identity.

POLICE AND TOWN REGULATIONS

Neighborhoods develop a variety of political institutions to manage neighborhood life and to establish order. The most important are town ordinances and regulations, particularly zoning regulations, and the police. For example, dogs, one of the prime proximity problems, are typically controlled by a dog officer attached to the police department. Towns vary greatly in the resources they invest in dog control and in their willingness to respond to dog complaints. Both Jackson and Hamilton have leash laws, but the residents of Hamilton seem more satisfied with the way their dog complaints are handled. Riverdale residents complain that the leash laws are never enforced. In Hamilton, the leash law is enforced by an escalating system of penalties and a mechanism that permits anonymous complaints. Hamilton also has an "excessive barking law" that prohibits barking between 11 P.M. and 7 A.M.[8]

The police are often called upon to handle proximity problems in all four neighborhoods, but their use is particularly striking in Hamilton. Hamilton residents seem far more satisfied with their police services than the Jackson residents and use them more often. Ninety-one percent said that they had called the police about a problem at some point in comparison to 78% of Oldtowne respondents, 64% of Hilltowne respondents, and only 56% of Riverdale respondents. This variation is statistically significant at the .01 level by chi-square. Hamilton residents only call about particular kinds of problems, however. The police are viewed as an appropriate resource for public-order problems such as noise and dog control, for teenage parties and drinking, and for crimes and accidents. But they do not want police intervention in family matters nor in their personal relationships with neighbors. One elderly resident said that she does not call the police for problems with her neighbors because "you have to live with your neighbors," but she does not hesitate to call for ambulance services or about prowlers. Another respondent said that police are helpful with problems of speeding cars and teenagers, but they are not good for family things. Hamilton residents

[8]In Hamilton, offenders receive a warning at the first complaint, $25 fines at the second and third complaints, and $50 fines for the fourth and subsequent complaints. The dog officer receives about 25 complaints daily. Many are "vague": The caller does not identify himself or herself and may even say that it is a another neighbor who is complaining about the dog. The dog officer talks to the owner of the dog, gives him or her the fine if necessary, and tells him or her that he or she can either pay or go to court. About 10 go to court a month, but most pay the fine without appearing. The court clerk estimated that only 14 cases a year actually have hearings. In Hamilton, both the dog officer and the court clerk, when the case goes that far, are careful not to reveal the identity of the complainant. At the hearing, the dog officer, not the neighbor, presses the claim.

do not often call about interpersonal matters.[9] Another reason they fail to call about family disputes is the distance between houses. One Hamilton woman said she did not think that people have fights in their families:

> It's not that kind of neighborhood. But then, how do we know? We're spread out enough so that we don't know what's going on.

Riverdale respondents express a similar view that the police are appropriate for problems with strangers, such as crimes or accidents, but not for family or interpersonal problems. They seemed more reluctant to call the police than Hamilton residents even for neighborhood-order problems, however. Several said that the way to deal with problems with neighbors was to avoid all contact with the offending parties, resorting to the police or the courts only as a very last resort. A few families were known as "court happy" or "police happy" because they called the police or went to court so often. They were typically avoided by their neighbors. Calling the police too frequently carried with it a stigma of lower-class status. With less space between their houses than Hamiltonians, Riverdale residents sometimes experienced considerable discomfort when they were able to overhear violent fights inside a neighbor's house, yet hesitated to call the police for fear of antagonizing the combatants.

One reason the police function differently in the two towns is the class status of the towns (cf. Black, 1980; Wilson, 1968). In a predominantly working-class city like Jackson, the police are likely to be the social equals or superiors to most of those they serve. In a upper middle-class town such as Hamilton, however, the residents are typically of a higher social class than the police. The police are viewed as serving the needs of the community as it defines its needs, and it is clear to the police that privacy is highly valued. Hamiltonians frequently comment on how polite and cooperative police officers are and how satisfied they are with the police. Jackson residents were far less likely to say the same thing. The police strategy of disposing of a problem on the spot, neither making an arrest nor encouraging the complainant to file charges, seems to satisfy Hamilton residents and to minimize the escalation of conflict. One man in Hamilton said that he had been afraid to complain directly

---

[9]For example, during the first 6 months of 1985, 211 calls for police assistance were recorded in the police log from the neighborhood studied. The most frequent were 68 responses to alarms, 17 ambulance runs, 11 accidents with property damage, 10 vandalism, and 9 animal complaints. There were 11 calls about larcenies and burglaries, 8 about disturbances, and only 2 about assaults.

to the neighbor teenagers when they had a loud party, but when he called the police, they broke up the party quietly, with no arrests. This was exactly what he wanted. In general, Hamilton allows anonymous complaints: People are able to complain about their neighbors' noise or dogs without having their identities revealed to the accused. This policy minimizes the escalation of interpersonal conflict while lodging more of the social-control task in the hands of the local government.

Town ordinances and zoning regulations are important to neighborhood social order (cf. Perin, 1977). Zoning regulations, that detail what kinds of buildings and activities are permissible in different areas, are important in maintaining socially homogeneous neighborhoods and eliminating eyesores that others view as intrusions. Hamilton, for example, has zoning regulations that prohibit leaving an unregistered vehicle where it is visible from the street. The zoning officials identify such vehicles and bring them to court without the need for a citizen complaint. This regulation prevents the accumulation of junked cars and discourages home repair of old cars. Both of these practices serve as markers of lower status neighborhoods and could lead to conflict. Quiet hours and leash laws are similarly important in preventing neighborhood conflict. Clearly, these regulations are effective only when they are enforced by the police and town officials.

PRIVACY

A cultural value on privacy regulates neighborhood life by diminishing social contact. Privacy has both social and spatial dimensions. Physical separation between houses, barriers such as fences and bushes, and private parking spaces facilitate privacy. But privacy is also a social and cultural phenomenon. In essence, it is the ability to limit social contact to those one chooses (cf. Altman, 1975). Private social lives are those in which social interactions are based on choice: The individual constructs a set of relationships based on those he or she wishes to see and avoids others. Neighbors, however, are not chosen. They are simply the people who happen to live nearby. Consquently, individuals intent on constructing a private social life will avoid intimate contact with them unless they seem desirable social companions on the basis of criteria other than where they live. In fact, too great intimacy with people who live nearby undermines privacy. One of the social mechanisms for maintaining privacy despite density is to keep those nearby at a distance, to treat them as if they were strangers. Norms that stress the privacy of the household and the importance of leaving others alone, of maintaining only superficial friendliness with neighbors, and closing off private spaces such as backyards with fences and shrubbery facilitate constructing social lives based on choice. The ability to complain about one's neighbors anonymously, through town officials such as the police or the zoning board, makes social order possible without the informal social control that neighborhood social relationships provide.

The survey respondents indicated that Hamilton, Riverdale, and Hilltowne were all more private places than Oldtowne. Seventy percent of the respondents in Oldtowne said that people in their neighborhood talk about each other, but only 25% in Hilltowne, 21% in Hamilton, and 19% in Riverdale felt that others talked about them. This variation is significant at the .01 level by chi-square. Respondents in Riverdale and Hamilton repeatedly emphasized that in their neighborhoods, people keep to themselves and avoid intimacy with their neighbors. As one Riverdale resident put it, "Here we only talk about the outsides of houses—yards, the paint, the appearance—not the insides of houses." One woman in Riverdale said, "This is a neighborhood where people don't bother each other too much, where they mind their own business." Many of the survey respondents commented that both parents in their families were full-time workers and they had little time to socialize with their neighbors but that this did not bother them at all. They preferred to have their own private space in which others could not intrude. They were generally reluctant to talk about their neighbors, both because they did not want to impose their views on others and because they do not want to be "gossipy." They typically did not talk much about one another's private lives, although they were very concerned with the exterior appearance of their neighbors' houses and were anxious to keep up the image of middle-class suburbia.

Privacy and keeping neighbors at a distance were similarly valued in Hamilton. Individuals in Hamilton who were too open and friendly found that they did not "fit in." One Hamilton resident, for example, who had come from another part of the country prided herself on her easy friendliness, saying that her door was always open and she was happy to have people of all kinds come to visit her home. Her neighbors were not friendly to her, which puzzled her. They complained about the traffic in and out of her house and her son's car-repair work in the driveway. Another newcomer said that it was hard to get to know people, that they do not talk to each other much or pay much attention to each other. Often, Hamilton residents do not really want to have close ties with their neighbors. Residents often described their neighborhood as having a "good feeling" but "not close." At the same time, they frequently said it was a peaceful and quiet neighborhood. One woman was explicit about the link between social distance and peace:

> We're not really close social friends with our neighbors, so we don't have the chance not to get along. Unless someone is being totally obnoxious, there wouldn't be a problem.

These suburban residents avoid proximity problems by keeping to themselves.

Residents of the suburban neighborhoods seek privacy because they desire peace and because they can afford it. Privacy is one measure of power in American society. To be able to regulate social interaction to those one chooses—to protect oneself from contact with the unselected—is one way to express elite status. Privacy is the regulation of contact in desirable, coveted spaces, where competition for space is intense. This kind of privacy is expensive. From private retreats with "No Trespassing" signs to private offices with secretaries standing guard to private limousines, jets, yachts, and so forth, American culture proclaims that resources buy privacy. An ad for an expensive resort in an elite magazine reads, "Because privacy is the ultimate luxury." Standards of privacy are cultural norms, defining particular spaces and social settings and varying by group and class. Hamilton is a town devoted to the enactment of this value as its competitive residents seek to achieve elite status. Riverdale is pursuing the same vision. The price is some degree of isolation from neighbors and neighborly assistance, but the reward is peace and quiet within a chosen rather than an imposed social world.

Although I have described this cultural value on privacy as distinctive of widely spaced suburbs, I suspect that it is equally strong among dwellers in denser housing, such as urban apartment buildings. Here, doormen, thick walls, and relatively large apartments may provide the spatial basis for privacy for those who desire it and can afford it, whereas norms of noninvolvement and minding your own business serve as the cultural expression of privacy between neighbors of all social classes.

WEALTH AND SOCIAL CLASS

Wealth is necessary to achieve high levels of privacy and local government regulation. It is more expensive to space houses farther apart, to build single-family detached homes rather than duplexes or apartment buildings. In cities, this calculus is somewhat different because everyone lives at higher densities. However, elite housing in cities is still built to be larger and more private than nonelite housing. Wealth buys better town services and schools, a more polite, dutiful, and subservient police force, and a more secure neighborhood identity. Wealth fosters local political power that protects a neighborhood from externally generated change and resists transitional pressures such as those experienced in Oldtowne. Wealth creates a reputation that maintains stable house prices and rents. High house prices, and perhaps real estate agents, serve as a filtering mechanism for an expensive neighborhood. Thus wealth produces social homogeneity despite transiency, for it insulates a neighborhood from change.

Less affluent neighborhoods adopt different strategies to defend their homogeneity and order: Some hand down houses within the family and rent to relatives and friends, as Hilltowne residents do. In other neighborhoods, teenage gangs may perform the same function (Suttles, 1972). But these strategies depend upon networks of social relationships within a neighborhood, upon particularistic social ties, upon a willingness to cooperate and reciprocate, and upon some informal social control. Rapid transition in the membership of a neighborhood tends to undermine these social relationships and patterns of cooperation. As the example of Oldtowne demonstrates, under conditions of neighborhood social transformation, the intrusions of neighbors upon one another are less likely to be managed without conflict.

NEIGHBORHOOD TRANSITION AND UNCERTAINTY

When the social composition of a neighborhood is changing, its residents experience uncertainty. They often feel unsure about who belongs in the neighborhood and what kind of neighborhood it is. Local conflicts escalate because of this uncertainty. At the same time, they are part of the process by which the neighborhood is redefined and new norms are created.

The three neighborhoods with secure social identities have relatively few proximity problems. Oldtowne, on the other hand, is a neighborhood whose residents feel considerable uncertainty about how it is changing or where it is going. There are numerous political conflicts in Oldtowne between those who wish to upgrade the neighborhood into a historic district and those who wish to preserve it as an area of low-priced housing. The gentrifying young professionals have joined with a few of the old Polish families to push for an identity as an elite historic area, whereas the more transient residents and the poorer Polish families try to block this process, fearing that they will be priced out of the neighborhood. Neighborhood conflicts are microlevel political battles around the same issues. For example, one young professional moved into a period house and carefully restored it. She was active in trying to upgrade the neighborhood and to increase its historic identity. She said she was willing to put up with the noise and the loud parties of her neighbors who lived in a frame three-decker building, but when she found a bra in the street, that was too much. She was willing to tolerate differences but felt that the life-style of the residents of this building, with their wild parties and underwear left in the street, was beyond what she wanted to endure. She called the police about the noise and hoped the bothersome residents would move away.

When residents assume that there are shared standards for neighborhood behavior, they are less likely to have proximity problems. Shared standards for neighborhood life facilitate the management of neighborhood problems by providing a clear measure against which behavior can be judged. Oldtowne residents frequently commented that different people have different ways of life, and how was anyone to decide what was fair. Residents of the other neighborhoods did not say this. In contrast, particularly in Hamilton, they felt completely justified in calling the police over a loud teenage party late at night or a barking dog. Their greater willingness to use the police to enforce standards of order was based on their assumption that these standards were clear and widely shared.

Transiency, the turnover of population in a neighborhood, has very different social implications than transition, the change in the social-class identity of a neighborhood. In neighborhoods of stable social identity, transiency simply means replacement of one individual with another of similar identity. This kind of replacement does not challenge the existing normative order. The newcomers enter a social world in which the standards are already clear and the mechanisms for enforcing them institutionalized in the form of police and town regulations. Hamilton respondents frequently commented on the amount of change in their neighborhood—the number of new people moving in—but the new people were very much like the people who left. This change was transiency, not transition. This situation contrasts with that of Oldtowne, which is experiencing both transiency and transition.

The factors that preserve the social identity of a neighborhood are economic, political, and historical. Hamilton is protected from change by its long and consistent history, and both Riverdale and Hilltowne have fairly stable past identities, whereas Oldtowne is vulnerable because of its shifting fortunes over the years. Outside factors are very important. Oldtowne is changing in large part because of an extensive urban renewal project on its borders that has renovated old wharves into a complex of trendy shops and a large condominium development. The recent changes are in large part engineered by external forces such as government decisions. Wealth serves to protect a neighborhood from this kind of externally induced change.

TWO CASES OF NEIGHBORHOOD CONFLICT

Two cases illustrate the way neighborhood disputes function as political struggles over neighborhood definition and order and contribute to the creation of a new order and a new definition of the neighborhood. In the first case, the density of the housing contributed to the conflict. However, if there had been greater consensus about neighborhood standards, these neighbors could probably have managed living in such a dense setting, as the other residents of this street did. This conflict occurred because the ethnic and life-style differences between the parties undermined their ability and willingness to negotiate. The conflicts over parking and noise became the language with which they struggled over to whom the neighborhood belonged and whose rules should apply.

The Case of the Neighborhood Fishing Boat

An elderly Polish lady, 67 years old, was angry at the middle-aged man living next door because he was building a large boat in his front-yard, parking in front of her house, refusing to let a workman onto his land to set his ladder to replace her gutters, and hitting her house with his car when he parked. This Jackson neighborhood had been built in the mid-19th century in an era when no one conceived of cars, much less the full-sized models favored by the residents of this neighborhood in the late 20th century. The street was extremely narrow, the houses close, and the sidewalks miniscule. Because of the lack of parking spaces, residents often parked on the sidewalks. The woman believed that cars parked on the narrow sidewalk undermined her house's foundations. Furthermore, in the process of parking his large car, the neighbor had occasionally hit the corner of her house, knocking things off the shelves inside. When his children played ball in the only level part of the street, directly in front of her house, the ball constantly banged into her house, making her very angry. The noise of the children and their friends had been a constant irritation to her and to her father and, she believed, had precipitated his death by heart attack 5 years earlier. The elderly lady felt alone and vulnerable, unable to protect her property and to stop her neighbor from building his boat, a loud project carried out in a very small space, or from storing his smelly lobster traps in his yard. She became particularly incensed when he prevented her from building a fence between the houses, claiming that she did not have enough land. She had worked for many years in a secretarial job but, now retired, lived on a small social security income and felt very short of money. She finally went to the zoning board to complain about the boat, and the case was referred to the court mediation program that held a 3-hour discussion of the problem and worked out an agreeement between the parties.

The man claimed that he was a fisherman and needed the boat for his livelihood. His income was low, and because of a back problem, he had difficulty getting work. He hoped to be finished soon and take the boat out of his yard. He was furious that she had complained to the zoning board. He complained that parking was difficult for everyone and that his daughter and husband, who rented a house next door to him, and his brothers, who often came to visit, generally had trouble finding places to park on the street. Sometimes they had to park in front of her house. His brash, aggressive manner overwhelmed her timid protests about the boat and the parking. He and his wife felt that the elderly lady was an unhappy and unpredictable person who would be nice one day and nasty the next, very difficult to deal with reasonably.

The man was a relative newcomer to the neighborhood. The elderly lady had owned her house for 41 years, whereas the man had lived there for only 10 years. Neither the man nor his wife nor many of the new neighbors are Polish. The neighborhood itself is shifting: It was near an old Polish community that is now breaking apart as younger, more affluent members of the community move away. The elderly lady perceived that the neighborhood was changing: She said it used to be all elderly people, nice people, but was now full of new people who drank, smoked, and used filthy language. She was proud of the street and its history but felt increasingly estranged from her new neighbors.

The physical design of this street clearly exacerbated the conflict between these neighbors. Yet the differences in age, life-style, personality, and ethnicity blocked their ability to negotiate an agreement on their own. The neighborhood is changing, and this particular dispute is simply a piece of the change; the elderly woman is trying to recreate the old order in the face of the new one that is coming.

THE CASE OF THE BOOMING STEREO

In a second case, an elderly man living alone in a home he had owned for many years went to mediation to complain about the noise from his neighbor's stereo. The houses were so close together that the stereo reverberated against his walls, making a loud boom in his house. The man had a wide range of health problems, and the sound of the music that he could not control exacerbated them. The other side of the dispute was a young couple who had recently purchased a dilapidated house and were energetically fixing it up. The neighborhood was beginning a gentrification process. The couple were young and expecting a baby. They denied playing the stereo excessively loud and felt that the elderly man should have been pleased by the improvements they were making in their house. The elderly man also complained about their leaving the trash cans on the sidewalk so that the trash blew around and was vulnerable to roving dogs, rather than putting it out just before the trash collection and tying it up carefully. Again, the young family denied doing this.

As in the previous conflict, density created the conditions for this conflict. Differences in age, life-style, and the gap between old-timers and newcomers intensifies the conflict and impedes a quick resolution. Personality factors—the elderly man's sense of vulnerability, the younger man's unwillingness to admit responsibility—further exacerbated the problem. Behind this case, as behind the other one, is neighborhood change. Conflicts between neighbors are the form that struggles over the identity of the neighborhood assume as newcomers and old-timers fight over whose rules should govern neighborhood life. Uncertainty over which rules or whose rules should prevail seems to escalate neighborhood conflict.

THE PRIVATE NEIGHBORHOOD

A comparison of these four neighborhoods suggests that they fall into three distinct types, according to the ways they deal with proximity problems. In Hilltowne, residents tend to rely on informal social control and networks of personal relationships, as they do in the urban ethnic villages described in the sociological literature. In Oldtowne, because of the changing identity of the neighborhood and the heterogeneity of its population, residents fight about proximity problems as they struggle over control of the neighborhood. In Riverdale and Hamilton, residents deal with proximity problems by leading private lives with minimal contact, by trying to insulate their neighborhoods from change, and by carrying out their struggles over neighborhood standards in political forums like town meetings and zoning boards rather than in the street.

I suggest that this third pattern of regulation represents a particular neighborhood type: the private neighborhood. It is characterized by the use of space, privacy, and formal means of social control to manage proximity problems. In such neighborhoods, order is based on alikeness rather than cohesion; the sense of belonging comes from a stable social identity rather than enduring social relationships; and peace and social order are achieved through privacy and government regulation rather than cooperation, compromise, and informal social control. Neighbors help each other by staying away from each other, comfortable in the anticipation that the person they do not know will help if necessary because they expect the same thing of themselves. Wealth—the price of houses and the rent of the few available rental units—insulates this kind of community from residents of different life-style or social class. People do not fight with their neighbors because they have shared standards of life, yet they do not know these neighbors. This is a neighborhood of transients, in that people move in and out, but it is not a neighborhood of transition. Those who move in replicate those who have left, maintaining shared norms of neighborhood life despite a shift of personnel. It is a neighborhood that offers peace without intimacy. Its residents avoid conflict by avoiding one another.[10]

The social life of private neighborhoods is based on choice rather than propinquity. The neighborhood is chosen for the houses, the prestige, or the schools rather than family relationships or the accident of birth. Order is maintained by shared standards of behavior enforced by local government rather than by informal social control. People in these neighborhoods do not gossip much about each other because they do not know each other and are not particularly interested in each other. Their close friends live elsewhere and are contacted through the workplace, organizations, or informal socializing. Neighbors do engage in casual sociability with each other, saying "hello" on the street, but generally avoid deeper entanglements. They generally feel too "busy" to visit with neighbors, although this "busyness" is simply a reflection of the way they have chosen to organize their lives. To be busy is to be important.

This kind of neighborhood is preoccupied with status, competition, individual growth and fulfillment, and constant activity. Status is defined not simply by wealth but by education, taste, individual accomplishment, and life-style. When one walks through the streets of Hamilton and Riverdale, it appears that no one lives there: People rarely sit on their steps or in their frontyards, and when they do appear, they typ-

---

[10]Baumgartner reports similar social organization in her study of conflict in an affluent American suburb (1980) (see further, on a similar social system, Beer [1985]).

ically work on the lawns or the shrubbery. They are not in front of their houses to sit and visit with whomever chances by; they are not interested in "passing the time" with a casual visit because they have already filled up their time with chosen activities, usually outside the home. The house and the neighborhood are not the places to be, the places where things are happening: Activity is at the school, the church, the office, or the beach. The home is a place to seek repose and renewal. Its external appearance is important to the neighbors, but its interior privacy is scrupulously guarded.

The private neighborhood is a place of paradoxes. It is a bastion of individualism, in which each person competes to assert his or her own autonomy. Yet it is also a place of alikeness, in which the houses look alike, the people dress alike, drive the same cars, and live similar lives. It is a neighborhood that values freedom highly: freedom from the prying eyes of neighbors and gossip, freedom from central government regulation and big brother social welfare policies. Yet it achieves its level of order and peace by permitting extensive regulation of neighborhood life by the town and the police. Freed from the pressures of informal social control, these residents are subordinated to the control of the more remote town political authority.

DIRECTIONS FOR FUTURE RESEARCH

This small study suggests that working-class neighborhoods develop different kinds of regulatory mechanisms for dealing with proximity problems than do middle- and upper-class neighborhoods. Further, it indicates that a major reason for proximity problems is neighborhood change: the social transformation of a neighborhood with the resulting uncertainty of its present and future social identity. Residents of neighborhoods in which no group is clearly dominant are uncertain about whose rules should govern neighborhood life. Furthermore, in neighborhoods in which the dominant group is changing, there is uncertainty about whose rules will come to prevail. Changing neighborhoods often experience frequent conflicts over shared space. However, conflict is part of the process through which new rules are developed and a new order is created.

This research covers only four small neighborhoods; we do not know if these patterns occur more widely. The private neighborhood type that I have characterized comes from a detailed study of only two neighborhoods. Further research is necessary to document when and where each of these neighborhood types appears.

This analysis of neighborhood conflict and regulation shows that it is valuable to look at the social, cultural, and political processes by which humans adapt to density. These processes include the generation of norms, the use of space, cultural values concerning privacy, political systems of regulation and policing, and confrontations over neighborhood order. All of these factors together explain when density feels like crowding. The amount of space between houses is related to the frequency of problems in these four neighborhoods, with the densest neighborhood having the most reported problems and the least dense neighborhoods the fewest reported problems; yet the detailed analysis of neighborhood social structure, political organization, and history shows that the relationship between space and conflict is very complex. Even in dense neighborhoods, noise, dogs, and children do not always lead to conflicts. Regardless of space between houses, conflicts occur only when normal neighborhood regulation mechanisms break down. The vast majority of interactions about noise, dogs, children, and trash are peacefully settled by a polite request and a cooperative response based on a shared expectation about how neighbors should behave toward one another. Most neighbors value good relations with those they live near and are willing to give in or to change their behavior in response to a complaint.

Only a few situations escalate: The request is rebuffed, the word is ignored, the gentle prod is perceived as offensive. Personality and idiosyncratic factors are clearly important in these failed exchanges; here, I am concerned with explanations based in the social world. I argue that one reason these situations escalate into conflicts is that they acquire a broader significance: They come to symbolize differences of class, ethnicity, or life-style. They become conflicts because they are arenas for struggle over the definition of the neighborhood and the rules that govern neighborhood life. Conflicts are more likely to take on this added significance in changing neighborhoods than in those with fixed and secure social identities. Under these conditions, conflicts may occur because people who live nearby have different values about the obligations neighbors have to each other and about standards of quiet, privacy, supervision of children, control of dogs, car repair at home, and so forth. Neighborhoods that can insulate themselves from residents of different values and life-styles through wealth or kinship ties tend to have fewer problems than those inhabited by people of different values.

Under conditions of uncertainty, density is more likely to be experienced as crowding and to produce stress and aggressiveness. As Baum suggests, in naturalistic settings, the effects of crowding are produced by a combination of overload, constraint, fear, and lack of control (1987).

In the neighborhood setting, the negative effects of crowding depend not just on space but also the wider political and social context. This model takes the investigator into terrain relatively unfamiliar to psychology; yet it shows the complexity of the ways space affects social life and the need for incorporating a wider social context than has been characteristic of much research on crowding and personal space (Aiello, 1987). Future research on environment and neighborhood could incorporate the examination of wider contextual factors. Research that examines the effect of space on social life could compare its impact in neighborhoods of different social class, different ethnicity, and different forms of political organization. Longitudinal research on the effects of space are also important. As the neighborhood studies show, the history of a neighborhood contributes to certainty about its future.

An understanding of culture is particularly important. Social settings are defined by standards of acceptable density that are shared by members of the same cultural group. These are learned through experience rather than innate and are generally not consciously recognized. Yet they constitute patterns of expected and appropriate behavior tagged to particular settings. As the discussion of privacy indicated, these cultural ideas are a significant aspect of coping with neighborhood density. Crowding is experienced when cultural standards for appropriate densities in particular social settings are violated. But one person's crowding may be another's feelings of good fellowship, depending on his or her cultural background and interpretation of the situation. In the United States, for example, people of elite social classes may search out and take for granted levels of density in their neighborhoods that people of working-class background would find lonely and isolated. Furthermore, a dense collection of people who think they share one another's values and standards may feel uncrowded, whereas the same density of people of different values feels like crowding. And a dense setting in which the individual can control the behavior of others may feel less crowded than one in which they cannot be controlled.

Finally, understanding coping mechanisms is very important in research on crowding. It is not density *per se* but the failure of mechanisms to cope with density that produces a sense of crowding. As this chapter illustrates, coping mechanisms cover a broad range of behavior and extend far beyond interactional strategies. They include systems of informal social control, political organization, cultural norms, and institutional barriers to neighborhood change. Many are not consciously directed to the control of density; yet they perform that function. An examination of a broader range of coping strategies beyond those of interpersonal interaction would enhance the capacity of environmental psychology to assess the impact of density on neighborhoods, communities, and other social settings.

Acknowledgments

I am grateful to Ann Webster for her contributions as a research assistant during the last phase of the research. Austin Sarat and the editors of this volume provided valuable comments on earlier drafts of the chapter.

REFERENCES

Aiello, J. R. (1987). Human spatial behavior. In D. Stokols & I. Altman (Eds.), *Handbook of environmental psychology*. New York: Wiley.

Altman, I. (1975). *The environment and social behavior: Privacy, personal space, territory, and crowding*. Monterey, CA: Brooks/Cole.

Baum, A. (1987). Crowding. In D. Stokols & I. Altman (Eds.). *Handbook of environmental psychology*. New York: Wiley.

Baumgartner, M. P. (1980). *Social control in a suburban town: An ethnographic study*. Unpublished doctoral dissertation, Department of Sociology, Yale University.

Beer, J. (1985). *Peacemaking in your neighborhood*. Philadelphia: New Society Press.

Black, D. (1976). *The behavior of law*. New York: Academic Press.

Black, D. (1980). *The manners and customs of the police*. New York: Academic Press.

Black, D. (Ed.). (1984). *Toward a general theory of social control*. 2 Vols. New York: Academic Press.

Cressey, P. (1932). *The taxi-dance hall*. Chicago: University of Chicago Press.

Freedman, J. L. (1975). *Crowding and behavior*. New York: Viking.

Gans, H. J. (1962). *The urban villagers: Group and class in the life of Italian Americans*. New York: Free Press.

Greenberg, S. W., Rohe, W. M., & Williams, J. R. (1984). *Informal citizen action and crime prevention at the neighborhood level*. Research Triangle Park, NC: Research Triangle Institute.

Hannerz, U. (1969). *Soulside: Inquires into ghetto culture and community*. New York: Columbia University Press.

Hannerz, U. (1980). *Exploring the city*. New York: Columbia University Press.

Hunter, A. J., & Suttles, G. D. (1972). The expanding community of limited liability. In G. D. Suttles (Ed.), *The social construction of communities* (pp. 44–82). Chicago: University of Chicago Press.

Jacobs, J. (1961). *The death and life of great American cities*. New York: Random House.

Loo, C. (1977). Beyond the effects of crowding: Situational and individual differences. In D. Stokols (Ed.), *Perspectives on environment and behavior* (pp. 153–169). New York: Plenum Press.

Merry, S. E. (1981a). *Urban danger: Life in a neighborhood of strangers*. Philadelphia: Temple University Press.

Merry, S. E. (1981b). Defensible space undefended; social factors in crime control through environmental design. *Urban Affairs Quarterly, 16*, 397–422.

Merry, S. E., & Silbey, S. S. (1984). What do plaintiffs want? Reexamining the concept of dispute. *Justice System Journal, 9,* 151–179.

Murray, C. A. (1983). The physical environment and community control of crime. In J. Q. Wilson (Ed.), *Crime and public policy* (pp. 107–122). San Francisco: ICS Press, Transaction Books.

Newman, O. (1973). *Defensible space.* New York: Macmillan.

Perin, C. (1977). *Everything in its place: Social order and land use in America.* Princeton: Princeton University Press.

Schwartz, R. (1954). Social factors in the development of legal control: A case study of two Israeli settlements. *Yale Law Journal, 63,* 471.

Silbey, S. S., & Merry, S. E. (1986). Mediator settlement strategies. *Law and Policy, 8,* 7–32.

Stack, C. (1974). *All our kin: Strategies for survival in a black community.* New York: Harper & Row.

Stokols, D. (1977). Origins and direction of environment–behavior research. In D. Stokols (Ed.), *Perspectives on environment and behavior* (pp. 5–37). New York: Plenum Press.

Suttles, G. D. (1968). *The social order of the slum.* Chicago: University of Chicago Press.

Suttles, G. D. (1972). *The social construction of communities.* Chicago: University of Chicago Press.

Unger, D. G., & Wandersman, A. (1985). The importance of neighbors: The social, cognitive, and affective components of neighboring. *American Journal of Community Psychology, 13,* 139–169.

Wandersman, A., Andrews, A., Riddle, D., & Fancell, C. (1983). Environmental psychology and prevention. In R. Felner, S. Farber, L. Jason, & J. Moritsugu (Eds.), *Preventive psychology: Theory, research, and practice* (pp. 104–127). New York: Pergamon.

Whyte, W. F. (1943). *Street-corner society: The social structure of an Italian slum.* Chicago: University of Chicago Press.

Wilson, J. Q. (1968). *Varieties of police behavior: The management of law and order in eight communities.* Cambridge: Harvard University Press.

Wirth, L. (1928). *The ghetto.* Chicago: University of Chicago Press.

Wirth, L. (1938). Urbanism as a way of life. *American Journal of Sociology, 44,* 1–24.

Young, M., & Willmott, P. (1957). *Family and kinship in East London.* London: Routledge & Kegan Paul.

Zorbaugh, H. F. (1929). *The gold coast and the slum.* Chicago: University of Chicago Press.

Community Dynamics in Coping with Toxic Contaminants

MICHAEL R. EDELSTEIN
AND ABRAHAM WANDERSMAN

INTRODUCTION

> This was a crisis situation with no specificed reaction. There was no "grief" ritual. You don't know what to do. There are divergent emotions and reactions needed to cope. People prefer that this didn't happen. They can't see water pollution; they don't feel bad. They believe it, yet they can't cope, so they rationalize it. Even I have a point where I said, "Enough, I can't believe anymore." When the [neighbor's] child died, I reached my breaking point. I couldn't believe that he died from the water because I couldn't live here with the kids if I believed this. Other people shut off at the beginning. One person got an ulcer and the next didn't believe that there was anything wrong. . . . We didn't know what we were supposed to be doing! Are we paranoid, hypocritical crazies?
> —Comment of a community leader, Legler section of Jackson, New Jersey (quoted in Edelstein, 1982, p. 132)

MICHAEL R. EDELSTEIN • School of Social Science and Human Services, Ramapo College of New Jersey, Mahwah, NJ 07430. ABRAHAM WANDERSMAN • Department of Psychology, University of South Carolina, Columbia, SC 29208.

Love Canal served to place toxic contamination into the American consciousness. The canal is the symbol of abandonment. It was initially dug by an entrepreneur seeking to capture the power of Niagra Falls for burgeoning industry before the turn of the century. The effort was stopped by a lack of capital. In the mid-20th century, the site was used by Hooker Chemical Company for waste disposal. After the dump site was abandoned in the 1950s, the Love Canal was developed into a residential neighborhood, complete with an elementary school. But in 1978, the discovery of widespread chemical contamination of the neighborhood led to a major controversy over the habitability of the area that still continues. As the result of a series of political decisions, residents of the canal were given the option of resettling elsewhere. Today, the canal is again largely abandoned (e.g., Fowlkes & Miller, 1982; L. Gibbs, 1982; Levine, 1982; Shaw & Milbrath, 1983).

Since the Love Canal disaster served to introduce Americans to the threat of residential exposure to toxic materials, thousands of additional sites have been identified where there is the potential for contamination (e.g., Office of Technology Assessment, 1983). For example, for just one type of exposure source, hazardous waste dump sites, 1979 estimates identified as many as 50,000 sites nationwide with as many as 2,000 posing imminent danger (Anderson & Greenberg, 1982). When the entire array of sources of contamination is examined, it appears that few if any are safe from the threat of toxic contamination. The exact health implications of the exposure to chemical and other contaminants escaping from these sites is subject to controversy due to such factors as the long latency for diseases such as cancer to develop. It is extremely difficult to show causal relationships between a given exposure to contamination and most potential health outcomes (Tucker, 1981). At the same time, there is ample evidence to suggest that exposures can have a variety of short-term and long-term effects. These include carcinogenic outcomes (cancers), somatogenic effects (ranging from skin lesions and rashes, to kidney failure and neurotoxic effects), mutagenic effects (upon genetic material), and teratogenic effects (upon children *in utero*). The later effect (e.g., miscarriages) may be the most sensitive short-term measure of toxic health effects (Paigen, 1979).

Given the emotional impact of the toxic contamination issue, it is not surprising that the issue is central to current political debate. Major national organizations, such as the Citizen's Clearinghouse for Hazardous Waste, have developed to assist citizens affected by toxic exposure. A number of pieces of legislation at the federal level have been written with the intent of protecting the air and water, regulating toxic materials, and cleaning up hazardous sites. The laws have only been partially successful. The most important legislation from the standpoint of victims of toxic contamination, the Comprehensive Environmental Response, Compensation, and Liability Act ("Superfund"), theoretically addresses the bottom line for existing sites causing toxic contamination, their containment, and cleanup. However, Superfund was woefully inadequate in its first incarnation (Anderson & Greenberg, 1982). Under the Reagan administration's attempts to weaken environmental legislation and regulation, the Superfund bill was threatened with a presidential veto. However, facing a congressional override, Reagan signed a $9 billion extension (Crawford, 1986).

Beginning with the work of several sociologists (Fowlkes & Miller, 1982; Levine, 1982) and psychologists (Edelstein, 1982; M. Gibbs, 1982), exposure to toxic substances has come to be recognized as a significant environmental stressor (e.g., Wandersman & Hess, 1985; Wandersman, Andrews, Riddle, & Fancett, 1983), having social and psychological ramifications for the individual, the family, the community, and the society.

There is a tendency for psychologists to be concerned with how the environment affects the individual. Therefore, researchers employ dependent measures such as stress, problem solving, individual coping, and psychopathology (e.g., Fleming & Baum, 1985; M. Gibbs, 1986; Jacobson, Jacobson, & Fein, 1985). However, toxic exposure is also responsible for influencing community dynamics and structure such as social networks, community solidarity, and community conflict (e.g., Edelstein, 1982; L. Gibbs, 1982) that are influenced by and, in turn, affect individual responses. The purpose of this chapter is to explore these community dynamics in coping with toxic exposure.

The community has been identified as one of the victims of disaster (see Barton, 1969; Erikson, 1976; Wallace, 1957). Erikson's work on the Buffalo Creek flood revealed a cultural setting where the individual was deeply dependent upon the community prior to the disaster. The flood led to the destruction of more than the physical community, resulting in the loss of social networks as well. Speaking of this lost "communality," Erikson noted that

> people are not referring to particular village territories when they lament the loss of community but to the network of relationships that make up their general human surround. (1976, p. 187)

This loss left survivors without direction in their individual and family lives, resulting in long-term disruption.

Destruction of the community fabric in the face of large-scale physical disruption and loss of life from acute and catastrophic disaster also characterizes some incidents of toxic contamination, such as that experienced by the residents of Bhopal, India, where methyl isocyanate was released from a Union Carbide plant. Yet disaster from toxic contamination often occurs in a chronic and perhaps undetected manner. The announcement of the discovery of the contamination is frequently the first awareness that many residents have of the disaster. Is the community likely to be destroyed in this later situation?

In examining the effects of chronic, low-level contamination on neighborhoods characterized by less intense proximate social relationships, an opposite effect has been found. Specifically, the circumstances surrounding toxic exposure appear, in many cases, to be conducive to the development of a sense of community (Edelstein, 1982; L. Gibbs, 1982; Levine, 1982). Drawing from these sources, it is possible to begin to sketch a process of community organization that can be related to toxic exposure.

In this chapter, we will discuss how communities respond to toxic contamination and why existing resources are often inadequate for this effort. We present a framework that helps us to explore how grass roots organizations develop to help cope with the stresses and strains of living in a community affected by toxic pollution. As an initial map of these community dynamics, based upon current research on this topic, this effort may help to guide further research leading to the development of theory in this area. Although other types of human-caused disasters also generate community dynamics (e.g., the Three Mile Island disaster [e.g., Gricar & Baratta, 1983] and presumably the recent Chernobyl incident as well as more chronic instances of exposure to radioactive materials), this chapter focuses specifically upon residential exposure to contamination by toxic chemicals.

COMMUNITY RESPONSE TO TOXIC CONTAMINATION: AN OVERVIEW

In this section, we present an overview of the process of community response to toxic exposure (see Figure 1). As the result of the announcement of toxic exposure, the affected community is thrown into turbulence. In their attempts to cope with this turbulence, residents of affected areas (newly labeled as *victims*) turn naturally to key components of their social environments: (a) the "social network" or existing group of friends and relatives who can normally be expected to offer support in the face of crisis; and (b) the "institutional network" of government agencies that is believed to be responsible for helping citizens in need.

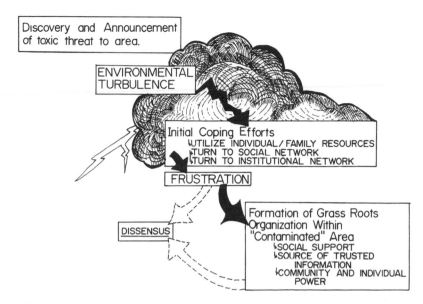

Figure 1. An exploratory map of community response to toxic contamination.

Often, neither of these networks is adequate in assisting the victims to deal with their situation. In fact, toxic exposure frequently appears to result in a virtual isolation of victims from outside sources of support.

As toxic victims discover that their previous channels for participation and problem solving appear to be ineffective, they are forced to innovate to create new alternatives. The result of this isolation from key support networks combined with the common geographic proximity of victims contributes to the creation of a "spatial network," a community group corresponding to the boundaries of contamination. This local grass roots organization appears to play a key role in attempts to cope with the demands of toxic exposure for individuals, families, and the newly defined community as well (aspects of these community dynamics are discussed in Bass, 1985; Creen, 1984; de Boer, 1985; Edelstein, 1982; Freudenberg, 1984a,b; L. Gibbs, 1982, 1983; Levine, 1982; Shaw & Milbrath, 1983; Stone & Levine, 1985; van Eijndhoven & Nieuwdorp, 1985).

The dynamics that lead to the development of community organization in response to toxic contamination are summarized in Figure 1. Before explaining the figure, it may be helpful to briefly outline a case study of an affected community in order to ground the discussion.

The Legler section of Jackson Township, NJ, shared in the high rate of growth found in the New York Metropolitan Area in the 1960s and 1970s. Adjacent to the sandy Pine Barrens region, Legler's custom-built ranches and bilevels offered new residents a rural/suburban escape from dense and crowded cities at a reasonable price. The bulk of the residents were young families with children.

Part of Legler had previously been mined by Glidden Paint Company for a mineral used in its products. In the early 1970s, the abandoned mine site was given to Jackson Township for use as a landfill. This facility operated through the 1970s with apparently poor safeguards. Beginning on November 8, 1978, the township notifed residents that their water, taken from wells tapping the vast Cohansy aquifer, was contaminated by chemicals and was not to be consumed. Bathing in the water was later discouraged as well. Some 300 residents went without tap water for 2 years, relying upon large containers of water delivered by the township.

Various state and local agencies played roles in the Legler case. Legler residents came quickly to distrust most local officials, whereas the state was seen as unlikely to provide help. About two thirds of the Legler residents banded together to form the Concerned Citizens Committee. This organization played an ongoing and significant role in guiding neighborhood response to the initiatives of regulators. A major step was the hiring of lawyers to seek damages on behalf of the residents. After a successful trial, Concerned Citizens Committee members won an award of more than $15 million from Jackson Township for health monitoring, psychological damage, and loss of quality of life (the verdict and award are in the midst of appeal). Once residents were supplied by a new water source and the lawsuit was in the hands of lawyers, the Concerned Citizens Committee became less active in the community.

With this case in mind, we will now explore the major concepts reviewed in Figure 1.

ENVIRONMENTAL TURBULENCE

News of toxic contamination threatening one's home involves an intrusion into the neighborhood via the environment. In this sense (following Katz & Kahn, 1978), the environment refers not only to the geographic "facts" of contamination, but to the social and economic significance of pollution; the uncertainties surrounding questions of health risk, the extent of damage, those responsibile for causing the contamination, and the reliability of information given by government officials and the press; the costs and assumptions behind technological solutions to contamination; and the politicized nature of the response of various bureaucratic agencies that comprise an institutional environment for toxic victims.

Thrust into such an anomalous environment, these victims further find that this environment has a number of specific characteristics that greatly affect the degree of stress associated with contamination incidents. These characteristics include four factors.

First, there is turbulence resulting from the disruption of everyday life, the various uncertainties, anticipatory fears, and the complexities of the situation.

Second, there is a fairly uniform response of the outside social environment to the afflicted community including stigma, blaming the victim, and uncertainty as to how to be of assistance. Victims may not recognize this pattern at first.

Third, the initial appearance of a random environmental response may be suggested by both social and physical responses. Outsiders who are expected to help may instead display contradictory interests and actions (as when several regulatory agencies become involved but act at cross-purposes). And even the physical condition of pollution may vary over time and place (e.g., varied test results over time for a given well or differences in detected contamination among neighbors).

Fourth, there is an overall scarcity of resources for "solving" the problem and restoring the victims' former lives. As illustrated by the Superfund experience in the United States involving the taxing of chemical industries in order to generate resources to be used for toxic cleanup, this scarcity may involve a lack of funds, a lack of political will to use available funds, the lack of a definitive agreement about the effectiveness of technological responses, and the use of rational technocratic criteria to evaluate and prioritize exposure sites. This results in a virtual "zero-sum" game between communities contending for the top of the list (e.g., L. Gibbs, 1985; Janis, 1981). It appears that the Dutch experience in conducting remediation of toxic incidents has had similar results (van Eijndhoven & Nieuwdorp, 1985).

In sum, the environment of the resident faced with pollution is turbulent. In the face of this development, these residents can be expected to take steps to create some form of stability and certainty.

INITIAL COPING EFFORTS

In a society based upon the autonomous nuclear family within an independent home, the family initially faces the news of contamination as a private challenge or problem. It is a complex and confusing situation. However, when the family seeks clarification, support, and assistance, they often discover that neither their social relationships nor "responsible" institutions are in a position to help in this time of need.

SOCIAL NETWORKS

Support from one's social network is commonly identified as essential to attempts to cope with a variety of stressful situations (e.g., Gottlieb, 1981). Yet the response from social networks based upon relatives, friendships, and co-worker ties outside the area of contamination is frequently disappointing to the victimized family. Various reasons for the failure of the social network can be cited (see Edelstein, 1982). First, toxic victimization exhibits an "insider/outsider" effect. Many of those outside the situation have difficulty understanding the impact of the incident upon the victims and thus fail to fully sympathize with them. The tendency for many victims to become wrapped up in a continuing concern for their situation to the exclusion of other concerns can drive off friends and relations who tire of this obsession; to outsiders, victims may appear to be overreacting to the situation. In addition, victims may have changed perceptions of themselves, their families, and their homes that also contribute to changed behavior on their part. Their temperament may reflect the stress load added to their lives. They often lose their desire to entertain guests. Their allocation of time may change; for example, recreation activities are replaced by efforts to address the pollution. These various changes can adversely affect social relationships, as this statement by a Legler resident suggests (Edelstein, 1982, p. 173):

> Our friends say that they don't want to be with us anymore because we are so caught up in the water problem.

Second, friends and relations who have spent time at the victims' home may be concerned with the risk to themselves from past visits and may greatly limit further visiting. In this sense, the victims and their homes are stigmatized in that they are seen as potential threats. They are "negatively different" now. This is illustrated by the comment of this Legler resident (Edelstein, 1982, p. 171):

> Only my mother will come here. It's like we have the plague the way they avoid Legler. They feel that they don't want to expose themselves to our house. My wife's parents don't even want to know about it.

Finally, toxic exposure situations frequently involve attempts to "blame the victim" (see Lerner, 1980). Extended family members may resent an "unwise" investment in a suburban home that distanced them from the "victims." Such masking of resentment is illustrated by this Legler resident's reflection (Edelstein, 1982, p. 173):

> Our parents hate our lifestyle. They think that this place is a step down from our former bi-level. The water just emphasizes our mistake in moving. It reinforces their belief that this was a bad idea; they won't accept our lifestyle.

Outsiders look at the victimization as suggesting a deficiency in vigilence ("only a fool would get themselves in a situation like this"). Such blaming is exacerbated by the dynamics of exposed communities, where lawsuits, publicity, and political pressure may serve to punish "surrounders" (Melief, 1985), those living outside of the boundaries of contamination but close enough to be affected by publicity and stigma. Taxpayers may resent what they view as an exaggerated crisis that proves costly to municipal budgets.

Although it is not suggested that none of the victims' prior social relationships is supportive in this situation, victims frequently note that there are limits to how helpful their friends and relatives could be. In the face of water contamination, for example, relatives might bring them bottles of water or offer a place to occasionally shower, but such assistance does not address the fundamental crisis experienced by victims. Just as the situation is beyond the competency of victims, so it appears to be for their social relations. One Legler resident noted of his friends (Edelstein, 1982, p. 172):

> There was nothing they could do. We didn't discuss the health problems with them. We did talk about the situation. They would see how I had to cook and ask, "How can you live like that"? They meant well. They were sympathetic. But I told them I had no choice.

Ironically, when outsiders inquire about the situation in an attempt to be supportive, they may find that victims are tired of explaining and being reminded of a situation in which they feel trapped with no effective recourse.

In sum, toxic exposure serves to distance victims from their prior social networks. The result is a loss of emotional support and effective assistance that produces a feeling of social isolation (Edelstein, 1982).

INSTITUTIONAL NETWORKS

Beyond looking to friends, relatives and co-workers, people respond to environmental turbulence by seeking information and assistance from those having institutional roles commonly believed to give them expertise, power, and responsibility to address the situation. As taxpayers, toxic victims appeal to their elected and appointed officials for assistance. Yet in few cases are they satisfied with government's response. Government procedures and offical actions frequently serve to "disable" concerned citizens by effectively excluding them from decision making and full information, further limiting their sense of control over their circumstances. The result is a loss of trust in government officials (e.g., Creen, 1984; Edelstein, 1987; Levine, 1982).

The impact of isolation is illustrated by Levine's (1982) description of the shared beliefs held by residents at Love Canal who joined the Love Canal Homeowners Association (LCHA). These beliefs include:

- Belief 1: We are the blameless victims of disaster.
- Belief 2: The problems we face are too large for us. We need help.
- Belief 3: We are good citizens. We deserve help from the government.
- Belief 4: The government can and should help us now. (pp. 176–177)

When residents in the outer ring of the neighborhood were omitted from the initial resettlement plan provided by the government, they further came to believe:

- Belief 5: We are being treated unfairly.
- Belief 6: We must stick together to take care of ourselves.
- Belief 7: Family and community help is not enough for our needs.
- Belief 8: No one but the government has enough resources for our pressing needs.
- Belief 9: We must work together to force the government to provide us what we are entitled to.
- Belief 10: We are the only ones who can understand each other. (p. 184)

Levine noted that these "beliefs provided a framework from which actions could flow logically to restore to the affected people some sense of control over their lives" (1982, p. 186). Similarly, Creen (1984) describes a parallel situation in Canada, noting that in the absence of either external validation of fears or correction of fears, those suffering fear were forced to turn to each other.

PARTICIPATION IN COMMUNITY ORGANIZATIONS

In this section, we will use a version of Wandersman's (1981; Heller, Price, Reinharz, Riger, & Wandersman, 1984) framework of participation in community organizations to explore the literature on the development of community organizations in response to toxic exposure (see Figure 2). In brief, the framework suggests that the community can be described in terms of environmental characteristics (e.g., noise, density), ecological characteristics (e.g., aspects of human ecology such as

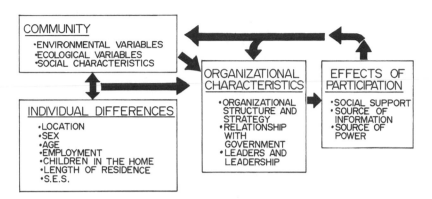

Figure 2. A framework of participation in community organizations formed in response to toxic contamination.

geographic factors, size, and boundaries and concepts from ecological psychology such as behavior settings), and social characteristics (e.g., social networks, norms, the delivery of services, etc.). This information about the community defines the opportunity and resources available for participation, the pressures and politics with which a citizen's group must contend, and the environmental press or problems that influence their involvement.

Citizens' perceptions of the environment are affected by individual difference characteristics (e.g., demographics and personality) that affect who participates and to what extent. The organizational characteristics of the citizen group can be assessed, such as the form (e.g., government-mandated or grass roots), size, and structure. The organizational characteristics help to define the type of participation (and thus power) that is available. These variables often influence the viability and success of the community organization.

Participation in community organizations produces effects upon individuals, the organization, and community. At the individual level, such factors as satisfaction, feelings about authority figures, sense of control, experience of alienation, and degree of social interaction are affected by participation. At the organizational level, legitimacy and organizational growth are affected by participation levels. At the community level, participation may affect the environmental and social aspects of the community.

The framework will be used as a guide to help us describe what has been found in the literature so far. We will examine the Legler case study, with additional references from other studies of communities affected by toxic exposure. Although relatively few studies are currently available, the importance of the issue suggests that the literature will grow. The framework suggested here may prove to be a useful guide for further research.

ENVIRONMENTAL, ECOLOGICAL, AND SOCIAL CHARACTERISTICS OF THE COMMUNITY

Environmental Characteristics

Legler is adjacent to the Pine Barrens of southern New Jersey, sitting on sandy soils atop the Cohansey aquifer. At the time of the water pollution incident in 1978, it was a recently developed suburban area set in a rural section off of a heavily trafficked road. Substantial tracts of parkland are in the immediate area as is a major airforce base.

Legler's geographic location influenced its choice as a landfill site. This was less because the site was suitable for a landfill than because it was in a peripheral part of Jackson Township, a municipality covering some 100 square miles. Additionally, the previous owner of the land had used it for a mining site. When the site was depleted, it was transferred to the township, avoiding reclamation costs.

The contamination introduced into the aquifer changed the environmental characteristics of the area. One report, issued by the Division of Epidemiology and Disease Control of the New Jersey State Department of Health (1980), listed some 34 organic chemicals discovered in Legler groundwater in 1978 and 1979. The report suggested the increased long-term likelihood of cancer as a plausible health outcome of consuming this water. Other somatic (injury to the body), teratogenic (injury to the fetus), and mutagenic (injury to the genetic material) health effects were not dismissed as possible outcomes by the report.

Human Ecology and Ecological Psychological Factors

In addition to the physical environment, one can also examine ecological factors related to impacts and patterns of life-style in the area such as size and boundaries. There was a lack of community definition in the Legler section prior to the contamination incident partly due to such ecological characteristics. Legler residents lacked amenities on their end of town. They either needed to shop in the more developed parts of Jackson Township or in the communities where they worked. Other than a vegetable stand, no functional ties fostered development of community identity in Legler.

In Legler, an area demarcated by no discernible physical features, most residents had never heard of the section's name before it was labeled as Legler during the pollution incident. They did not think of it as a discrete and identifiable neighborhood but rather as "the boonies" of Jackson Township.

After the incident, a careful mapping of the boundaries of the community occurred. People became very aware of these boundaries, which corresponded to the warnings about water contamination. Later these boundaries would serve as the approximate basis for the new water district, thereby taking on a political/legal significance.

During the contamination incident, however, the Concerned Citizens Committee itself served a key functional role. Its meetings became behavior settings where community members had the opportunity to interact. The homes of its board members were communications centers. In a parallel vein, the Legler fire hall became the meeting center for local residents. Both the leaders' homes and the fire hall became functional loci for a sense of community.

Social Characteristics

As residential development occurred in Legler, it progressed from a quiet rural area to a suburban section populated by approximately 150 families. The earliest residents shared a self-reliant community based upon mutual help but also substantial privacy. The first major group of newcomers in the 1960s and early 1970s used Legler as essentially a bedroom community. They made their neighbor's acquaintance, but the key thrust of their activity was family and home-oriented. They actively sought privacy. The final group, those arriving in the mid-to-late 1970s, lived on the less trafficked streets furthest from the highway. Generally, these residents established close and intimate relationships with their neighbors. Privacy was less important than the opportunity to socialize and share child-rearing activities. Although the early residents valued the rural character, the new arrivals looked forward to further development, particularly of amenities such as shopping. It would be hard to anticipate these different populations merging together as one community.

Sense of Community

Sarason (1974) suggested that the ingredients of sense of community are

> the perception of similarity to others, an acknowledged interdependence with others, a willingness to maintain this interdependence by giving to or

doing for others what one expects from them, the feeling that one is part of a
larger dependable and stable structure. (p. 157)

Prior to the contamination incident, not only was the term *Legler*
unknown to most residents, but there was no other basis for a collective
"sense of identity" that might bring about an identification of the individual family with the community. Rather than the "communality" identified by Erikson (1976) in Buffalo Creek, West Virginia, where a "state of
mind [was] shared among a particular group of people" (p. 189), Legler
was much more indicative of the suburban community studied by Gans
(1967), which was "clearly not a symbolic unit" (p. 145).

Later, Legler became a very meaningful symbol by which the exposure victims were collectively identified. Its stigma was their stigma.
The solutions to its problems were essential to their own life-styles. In
the words of Heider (1958), a "unit relationship" had been created between the residents and their neighborhood. It became a psychological
community.

Neighboring and Formal Organizations

Prior to the incident, different areas of Legler developed very different patterns of neighboring, some establishing an aloof acquaintanceship
featuring strong norms of privacy, whereas others engaged in an interactive "coffee klatch" networking based upon a coincidence of proximity
with homogeneity (e.g., Gans, 1970). There appeared to be minimal
development of formal organizations and minimal involvement in such
organizations outside of Legler (only 1 family out of a sample of 25
reported a family member as belonging to a community organization).

After the residents were notified of the contamination, neighborhood communication became an important element in residents'
coping. Not only was there more informal social contact, but the Concerned Citizens Committee became a central formal statement about the
development of community.

Using the preceding dimensions, we can see how environmental,
ecological, and social aspects of the situation contributed to the development of a sense of community in Legler. One could similarly chart the
creation of community feeling in other locations, such as Love Canal,
where toxic incidents have occurred.

INDIVIDUAL DIFFERENCES IN PARTICIPATION

Who participates in efforts to organize such a community? Looking
beyond Legler, several researchers have discussed the profile of community activists responding to toxic incidents.

Using a mail questionnaire, Freudenberg (1984b) sampled 110 community groups from 31 states that had as their main concern human-caused environmental hazards with possible adverse health outcomes. Because the study has major methodological limitations and many of the sampled groups were local affiliates of national organizations, it is not clear how well this study generalizes to the grass roots type of organization that forms to respond to toxic disaster at the local level. However, the study can serve as a starting point for profiling the typical activist and community group. Freudenberg's data suggest that the typical member of the groups he sampled is between 26 and 40 years of age and a homemaker. The community groups had a modal membership of 200, with 20 core members. The leaders often were found to have professional careers, yet represented a diverse socioeconomic spectrum.

A more in-depth picture at the local level can be found in Stone and Levine (1985) who analyzed community activism at Love Canal. Several community groups had formed at Love Canal in response to the toxic incident that began there in August 1978. The most prominent of these groups was the Love Canal Homeowners Association, led by Lois Gibbs. This organization worked to create media events in order to generate political pressure necessary for government action to be taken. The members were recognized as legitimate spokespeople for the community and were sometimes invited to government decision-making meetings. The group conducted its own health research with the expert help of a leading health researcher. Efforts to expand an initial government relocation effort to the outer areas of the neighborhood eventually succeeded through the organization's efforts (e.g., L. Gibbs, 1982; Levine, 1982).

Respondents to two sets of interviews, one in the fall of 1978 and one in the spring of 1979, were classified by two judges as being either activists or nonactivists according to their involvement in trying to alter their circumstances (Stone & Levine, 1985). The judges' ratings of the interview records correlated highly with records of the respondents' membership in organizations and their self-reports of their actions and memberships.

Although their analysis is limited to one community case, Stone and Levine's comparison of activists and nonactivists provides useful information:

> In aggregating the social characteristics of the "activists" we arrive at a generalization of people with "new roots" in the community. They were not the old-timers who had lived in the community from the beginning (those with the longest exposure to the dangers), and they were less likely to work in chemical industries (though some did). They were also not the youngest members of the neighborhood, nor those who had lived there the least amount of time (renters, or homeowners with short length of exposure).

They were "rooted" in the community, having lived there for several years
(typically more than five, most 6–10 years), owning homes (their major as-
set), employed, with young or school-age children. Most had one full-time
wage-earner. They had moderate incomes, and as income increased, so did
the tendency to activism. The activists were better educated and had somewhat smaller families than the non-activists. These characteristics are typical
of young, stable working-class families in the late 1970's, when the data were
collected. (1985, p. 166)

Some additional characteristics of activists in this study deserve
further note. Age was clearly a factor in activism. Activists tended to be
under the age of 40, with only one activist in the sample over 60. Age of
children was a second factor that appears to be an important correlate of
activism. A strong correlation between presence of younger children
and activism was found.

There were significant correlations between education and activism
and between family income and activism. Freudenberg's mention of
homemakers as activists fits with the Stone and Levine's finding that
activist families were most likely to have one person working, whereas
nonactivist families either had no one working (e.g., elderly families) or
more than one worker (it is difficult for a family to become active when
both adults are busy working).

Interestingly, a negative correlation was found between location
closest to the canal and activism. Although this finding is not particularly strong, it raises some fascinating questions. Is activism more necessary for the marginal victims who are least likely to receive government
aid or compensation for damages? Are some closest to the pollution site
immobilized by defensive avoidance (see Hatcher, 1982) and thus given
to denial? An alternative explanation involves a characteristic of the
Love Canal environment. Branching out from the canal and crossing the
neighborhood are swales or wet drainage areas. Exposure to toxics correlated less with proximity to the canal than to wet areas along the
swales (L. Gibbs, 1982; Levine, 1982; Paigen, 1979; Vianna & Polan,
1984). If proximity to wet areas was used, rather than their location in
the rings surrounding the canal, the results might differ.

Overall, the Stone and Levine findings suggested that activists were
most likely to be drawn from among residents who lived in the community long enough to identify with it but who were not there so long that
they became adapted to the dangers present at Love Canal. Some explanation for this finding may be found in interviews conducted by Edelstein at Love Canal. In speaking to a few "newer" residents, it was clear
that they had neither known about the existence of the canal nor the
dumping that had occurred. In contrast, it is likely that older residents
knew that dumping had occurred at the site. They may have engaged in

some type of defensive avoidance regarding the possible dangers. Thus residents with "new roots" in the community may well have been the most surprised by the presence of danger lurking in the soil.

Based upon analysis of available resources and interviews with key respondents, Shaw and Milbrath (1983) report that few Love Canal activists were highly educated and most were blue collar. Finally, they assert a finding hinted at but not stated by either Freudenberg (who speaks of homemakers) or Stone and Levine (who discuss one-worker families), that most leaders (at least at Love Canal) were women. Shaw and Milbrath offer several tentative hypotheses regarding why women emerged as leaders. These include the idea that women have more time at home, that men were more likely to be employed in the chemical industry, that men might have felt that they had failed in their role as protector of the home, that it is unmasculine to publicly admit fears and concerns over health and safety, and, finally, that the social networks previously established by women were most available for quick action.

A number of other possible hypotheses might be added to this list. For example, in her autobiography, Lois Gibbs (1982), the leader of the LCHA, suggests that her motivation for activism rested heavily upon her concern for the safety and health of her children and the potential dangers involved in their attending the local elementary school. At least at Love Canal, the mother role may have led women to be particularly concerned with taking actions to protect children, to deal with school-related problems, and probably to deal with health problems. At both Love Canal and Legler, it appeared to be women in the community who compared their children's health records to discover clusters of problems.

L. Gibbs (1985) summarizes her observations of this issue in the following discussion of toxic exposure incidents:

> Most communities faced with this problem are blue-collar, lower middle-class or poor communities. The normal social family pattern in these neighborhoods is that the husband works while the wife stays home and cares for the house and children. The male is the "protector and provider" while the wife has a more passive role. Because of this situation, it is the woman who generally becomes most involved. Maybe this happens because she is home and thus has the time. Maybe, it is because she sees and feels the effects more since she carries the baby and nurses the sickly children. Or, maybe it's because she's better able or qualified to deal with the role. In any case, women usually take the lead and thus significantly change their lives and the life of their family. (p. 5)

Women who work at home do not have the release from residential stress available to those who leave the neighborhood to go away to work. The nature of the husbands' work is also a possible factor. At Love Canal, many men worked in the chemical industry. They were more likely to engage in denial over the potential ill effects of chemical exposure. They may also have felt loyal to their employers and/or feared that the toxic issue might cause them to lose their jobs (Fowlkes & Miller, 1982; Francis, 1983).

Finally, there may be a difference between the degree of risk that people are willing to tolerate at home and at work. When Edelstein's students questioned workers in hazardous chemical factories, they found that many workers were aware of the dangers. They engaged in various forms of rationalization to justify taking such risks. For example, many claimed to be trading off personal risks for the opportunity to work at a high-paying blue-collar job that might provide the ticket for their children to go to college and escape such work.

Although risk at work may be acceptable to many workers, risk at home is not. This may be partially due to the influence of women over home environments. Although men appear to dominate work in hazardous environments, women have a large role in defining appropriate levels of risk in the home. They may be less swayed by macho behavior in favor of a concern for health, particularly regarding children. Where the home is the domain of the woman, it is not suprising that it is the woman who defends it. Furthermore, women may be a little more distanced than men from the dominant social paradigm of economic growth and thus less willing to make trade-offs for safety (see Milbrath, 1984).

In profiling community activists, one must be cautious not to overgeneralize from such findings. For example, in Legler, three of the seven key leaders were male, including the principal leader. However, none had demanding work schedules away from home. Two were on disability, and the third had the somewhat flexible schedule of a teacher.

In other respects, Legler's Concerned Citizens Committee tends to fit the profile offered. Its key activists had young children as did the majority of its residents. They also tended to reflect the group of residents who had come to Legler in the period from the mid-1960s through the early 1970s. They had sunk roots but were not "old-timers" (similar to activists at Love Canal).

ORGANIZATIONAL CHARACTERISTICS

The nature of participation and its effects are influenced by the characteristics of the community organization.

Organizational Structure and Strategy

van Eijndhoven and Nieuwdorp (1985) differentiate between several forms of organization in their study of three Dutch communities that have suffered major toxic incidents involving soil pollution with such contaminants as dioxin. In Merwedepolder, they found a highly centralized and hierarchical organization; in the Volgermeerpolder, rather than a general mobilization of residents, a group of experts worked for the community with the community's support. In contrast, in Griftpark, residents acted in a very consensual decentralized structure. The organizational differences in the three Dutch communities contributed to different strategies among community groups. In Griftpark, the organization made effective use of direct actions in which all could participate, such as public demonstrations. This stands in contrast to the other communities, where the organizations avoided direct action in favor of petitions and public meetings. In Merwedepolder, dissenting community members veered from the general strategy to take expressive measures on their own (such as occupying a town hall and cutting bridge cables).

At Love Canal, the LCHA appeared to bridge two of these models; it was run principally by a core of key members and yet frequently undertook broad participatory actions. Lois Gibbs, the organization's president and dominant force, deliberately used direct action as a means of controlling dissenters within her organization (L. Gibbs, 1983). Fowlkes and Miller (1982) suggested that the strategies of the LCHA varied over time. The early use of direct action was primarily expressive, whereas later use was more focused and instrumental (as evidenced by the attempt to halt remedial work at the canal through an injunction).

Relationship with Government

Variations in strategy appear to depend on more than the organizational structure. As the Love Canal example suggests, community groups spend much of their effort responding to an institutional and cultural context. Thus American regulators respond to toxic exposure by attempting to minimize the risks and, therefore, their own responsibility to respond. This forces community groups into a confrontational mode with government, where the media and direct action are used to apply political pressure to override the regulators (e.g., L. Gibbs, 1982; Levine, 1982). In contrast, community groups in the Netherlands enter into a semipermanent negotiation structure with government, providing a legitimate forum for communication (Bass, 1985; van Eijndhoven & Nieuwdorp, 1985). Although Dutch toxic victims still appear to distrust their government's response (Bass, 1985), the community group is accorded a legitimacy that is rarely acknowledged in the United States. In both cases, however, the internal development of the organization can be related to the development of its representative role in the relationship between citizen and government (Bass, 1985).

Leaders and Leadership

The patterns of individual participation within a community organization have implications for its ongoing functioning. A frequent scenario in the United States involves the isolation of a core of leaders who become systematically burned out over time. This can be seen by briefly reviewing the history of the community group in Legler.

Legler's Concerned Citizens Committee formed around a core of local activists. The initial leadership of Concerned Citizens stemmed from a cluster of early residents who had previously fought the location of the landfill in their section. These leaders began to network almost immediately upon the announcement of the water contamination. They became additionally visible when they and others spoke out at township meetings early in the incident. As issues became crystallized, increased networking and attempts to share information occurred. The leadership expanded to include newer residents who, as a group, had been heretofore fairly isolated from long-term residents in the neighborhood.

Edelstein interviewed the entire executive board of the organization as well as a good representation of the membership. It was clear from these interviews that the brunt of the organization's work was done by a few key people (generally the executive board). Most of the other residents regularly attended general meetings but did little else. Therefore, it was not surprising that the leaders showed signs of extreme overload, as is reflected in these comments (Edelstein, 1982, p. 183):

> This made our house like an insane asylum. We got 65 calls a day sometimes. I'm tired of being harassed and being the guiding light. I've lost my privacy. Home is like Grand Central Station. Anyone with a problem can come here anytime. I've come to resent the intrusions. And I don't like knowing everybody's business. We executive members are always coiled with tension. The town lies, it puts us down—it's frustrating. We're all edgy on the board. If anything goes wrong, everyone calls the executive. There's a lot of stress.

In general, the members of the executive board of the organization appeared to be exhausted and felt unappreciated. They detested personal rumors that spread about town. Although interviews with a sample of the membership of Concerned Citizens showed consistently positive support for the leadership, this support was not perceived by board members. Somehow it was not being communicated upward within the organization. Typical of the accolades recorded was (Edelstein, 1982, p. 184) that "they try to help. I respect them. They always offer to help. . . . They are conscientious."

This outcome can, in part, be laid to the organizational structure of the Concerned Citizens Committee. The major roles of the organization were invested in the executive board. Particularly after concerns developed that a spy was feeding Jackson Township information about the Concerned Citizens Committee's plans, the members of the executive board became highly secretive. As they became less open, their isolation contributed to their feelings of abandonment.

An additional contributor to leader burnout was the course of the Legler disaster, which intimately involved the response of government. Initially, the group utilized broad participatory actions needed to capture attention and bring power to bear. But after the community entered the waiting period after decisions had been made, the maintenance tasks required to keep the organization working toward its goals were handled best within the executive committee structure. As they no longer were forced to go back to their membership for support, the leaders became increasingly isolated.

Effects of Participation

Although leaders paid a price for their activism, the outcomes of community activism can have an overall positive effect upon attempts to cope with toxic exposure for the individual, organization, and community.

The community group served as a "therapeutic social system" (Barton, 1969) for a very stressed neighborhood. Such therapeutic communities help compensate for the stress found in disasters by sharing information, warmth and help, providing for a rapid consensus for actions taken to meet collective needs, and engendering a high degree of motivation among victims to work for common purposes (Barton, 1969, pp. 206–207).

The nature of this help is important to establish. At least three outcomes can be identified as measures of the effectiveness of the group in addressing the needs of members and in changing its environment: social support, provision of information, and achievement of power. Although these factors emerged in the analysis of the Concerned Citizens Committee in Legler (Edelstein, 1982), the same three factors are also mentioned by others who have researched community response to toxic exposure (Bass, 1985; de Boer, 1986; L. Gibbs, 1983, 1985; Stone & Levine, 1985; van Eijndhoven & Nieuwdorp, 1985). Each type of outcome will be discussed briefly as it pertains to the Legler case:

Social Support

Earlier, we suggested that isolation from social and institutional networks in the face of toxic exposure forces interaction within the community. Even in a "bedroom community" such as Legler, where social interaction within the neighborhood is generally limited, increased interaction among neighbors is a consequence of the inability of the existing institutional and social networks to ameliorate the contamination. Within the neighborhood, three different but interactive dynamics might be identified (Unger & Wandersman, 1985):

1. The development of a sense of neighborhood
2. Participation in neighborhood organization
3. Neighboring

We have already looked at the development of a grass roots organization in the face of toxic exposure; and with the Legler example, we have seen how a cognitive definition of an area can emerge through this crisis situation. Neighboring, the third element, is a key one for the provision of social support. In their discussion of social support as part of normal neighboring, Unger and Wandersman (1985) suggest that support may be instrumental or personal/emotional and may involve the creation of networks that address individual needs as well as those that address neighborhood needs (see also Bass, 1985; M. Gibbs, 1986).

In pulling together to address their common problems, toxic victims not only build an organization, but they build relationships as well. Their need for social support as a result of the isolation of their situation (see also Bass, 1985) is met, in part, by the neighboring process. Levine's description of the Love Canal Homeowners Association (1982, pp. 185–186; see also L. Gibbs, 1983, 1985) illustrates this well:

> As time passed and discouraging incidents piled one on the other, residents felt more and more that no one but people undergoing the experience themselves . . . could understand them. Only fellow sufferers could share the feelings of uncertainty. . . . As they confided in each other more and more, both privately and in public; as they worked together and participated in individual and group actions . . . ; as they interpreted their beliefs, their goals, their behavior; and as they thought and planned together for a better and happier future, free of Love Canal, they became essential supports for each other—a sort of large self-help group, a substitute for a strong, supportive, and ever-understanding family.

Similarly in Legler, the Concerned Citizens Committee helped people get to meet others with similar problems. People were reassured that they were neither crazy nor alone. They were able to meet others with whom they shared what otherwise seemed to be a private experience that was inaccessible to the understanding of nonvictims.

Affiliation among those in a similar predicament has been associated with the obtaining of reassurance and support, particularly when people are afraid (Schacter, 1959). Forming a group also helps victims avoid the feeling of being abandoned and may help increase the accuracy of the estimation of danger (Wolfenstein, 1957). The presence of social support is generally viewed as a key aid to successful coping with technological disaster (Baum, Fleming, & Singer, 1982; M. Gibbs, 1986).

It is important to note that not all those exposed feel equally isolated. Thus, in their analysis of activists versus nonactivists at Love Canal, Stone and Levine (1985) reported that although the community group was the main source of help for activists, nonactivists got their principal support from family and relatives. Relations of activists may not have helped for a number of reasons: They may not have been convinced that help was needed; they may have lacked a means to help; they may have been too far away to be of help; or they may have been in the situation themselves. Because the same problems may have confronted relations of nonactivists, this does not explain why the social network of nonactivists remains functioning whereas that of activists fails.

There are a number of other possible explanations for the Stone and Levine findings. Those believing that the threat was strongest would naturally be the most concerned with the situation. Their behavior would be likely to be more affected than would the actions of those unconvinced of any significant risk. Their relationships would probably be more strained by their attempts to cope with the situation than would those of nonbelievers, who may act less like victims in the presence of their friends and relatives.

Furthermore, those most denied their existing support structures will be the most likely to seek new sources of support. In other words, those with strong support networks that remained helpful during the crisis may have been able to cope effectively with the situation. They were neither motivated to develop new associates nor to become activists. In contrast, those who find that others not experiencing the disaster cannot or will not understand their predicament and/or help them are more motivated to seek out common sufferers. Activism may be nurtured by the interaction between victims, involving such types of mutual influence as the confirmation of concerns and ideas, role modeling of effective responses, bolstering of spirits and motivation, and contagion or reflected excitement.

Finally, it may simply be that those least affected by the exposure are least likely to become activists. Thus, although Stone and Levine (1985) found that all residents generally share problems relating to physical health and illness, worry and anxiety and property damage, certain key differences were found within the sample. Nonactivists at Love

Canal viewed their health as less severely affected and their homes as safer than did the activists. They also were more likely to see the pollution as a solvable problem.

These three explanations all mesh. Thus, those perceiving the greatest impact became believers and activists. In doing so, they distanced themselves from some former relationships. The result is that their need for support further encouraged their activism. Support for this interpretation comes from the finding by Stone and Levine that activists exceeded nonactivists in the loss of friends (44% to 25%) as well as in finding new friendships (63% to 40%). Both develop new friendships, but activists appear to undergo greater change, presumably because they sustain a greater loss of the old and have more opportunity to find new friends. However, competing explanations exist. For example, given that activists have newer roots in the community, it is possible that their changes in relationship patterns reflect, at least in part, their recent mobility. Clearly, more research is needed to understand the networks and support of activists and nonactivists.

In summary, one outcome of the toxic exposure appears to be the development of new sources of social support, particularly where an area is isolated because of a shared exposure situation. This occurs through neighboring, which accompanies and influences the development of a sense of community and participation in a grass roots effort to address the problem.

Source of Information

Neighbors, as they interact and offer social support to one another, share information about the neighborhood (Unger & Wandersman, 1985). In Legler, such communication was minimal before the pollution crisis forced lines of intraneighborhood communication to be opened. Then the community had to contend with an informational context far different from that of a stable neighborhood. One of the major stressful components of disasters, such as Legler's, is the extreme degree of uncertainty in which victims find themselves (see Edelstein, 1982; Fleming & Baum, 1985; Freudenberg, 1984a; Levine, 1982; Slovic, Fischhoff, & Lichtenstein, 1980).

The Concerned Citizens Committee helped to supply information to Legler residents at a time when there was real confusion of facts and denial of responsibility for clarification on the part of responding government agencies. The community organization worked largely through informal networks. If anything suspicious happened in the neighborhood or if anything important was learned, this information was channeled immediately to the group's leadership. Perceptions were frequently checked out with members of the executive board as rumors passed through Legler. The group's periodic meetings came to be seen as *the* one authoritative place where one could get straight answers to questions.

When respondents were questioned about sources of information during the water crisis, they gave government and the press negative ratings as sources of information. Government at both the township and higher levels was not seen as open or truthful. The press was seen as depending upon the township government for information. Television was too sporadic in its coverage to be useful for information. Only the meetings of Concerned Citizens Committee and its informal communications network were consistently seen by group members as being reliable sources of information.

L. Gibbs (1982) reported that the LCHA provided residents with information about chemical hazards, translation of scientific reports, and directions for filing relocation papers. Bass (1985) reports very similar findings for community organizations serving as sources of information in four Dutch communities. Although there were major differences between communities, residents of exposed communities reported heavy use of resident organizations for information, whereas authorities played a much less central role in providing information.

A Source of Power

The development of community organizations tends to provide for a new sense of power in the midst of a situation where there is an overall sense of loss of control. This can be seen at the community and organizational levels as well as at the individual level.

Community Power. As a source of collective power, Concerned Citizens helped people overcome their sense of powerlessness in a difficult situation. This is reflected in the following comment by one resident (Edelstein, 1982, p. 185):

> We felt support. We were powerful enough not to have to take it. The Township underestimates us "hicks." We made the Township accountable.

By forming a group that could wield power and be effective, residents had a direction in which to channel their frustrations constructively. For example (Edelstein, 1982, p. 185):

> We helped each other not overreact. Some of us were going to Township meetings with guns, we were that frustrated and angry. We felt like our arms were pinned back.

> We all channeled our frustrations into Concerned Citizens. Otherwise, there
> would have been vigilante violence.

The group also allowed families to take actions that they might not
have been able to individually undertake. Media coverage was sought
and coordinated. The lawsuit was particularly mentioned by respondents as a course of action made possible by their union.

By turning to legal expertise, the Concerned Citizens Committee
undertook to attain some balance of power between citizens and the
experts brought forth by government and those responsible for the contamination. The lawyers, in turn, hired specialists able to address the
issues faced by the Legler neighborhood. In other instances, community
groups have directly attracted experts to work with them in an advisory
role. The experts help them understand the significance of new developments, to plot strategy, and even to take on adversaries directly.

The LCHA made extensive use of such expertise, some volunteer
and some government sponsored. Particularly important was the work
of a cancer researcher, Beverly Paigen, in helping to reinterpret government data, develop the capacity to collect additional information, and
interpret this information credibly inside and outside the neighborhood
(Fowlkes & Miller, 1982; L. Gibbs, 1982; Levine, 1982).

In the Netherlands, mobilization of expertise has been shown to be
a key to community power, allowing citizens to demonstrate weaknesses in the reassurances given by the authorities and to put forward
alternative plans of their own (van Eijndhoven & Nieuwdorp, 1985).

Bass (1985) studied four Dutch communities where there was little
confidence in the solutions proposed by government. In each case, community groups served a representative function well enough to earn
overwelming ratings of confidence from residents. These groups gained
some control over community process by providing independent
sources of information, criticizing technical investigations, and keeping
authorities informed of local developments and the desired solutions. L.
Gibbs (1983) further notes that the office of the LCHA served as a base
for commuity member participation. She stresses the importance for
community organizations to provide such a setting.

Similarly, by creating a context for social support, a source of reliable information and a basis for collective power, Legler's Concerned
Citizens helped residents to cope with what otherwise might have been
an unmanageable situation. The individual family was buffered somewhat from the ongoing stresses that resulted from dealing with government in seeking solutions to the crisis.

Individual Power. The importance of the community group as a path
to power appears in at least two senses. On one hand, it is a collective

. means to achieve commonly shared individual goals. On the other hand, it is a means to reverse some of the psychological damage that occurs from the inherent powerlessness of the situation.

Numerous personal growth outcomes are associated with activism. Shaw and Milbrath (1983) suggested that leaders of Love Canal groups experienced enhanced self-control, self-worth, and personal efficacy. Stone and Levine (1985) similarly suggested an association between activism and positive individual change at Love Canal. They show, for example, that nonactivists report substantially more negative effects than do activists. Furthermore, nonactivists did not appear to change their behavior during the incident, whereas activists learned to assert their rights. Thus

> if we assume that people feel better about themselves after they meet difficult challenges with action, we can speculate that the organized citizens' groups provided a means for people to feel more in control of events, even though active membership entailed a change in personal behavior that was surprising to the actors themselves. (p. 173)

There is, of course, a relationship between this growth and the ability of the organized groups to achieve their desired ends. Thus power is achieved in part by increasing the competence of the community group. Although some expertise is achieved through the use of consultants (see, e.g., L. Gibbs, 1982; Levine, 1982; Shaw & Milbrath, 1983), at least equally as important is the learning evidenced by community leaders (Stone & Levine, 1985).

The real importance of consultants to the citizens' groups may at times be less as technical experts than as educators. The power of such citizen/consultant teams was strongly evidenced at Love Canal (L. Gibbs, 1982; Levine, 1982). The most dramatic outcome may have been the swale theory, the inspiration of L. Gibbs (1982) but developed for its scientific implications under the guidance of Paigen (1979). This theory involved the realization that proximity to wet areas in the neighborhood rather than to the canal itself was the crucial variable in identifying health impacts from toxic exposure. This theory successfully challenged the conceptual framework depended upon by the state experts. Similar examples of citizen competence are evidenced in other cases. Collectively, they suggest that individual learning is a major component of group power.

Several writers referred to a growing sophistication of citizens (Freudenberg, 1984a; Shaw & Milbrath, 1983) that reflected a similar development of community organizations. As Shaw and Milbrath noted:

> Nearly everyone who became deeply involved at Love Canal experienced
> some significant change in their understanding of how the world works
> physically, socially and politically. (p. 25)

It would follow that they correspondingly became more effective to
the benefit of the overall power of their organizations. A powerful grass
roots organization, in turn, has benefits for the sense of security and
control felt by its members. Rather than merely being dependent upon
government to meet their needs, the organization provides a vehicle for
taking back some of the control over the response to the situation. This
security was rooted in activism as indicated by Stone and Levine (1985):

> Resident's own organizations became important means of dealing with the
> problems they faced, in part because their own organizations would not
> consider the matter "closed" as long as people were still having problems
> related to Love Canal. (p. 158)

In summary, grass roots organization provides an important source
of power for toxic victims. Shaw and Milbrath (1983) noted that the
success of a community group's influence on policy rests particularly
upon its ability to put forward clear goals and to develop good strategy.
The Concerned Citizens Committee in Legler was, in fact, successful in
meeting its two major objectives: An alternative water system was installed, and their law suit against Jackson Township was won (pending
appeals). The LCHA succeeded in bringing political pressure to bear,
resulting in a buyout of homes. Such success may not be uncommon.
Thus, Freudenberg (1984a) found that 37% of the sampled community
groups perceived themselves to be very successful and another 46%
somewhat successful. Half reported the elimination or reduction of the
hazard that was the group's main focus. Although these findings may
have been subject to a sampling bias favoring successful groups, the
importance of participation at the community level by toxic victims in
affecting the course of events is clearly demonstrated.

PROACTIVE ATTEMPTS TO COMBAT POTENTIAL HAZARDS

Roughly 350 pounds of hazardous wastes are produced annually for
every American citizen (Epstein, Brown, & Pope, 1983), creating the
need for appropriately designed disposal sites. Among attempts to locate potentially noxious facilities, efforts to locate permanent disposal
sites for nuclear waste have also received widespread attention. Although most of the studies on community response to toxic exposure
have investigated reactive attempts by communities to cope with existing sources of exposure, two studies have examined proactive commu-

nity responses that attempted to halt the siting of a nearby hazardous waste facility. The studies focused on the indvidual characteristics of residents who became involved in attempts to halt the facility versus those who did not.

In a North Carolina community, Cook (1983) found that residents who participated in a minimal way (i.e., signed a petition, attended a meeting), as contrasted with nonactivists, were more likely to have lived in the neighborhood longer (suggesting attachment to the community) and have children in the home. Residents who were more involved (i.e., contributed money, distributed petitions) also had higher incomes and more valuable homes, suggesting that they had more to lose if the hazardous waste site was developed. In an Arizona community, Bachrach and Zautra (1985) found that living in the community longer was the only demographic characteristic differentiating participants versus nonparticipants (no differences in income, education, sex, race, or marital status were found). They also found that activism was associated more with perceptions of the community (sense of community) than with perceptions of personal attributes.

These studies are limited by small numbers of subjects. And because they used different measures, consistencies are obscured. Regardless, several commonalities can be identified. Attachment to the community (either directly or indirectly measured) was related to activism in both studies. Length of residence was found to be a key variable, with activism requiring enough time in residence to both hold a stake in the community and to be concerned about the degree of exposure. This finding also fits with the profile of opposition found in Legler in 1971 to the proposed landfill that later came to be the source of water contamination (Edelstein, 1982) as well as with the Stone and Levine findings (1985). Finally, a further commonality involves the belief by some residents that the proposed facility (in the case of proactive community groups) will represent a source of future danger. Edelstein (1987) terms this effect "anticipatory fear." He first identified it in a social impact assessment of a sanitary landfill (Edelstein, 1980) where residents used the example of Love Canal to imagine worse-case scenarios for the effects of the landfill on area groundwater and health.

It would appear that the results of the proactive studies do not correspond completely to those of Stone and Levine's findings (1985) describing Love Canal. This may be due to differences in the three communities: urban working class (Stone & Levine, 1985), rural (Cook, 1983), and suburban (Bachrach & Zautra, 1985). It may also reflect differences between proactive and reactive community environments. Further research is needed to elucidate this.

However, the reactive/proactive distinction may benefit from refinement. In both cases, community concern occurs as a reaction to an environmental threat. In one case, the threat is a result of a past-documented release of toxins into the environment. In the second case, the threat stems from plans to create a facility that may release toxins into the environment at some future time. In both cases, there is a reaction to a threat, one "real," the second anticipatory ("imagined" or "perceived"). Therefore, the key distinction may be between contamination that is anticipated versus that that has occurred. The anticipatory situation is likely to be even less clearly defined than a labeled toxic exposure, allowing for a much greater projective definition by the community.

The widespread opposition to hazardous facilities attests to the power of anticipatory fears as well as environmental stigma (Edelstein, 1984, 1986) in motivating citizen involvement in community activity. This so-called "not-in-my-backyard" phenomena is a rich area for further research (see Armour, 1984; Edelstein, 1987).

LIMITS TO COMMUNITY: CONSENSUS AND DISSENSUS

In the prior sections, we have explored the development of grass roots organizations as a response to toxic contamination. However, it would be misleading to suggest that contamination only causes community cohesion.

Quarantelli and Dynes (1977) suggested that there are two types of crises (p. 23):

> Dissensus types of crises are conflict-containing situations where there are sharply contrasting views of the nature of the situation, what brought it about and what should be done to resolve it. . . . Consensus-type crises are those where there is an agreement on the meaning of the situation, the norms and values that are appropriate and priorities that should be followed.

They argue that both natural and technological disasters exemplify the consensus crisis. In many respects, the examples discussed in this chapter support their contention. In other ways, however, even major toxic disasters involve differences in interpretation and strategy that can serve as the basis for conflict rather than cooperation (e.g., Fowlkes & Miller, 1982). Thus, according to Freudenberg (1984a), some one third of the community groups confronting toxic threats suffered from divisiveness between neighbors. At a given time, a particular community might be described at a place on a continuum between dissensus and consensus, but both are likely to be present.

CONSENSUS AND DISSENSUS IN LEGLER

As the Legler case illustrates, even incidents involving a fair degree of general consensus are marred by conflict. Perhaps, consensus and dissensus have a dialectical relationship such that elements of each are likely to be found in differing degrees in different aspects of any toxic incident due to the inherent uncertainties of the situation. Furthermore, the mix of consensus and dissensus may vary over the stages of toxic disaster (de Boer, 1985). For example, in the Legler case, the fact that an effective community organization emerged reflected an early consensus (at least among those who joined it) over certain common problems, goals, and approaches. But conflict based on dissensus was never absent from the picture. It occurred both within the Concerned Citizens Committee at key decision-making junctures where differing goals among members surfaced and also as a result of interpersonal tensions over time.

Conflict involved both the task and socioemotional environments of the Concerned Citizens Committee, the first relating to the accomplishment of the organization's objectives and the second involving the relationships among members of the organization. Several examples are provided.

Wells versus City Water

Legler was a community that lacked homogeneity in certain key ways. Most important was the division between earlier and later settlers. Both those who arrived in Legler during the first major wave of development in the 1960s and early 1970s and those who had preceded them valued the rural ambiance of the section and desired a high degree of seclusion and privacy from neighbors. They opposed further growth in the area. In contrast, most of the newcomers who arrived in the mid-to-late 1970s sought a more suburbanized "coffee klatch" community with opportunities for social contact between neighbors. They sought development-style living and the growth of amenities in the immediate area. Obviously, a basic clash of values existed between these groups.

As the Concerned Citizens Committee took shape around a shared need to respond to the water crisis, an early conflict nearly shattered the organization. This was a conflict over whether to fight for a central, municipally operated water district or for the digging of new, deeper individual wells. Generally, the longer term residents favored the replacement of wells; the newer residents thought that a "city water" system would provide the same kinds of safety they had in their prior (usually urban) homes. To the former group, wells were a sign of independence and rural living; city water was a sign of government interference, additional expense, and impure water. To the latter group, wells were a big responsibility and very uncertain (as the pollution experience confirmed); city water was a service that could (and should) be provided by government; a central water system would therefore be a sign of progress in the area. This conflict was resolved when the option of individual wells became unattainable. Local government claimed that public money could not be spent to improve private property. Consensus was then reestablished around the fight for city water.

To Sue or Not to Sue?

A second major area of conflict occurred around the initiation of the lawsuit against the township. This issue divided the neighborhood, eventually serving to discriminate who was in and who was not in Concerned Citizens. Although Edelstein's interviews were only with residents who were in the lawsuit, it became clear that diverse reasons accounted for the unwillingness of about one third of the families to join in the suit. Some refused to join because of their unwillingness or inability to risk an initial retainer for the lawyers ($100) or because they disliked lawyers and lawsuits. Others feared retaliation by the township either because they worked for the government or because they feared that the certificates of occupancy issued for their homes might be revoked. Some felt that "you just can't win against city hall"; others had personality conflicts with leaders of the community group. Finally, some people apparently were not able to cope with the situation well enough to join a suit or, as some resentful participants in the lawsuit felt, they may have believed that they could share in the benefits of a lawsuit without having to take the risks (these were "easy riders," according to Walsh & Warland [1983], cited by Stone & Levine [1985]). The question of participation in the lawsuit caused ongoing division in the community, although this conflict ceased to be internal to the community organization after nonparticipants in the lawsuits left the organization.

Trust

A third area of conflict arose when it was perceived that a "snitch" was operating within the group, passing information to the township. This was inherently divisive because it forced people to suspect each other. Within the organization, a decision was made to stop the open flow of information; the executive board became very secretive. This alienated some of the general membership who now were able neither to fully understand what was happening nor to participate in decisions.

Interpersonal Conflict

Finally, conflict also occurred as the group entered its third year without a complete resolution of its objectives. Leaders who had been mobilized for such an extended time began to show signs of fatigue. This surfaced in the form of personality conflict rather than disagreement over issues. It is possible that this conflict was always present but had been suppressed by the need for cooperation during crisis. But over time, feelings began to surface in arguments over the procedures to be used in meetings, the sharing of information among leaders and with members, and over the extensive media exposure of some leaders.

Conflict over the type of acceptable replacement water system and over the lawsuit involved task-oriented procedural decisions crucial to the organization's decision-making process. In contrast, the question of trust and particularly the interpersonal conflict illustrate tension within the socioemotional sphere of the organization. Cumulative tension developed over time among a group of leaders under intense pressure. These conflicts surfaced at a time when Concerned Citizens had succeeded in its first objective of getting a new water source installed. There was less need to suppress internal conflict. The lawsuit, the major continuing concern of the group, was almost totally in the hands of the lawyers. With external pressure now reduced, the interpersonal relationships among the leaders reflected the suppressed issues that arise when a diverse group of possibly incompatible individuals are thrown together under high pressure. Thus, at a time when the leadership might have begun to relax, rising internal conflict within the group kept tensions at a boiling point.

The outcome of this ongoing pressure appears to be the eventual disintegration of the community organization. In the aftermath of a major legal victory for the Concerned Citizens Committee, some residents were disgruntled with the court's allocation of awards. During the period in which the decision was appealed, residents were further frustrated by their inability to get their awards. Communication among residents and between leaders of the organization and lawyers eroded, fed by arguments over legal costs. This, in turn, eroded trust. With appeals continuing some 7 years after the incident began, dissensus appears to have replaced consensus in Legler.

Such group conflicts may reflect a normal response to prolonged stress, as suggested by several observers of disaster:

When disaster threatens over a long period of time, the cohesive forces that
hold a group together are subject to strain. (Lang & Lang, 1964, p. 58)

The Langs note that group effort may be disrupted by collective emotional disturbances, displacement or schismatic tendencies toward mutual withdrawal, and increasing subgroup solidarity reflected in distrust
of authority, charges of favoritism, and intensification of damages.

Barton (1969) cites research to suggest that a "therapeutic community" that pulls people together to face a disaster will break apart as it must
decide on questions of allocation of aid or resources and as fellow sufferers discover that their association becomes less comforting and more
painful over time because they continually remind one another of past
crises. Both of these factors can be seen as contributing to conflict within
Concerned Citizens. Similarly, Creen (1984) noted various characteristics of the stress associated with prolonged confrontations. Among
the pressures that invite internal division is depression associated with
the "next shoe syndrome" (p. 56), where organization members find
themselves waiting for the next piece of bad news. Finally, de Boer
(1986) suggested that in latter stages of a toxic incident, personal rather
than community issues become dominant, possibly contributing to a
loss of the strong ties of mutual interdependence found earlier. People
may no longer hold common objectives.

Interorganizational Conflict

Consensus often reflects conformity pressures, and so may dissensus. Thus, in Legler, some Concerned Citizens Committee members felt
that nonsupportive neighbors feared retribution by the township if they
joined. Such "uneasy nonriders" are kept from taking action by conformity pressure and fear of punishment.

Disintegration of community consensus may reflect legitimate differences between different sectors of the community with differing interests. In his study of community groups, Freudenberg (1984a) noted
that the most often reported source of opposition to local organizations
stemmed from industry. However, the community conflict surrounding
toxic exposure and threat is often more complex. Thus, many Legler
residents not only met with what they perceived to be a hostile reaction
from local government (the "polluter" in their instance), but they were
often stigmatized by outsiders as well. Not all residents of Jackson
Township agreed in their interpretation of events. For example, when
some Jackson Township taxpayers from outside of Legler were angered
by demands for public assistance for the neighborhood, conflict occurred over the legitimacy of these claims.

The existence of differing interest groups within the community may even lead to the creation of more than one grass roots organization. Thus, Shaw and Milbrath (1983) report the existence of several local groups at Love Canal. Besides the best known, the Love Canal Home-owners Association, the Lasalle Development Tenants Association rep-resented largely black renters in a federal housing project; the Love Canal Renters Association represented renters from throughout the community; the 93rd St. Group represented home owners who felt sold down the river (canal?) by the LCHA when they were placed just out-side a boundary for tax relief. Shaw and Milbrath report substantial inequality between these groups because of LCHA's informal power. This group had also gained formal power somewhat by chance; their participation in the state task force had been instituted because the governor of New York insisted at the time this group first asserted itself that there be improved relationships between the task force and resi-dents. The functioning of various groups raised a concern that the state might use a divide-and-conquer strategy with the residents.

THE DISSENSUS COMMUNITY

Toxic disaster may also produce a dissensus so fundamental that interneighborhood conflict may serve to remove an overall sense of community that was previously present. This is precisely the situation described by Couch and Kroll-Smith (1985; Kroll-Smith & Couch, 1984; Kroll-Smith & Garula, 1985) in their excellent study of Centralia, Penn-sylvania. They profile a "community" (in the sense of municipality) in which there was neither an overall consensus nor the successful devel-opment of community groups representing different points of view. Thus the benefits described for therapeutic community development are largely absent, whereas the level of stress may be exacerbated by con-flict. On a continuum, Centralia was truly on the dissensus side.

Let us look briefly at the story of Centralia. Since 1962, an anthracite coal deposit below the town has burned out of control, threatening the 1,000 largely elderly and ethnically diverse residents with toxic gases, explosion, and subsidence (land collapse). The fire began in a garbage dump located on an area that had been strip-mined. Kroll-Smith and Couch (1984) report divisions over three issues:

1. Disagreement over whether the fire is really under the town and in what direction it is moving.
2. Disagreement over the best method to fight the fire.
3. Disagreement over health and safety questions. Some residents

were not threatened, whereas others feared subsidence and various gases (carbon monoxide, carbon dioxide, and methane).

In this climate of uncertainty, government failed to clarify any of these issues. The fire was not located, a strategy for fighting it was not developed, and hazards were not defined. The situation was further confounded when government standards for gas exposure were changed three times (Kroll-Smith & Couch, 1984).

The researchers report that anger has been directed neither at the fire nor at government. Instead, it was directed inward at the community. Community violence was common. Unlike the therapeutic community described for Legler and Love Canal, "The primary stressor in Centralia is not the fire, but community conflict" (1984, p. 6).

Over a period of 3 years, these researchers observed the development of seven different community groups, each representing factions in the general conflict over goals. The differences in the ways these groups have tried to define the situation is well illustrated by these two examples (Kroll-Smith and Couch, 1984, p. 7):

> Our message is clear. This town is in severe danger from an underground mine fire and each person in the town should acknowledge that danger and help us do something about it.
>
> We are being duped by the government and a handful of greedy people who want government to purchase their home so they can leave. There is no danger here (from the fire).

Internal conflict affected other communities without destroying the possibility for therapeutic community development. For example, in Legler, internal conflict did not prevent the formation of one predominant community group to represent the bulk of the neighborhood. Similarly, at Love Canal, despite the presence of competing groups, the LCHA was the principal representative of the community. In neither neighborhood were all residents in agreement about the risks of exposure; however, community organizations were able to represent the shared interests of a substantial portion of the community.

Why then is Centralia so different? Centralia differs in several ways from these other communities. First of all, boundaries were never firmly drawn delineating the endangered area. The drawing of boundaries in the other two cases served to define the range of danger, to activate anger at government for the way the boundaries were drawn, and to legitimate fears felt by marginal residents (those just outside the boundary who were both threatened by the arbitrary separation between their homes and the danger zone and were at a disadvantage in receiving aid). Second, the danger was less actualized and more uncertain than in the other cases. Finally, the entire town was being asked to agree to a strategy for addressing the concerns that probably most belonged to those proximate to the fire.

Kroll-Smith and Couch imply that divisions within Centralia correspond to existing neighborhoods within the community. Not only were these neighborhoods the traditional basis of affiliation, but neighborhoods reflected different degrees of exposure to the fire and thus different levels of concern. For residents of the neighborhood adjacent to the fire, support for a goal of government-aided evacuation was logical. However, this strategy threatened residents of neighborhoods less at risk who wanted to stay in Centralia. Thus conflict was the result of trying to achieve consensus within a community that was in reality several communities of interest. In terms of the framework introduced in Figure 1, each of these neighborhoods varied in their degree of turbulence, the extent to which the turbulence was directly due to the mine fire (an ecological condition) or to the reaction of other neighborhoods and government to this fire, and in their definition of a successful response. These differences help to explain the existence of dissensus in this case. Because of their insight into such differences, Kroll-Smith and Couch were able to begin to intervene in order to recreate a basis for community discussion of the crisis. Neighborhood meetings were held rather than meetings of the entire community. Because people could meaningfully share issues at this level of participation, a process of discussion was begun that started to dissipate the hostile atmosphere in the town.

For community organization to be therapeutic, there must be a shared sense of concern and a consensus around goals. Because *community* is such a slippery concept, there may be dysfunctional attempts to create community support at a level that is beyond consensus. Thus in the absence of the isolation of the "victims," structures that represent both victims and nonvictims (both as self-defined and defined by others) hardly can be expected to serve as a basis for social support, information, and power on behalf of the victims. This supports the idea that the process of isolation from social and institutional networks may be a necessary basis for the development of grass roots community organizations focused on addressing contamination issues.

AN OVERVIEW: DILEMMAS AND DIALECTICS OF COMMUNITY AND COMMUNITY ORGANIZATIONS

It has been argued that toxic contamination of a residential community creates the conditions for community organization because environmental turbulence demands efforts to create stability and because the residents are isolated from sources of support previously assumed to be available. Yet the full development of a social community may not always result from toxic disaster or threat, as in the case of dissensus.

On one hand, community groups reflect innovation in their capacity to learn to play the roles demanded by the communities' needs. Such community groups are thus inherently organizations devoted to learning. They offer paths for personal self-actualization as well as collective actualization. Collective actualization is central to the development of the identity required of a sense of community.

On the other hand, several limiting aspects to this development of community are also in evidence. It has been demonstrated that contamination alters the way in which residents view the place where they live. Although activism is quite likely to help individuals regain a sense of control and to further the collective individual interests of families within the neighborhood, neighboring is unlikely to erase the changes in neighborhood perception that preceded it. Therefore, in fighting for the mutual individual needs of families sharing exposure, activists must overcome the loss of or injury to the place—the commons that binds them together. Although a "sense of community" may evolve, it ironically may take the form of a temporary community fighting for its own dissolution through government-sponsored relocation (as in the cases of Times Beach and Love Canal). Even where the community is "repaired," as in Legler, a substantial proportion of Legler residents expressed a desire to move away if a successful lawsuit made it financially feasible for them to do so. Community development, in this case, may never broaden beyond the original focal issue simply because many residents have lost their long-term committment to the neighborhood.

In this context, the development of community organizations in response to such hazards as toxic exposure may be more similar to the kind of temporary organization, described by Bennis and Slater (1968; also Katz & Kahn, 1978), that forms expressly for the duration of its problem-solving effort than it is to more permanent community organizations aimed at the maintenance of ongoing activities in a fairly stable environment. This may be true both for organizations responding to a known toxic exposure as well as those acting on anticipatory fear and stigma to proactively fight a community hazard.

As reactive community groups succeed in responding to their original crisis, some are able to make the transition to becoming anticipatory organizations (see Botkin, Elmandjra, & Malitza, 1979). Furthermore, as networking across groups occurs, national representation of the network is created (e.g., the Citizen's Clearinghouse for Hazardous Waste).

Affiliation with national groups occurs; real bases of participation in the central structure are sought. Community development then serves not a temporary purpose but the basis instead for a national social movement representing toxic victims.

FUTURE DIRECTIONS

There may be as many as 100,000 sites in the United States alone that potentially threaten residential areas with toxic exposure, tearing communities apart and causing physical illness and mental stress to individuals. This chapter represents only a beginning attempt to outline and understand what is happening in communities affected by toxic contamination. As such, it is likely to raise more questions than it provides answers. There is a clear need for additional research to explore these questions.

SOME RESEARCH DIRECTIONS

In most situations, the individual is unable to cope with toxic disaster. Litwak (1985) has proposed that a modern society must have large-scale formal organizations (e.g., courts, schools, hospitals) and small primary groups (e.g., family, neighbors, relatives, friends) to manage most tasks. He points out that all of our formal systems appear to have natural limits, and they have hit them. On the other hand, the informal systems cannot by themselves stop crime, educate children, or, as in this chapter, prevent toxic exposure. As indicated in our framework and review, the community organization can serve as a bridge between the informal and formal systems. This chapter suggests a theoretical framework for explaining the development of community organizations in the face of toxic exposure. Further research is needed to verify and refine this model. Additional questions for future research include:

1. What are the strengths and weaknesses of the informal system (e.g., family, neighbors, relatives) in coping with the problems involving toxic exposure?

2. What are the causes of alienation and mistrust by residents of the formal organizations?

3. What are the effective ways that community organizations can link the formal and informal systems to solve problems caused by toxic exposure? For example, a community leader and a mental health center administrator can discuss problems and possible solutions for improv-

ing mental health services to residents living in a community affected by toxic wastes (Hess & Wandersman, 1985).

4. What are the longitudinal dimmensions of toxic exposure? For example, one can chart the life cycle of community organizations responding to toxic contamination to better understand the dialectics between dissensus and consensus or explore such dimmensions as time, government action, legal action, and relocation to see how they affect individuals, families and communities.

Additional directions for future research can be focused upon specific components of the framework of participation in community organizations. For example:

5. How are community responses to toxic exposure affected by molar actions (e.g., federal or state legislation)? Communities do not function in a vaccuum—what types of governmental responses have been helpful or harmful?

6. What are the characteristics of communities that are most likely to develop a community organization in response to a toxic hazard?

7. What are the organizational characteristics of effective community organizations (e.g., Prestby & Wandersman, 1985)?

8. Can we use a person × situation approach to individual differences to help us explain why some people participate and others do not (e.g., Florin & Wandersman, 1984)? Can this approach be used to increase participation?

9. Do community organizations that form in response to a toxic hazard generalize their activism to other issues (e.g., Edelstein, 1984)?

10. What are the factors that influence consensus and dissensus within community organizations?

11. What helps victims of toxic contamination cope effectively? What kinds of "helpers" are effective? The list can go on and on.

The topic of community dynamics in coping with toxic exposure is at the nexus of several literatures including environmental psychology, community psychology, health psychology, clinical psychology, community organization, law, public health, risk analysis, social impact assessment, and the study of disaster. Although our chapter frames a number of issues important for understanding how individuals and communities cope with the toxic hazards, it is obvious that the cliche fits—much research needs to be done to fill in and expand the concepts and framework used here.

SOME ACTION DIRECTIONS

Given the deleterious effects of toxic exposure, there is a need to go beyond the model of "pure" research to incorporate elements of action and advocacy research. Because the level of stress among toxic victims appears to be greatly enhanced by the failure of institutional and social networks to meet the needs of those affected, an important area of applied research is suggested. The study of the impacts of various responses to toxic disaster can serve as the basis for experimenting with more effective and less stressful responses. Likewise, research can help to document and legitimate the plight of toxic victims, having important implications in the consideration of legislation and litigation. Kroll-Smith and Couch integrated into their study of dissensus in Centralia an intervention to enhance consensus. Paigen applied pragmatic research methods to test for health effects at Love Canal. Edelstein has used his findings in litigation in suggesting legislation and in designing programs to address environmental hazards. In short, the topic demands further research, but it also needs researchers committed to acting on the implications of their work.

Acknowledgments

We would like to thank David Altman, Steve Berman, Peter Fisher, Bill Hallman, Christine LoPresti, Deborah Kleese, Adeline Gordon Levine, and Donald Unger for their very helpful comments on earlier drafts.

REFERENCES

Anderson, R. F., & Greenberg. M. R. (1982). Hazardous waste facility siting: A role for planners. *APA Journal*, Spring, 204–218.

Armour, A. (1984). *The not-in-my-backyard syndrome*. Downsview, Ontario: York University.

Bachrach, K., & Zautra, A. (1985). Coping with a community stressor: The threat of a hazardous waste facility. *Journal of Health and Social Behavior, 26*, 127–141.

Barton, A. (1969). *Communities in disaster*. Garden City, NY: Doubleday.

Bass, L. (1985). *Impacts of strategy and participation of volunteer-organizations of involved inhabitants in living-quarters on contaminated soil*. Paper presented at the International Association for Impact Assessment Annual Conference, "Methods and Experiences in Impact Assessment," June 27–28, Utrecht, The Netherlands.

Baum, A., Fleming, R., & Singer, J. (1982). Stress at Three Mile Island: Applying social psychological impact analysis. In L. Bickman (Ed.), *Applied social psychology annual* (pp. 217–248). Beverly Hills, CA: Sage.

Bennis, W. G., & Slater, P. E. (1968). *The temporary society*. New York: Harper & Row.

Botkin, J. W., Elmandjra, M., & Malitza, M. (1979). *No limits to learning: Bridging the human gap*. New York: Pergamon Press.

Cook, J. (1983). Citizen response in a neighborhood under threat. *American Journal of Community Psychology, 11*, 459–471.

Couch, S. R., & Kroll-Smith, J. S. (1985). The chronic technical disaster: Toward a social scientific perspective. *Social Science Quarterly, 66*, 564–575.

Crawford, M. (1986). Toxic waste, energy bills clear Congress. *Science, 234,* 537–538.

Creen, T. (1984). The social and psychological impact of nimby disputes. In A. Armour (Ed.), *The not-in-my-backyard syndrome: conference proceedings, 1983* (pp. 51–60). Downsview, Ontario: York University.

de Boer, J. (1985). *Community response to soil pollution: A model of parallel processes.* Paper presented at the International Association for Impact Assessment Annual Conference, "Methods and Experiences in Impact Assessment," June 27–28, Utrecht, The Netherlands.

Division of Epidemiology and Disease Control. (1980). *Groundwater contamination and possible health effects in Jackson Township, New Jersey.* Report to the New Jersey State Department of Health, July.

Edelstein, M. R. (1980). *Social impacts of Al Turi Landfill, Inc.* Report prepared for the Town of Goshen, NY.

Edelstein, M. R. (1982). *The social and psychological impacts of groundwater contamination in the Legler section of Jackson, New Jersey.* Report to the law firm, Kreindler & Kreindler.

Edelstein, M. R. (1984). *Stigmatizing aspects of toxic pollution.* Report to the law firm, Martin & Snyder.

Edelstein, M. R. (1986). Disabling communities: The impact of regulatory proceedings. *Journal of Environmental Systems, 16,* 87–110.

Edelstein, M. R. (1987). *Inverting the American dream: The social and psychological dynamics of residential toxic exposure.* Boulder, CO: Westview Press.

Epstein, S., Brown, L. O., & Pope, C. (1983). *Hazardous waste in America: Our number one environmental crisis.* San Fransisco: Sierra Club.

Erikson, K. (1976). *Everything in its path.* New York: Simon & Schuster.

Fleming, I., & Baum, A. (1985). The role of prevention in technological catastrophe. In A. Wandersman & R. Hess (Eds.), *Beyond the individual: Environmental approaches and prevention* (pp. 139–152). New York: Haworth.

Florin, P., & Wandersman, A. (1984). Cognitive social learning variables and participation in community development. *American Journal of Community Psychology, 12,* 689–708.

Fowlkes, M., & Miller, P., (1982). *Love Canal: The social construction of disaster.* Report to the Federal Emergency Management Agency.

Francis, R. S. (1983). Attitudes toward industrial pollution, strategies for protecting the environment, and environmental-economic trade-offs. *Journal of Applied Social Psychology, 13,* 310–327.

Freudenberg, N. (1984a). Citizen action for environmental health: Report on a survey of community organizations. *American Journal of Public Health, 74,* 444–448.

Freudenberg, N. (1984b). *Not in our backyards.* New York: Monthly Review Press.

Gans, H. (1967). *The Levittowners.* New York: Vintage Books.

Gans, H. (1970). Planning and social life: Friendship and neighbor relations in suburban communities. In H. Proshansky, W. Ittelson, & L. Rivlin (Eds.), *Environmental psychology: Man and his physical setting* (pp. 501–508). New York: Holt, Rinehart & Winston.

Gibbs, L. M. (1982). *Love Canal: My story.* Albany: State University of New York Press.

Gibbs, L. M. (1983). *Community response to an emergency situation: Psychological destruction and the Love Canal. American Journal of Community Psychology, 11,* 116–125.

Gibbs, L. M. (1985). *The impacts of environmental disasters on communities.* Reprint of the Citizens Clearinghouse for Hazardous Wastes.

Gibbs, M. (1982). *Psychological dysfunction in the Legler litigation group.* Report to the law firm, Kreindler & Kreindler.

Gibbs, M. (1986). Psychological dysfunction as a consequence of exposure to toxics. In A. Lebovitz, A. Baum, & J. Singer (Eds.), *Health consequences of exposure to toxins* (pp. 47–70). Hillsdale, NJ: Lawrence Erlbaum Associates.

Gottlieb, B. (1981). *Social networks and social support in community mental health*. Beverly Hills, CA: Sage Publications.

Gricar, B. G., & Baratta, A. (1983). Bridging the information gap at Three Mile Island: Radiation monitoring by citizens. *Journal of Applied Behavioral Science, 19*, 35–49.

Hatcher, S. L. (1982). The psychological experience of nursing mothers upon learning of a toxic substance in their breast milk. *Psychiatry, 45*, 172–181.

Heider, F. (1958). *The psychology of interpersonal relations*. New York: Wiley.

Heller, K., Price, R., Reinharz, S., Riger, S., & Wandersman, A. (1984). *Psychology and community change* (2nd ed.). Homewood, IL: Dorsey.

Hess, R., & Wandersman, A. (1985). What can we learn from Love Canal? A conversation with Lois Gibbs and Richard Valinsky. In A. Wandersman & R. Hess (Eds.), *Beyond the individual: Environmental approaches and prevention* (pp. 111–124). New York: Haworth.

Jacobson, J., Jacobson, S., & Fein, G. (1985). Intrauterine exposure to environmental toxins: The significance of subtle behavioral effects. In A. Wandersman & R. Hess (Eds.), *Beyond the individual: Environmental approaches and prevention* (pp. 125–138). New York: Haworth.

Janis, J. R. (1981). The public and superfund. *EPA Journal*, 714–729.

Katz, D., & Kahn, R. (1978). *The social psychology of organizations* (2nd ed.). New York: Wiley.

Kroll-Smith, J. S., & Couch, S. (1984). *Fear and suspicion in Centralia: Doing fieldwork in a community in crisis*. Paper presented at the SSSP Conference, San Antonio, Texas, August.

Kroll-Smith, J. S., & Garula, S., Jr. (1985). The real disaster is above ground: Community conflict and grass roots organization in Centralia. *Small Town, 15*, 4–11.

Lang, K., & Lang, G. E. (1964). Collective responses to the threats of disaster. In G. H. Grosser, H. Wechsler, & M. Greenblatt (Eds.), *The threat of impending disaster* (pp. 58–75). Cambridge, MA: The M.I.T. Press.

Lerner, M. J. (1980). *The belief in a just world: A fundamental delusion*. New York: Plenum Press.

Levine, A. (1982). *Love Canal: Science, politics and people*. Boston: Lexington Books.

Litwak, E. (1985). *Helping the elderly: The complementary roles of informal networks and formal systems*. New York: Guilford.

Melief, W. (1985). *The social impacts of alternative policy approaches to incidents of toxic waste exposure*. Paper presented at the International Association for Impact Assessment Annual Conference, "Methods and Experiences in Impact Assessment," June 27–28, Utrecht, The Netherlands.

Milbrath, L. (1984). *Environmentalists: Vanguard for a new society*. Albany: S.U.N.Y. Press.

Office of Technology Assessment. (1983). *Technologies and management strategies for hazardous waste control*. Washington, DC: Congress of the United States.

Paigen, B. (1979). Health hazards at Love Canal. Testimony presented to the House Sub-Committee on Oversight and Investigations, March 21.

Prestby, J., & Wandersman, A. (1985). An empirical exploration of a framework of organizational viability: Maintaining block organizations. *Journal of Applied Behavioral Science, 21*, 287–305.

Quarantelli, E. L., & Dynes, R. R. (1977). Response to social crisis and disaster. *Annual Review of Sociology, 3*, 23–49.

Sarason, S. (1974). *The psychological sense of community*. Washington, DC: Jossey-Bass.

Schacter, S. (1959). *The psychology of affiliation*. Palo Alto: Stanford University Press.

Shaw, L. G., & Milbrath, L. W. (1983). Citizen participation in governmental decision making: The toxic waste threat at Love Canal, Niagra Falls, New York. *Rockefeller Institute Working Papers, 8*.

Slovic, P., Fischhoff, B., & Lichtenstein, S. (1980). Facts vs. fears: Understanding perceived risk. In R. Schwing & W. A. Albers, Jr. (Eds.), *Societal risk assessment: How safe is safe enough?* (pp. 181–214). New York: Plenum Press.

Stone, R. A., & Levine, A. G. (1985). Reactions to collective stress: Correlates of active citizen participation at Love Canal. In A. Wandersman & R. Hess (Eds.), *Beyond the individual: Environmental approaches and prevention* (pp. 153–178). New York: Haworth.

Tucker, R. K. (1981). *Groundwater quality in New Jersey: An investigation of toxic contaminants.* Report of the Department of Environmental Protection.

Unger, D., & Wandersman, A. (1985). The importance of neighbors: The social, cognitive, and affective components of neighboring. *American Journal of Community Psychology, 13,* 139–169.

van Eijndhoven, J. C. M., & Nieuwdorp, G. H. E. (1985). *Institutional Action in Soil Pollution Situations with Uncertain Risks.* Paper presented at the International Association for Impact Assessment Annual Conference, "Methods and Experiences in Impact Assessment," June 27–28, Utrecht, The Netherlands.

Vianna, N. J., & Polan, A. K. (1984). Incidence of low birth weight among Love Canal residents. *Science, 226,* 1217–1219.

Wallace, A. (1957). Mazeway disintegration. *Human Organization, 14,* 23–27.

Walsh, E. J., & Warland, R. H. (1983). Social movement involvement in the wake of a nuclear accident. *American Sociological Review, 48,* 764–780.

Wandersman, A. (1981). A framework of participation in community organizations. *Journal of Applied Behavioral Science, 17,* 27–58.

Wandersman, A., & Hess, R. (Eds.). (1985). *Beyond the individual: Environmental approaches and prevention.* New York: Haworth.

Wandersman, A., Andrews, A., Riddle, D., & Fancett, C. (1983). Environmental psychology and prevention. In R. Felner & L. Jason, (Eds.). *Preventive psychology: Theory, research and practice* (pp. 104–127). Elmsford, NY: Pergamon Press.

Wolfenstein, M. (1957). *Disaster: A psychological essay.* Glencoe, IL: Free Press.

4

Can Resident Participation in Neighborhood Rehabilitation Programs Succeed?

ISRAEL'S PROJECT RENEWAL THROUGH A COMPARATIVE PERSPECTIVE

ARZA CHURCHMAN

INTRODUCTION

Citizen participation and neighborhood rehabilitation have received considerable attention in the last two decades and, to a large extent, have been inextricably linked. It is in the context of neighborhood rehabilitation that citizen involvement has been most implemented, most prominent, and most controversial.

The focus of this chapter is the systematic description and evaluation of resident involvement in a particular program—Project Renewal—Israel's ambitious, comprehensive neighborhood rehabilitation program. The analysis is based upon a conceptual framework developed for coping with the complexity of the concept of citizen participation. We will also attempt to relate to the experience in other countries. How-

ARZA CHURCHMAN • The Samuel Neaman Institute for Advanced Studies in Science and Technology and the Faculty of Architecture and Town Planning, Technion—Israel Institute of Technology, Haifa, Israel.

ever, we will be limited by our dependence on published material that does not always relate to all of the dimensions that are part of our conceptual framework. Furthermore, there are undoubtedly many additional cases that either have not been published or have not come to our attention. Our comparison, therefore, does not pretend to be a thorough or systematic one. It will, however, allow us to look for common, or uncommon, threads.

Project Renewal was initiated in 1979 and by 1982 encompassed 82 neighborhoods (containing about 500,000 residents), with 78 more scheduled to be included in the near future. In view of Israel's small scale (population 4,064,000), the result is that almost every local authority already has at least one neighborhood in the project. Thus it is a truly nationwide project and of an unprecedented scale.

It is ambitious in another sense as well: It was established as an integrated, comprehensive program, rather than as a single-purpose one, attempting to affect positive change in virtually all aspects of life in the neighborhoods.

The material on resident participation in the project (Churchman, 1985) is based upon a 4-year comprehensive evaluation study carried out within the framework of the Samuel Neaman Institute for Advanced Studies in Science and Technology and funded by the International Committee for the Evaluation of Project Renewal and the Samuel Neaman Institute for Advanced Studies in Science and Technology. Ten neighborhoods, varying in geographic location, size, and length of time in the program were included in the study. Each neighborhood was assigned a field investigator who gathered data over the course of 2 years (1982–1984). Methods used were participant observation in meetings and events of all kinds, structured and unstructured interviews, informal contacts with local informants, and directed data collection. Individual, structured interviews were conducted with representatives of governmental authorities active in the neighborhoods. Information on resident attitudes was gathered in a household survey conducted in 9 of the 10 neighborhoods by an independent survey organization. A random sample of 150 residents in each neighborhood and a special sample of active residents was interviewed.

NEIGHBORHOOD PLANNING AND REHABILITATION

In recent years there has been renewed interest in neighborhoods as the basic building blocks of cities, and they have emerged as the principal unit of community development policy and program concern (Baroni, 1983; Stegman, 1979). Furthermore, there are many persons calling for the transferring of elements of government authority to the neighborhood level and for allowing neighborhood control of one sort or another (see, for example, Hawkins, 1983). This approach has stemmed from some of the same processes affecting the interest in citizen participation and has both influenced and been influenced by neighborhood rehabilitation programs.

Neighborhood improvement can assume many forms (Downs, 1981) and has a number of appelations, for example, neighborhood revitalization, gentrification, incumbent upgrading. We will be discussing the type of government-sponsored, initiated, or approved program that attempts to achieve rehabilitation without a change in the nature of the population or a radical change in the character of the neighborhood.

Although most recent rehabilitation programs throughout the world have been neighborhood-based, there are still those who challenge this approach and question its legitimacy. One issue raised when Project Renewal was first initiated was that of equity. Can or should need be geographically defined or limited? The neighborhood approach, by definition, provides benefits to those within the sometimes arbitrary borders of the neighborhood who may be less in need than those more deprived who by chance live outside those borders.

Others assert that many of the problems facing deteriorated neighborhoods are complex and deep-seated economic, political, and social problems, which cannot be solved at the neighborhood level. Thus Fisher (1984) argues that the neighborhood is neither the site nor the focus of its problems, nor the site of the power needed to address them. Because government programs are, however, not interested in the kind of radical change desired by Fisher, his argument is not considered relevant.

A further caveat is that neighborhood residents may have a limited, "conservative," and parochial approach and that they may not be interested in the larger, urban picture (Vonk, 1983).

Nevertheless, the general consensus seems to be that a neighborhood-based program enables a macrolevel and comprehensive approach to rehabilitation rather than more microlevel and individualized attempts to aid particular families. It is now generally recognized that the quality of life in a neighborhood is a function not only of the quality of the housing stock but also of the quality and level of public services, social relationships between residents, perceptions of safety and security, and accessibility to transportation, shopping, and cultural facilities (Ahlbrandt & Cunningham, 1979).

In terms of resident involvement, the neighborhood approach has been a critical factor encouraging and facilitating resident organization and participation in the rehabilitation program.

CITIZEN INVOLVEMENT AND PARTICIPATION IN DECISION-MAKING PROCESSES

A large body of literature exists on the subject of citizen participation, and it appears in many different fields: planning, political science, public administration, architecture, environment–behavior studies, community organization, and industrial relations. Concurrently, participation is dealt with in many different environmental contexts and levels—the home, the street, the neighborhood, the work environment, the city, and the state.

Not surprisingly, there are, as a result, many different definitions of *citizen participation*. This is true despite the fact that many do not feel the need to define it or give pseudodefinitions that deal with its goals or outcomes, rather than actually define what it is. Examples of definitions include:

From the field of *political science*, the term *citizen participation* refers to those activities by private citizens that are more or less directly aimed at influencing the selection of governmental personnel and or the actions they take (Verba & Nie, 1972).

From the field of *community organization*, citizen participation refers to the means by which people who are not elected or appointed officials of agencies and government influence decisions about programs and policies that affect their lives (Brager & Specht, 1973).

In *planning*, citizen participation exists where an individual has an option to be a party to an agreement that must be sought within reasonable limits, before a decision affecting him or her can be effected (Mulvihill, 1980).

In *environment–behavior studies*, the term refers to individuals taking part in decision making in the institutions, programs, and environments that affect them (Wandersman, 1984); or incorporating the actual or prospective users of a facility, program, or product into the planning and design of that environment, program, or product (Becker, 1977).

Within the context of this chapter, we will adopt Wandersman's definition. However, in our experience, it is important to add a descriptive phrase to the term *individuals*: Therefore participation exists when individuals who are not elected or appointed officials of agencies and of government take part in decision making in the institutions, programs, and/or environments that affect them.

We will distinguish between *involvement* and *participation*. *Involvement* is used to denote the initiative and actions of the authorities or professionals, who, for whatever reason, wish to "involve" the residents in the decision-making process. *Participation* is used to denote the activity of the residents who take part in that process.

Many writers find historical antecedents for the present-day concern with participation and with neighborhoods. However, the question still arises as to why it was that the zeitgeist of the 1960s in the United States and England (and somewhat later in other countries) turned these issues into central ones. Various factors have been proposed as explanations for this development:

1. The increase in the size of the government and its role in our lives, as a result of the weakening of mediating institutions such as the family and church. At the same time, the growing sense of distance and alienation from the government (Kasperson & Breitbart, 1974; Kweit & Kweit, 1981).
2. The fact that government was increasingly personified by the bureaucrats who administer the policies and who are less amenable to citizen influence than politicians (Kweit & Kweit, 1981; Warren & Warren, 1977).
3. The impact of the mass media—through their opening up of the government to the scrutiny of the ordinary citizen (Langton, 1978).
4. The demands of minority groups for political and social equality and their belief that the institutional structure and supposedly professional decisions were depriving them of their legitimate share of benefits (Fainstein & Fainstein, 1974; Hallman, 1973; Schmandt, 1973).
5. Negative reactions to the urban renewal and highway programs of the 1950s (Frieden & Kaplan, 1975; Landsberger, 1980). The concurrent recognition of the failure of the purely physical approach to planning and the assumption that action in the social arena would be more effective if those affected participated themselves.
6. Criticism of the power and prestige of "experts" and professionals (Wooley, 1985).
7. Increased recognition on the part of planners and architects of the need for more contact with the users and for concern with their needs as perceived by them (Wooley, 1985).
8. The changes that have taken place in education, both in the average length of formal education and in the pedagogical approaches that have deemphasized discipline and authority and encouraged the development of individuality (Sharpe, 1979).

Susskind and Elliott (1983) summarize these trends in their statement:

> For advocates of participation, citizen involvement in government decision making is synonymous with (1) *democratization* of choices involving resource allocation, (2) *decentralization* of service systems management, (3) *deprofessionalization* of bureaucratic judgements that affect the lives of residents, and (4) *demystification* of design and investment decisions. (p. 3)

These trends were so pervasive that, as we shall see, participation was an idea whose time had come in countries with very different political and economic systems and with very different historical and cultural traditions.

With the increase in the practice of citizen participation, there was a concomitant attempt to clarify, analyze, and systematize the concept on a more theoretical level. These attempts quickly revealed the difficulty of the task and the complexity of the concept.

Not only are there often different interpretations given to the notions of involvement and participation from situation to situation, but there are also many "actors" within a given situation, each of whom may interpret them differently. The same can be said for the goals of involvement/participation, the strategies developed for action and the criteria used to evaluate its functioning. This clearly makes difficult the comparison between separate instances of participation between countries, or even within them.

Rosener (1978a) has argued, indeed, that the lack of knowledge about the effectiveness of participation is probably related to the fact that the complexity of the concept is not sufficiently acknowledged. Furthermore, the idea of citizen participation has continuously been bedeviled by implicit, unrealistic, and conflicting expectations (Kweit & Kweit, 1981). Thus much of the criticism leveled against participation stems from a misunderstanding of its complexity, from the unrealistic goals attached to it, and from unsystematic approaches to its analysis or evaluation.

A CONCEPTUAL FRAMEWORK FOR CLARIFYING, PLANNING, AND EVALUATING CITIZEN INVOLVEMENT/PARTICIPATION

The conceptual framework to be presented here (Alterman, Churchman, & Law-Yone, 1981) grew out of a sense of dissatisfaction with the unidimensional character of many approaches. We proposed a multidimensional approach that drew upon many sources and owes much to them (particularly Arnstein, 1969; Burke, 1968; Fagence, 1977;

Fainstein, Fainstein, & Armistead, 1979; Glass, 1979; Glenn, 1978; Rosener, 1978b; Wandersman, 1979). We have attempted to be inclusive, not limited by a particular professional emphasis, and for the framework to be applicable to different environmental levels—to architectural as well as planning contexts. In our study of Project Renewal we found it possible to set up an evaluation procedure based upon this framework that allowed us to direct the data-gathering process, to organize the material, and evaluate its significance.

The dimensions of the framework are (a) the situational context and the subject domain within which participation takes place; (b) the goals of involvement and of participation; (c) the definition of the "public" participating; (d) the types and amounts of resources invested in involvement and participation; (e) the power relationships between the decision makers and the residents; and (f) the stages in the decision-making process where participation occurs.

Clearly, all of these dimensions are interrelated, and the specific nature of one has a significant effect upon the others and upon the participatory techniques that are appropriate. For example, the goals of the decision makers will affect the definition of the public that they wish to involve and the nature of the power relationship that they wish to maintain.

These dimensions enable the planning of a strategy for involvement—a conscious choice between the possible alternatives in each dimension and an initial examination of the possible ramifications of a decision on one dimension upon the others.

As noted before, our evaluation study of Project Renewal was guided by this framework, and the presentation here of the results (and of the experience in other countries) will focus on each dimension in turn.

THE CONTEXT AND SUBJECT MATTER OF RESIDENT PARTICIPATION IN NEIGHBORHOOD REHABILITATION PROGRAMS

INTRODUCTION

In general, relevant contextual aspects of the situation include factors such as political traditions and institutional structures, economic systems, cultural attributes, planning traditions and institutional structures, housing tenure distribution, the environmental and social characteristics of the relevant "community," the nature of the decision-making body and its authority, and the attitudes and experiences of decision makers and citizens as regards participation.

The subject domain refers to the level of the environment being addressed by the decision-making process—an individual dwelling or room, a building, a street, a neighborhood, a town, region, or country; and to the topics involved—physical, social, economic, cultural, and so forth. An alternative approach to categorizing this aspect is by defining the type of substantive issue under discussion; for example, whether or not the issue entails trade-offs and conflict among groups or individuals; whether or not it requires specialized knowledge; whether it entails tangible and visible impacts; and whether it has a long- or short-range time span.[1]

THE CONTEXT IN WHICH PARTICIPATION HAS TAKEN PLACE

Published reports on resident participation in neighborhood rehabilitation programs indicate that, in the last 20 years, such activity has occurred in many countries—democratic, nondemocratic, and communist; in planned economies and market economies; and in developed and developing countries. The nature and focus of the participation as well as of the program itself is affected, of course, by these differences. The significant factor, however, is that participation has occurred in them all.

Participation in developing countries and in communist countries includes a large component of self-help—of doing the physical work oneself—which is largely absent in developed countries. This is a function, to a certain extent, of different philosophies; but perhaps mainly, of the level of resources available and of the services needing to be provided. For example, the reports from Africa and Latin America are mainly in relation to squatter neighborhoods, where the quality of life and the level of services are clearly different from those of even the most deteriorated neighborhoods in the United States or Europe.

There seem to be commonalities between participation in countries with very different political, economic, and cultural contexts. In discussing political participation in the Soviet Union, Friedgut (1979) distinguished between (a) autonomous participation, where the initiative to be active as well as the content and forms of organization are principally determined by the individual participating; and (b) mobilized participation, where actors external to the community are the sole ini-

[1]See Alterman (1982) for a fuller exposition of these dimensions.

tiators of participation, and they establish its legitimate framework, agenda, and tone. This distinction can apply as well to neighborhood rehabilitation programs in democratic countries. Mobilized participation is very much the character of at least the initial framework of government-mandated participation in such programs.

In almost all of the aforementioned countries, the governmental structure is a very centralized one, and planning is recognized as a national public policy tool. The United States is an exception to this rule with no national planning bodies. Decentralization has long been part of its political culture, and there is a tradition of local initiative and participation, particularly in the field of education (Schmandt, 1973).

The centralized nature of European governmental systems coupled with different political philosophies and different economic circumstances has led to a further difference from the United States that is significant in the context of neighborhood planning: the degree of direct governmental involvement in the planning, construction, and management of housing developments (Harloe, 1982). For example, the Dutch central government subsidizes 76% of all new dwellings (Godschalk & Zeisel, 1983). In some communist countries, 70% of the total urban housing stock are socialized multifamily houses (Jajszczyk & Hlebowicz, 1980). In Israel, the majority of housing construction is government financed or initiated.

However, even within centralized systems there have been varied approaches to the institutionalization of citizen participation. In many European countries, the requirement was included in general planning legislation: the British Town and Country Planning Acts of 1971–1972, the Town Planning Promotion Act in the Federal Republic of Germany, and the Dutch Physical Planning Act of 1965. In these instances, there are highly refined rules indicating when and how citizens can participate (Susskind & Elliott, 1983). The constitutions and laws of the European communist countries have established the rights of citizens to participate in economic and physical planning and in the management of neighborhoods (Bruston, 1980).

Legal or institutional requirements for citizen involvement most often relate to the neighborhood level. However, in Yugoslavia and other Eastern European countries, tenants in public-housing developments have recognized rights to participate in decision making on maintenance questions (Mulvihill, 1980). A legal requirement for tenant organizations to take an active part in housing improvements and redevelopment exists in Sweden (Nilsson, 1985).

Resident opposition to urban renewal policies that were based upon their displacement led to the legitimization of resident participation in later rehabilitation programs in a number of countries, including the United States, Spain, and Holland.

In the United States, requirements for citizen participation were written into the laws setting up specific rehabilitation programs, such as the Community Action Program, the Demonstration Cities and Metropolitan Development Act, and the Community Development Block Grant (CDBG) program. The level of specificity embodied in these different acts varied from the broad and vague requirement of "maximum feasible participation" in the Community Action Program to the more specific and limiting language of the CDBG program.

The tendency in developing countries, such as Zambia and Transkei, South Africa, seems to be for both rehabilitation programs and the involvement of residents to be a more localized, sometimes planner-initiated, activity not anchored in some central action (see Finlayson, 1978; Rakodi, 1983).

Clearly, the fact that formal or legal requirements for participation exist does not guarantee that they are met or that the residents have an impact on the process. Perlman and Spiegel (1983), for example, assert that over the past 50 years there has not been a single substantive change made in a proposed plan in Copenhagen as a result of citizen participation. Nevertheless, the formal requirement represents a commitment, both symbolic and potential, which can be taken advantage of.

Citizen participation in Israel has begun to gather some momentum only since the late 1970s (Churchman, Alterman, & Law-Yone, 1979). On the whole, the principle of participation has encountered difficulty in rooting itself in Israeli life for several reasons: Israel does not have a political tradition of participatory democracy or of decentralized democracy. The central government plays the most important role in the planning of services of all kinds. Its basic attitude has been a paternalistic one, especially toward the various waves of new immigrants who arrived with nothing—from Europe after World War II, from the Islamic countries in the 1950s, from Russia in the 1970s, and recently from Ethiopia. The approach was that politicians, professionals, and experts knew what was best for them in all fields—housing, education, social and cultural services, and the like. Furthermore, almost all of these immigrants came from countries with nondemocratic regimes, and many of them were from cultures with very traditional authoritarian family structures.

Thus, the fact that Project Renewal stipulated that resident participation was to be an integral and required part of the decision-making process was a revolutionary step. There was no certainty as to how, or if, it would work. Many felt that as an "alien" concept imported from the United States, it would not succeed.

On the other hand, there were factors operating in a positive direction: When a centralized power structure decides to decentralize somewhat, it can mandate a pattern of involvement, require a basic minimum, and enforce it. Furthermore, there were residents who over the years had learned something about the use of influence in a democratic system. They were not characterized by the so-called culture of poverty and were not seriously alienated from the system. Protest among the disadvantaged in Israel is not revolutionary activity aimed at affecting change in the social order. It is, rather, an attempt to influence social policy, within the existing normative system (Azmon, 1983).

An additional factor was the influence exerted by American Jewish communities in support of the principle of resident participation in general and, in particular instances, in support of the residents' positions.[2]

The Subject Domain of the Program in Which Participation Has Taken Place

The Environmental Level

The environmental level with which this chapter is concerned is, of course, the neighborhood. However, this level subsumes other levels, such as subareas of the neighborhood, streets, buildings, and individual dwellings, each of which can be treated separately within a given program.

At the neighborhood level, an initial question that arises is the definition of the boundaries of the neighborhood. Warren and Warren (1977) argued that, in the Model Cities program, there were many instances of artificially defined administrative units. Most reports on other programs do not raise this point, perhaps because it was not an issue. Clearly, however, if the attempt is to organize a "community," this can be a critical factor.

Neighborhood size has not been identified in the literature as a critical variable, although it does have implications for the scope of the problems involved and the methods necessary in order to reach a given proportion of the residents.

---

[2]Each neighborhood was twinned with a Jewish community outside of Israel that contributed funds to the programs and was variably involved in the decision-making and implementation process.

The relative homogeneity or heterogeneity of the neighborhood in both physical and social terms has implications for the participation process. In terms of the housing characteristics, the topics of interest appear to be the building types (single or multifamily; low or high rise); the forms of ownership (private, municipal, cooperative, or state); and housing tenure (owner or renter). These characteristics affect the type of renovations that can be undertaken and the nature of resident participation that can be expected.

There is no doubt that more participation occurs with regard to individual homes than with regard to multifamily dwellings; and the larger these latter are, the more complex the question of involvement. Sharpe (1979) argued that the recent growth in owner-occupiers in the Western countries has strengthened the neighborhood and participation movements. Cooperative housing, which is based on the principle of self-government, is assumed to be particularly advantageous for citizen participation in the management of neighborhoods (Jajszczyk & Hlebowicz, 1980). There is clearly a problem in involving renters, although it may depend on the nature of the participation afforded. In socialist countries, where rents are independent of the real costs of maintenance, it has not been possible to create sufficiently strong economic and psychological motivation to induce people to participate in the maintenance of their homes and neighborhoods (Jajszczyk & Hlebowicz, 1980). This has also been a problem in Israeli project housing. On the other hand, where tenants are involved in decisions as to the nature of the planned rehabilitation of the building, then they are more likely to participate (Nilsson, 1985).

As to the population of the neighborhood, even within distressed neighborhoods there is always some degree of heterogeneity. However, the characteristics that are particularly relevant will vary. In some cases, it may be socioeconomic characteristics, in others, color, ethnic origin, or tribe, in others, differences between the original population and newcomers from other countries (as between the Dutch and "non-Dutch" residents of Oude Westen [Godschalk & Zeisel, 1983]). It seems that the dominant group will set the tone, and unless concerted, specific efforts are made to involve the exceptions, they will not participate.

Another contextual variable of importance for resident participation is the level of community organization in existence prior to the start of any government-initiated program.

The neighborhoods in our study of Project Renewal ranged from a population size of 2,100 to 10,260. There was no direct relationship between population size and the percentage of residents participating in the project. Division of the neighborhood into subareas with their own resident committees seemed to facilitate a higher level of participation. However, the creation of these subdivisions was not a simple function of size but of other factors as well.

An average of 75% of the buildings were multifamily buildings (as is typical of Israel as a whole), mainly three- to four-story buildings with 18 to 32 apartments. Such buildings are commonly owner-occupied in a condominium-type arrangement, where management is on a voluntary basis by a committee of residents. The percentage of owner-occupied dwellings ranged from 43% to 94%. (In Israel as a whole the figure is 70%.)

The relevant population characteristics tended to be length of residence in Israel, so that groups of relatively recent immigrants were not well-integrated in the participation process.

Despite differences in numbers, there was a core of active local residents and particular patterns of independent initiative and local organization in every neighborhood. The project organizers chose, on the whole, to view these active residents as the leadership core in the project. We will see later that this had far-reaching implications.

The Subject Matter of the Rehabilitation Program

Most of the Western European neighborhood rehabilitation programs in which participation has occurred have been limited to issues or topics with physical planning implications. They have been programs of neighborhood improvement dealing with basic infrastructure development, such as roads, sewage, water and so forth, for example, Madrid (Perlman, 1983), also Lusaka (Rakodi, 1983); and/or improvements to the public areas and green spaces of the neighborhood, for example, Stockholm (Elliott, n.d.); and/or building improvements and renovations, as in Rotterdam (Godschalk & Zeisel, 1983) or Cambridge, England (Elliott, n.d.).

There does seem to be a tendency in Holland to extend the issues to be treated in such programs. For example, the program in Schilderswijk, The Hague, included developing a structure plan dealing with housing, green spaces, the traffic system, recreational facilities, schools, and economic and business location decisions (Draisen, 1983). However, an interim report of a study of Economic Commission for Europe (ECE) countries stated that it was difficult to find cases in which the approach to social and economic revitalization was conducted with a substantial amount of resident participation (Basel, Grieff, & Muhlich, 1978).

The policy orientation in the United States has been more comprehensive, with relatively more attention given to social and economic issues in concert with housing and physical issues. There have, nevertheless, been variations in emphasis in different programs. Thus, the Community Action Program focused on social and economic issues, schools, social services, job opportunities, and on the empowerment of the poor as part of the War on Poverty (Kasperson, 1977). The Model Cities program was a more comprehensive and coordinated effort in that it added the domain of physical rebuilding to make it a "total" approach (Frieden & Kaplan, 1975). The later Community Development Block Grant Program encompassed all of these areas in principle; but in practice, the housing aspect was central to the program, with economic development and social services relatively less emphasized (Armistead, Fainstein, & Fainstein, 1980).

The general experience seems to indicate that residents are more interested in participating when the matters discussed are immediate ones and directly affect them. In most neighborhood programs, these are indeed the kinds of issues raised. Godschalk and Zeisel (1983) reported that, in general, Dutch citizens were more interested in "doorstep issues" (like the Woonerf) than in general policy questions. Appleyard (1983) also stated that citizens were more directly involved at the street committee level than at the neighborhood or city level. Even at the level of apartment design, the more detailed and less abstract the decision, the more participation there was (Perlman, 1983).

Israel's Project Renewal was greatly influenced in its formative stages by the Model Cities Program. It was established as a comprehensive program and dealt with housing renovation and expansion, physical improvement of the neighborhood infrastructure and open spaces, educational enrichment programs, the improvement of school facilities, health, vocational training, and social service programs, and community organization. Employment issues have only recently become a focus of activity.

On the whole, Project Renewal focused on issues that were tangible and with short-range implications. No attempts were made to formulate general types of plans. Thus there were no reactions similar to those of some residents in Schilderswijk, Holland, who were opposed to the concern with "useless long-term planning" (Draisen, 1983).

THE GOALS OF INVOLVEMENT AND PARTICIPATION IN NEIGHBORHOOD REHABILITATION

THE GOALS OF CITIZEN INVOLVEMENT AND PARTICIPATION

Six higher order goals may be identified, each of which can be broken down into lower order goals and objectives. Table 1 presents

TABLE 1. THE GOALS OF CITIZEN INVOLVEMENT AND PARTICIPATION

The Planner/Decision Maker	Participants
Goal 1—to further democratic values	
To permit those affected to make the decision	To make their own decisions
To redistribute power	To redistribute power
To make decision makers more accountable	To make decision makers more accountable
Goal 2—to achieve planning that is attuned to the preferences of different groups	
To learn about the preferences of the various groups	
To attempt to fit planning to the preferences of the various groups	To obtain plans that are more attuned to their own and their community's preferences
To prevent mistakes that could arise by not taking needs into account	To prevent negative impacts of public policies on them and their community
Goal 3—to educate the public	
To educate the public regarding the planning process	To learn about the planning process
To educate the public regarding the need to compromise and consider constraints	
Goal 4—to bring about social or personal change	
To enable the emergence of local leadership	To have the opportunity to become a local leader
To increase community involvement	To become more active
To reduce feelings of anonymity and alienation	To feel less alienated
To strengthen the feeling of self-reliance, competence, and control	To strengthen the feeling of self-reliance, competence, and control
	To gain recognition from others
	To meet people, socialize
	To obtain political power
Goal 5—to build support and legitimacy for planning	
To gain support for the plan	
To prevent opposition during implementation	
To share responsibility for mistakes	
To enable the planner to control the situation through cooperation with the public	
Goal 6—to bring about political change	
To weaken the legitimacy of public planning	
To show that the authorities cannot be trusted	
	To get the establishment and its programs entirely out

these six goals with a few selected examples of lower order goals. An important distinction emphasized in Table 1 is that between the goals of the official decision makers (why they wish to involve residents) and the goals of those citizens who participate in the process. These two sets of goals may not be similar or compatible in a given situation. Some goals appear in both columns of the table, whereas others are the province of only one group. For example, the planner may wish to educate the public on the need to compromise; participants are not likely to share this goal at all.

The literature in different fields tends to stress different goals. Political scientists are more likely to stress Goal 1—to further democratic values and to view involvement as an end in itself. However, there are political philosophers who see involvement as a means to educating the individual citizen and enabling the realization of his or her potential human development (Cole, 1974). Friedgut (1979) reports that Soviet social scientists look to involving institutions as a major source of socialization-participation as increasing people's control over each other. Public administrators speak primarily in terms of Goal 5—building support for government or for planning and increasing efficiency. Political activists emphasize involvement as a means to raising political consciousness and thus begin a process of political change (Goal 6). Community workers are concerned with Goal 4, involvement as a means toward bringing about change in the community and among its members. Within the fields of architecture, planning, and environment–behavior studies, the main focus is upon Goal 2—involvement as a means to improving the optimization of the environment and increasing the congruence between the environment and the individual's needs and values (Wandersman, 1978).

Clearly, the strategy of involvement that fits the achievement of one goal may not serve to attain another one.

THE INVOLVEMENT GOALS IN NEIGHBORHOOD PROGRAMS

Although the goals of involvement and participation are much discussed in the theoretical or ideological literature, they are relatively neglected in the literature that describes or analyzes particular cases. This may reflect awareness of the complexity of the topic and a deliberate decision to adopt a goal-free stance. It is our contention, however, that the goals play too critical a role in the process to allow them to be ignored.

Any particular involvement process includes many actors, each of whom may, by virtue of his or her role in the process or his or her personal attitudes and values, hold different views as to the goals of resident involvement. At the initial level, there may, or may not, be the declared goals of the overall authority for the official rehabilitation program.

The declared goals in the various U.S. programs ranged from Goal 1 (to further democratic values) and 4 (to bring about social and personal change) and perhaps Goal 6 (to bring about political change) in the Community Action Program (Frieden & Kaplan, 1975; Kasperson & Breitbart, 1974); to Goals 1 and 2 (to achieve planning attuned to the preferences of different groups) in the Model Cities Program (Frieden & Kaplan, 1975) to Goals 1, 2, and 5 (to build support and legitimacy for planning) in the CDBG program (Johnson & Associates, 1978).

In the Lusaka project, the main goal for involving residents was Goal 5, "to facilitate speedy implementation, lower costs and improve the collection of services charges and loan repayments" (Rakodi, 1983, p. 22). Additional objectives were Goals 2 and 4. The only goal reported in the Transkei case was Goal 2—to allow the residents to have input into the particular decision-making process (Finlayson, 1978).

Goals at this level are often expressed vaguely, and Alterman (1982) argues that this may be a purposeful act that is an indication of the political nature of participation. However, whether overtly expressed or not, any government-mandated program can be considered to contain Goal 5 as an aspect of the involvement process.

At any level, but perhaps particularly at this one, the goals may be unrealistic ones and thus may inevitably result in a failure to achieve them and in an unreasonably negative evaluation of this aspect of the program.

The second level of goals are those held and promulgated by the individuals who operate or function within the program. Their goals for resident involvement may not necessarily be the same as the official goals. For example, the World Bank's goals in the Lusaka project focused on speedy implementation, whereas the professional planners were concerned with involvement as a means of "producing policies appropriate to the needs of the local population, and acceptable to various, possibly conflicting local interests thus reducing opposition to their implementation" (Goals 2 and 5) (Rakodi, 1983, pp. 20–21). Fainstein & Fainstein (1974) report that studies of Community Action programs showed that only 3% to 5% of those interviewed considered organizing the poor so as to increase their political power as their agencies' best developed goal.

The third level of goals are those of the residents themselves, their motivation for participating in the process. As expressed in our conceptual framework, their goals may parallel those of the involvers, may conflict with them, or may be unique to the residents.

Kasperson (1977) summed up some general lessons from the experience in the United States and said that policymakers, planners, and bureaucrats tended to see involvement primarily as a means for achieving other ends (and the ones he described are in the realm of Goal 5). Citizens, on the other hand, tended to view participation as an end in itself.

Cole (1974) reported on two studies (his own and that of Gilbert) that directly ascertained the motives and goal orientation of the participants. Gilbert found that the participants in Pittsburgh's Community Action Agency boards were motivated by what we would term Goals 2 and 3 (education). Cole's sample from 26 programs across the United States predominantly (64%) claimed "concern with general neighborhood improvement" (Goal 2). Only 11% mentioned a desire for political influence (Goal 1 or 4) as their first motive, but another 50% mentioned it as a second or third motive. West Oakland residents (May, 1973) were reported to have wanted control, in order to attain programs that met their needs (Goal 2).

The significance of the distinction between involver and participant goals lies in the obvious, but often forgotten, fact that residents have the choice as to whether or not they will participate. If they do not perceive that they can satisfy *their* goals, they will not participate.

The officially expressed goals of Project Renewal on the governmental level were basically Goals 1, 2, and 4 (Shimshoni, 1983). In our study, we focused on the second level of goals—those held by the officials and professionals directly involved in the neighborhoods.

According to the assessments of the field investigators, the various authorities working in the neighborhoods placed most emphasis on Goals 1, 2, and 3. On the other hand, the representatives of the authorities themselves ($N = 71$) stated when interviewed that their goals for involvement were Goals 1, 2, and 4. Goal 5 was mentioned in five neighborhoods, and Goal 6 was not mentioned at all. The goal of social and personal change was the most frequently mentioned.

The active residents ($N = 90$), when asked how they perceived the goals of the authorities, mentioned Goals 1, 2, and 4. Goal 5 was mentioned in three neighborhoods, although in a negative-cynical context, as though this was the ulterior motive behind the authorities' ideology of involvement.

The difference between the findings obtained from the various sources may reflect a difference between theory and practice. On the level of declared objectives (expressed in the answers to the interviewer's questions), there was an acceptance of the importance of involvement as a means of attaining long-range social and educational change, whereas on the practical level (based on the investigators' assessments of the authorities' actions), the emphasis was on the attainment of legitimacy and the prevention of resident interference with the execution of plans that the authorities found desirable. From the active residents' viewpoint, the goal of involvement was not to change the residents but rather to influence the project's plans by expressing their wishes and participating in the determination of the project's goals. To sum up, an examination of the various attitudes showed that the principle of resident involvement was accepted by all parties as a general and binding norm, at least in theory. This is not an unimportant finding given the Israeli context described previously, where the principle was until then virtually unknown.

THE PUBLIC PARTICIPATING IN NEIGHBORHOOD REHABILITATION

THE DEFINITION OF THE "PUBLIC" PARTICIPATING

The public who participates in the decision-making process must be defined and described. One aspect that is relatively well researched is the participants' description in terms of demographic, socioeconomic, and sometimes, attitudinal and behavioral characteristics.

In addition, however, one can distinguish between situations in terms of the number participating and in terms of the manner in which they come to participate, whether by election, appointment, selection, or by choice.[3]

Any program for involving residents requires the cooperation and favorable response of the residents to the initiative of the involvers. Who, in fact, participates is the result of an interaction between the actions of the involvers (how and for whom they encourage or discourage participation and in what context and subject domain) and the choice of the residents.

This section examines first the manner in which the participation of the residents came about and the nature of their organizations. We then turn to the question of who participates and their representativeness.

[3]See Alterman (1982) for the specific categories suggested.

How Participation Came About and the Nature of Resident
Organization

A summary comparison of the situation in Project Renewal with that in other neighborhood rehabilitation programs reveals the following similarities and differences:

1. Many of the resident participants in such programs were active previously in other forums (Cole, 1974; May, 1973). In virtually all neighborhoods, as in the ones we studied, there were existing leaders or activists who then became central in the involvement process.

2. Varied approaches existed as to the specificity with which the criteria of representation were defined. For example, the guidelines for the U.S. Community Action Program never determined exactly who was to participate—poor, nonwhite, neighborhood residents, beneficiaries, or the citizenry at large—or how the representatives were to be selected (Kasperson & Breitbart, 1974). Project Renewal stipulated that the representatives had to be residents who were not officials. However, no uniform system for choosing the representatives was determined.

The mixed picture that then resulted, wherein representatives in some instances were elected by the residents, in some self-selected, and in some appointed by mayors, was found by Cole (1974), by Johnson and Associates (1978), and in our study. In most cases, even those appointed were "ordinary" residents. However, the Road Planning Group in Lusaka consisted of residents who were councillors, officials, or representatives of organizations (Rakodi, 1983).

3. Elections held to choose the residents' representatives were not always successful, as levels of participation were low. In the Community Action Program, percentages ranged from 1% to 6% (Kasperson & Breitbart, 1974). The range in the Model Cities Program—from 10% to 25% (coincidentally the same as in Project Renewal) was more encouraging (Frieden & Kaplan, 1975).

4. Division of the neighborhood into subareas, as existed in some Project Renewal neighborhoods, was also found helpful in Schilderswijk (Godschalk & Zeisel, 1983) and in Birmingham (Paris, 1975).

5. Variability in the degree of openness of the process to residents other than the elected members of the boards existed in the CDBG program (Johnson & Associates, 1978). In Project Renewal, the pattern of involvement of the resident representatives in the steering committees and the subcommittees required by the regulations was a minimal demand that neither necessitated nor prevented a wider involvement of residents. In practice, the minimum pattern became the maximum pattern in most places, and other residents had almost no opportunity to

take part in the decision-making process on the public level. There were, however, neighborhoods that were more open to other residents, particularly within the framework of the subcommittees. Working groups (similar to these subcommittees) were active and open to anyone who wanted to attend in Schilderswijk (Draisen, 1983) and in Milwaukee (Harris, 1984).

6. The critical role played by an individual leader was mentioned in Orcasitas (Perlman, 1983) and in Schilderswijk (Draisen 1983) and was evident in most of our study neighborhoods.

7. The tendency for leaders to cling to power once they attained it was mentioned with regard to the Community Action Program (Kasperson & Breitbart, 1974) and existed in a number of Project Renewal neighborhoods.

8. A neighborhood council was the organizational focus of the residents in Rotterdam (Godschalk & Zeisel, 1983), in Birmingham (Paris, 1975), in some Model Cities programs (Frieden & Kaplan, 1975), in some CDBG programs (Armistead et al., 1980), and in the Project Renewal neighborhoods.

Another format adopted in other instances was that of a central group that consisted of representatives of all or most of the resident groups in the neighborhood. Harris (1984) reported that this kind of coalition presented difficulties because of the delays occasioned by the need for each member organization to discuss the issues before a council decision. On the other hand, the West Oakland Planning Committee was reported to function well (May, 1973).

9. Support to resident groups that existed before the initiation of the rehabilitation program occurred in Rotterdam (Godschalk & Zeisel, 1983). In the CDBG program, there were places where existing groups were incorporated into the program and others where the program helped to develop new neighborhood organizations (Johnson & Associates, 1978). Such was also the case in Project Renewal. However, there was a marked difference between those neighborhoods in which a neighborhood council was active before the start of the project and those neighborhoods in which new councils were created. The former councils generally did not try to expand the circle of participants or to involve other residents in responsible positions. These councils were essentially assimilated into the project's institutional framework. They had no independent budgetary support and hardly ever met, except to prepare for meetings of the steering committee.

The new councils, on the other hand, demonstrated more openness to attempts to enlist additional active residents and even displayed some initiative of their own in this direction. The council members in these neighborhoods acted more independently. They met regularly and dealt with a wider range of topics instead of merely preparing for the next meeting of the steering committee.

10. In many cases, the formation of neighborhood groups was aided and encouraged by professionals working in the program. There were also cases of self-initiation, groups started by residents that then developed into full-fledged and recognized organizations (e.g., Orcasitas [Perlman, 1983]; Copenhagen [Perlman & Spiegel, 1983]; Schilderswijk [Draisen, 1983]). The former was the pattern most typical in Project Renewal.

11. The problem of the lack of regular channels of communication between the resident's organization and the residents as a whole that existed in Project Renewal was also reported in Schilderswijk (Godschalk & Zeisel, 1983) and in the Model Cities Program (Kasperson & Breitbart, 1974).

WHO PARTICIPATES IN NEIGHBORHOOD REHABILITATION PROGRAMS

Virtually all descriptions of participants relate to traditional demographic variables, usually some or all of the following: age, sex, education, income, length of residence, homeownership tenure, marital status, race, or ethnic origin (where relevant). Unfortunately, it is impossible to summarize these data because in the various cases mention is usually made of only a few of these variables.

Most of the residents who participated in the Project Renewal decision-making process were male. Women were more likely to participate as volunteers in programs or as paraprofessionals. By contrast, some studies in the United States reported women to be more predominant in leadership, although not always in the top positions (Fainstein & Fainstein, 1974; Wandersman, Jakubs, & Giamartino, 1981). In the Lusaka project, most of those attending the meetings to discuss the self-help projects were men, whereas most of those who did the work were women (Rakodi, 1983).

The representatives on the steering committees in our research neighborhoods were middle-aged (30–50). Only in four neighborhoods was there any representation of younger people, and nowhere were there teenagers or pensioners. Scattered instances of attempts elsewhere to involve children have been reported, for example, Transkei (Finlayson, 1978) and Planwinkel, Holland (Draisen, 1983), where some attempts were also made to involve the elderly.

On the whole, the Project Renewal resident representatives were from the same countries of origin as the majority of neighborhood residents. However, there were neighborhoods in which there was minimal or no representation of other ethnic groups. A similar, though more extreme phenomenon occurred in Oude Westen, Rotterdam, where participants were all "Dutch" residents despite the fact that half the population consisted of people who had moved to Holland from other countries (Godschalk & Zeisel, 1983). Draisen (1983) reported that in Planwinkel special efforts were made to involve foreigners, but few came to meetings, and none were regular members. This variable may be related to another characteristic, that of length of residence in the neighborhood. Participants in Project Renewal were, on the whole, long-term residents, as were those active in the block organizations studied by Wandersman et al. (1981).

In a study of the CDBG Program, participants were found more likely to be homeowners, rather than renters (Armistead et al., 1980). We did not find such a difference in Project Renewal, probably because the program was a more comprehensive one.

Socioeconomic status has been the most common characteristic considered of interest. Most studies have found, as did we, that the active participants were of a higher socioeconomic status relative to the neighborhood population. Some reported greater differences (Cole, 1974; Kweit & Kweit, 1981) and others only marginal ones (Fainstein & Fainstein, 1974). This does not mean that there were no relatively low-income individuals participating (Armistead et al., 1980; May, 1973). Nevertheless, all who mention this variable report, as do we, that there was virtually no participation by the very poor or the unemployed (Fainstein & Fainstein, 1974; Kasperson & Breitbart, 1974).

Although the study is not strictly within the purview of this chapter, it should be noted that an attempt has been made to broaden the approach to the description of participants. Florin and Wandersman (1984) have proposed a cognitive social-learning approach that adds cognitive variables to the traditional demographic and personality variables used. They found the cognitive variables able to account for more of the variance in the dependent variable (membership or nonmembership in a block organization) than the traditional variables.

THE REPRESENTATIVENESS OF THE ACTIVE RESIDENTS

Within the context of neighborhood rehabilitation programs, the question of who participates has been of interest mainly in terms of the degree to which these participants (who are usually a relatively small group) may be considered to represent the population of the neighborhood.

Although this is indeed a critical question, it should be noted that it is not necessarily relevant for the goals of involvement that relate to education or personal change. In such cases it does not matter who participates; the more important question may be how many people participate. At first glance, it may seem that the question is less important at the individual-dwelling level. However, unless all family members participate in the design process, it is also relevant in that situation. The goals of involvement, however, relate on the whole to more communitywide implications, and thus the issue of representativeness becomes critical.

Representation is not a simple concept, despite the fact that it is often examined solely in terms of the indicator of demographic characteristics. Pitkin (1967) distinguished between four aspects of representation:

1. Formal representation—one is representative if one has been elected or selected by an elected official and if mechanisms for accountability exist.
2. Descriptive representation—the representatives are like their constituency in terms of demographic, attitudinal, or behavioral characteristics.
3. Symbolic representation—the representative is believed in by his or her constituency.
4. Substantive representation—representatives act for their constituency by either doing what the latter want or what is in their interest.

One can see that, in any given situation, any combination of these aspects may exist. The question of which aspects are more important within the context of neighborhood rehabilitation is an open one. It could be linked to the goals of involvement. For example, formal representation might be considered sufficient for Goal 5; substantive representation would be necessary for Goal 2.

From the aspect of *formal representation,* only situations in which the participants were self-selected would not meet the criterion, and this was the case at least part of the time for at least some of the representatives in six Project Renewal neighborhoods. The central administrative arm of the project looked upon elections as the best form of legitimation. However, because local election processes and the number of voters were not without limitations, it is not clear that elections *per se* can always be considered to meet this criterion. Furthermore, in none of the neighborhoods were there well-defined mechanisms of accountability.

This kind of variable picture seems to have also characterized the

U.S. programs (Cole, 1974; Johnson & Associates, 1978). Many Western European groups, on the other hand, were begun by self-selected individuals and only later became more formalized by elections (e.g., Perlman, 1983).

Descriptive representation in Project Renewal was objectively low. Although the active residents were similar to the nonactive residents in ethnic origin, type of housing, housing tenure, and length of residence, they were significantly different in sex, age, and socioeconomic status.[4] In the subcommittees, there was at least some representation of women, of additional age groups, and of people from different countries of origin and other socioeconomic strata.

Fainstein and Fainstein (1974) argued that "creaming" in the Community Action Program was not extreme. Nevertheless, most writers argued that in the U.S. programs, the representatives were, on the whole, on a relatively higher socioeconomic level (Cole, 1974; Kasperson & Breitbart, 1974). In Holland, there were many instances of under-representation of minority groups (Godschalk & Zeisel, 1983).

The fact that studies reported by Kweit and Kweit (1981) have found active residents to be more highly motivated is not surprising, nor should it be taken to question their representativeness. More critical is Cole's (1974) finding that

> as demographic discrepancy increases, internal conflict tends to increase, the program's effect on the residents' confidence decreases and the proportion of neighborhood residents aware of the program decreases. (p. 97)

Another approach to descriptive representation compares the attitudes and behavior patterns of the residents. In Project Renewal, a higher degree of involvement and social activity in the neighborhood was found among the participants. No difference was found between participants and nonparticipants in the majority of attitudes toward the neighborhood. On the other hand, there was a difference between the two groups in their evaluation of the project. The participants were more likely to believe that there had been an improvement in the situation and that the Project had contributed to the neighborhood, but they were less satisfied with the level of services that had been achieved. We do not know whether their expectations were higher to begin with and that is what motivated them to participate, or if their level of expectation rose as a result of their activities, or if both are true. Regardless, this difference can be seen as a positive one, insofar as it was likely to encourage the active residents to strive toward greater achievements.

---

[4]Based upon the household survey with 982 nonactive residents and 153 active residents.

Studies by Ahlbrandt and Cunningham (1979) and by Wandersman *et al.*, (1981) that included variables of this kind do not relate to neighborhood programs of the kind delimited as our concern, but they found similar, closer neighboring patterns among participants in community organizations. However, the causal sequence may be one in which this social interaction is a result of participation, and not vice versa (Unger & Wandersman, 1983). Ahlbrandt and Cunningham (1979) also found active members to be more dissatisfied with community services. Wandersman *et al.* (1981) found no differences in satisfaction with the block but did find a curvilinear relationship between perception of block problems and participation.

The aspect of descriptive representation is strongly linked to that of substantive representation. The explicit or implicit assumption behind it is that people with similar characteristics have interests in common and that, therefore, an individual whose characteristics are similar to those of a group can represent and further the interests of the group. This may be true on a very basic level, but it is both a simplistic approach to the complexity of groups that any individual belongs to and ignores the question of the degree of that individual's identification with the group's interests.

The aspects of *substantive* and *symbolic representation* are much more difficult to examine directly, unless they are built into the research framework. Because this was not the case in our research, we will attempt to address these issues through the limited and indirect data available on resident attitudes.

One indication of possible substantive representation was the similarity found between the participants and nonparticipants in their identification of the priorities that Project Renewal should adopt in their neighborhood.

Another indirect indication was the subjective assessment of the degree of representativeness. Fifty-three percent of the nonparticipants felt that the representatives did not represent them at all. Where there were coalitions of groups within the neighborhood, the resident group was able to present itself as speaking for a wide range of groups (Harris, 1984; May, 1973).

A survey conducted among Schilderswijk residents showed that the leaders did, for the most part, accurately represent the views of their members (Draisen, 1983). However, the fluidity of the situation was such that at a later point the same resident organization was reported to have lost its unanimous support (Godschalk & Zeisel, 1983). Kweit and Kweit (1981) report on studies of CDBG programs where citizens were not satisfied with their representatives. These reports, however, may be construed as relating to symbolic representation; they are only indirect measures of substantive representation.

In all of the programs surveyed, there seems to have been relatively little serious attempt to reach out to other groups; there was a tendency to work with those already motivated or those easier to reach. On the one hand, it must be recognized that participation in democratic countries is a right, not a duty. This means that people have the right to choose not to participate. On the other hand, no program has yet reached the point where one could argue that every attempt has been made to offer the opportunity to all in a manner geared toward them.

RESOURCES INVESTED IN RESIDENT INVOLVEMENT AND PARTICIPATION IN NEIGHBORHOOD REHABILITATION

Involving residents in a planning process is not without its costs. The resources invested by the authorities towards this end can be divided into three categories: (a) time spent by officials or staff in contact with residents or in matters related to their involvement; (b) manpower—persons hired specifically for planning or implementing resident involvement or existing personnel whose role was defined mainly in these terms (usually community workers but in some instances also consultants hired to develop and/or implement resident involvement); and (c) budgets allocated for resident involvement. These can be subdivided into three categories: (1) payment for salaries of community workers or consultants; (2) allocations for activities of neighborhood councils both in the organizational and the programmatic fields; and (3) training and technical assistance funds.

Concurrently, of course, the residents themselves invest resources in the participation process. Although often overlooked and underrated, these in-kind contributions maintain the neighborhood organization and can supplement and coproduce services and functions performed by the public sector (Haskell, 1980). These resources may be divided into three parallel categories: (a) time spent in committee meetings of various types, in volunteering activities, and in employment on a salaried basis; (b) self-help; physical labor—in cleaning and maintaining multi family buildings, in renovating dwellings, in building community facilities or in preparing the neighborhood infrastructure; and (c) money—by partial funding of programs.

Space limitations do not allow the presentation of details as to the nature of these resources invested in various rehabilitation programs.

BALANCE OF POWER BETWEEN RESIDENTS AND AUTHORITIES IN NEIGHBORHOOD REHABILITATION

The question of the power attained by the residents is viewed by many as the very essence of the principle of participation. It is clearly a critical aspect, but its saliency is not unrelated to the goals of involvement and may be more or less central, depending upon which goal is paramount.

Table 2 presents the scale that we have proposed for this dimension. The scale was influenced greatly by the analyses of Arnstein (1969) and Fagence (1977). This section examines the nature of the balance of power occurring in rehabilitation programs and the opportunities open to the residents for exerting influence on the process and on the decisions taken.

THE SOURCES OF POWER OF THOSE TAKING PART IN THE PROCESS

The influence of the representatives of the authorities stemmed first and foremost from their control over budgets, manpower, information, and implementation systems. Also, the bottom line was that they had the final authority to authorize budgets and put plans into action.

This was true to a large extent in most government-mandated involvement programs. However, the particular aspect emphasized varied. For example, control over the shaping and selecting of information was stressed as a source of power for bureaucrats and authorities (Armistead et al., 1980; May, 1973) as was the power of professional knowledge (Armistead et al., 1980; Mamalis, 1983). Control over funds was mentioned particularly by Frieden and Kaplan (1975) in terms of the Model Cities Program. In that program, as well as in the CDBG program, the specifications determined by the federal government were critical in defining the authority of the local government (Johnson & Associates, 1978). However, in Project Renewal, over and above their initial power, the authorities enjoyed another source of influence, granted by the residents themselves, by the tendency of the residents to accept their opinions.

On the other side, the legitimation given to the residents by the authorities has played an important role in all of the government-mandated programs around the world and has been the basic source of their power. Clearly, it has had a stronger effect where the rights of the residents were stated unambiguously. For example, landlords in Sweden are required by law to obtain the tenants' consent to renovations before they can obtain a planning permit (Nilsson, 1985). In the United

TABLE 2. BALANCE OF POWER OF INVOLVERS/PARTICIPANTS

	Project Renewal		
	Assessment of field investigators	Assessment of authorities	Programs in other countries
1. Involver control—one-way communication of information from involver to participant or from participant to involver			Community Action Program (CAP) (Arnstein, 1969), CDBG (Armistead, Fainstein, & Fainstein, 1980), Mamalis (1983)
2. Involver control—two-way communication of information		Netivot	Transkei (Finlayson, 1978)
3. Token involvement of residents in decision making	Netivot		Lusaka (Rakodi, 1983), Cole (1974)
4. Obligation to consult residents			CDBG (Armistead et al., 1980), Copenhagen (Perlman & Spiegel, 1983), Covent Garden (Appleyard, 1983), Docklands (Spiegel & Perlman, 1983), Nilsson (1985)
5. Right to voice opposition given to residents		Neve Israel	
6. Cooptation of residents	Neve Eliezer, Neve Israel		
7. Vesting of some decision-making authority in residents	Ir Ganim, Canaan, Givat Olga	Ir Ganim	Detroit (Bachelor & Jones, 1981); Mamalis (1983)
8. Partnership in which involvers have veto	Or Akiva		
9. Full partnership	East Akko, Hatikva	East Akko, Hatikva, Canaan, Givat Olga, Neve Eliezer,	Schilderswijk (Draisen, 1983)

(*continued*)

TABLE 2 (*Continued*)

	Project Renewal		
	Assessment of field investigators	Assessment of authorities	Programs in other countries
10. Partnership in which participants have veto		Or Akiva, Givat-Harakafot	Orcasitas (Perlman, 1983), Model Cities (Frieden & Kaplan, 1975), Oakland (May, 1973), Cole (1974), Nilsson (1985)
11. Planner chooses group to represent			
12. Advocacy planning			
13. Resident control without planner	Givat-Harakafot		CAP (Arnstein, 1969), Dayton (Frieden & Kaplan, 1975)

States, there were many more conflicts over the power of the residents in the Community Action Program than in the Model Cities or CDBG programs. The definition of the scope of resident authority was both clearer and more delimited in the latter programs (Wandersman, 1984). Even then, however, there were no specific requirements as to the proportion of residents on boards, and the situation in practice varied (Cole, 1974). In Project Renewal, the stipulation was that residents were to comprise 50% of the local steering committee.

As in Project Renewal, the backing of the central government was often useful in countering the resistance of local authorities to the granting of authority to the residents (James, 1973), and its absence weakened their position (Perlman, 1983). The experience in Holland indicated that even with central government support, there were still cases where resident control was only wrested after a process of conflict and protest (Draisen, 1983).

The Dutch institution of coproduction contracts is unique. It is a mechanism to make more visible the responsibilities each group (residents and authorities) expects the other to meet (Godschalk & Zeisel,

1983). These contracts thus spell out the authority of the residents, but their unique significance lies in the fact that they are jointly formulated, rather than one-sidedly stipulated.

The recognition on the part of the authorities of their obligation to involve the residents in decisions relating to the neighborhood was therefore the residents' basic source of power in all the Project Renewal neighborhoods (as well as in most rehabilitation programs). In some of the neighborhoods there were also additional sources of power: (a) the potential electoral power of the active residents; (b) the backing—either proven or assumed—that the active residents received from the neighborhood residents; and (c) the fear that the public would make a particular plan or program unworkable because they were not involved in the decision to accept it.

Points b and c were probably factors in many instances in other contexts: They were specifically mentioned by Perlman (1983) and by Draisen (1983).

Then there was the fact of (d) the active residents' ability to maneuver between the various authorities and to enlist support from an element such as the Twinned Community, or higher political levels. This could be seen as reflecting a certain degree of weakness because the residents were shown to need the support of a powerful outside element. However, this also expressed a correct understanding of the balance of power between the various authorities and the refusal of the active residents to accept dictates from above without putting up a fight.

In the Model Cities program, there were some instances termed *reverse co-optation* where agency experts were radicalized and began to act as neighborhood advocates, thus strengthening the power of the residents (Kasperson & Breibait, 1974).

Finally, there was (e) the personal influence of the chairman.

On the other hand, internal conflicts sometimes weakened the power of the residents (see May, 1973; Perlman & Spiegel, 1983; and also in Project Renewal).

PATTERNS OF EXERTION OF INFLUENCE

Most of the rehabilitation programs included in this survey can be categorized as essentially representing a pattern of negotiation, discussion, and consultation between the residents and the authorities. This was true in the Model Cities and CDBG programs (Armistead *et al.*, 1980; Cole, 1974; Johnson & Associates, 1978), in Schilderswijk (Draisen, 1983), and in Lusaka (Rakodi, 1983).

This was also the pattern in Project Renewal. The tactics used by the authorities to obtain the cooperation of the residents and to increase their own influence included influencing the composition of the resident representation; coalitions between the residents and one particular authority; co-optation of one or more of the resident representatives; and bringing in experts on a specific subject.

If these tactics failed, the authorities could always fall back on their main trump card—refusal to allocate budgets or the threat of such refusal. Also, the authorities' control over the implementation process sometimes made it possible for them to make changes in a plan that had been passed by the committees, thereby creating facts to be approved *ex post facto*.

The residents in turn can use various tactics to increase their influence. Lobbying of local political figures for support against staff and bureaucrats was the tactic of choice in many CDBG programs (Armistead *et al.*, 1980). Appeals to officials at higher levels of government were reported in instances in the United States (Harris, 1984; May, 1973) and in Madrid (Perlman, 1983).

Confrontational tactics were much more common in Western European countries. Demonstrations were organized and use of the media made in Schilderswijk (Draisen, 1983), Copenhagen (Perlman & Spiegel, 1983), Covent Garden (Appleyard, 1983), and the Docklands (Spiegel & Perlman, 1983). More disruptive tactics were also adopted in Copenhagen and in Schilderswijk.

The residents in Project Renewal entered into coalitions with representatives of various authorities, developed mutual co-optation relationships, made occasional use of demonstrations, turned to the national media to enlist public support or to embarrass the authorities, and appealed to national political figures for support. However, the confrontational tactics were only employed in a handful of cases.

Citizen action groups were prevalent and active in the United States and in Western Europe, where in some instances they were the only or dominant resident force in the neighborhood. These groups were often radical in nature, with wider goals than the authorities were interested in, and for this reason came afoul of them. This was true in the U.S. Community Action Program (Wandersman, 1984), in Copenhagen (Perlman & Spiegel, 1983) in the Docklands and Coventry (Spiegel & Perlman, 1983), and in Madrid (Perlman, 1983). Many groups began as grass-roots, ad hoc groups protesting a particular proposed plan—a road through the neighborhood, renewal plans, and so forth, and then continued to act as a neighborhood organization. These groups were more likely than other neighborhood groups to prepare alternative plans of their own and to operate services on their own (Perlman & Spiegel,

1983; Spiegel & Perlman, 1983). In these instances, conflict and confrontation characterized much of the relationship between the residents and the authorities.

In Project Renewal, there was one council that adopted an anti-establishment ideology, three neighborhoods where groups opposed to the existing leadership arose, and one neighborhood where there was a grass-roots student organization for the betterment of the neighborhood's social and cultural life. Thus, in Susskind and Elliot's (1983) terms, we found instances of paternalism, conflict, and coproduction.

On the level of individual buildings, the relationship was essentially one of discussion rather than confrontation in Project Renewal and elsewhere (Mamalis, 1983; Nilsson, 1985; Perlman, 1983).

NATURE OF RESIDENT INFLUENCE

The residents' influence on the decision-making process may manifest itself on a number of planes: the definition of the neighborhoods's problems and the goals and priorities that the project should set for itself; the initiation of programs; support for a program proposed by the authorities; changes made to the programs of other elements; the rejection of programs; influence on the speed with which a program is implemented; changes in the project's administrative procedures; and changes in the staff employed by the project.

The influence of the residents on these planes may be direct and open and exerted through the use of the tactics and sources of power described previously. However, they may also have an indirect and subtle influence, in that the representatives of the authorities may refrain from the outset from bringing up subjects that are likely to arouse their opposition, or they may try to present programs in a manner that would be likely to win their support.

The latent function of resident participation in committees was noted by Zawadzki (1974) who found that even when the representatives do not use their power, the fact that they examine the budgets affects the decisions taken.

In all of the references where residents were reported to have influenced decisions on defining problems and goals, the residents insisted on rehabilitation and improvement of the neighborhood rather than demolition or redevelopment (Bachelor & Jones, 1981; Draisen, 1983; Paris, 1975; Perlman, 1983). Understandably, their priority was for the interests of the existing residents of the neighborhood. In Project Renewal, this was not an issue, and the residents' influence was on the relative emphasis given to program areas.

The initial approach of the professionals was that it was important to begin the project with visible and "concrete" actions. They felt that they could thus win the trust of residents suspicious of promises and plans not always brought to fruition. The residents in many instances pressed for new construction and physical improvements as lasting benefits that could not be cut back or eliminated in the future, as could educational programs or staff. Thus a significant degree of environmental change occurred: In the 10 neighborhoods, a total of 24 new public buildings were built, including day-care centers, community centers, and health clinics; and 55 public buildings were enlarged or renovated. On principle, no new housing was constructed; rather, dwellings were enlarged or renovated. On average, 37% of the families benefited from some improvement in their housing conditions (Alterman & Frenkel, 1985).

Initiation of programs was often the province of the authorities; in Project Renewal it was overwhelmingly so. It is interesting that the approach to planning in the instances where they were initiated by the residents was somewhat less conventional and institutionalized than that of the government ministries. The same might be said of at least two other cases of resident initiative: a low-rise housing complex in one Rotterdam neighborhood and a congregate housing project for older people in another (Godschalk & Zeisel, 1983).

Resident support for a program initiated by another element was important because it basically ensured its acceptance. The time and effort invested in the persuasion of residents was evidence of the recognition of the importance of their support.

Changes in programs introduced by residents included changes in the scope of the program, the venue of the activity or service, and the level or scope of subsidization. This kind of influence was the basic element of most involvement programs. Some examples of the nature of the changes made elsewhere as a result of resident influence are the rerouting of city traffic around the Schilderswijk neighborhood and a series of smaller parks instead of one linear one (Draisen, 1983), the number of jobs guaranteed to residents, and the number of residents to be served by the program (Frieden & Kaplan, 1975). Residents in Milwaukee rejected the proposal that a large percentage of CDBG funds be spent on administration and urban renewal. They instead won increased funds for social service programs, home repairs, and rat control (Harris, 1984). A comparison of resident and executive board recommendations found that the residents distributed the funds more widely among neighborhood organizations, accorded a high priority to community support for a project, and were more supportive of residential than commercial projects (Bachelor & Jones, 1981).

On the building or dwelling level, residents have had the most influence on detailed design aspects, such as covering materials, textures and colors (Nilsson, 1985; Perlman, 1983), and interior layouts (Godschalk & Zeisel, 1983; Mamalis, 1983; Nilsson, 1985; Wooley, 1985)—more than on such issues as site layout or building materials.

Influence on the speed of implementation of plans was exercized in Project Renewal through both the speeding up and the slowing down of the implementation. The only reference to this type of influence that we found was the report that the residents in Schilderswijk insisted that plan implementation be fitted to a time schedule rather than left ambiguous (Godschalk & Zeisel, 1983).

Project administration in terms of the nature and extent to which resident power could be expressed was in many cases the main bone of contention, and as Draisen (1983) commented, there was often more conflict on the demand for participation than on substantive issues. Residents in Orcasitas won the right to hire their own experts and to approve or disapprove the city technicians' plans (Perlman, 1983). In West Oakland, the residents gained 51% representation on the Model Cities Steering Committee and had a hand in defining the role of the city manager and choosing the director (May, 1973). The question of the number of residents who would be members of policy boards was one on which many communities in the Community Action and Model Cit ies programs fought and won (Frieden & Kaplan, 1975). It was pressure from the residents in Project Renewal that brought about the change in the guidelines with regard to the relative number of residents on the steering committee. They also influenced appointments to project positions.

SUMMARY ASSESSMENT OF THE BALANCE OF POWER BETWEEN THE RESIDENTS AND THE AUTHORITIES

The balance of power between the authorities and the participating residents can be described by means of a scale based on the extent of control of the "involver," on the one hand, and the extent of influence of the participants on the process, on the other hand.

Table 2 presents the grading of the Project Renewal neighborhoods according to our field investigators' assessments of the *highest* level of resident influence attained *at a given point in time*, while being represented *by the dominant body* in that neighborhood (the representatives on the steering committee, the neighborhood council, or the neighborhood council chairman).

The table indicates that there were great differences between the neighborhoods. The overall assessment was not high: Six neighborhoods did not exceed Grade 7—vesting of some of the authority for decisions in the residents—and some of them did not even reach this grade. Only in three neighborhoods was there full partnership or even almost total resident control over the decision-making process. The authorities when interviewed made fewer distinctions between the neighborhoods and placed most of them under Grade nine—full partnership.

In the third column of Table 2 we have attempted to place other programs on the scale according to the published descriptions. Where a reference appears at more than one level, the meaning is that within the program there was variability between places and that some fell at different points within that range. From the references we see that this variability existed at different environmental levels: in neighborhood programs (Cole, 1974), building renovations (Nilsson, 1985) as well as apartment designs (Mamalis, 1983).

Many of the neighborhoods in which citizen action groups were very active were those in which the basic relationship was Grade 4, the obligation to consult residents, but where decision-making authority was not given them (Copenhagen, Covent Garden, Docklands). The residents' response, then, was to demand particular decisions and to adopt demonstrative tactics to achieve them.

EVALUATION OF RESIDENT INVOLVEMENT AND PARTICIPATION IN NEIGHBORHOOD REHABILITATION PROGRAMS

The determination of the success or failure of resident involvement in any given program is a complex task, as complex as the process of resident involvement. Evaluations have often consisted of sweeping, generalized statements negating the experience rather than specifications of what was achieved and what was not. Part of the difficulty in evaluating resident involvement may be a function of conflicting and inconsistent standards as well as expectations that are so value-laden that they are not amenable to compromise (Kweit & Kweit, 1981). A further problematic aspect in evaluation arises when involvement or participation is seen as having only one purpose. For example, the statement is often made that citizen participation is not effective for achieving major social reform; with the implicit or explicit implication that it is therefore a useless exercise. Such a position ignores the fact that participation may be very effective for achieving other legitimate and worthwhile goals.

The involvement and participation experience can be evaluated in terms of each and every one of the dimensions presented previously.

We have chosen to take the goals of involvement as the framework and criteria for evaluating resident involvement in Project Renewal and in neighborhood rehabilitation programs in other countries.

THE EXPERIENCE IN OTHER COUNTRIES

This section relates to resident involvement in the other programs encompassed by our survey, based on the evaluative statements made by those authors.

Goal 1—To Further Democratic Values

Representation of the residents in some manner existed at least minimally in all government-mandated programs. One could therefore say that there was some achievement of this goal in terms of resident involvement in the decision-making process.

Problems as to the representativeness of these representatives were specifically raised with regard to the Community Action Program (Kasperson & Breitbart, 1974) and some Dutch programs (Draisen, 1983). It is probably safe to say that the question could be raised with regard to most programs. May (1973) is the only one to argue that the particular program she examined (West Oakland) succeeded in this respect to a large extent.

Nowhere was there a situation that could be termed participatory democracy. True, in some cases relatively large numbers of residents were involved, but this was usually in special projects and in demonstrative actions.

An increase in the accountability of the authorities to at least some extent was mentioned with regard to the Community Action Program (Kasperson & Breitbart, 1974) and in relation to Poland by Zawadzki (1974). An important point raised in this regard is the fact that one aspect of the problem is the willingness or unwillingness of the authorities to divulge the information they have. However, the problem may sometimes be that the information does not exist in the form required (Committee on Housing, Building and Planning, 1980). The need to supply information to residents may thus play a salutory role in prodding the authorities to collect it or to analyze what is available.

The goal of redistribution of power is considered to have been achieved to some extent in the Model Cities Program (Kasperson & Breitbart, 1974) and in a variable manner in all of the U.S. programs (Kweit & Kweit, 1981). On the other hand, Susskind and Elliott (1983) stated that paternalistic patterns such as occurred in Copenhagen have not led to a substantial redistribution of power. In the CDBG program, as in Project Renewal, delegation of authority to residents did not encompass the implementation process (Armistead *et al.*, 1980).

Goal 2—Planning Attuned to the Preferences of Different Groups

Most reports state that residents were able to have some effect on the content of the neighborhood program and on the resultant neighborhood environment (Committee on Housing, Building and Planning, 1980; Draisen, 1983; Godschalk & Zeisel, 1983; Perlman, 1983; Spiegel & Perlman, 1983; Wooley, 1985). In the American programs, the general consensus seems to be that resident participation altered and improved patterns of service delivery (Kweit & Kweit, 1981).

On the other hand, the limitations placed on the scope of this influence have been mentioned with regard to the Lusaka program (Rakodi, 1983), the CDBG program (Armistead *et al.*, 1980), and some British housing schemes (Wooley, 1985). These suggested that as a result, the "product" was not substantially altered or affected by the residents.

Goal 3—Education

This goal was achieved to at least some extent in many programs (Draisen, 1983; Kasperson & Breitbart, 1974; Spiegel & Perlman, 1983), even in places such as Transkei where it would be hard to say that other goals were achieved (Finlayson, 1978). One of the aspects stressed is that the active residents learned the "rules of the game."

As to the education acquired by the involvers, it was mentioned specifically by Perlman and Spiegel, (1983) in terms of their becoming sensitized to the residents' needs and to the issues important to them. The need for specialized knowledge as to how to involve residents was recognized by Wooley (1985) in relation to architects working on cooperative housing schemes.

Goal 4—Social and Personal Change

Social change, particularly in terms of the development of indigenous leadership and community organizations, was deemed to have been achieved in virtually all programs (Bachelor & Jones, 1981; Baroni, 1983; Committee on Housing, Building and Planning, 1980; Draisen, 1983; Godschalk & Zeisel, 1983; Kasperson, 1977; Kweit & Kweit, 1981; Perlman, 1983; Pressman, 1973; Spiegel & Perlman, 1983). It is clear that in each of these cases some personal change occurred within the leadership cadres even if it was not always mentioned in the written reports.

Kasperson and Breitbart (1974) reported that in the Community Action Program not enough was done to provide the kind of training and professional development that was needed for the long-term growth of the residents who were employed by the program.

With regard to the question of conflicts within the neighborhood, some reports found them to have been intensified (e.g., Perlman & Spiegel, 1983), whereas others found them to have been reduced (Draisen, 1983). May (1973) reported that the West Oakland Planning Committee developed a structure that encouraged the resolution of conflicts within the community rather than by appeals to outside elements.

Goal 5—Support and Legitimacy for Planning

Fundamental support for the rehabilitation program was reported to have been achieved in virtually all government-mandated programs (Armistead *et al.*, 1980; Finlayson, 1978; Kasperson & Breitbart, 1974; Kweit & Kweit, 1981; Rakodi, 1983). Cole (1974) found participants to have a higher degree of trust and confidence in the government than did nonparticipants.

As to the effect of resident involvement on the time span of the decision-making process, Nilsson (1985) reported that it has both lengthened and shortened the process in different instances. Zawadzki (1974) argued that participation does not impede the process, provided the experts cooperate with the representatives. This question seems to be a particularly value-laden one. For example, Trapero (1980) refused to accept the concept of the

> impact of participation on the planning process, for that would be tantamount to considering participation as an external event which supervenes to interrupt the autocratic process of planning without participation, diverting it from an assumed predetermined course. Participation must, on the contrary, be understood as a fundamental component of the planning process proper, without which there is no planning (just as a vehicle without an engine has the outward appearance of a motor vehicle; but is incapable of movement). (p. 4)

Goal 6—Political Change

Significant social or political change was not reported in any instance, except one. Perlman (1983) reported that in Madrid the residents succeeded in turning the city-planning process on its head, initiating decisions from the bottom up rather than from the top down.

The more limited aspect of the political advancement of individuals or neighborhoods was referred to with regard to the Community Action Program (Baroni, 1983).

Spillover effects of particular resident participation experiences to other neighborhoods or to later programs occurred as a result of the Community Action Program (Kasperson & Breitbart, 1974) and in Madrid. In Milwaukee, the experience in the CDBG program led to resident participation in the Department of City Development and to a resident chairing the advisory committee that helped choose a cable television franchise for the city (Harris, 1984). Project Renewal can be seen as a spillover effect of the Model Cities Program, though further afield, because its structure and philosophy were very much influenced by the Model Cities experience.

PROJECT RENEWAL

In evaluating Project Renewal, we adopted an approach that examined the extent to which the goals of resident involvement were achieved regardless of whether or not they were the proclaimed goals of any particular party connected to the project. It is based on the assumption that it is possible to achieve a goal without proclaimed or explicit intentions. Our assessment is an overall one, while recognizing that in practice, the generalization applies differently to the various neighborhoods and sometimes to various periods of time or specific cases.

An important achievement of Project Renewal in the area of resident involvement was the creation of a process unique in the State of Israel: public decision making in which rank-and-file residents were involved by virtue of right and in a proportion that afforded them some influence. Although the residents did not succeed in realizing this potential to a significant degree in all the research neighborhoods, the very existence of such a possibility represents a revolutionary change and a considerable achievement. It is unlikely that the situation will easily revert to the remote and high-handed manner in which decisions were previously made.

All the goals of resident involvement were promoted to some extent, even though there were neighborhoods in which some of the goals were not advanced at all. Considering the nature of these goals and the various constraints, it could not be expected that all would be fulfilled in entirety: accordingly, the partial achievement is indeed an achievement. The project's lack of success should be seen in terms of the failure to realize the potential and possibilities opened up by the project to a greater extent.

Goal 1—To Further Democratic Values

The goal of furthering democracy, in terms of the principle of representative democracy, was advanced, though not without difficulty. The residents' representatives did participate in all the project's institutions, but the nature of their representation in many of the neighborhoods was deficient, and this problem was not resolved.

Participatory democratic principles were not furthered in the public decision-making process, because for the most part, only a small number of individuals participated in it. On the semipublic level (apartment block) and the private level (apartment), the situation was closer to participatory democracy, as decisions were made by the relatively larger number of people affected and not just by their representatives.

Increased accountability of the various authorities was achieved partially and to a limited extent, but this, too, represents some change from the past situation.

In contrast, there was almost no accountability of the representatives of the residents. There was no regular contact between these representatives and the neighborhood. Such lines of communication might have considerably moderated the problems of representation, especially if they had been two-directional.

Delegation of authority from the authorities to the residents' representatives was carried out to a limited extent, enabling them to exert some degree of direct and indirect influence. This related, however, only to matters of planning and did not include implementation.

The residents were thus able to participate in the process at an entirely different level than that formerly open to any group of residents in urban areas. This is significant in and of itself, regardless of the issue of the degree to which the process was actually influenced.

Goal 2—Planning Attuned to the Preferences of Different Groups

There is no doubt that the decision-making process within the project was affected by the involvement of the residents and was different than it would have been without their participation. The most relevant question in terms of the goal of appropriate planning is whether the product of the process was also different than it would have been had residents not participated.

A common assumption among professionals is that a planning process that is professional and "rational" is more efficient and results in a better plan than one that is not. In the case of Project Renewal, it was not possible to judge whether the product of the planning process suffered from the participation of the residents. There was no controlled comparison with a similar process carried out without residents, and it was not possible to determine whether the process that was common prior to the project (which did not include residents) was actually professional, rational, and efficient. Political, economic, and personal considerations irrelevant to the matter itself and completely unrelated to the neighborhood probably played a part, even when professionals or officials were the sole decision makers.

In practice, the professionals tried to overcome the problem of lack of professionalism by attempting to persuade the residents of their professional opinions. In most cases, the residents were in fact persuaded or accepted the expertise of the professionals from the outset.

Nevertheless, the residents did indeed have an effect in various spheres of the project programs. However, the limitation of the types of decisions open to the residents and the fact that the range of power transferred to them was limited precluded the possibility that the plan would be significantly or in essence different from that that would have resulted had the residents not participated. Environmental change did take place, much of it because of the expressed or anticipated preferences of the residents.

On the neighborhood level, sufficient steps were not taken to ensure representation or input of the entire spectrum of desires of various groups of residents, and particularly of the relatively weak. On the building and dwelling levels, the process of involvement made possible planning that more directly reflected the desires of various groups and individuals. At the building level, however, there were many cases in which preference was given to professional opinions and, beyond minor details, the preferences of the residents were not always taken into account. The process of participation at the dwelling level was generally carried out with the intention of planning as much as possible in accordance with the residents' wishes.

Goal 3—Education

This goal was achieved to a great extent but unfortunately only among a small number of residents. Some of the material learned was dependent on experience over a long period and the investment of much time; thus it could not have been expected that each and every resident would do so. It was certainly possible, however, to provide more information about planning and about programs to the wider public and thus to greatly increase the number of residents who could benefit from this achievement.

The active residents became more familiar with the institutional structure and the decision-making system of the local authority and the government ministries, and with the personnel involved. They came to recognize their power as representatives of the neighborhood, to know their rights, and to stand up for them.

The manner in which residents were involved in Project Renewal indicates that there was a lack of recognition of the need for knowledge and experience in resident involvement and the need for planning the form of involvement. Evidently, it was assumed that the matter was simple and intuitively understood. This was a mistake, particularly given the minimal degree of experience in Israel with any kind of resi dent involvement and participation in decision-making processes.

Goal 4—Social and Personal Change

The degree and the scope of resident concern with what was being done in the neighborhoods increased. There was some increase in independent resident activity and in the personal responsibility taken for community activity, in terms of participation in payment for services as well as the willingness to volunteer for the sake of the neighborhood. The achievements in the area of care for jointly owned buildings were much more limited. Although a large number of building committees were organized, most of them did not last for long and did not persevere in the upkeep of their buildings.

In each neighborhood there were a few individuals who achieved personal advancement through the experience they acquired or through a more formal educational framework. The goal of personal change, thus, was only achieved among those residents who were active within the project; in particular, those who participated in the decision-making process and to a somewhat more limited extent, those (both employed and volunteers) who participated in the implementation and operation of programs.

In terms of employment of residents in Project Renewal, a very small step forward was taken, but the opportunity to provide training and guidance so as to widen possibilities of future employment for the individuals involved was not exploited in full.

In the neighborhoods where new councils were created, new leadership that was relatively open and democratic arose and was encouraged. On the other hand, in the other neighborhoods the opportunity to change the former leadership was missed. One-person leadership, which was not particularly democratic, was supported, rather than being replaced or at least expanded.

There was some intensification of the rifts within the neighborhoods. In some of the neighborhoods, these impaired the functioning of
the residents in the framework of the project.

Goal 5—Support and Legitimacy for Planning

Fundamental support for the project was attained, and support for
demands for radical social-political changes were prevented; the cooperation of the residents was achieved. The widespread pattern of cooperation and compromise between the authorities and the residents benefited the authorities.

All in all, it was to be expected that a process with many parties
would increase the chances of disagreement between them and that this
would lead to delays. Such disagreements are legitimate, and the guiding principle of resident involvement in this context is that if objections
are dealt with at the planning stage, they are less likely to crop up later.

In Project Renewal, many cases of delays that might have been
caused by disputes were prevented through prior settlement of conflicts, advance coordination, and the persuasion of the residents. Sometimes the residents were able to speed up the implementation of programs through applying pressure on the authorities who were delaying
implementation. The few serious delays in the process were caused
when both sides (the residents and the authorities) were not prepared to
make concessions, or where there were bitterly fought power struggles
within the resident group.

In the final analysis, the answer to the question of whether the
process of involvement delayed project activity is related to one's perspective: It depends whether the emphasis is on results or on the means
by which the results are achieved. Those who consider the involvement
of residents as an important aspect will consider the time and effort
invested as an integral part of project activity, and, subsequently, as
important and worthwhile. Those who do not think that resident involvement is important may view this investment as a waste.

Goal 6—Political Change

Within the neighborhoods, there were hardly any manifestations of
radical political changes. There were also no such aspirations. In a
number of neighborhoods. political advancement or increased political
power was attained, sometimes for one or two people within the neighborhood and sometimes for the neighborhood as a whole in relation to
the local authority.

In our estimation, the process of resident involvement in Project Renewal led to a very significant political change, in that, for the first time in the history of Israel, it was required that rank-and-file residents participate directly in making decisions that affect them. Representatives of authorities of varying ranks were forced to leave their offices, to go into the neighborhood, to meet with residents, to talk to them, and listen to them. For most of these officials, as for the residents, this was the first experience of its kind.

There have already been visible spillover effects. The concept of resident involvement has spread to other neighborhoods that were similar to those already included in the project. The principle has also penetrated additional frameworks, both through government and resident initiatives.

CONCLUSIONS AND DIRECTIONS FOR FUTURE RESEARCH

The preceding discussion has clarified just how complex the subject of resident involvement is. The evaluation of its functioning is, thus, by necessity complex and multidimensional and cannot yield unequivocal conclusions. The breakdown of the concept of involvement into numerous aspects has shown that achievements have been attained in every program, some more significant and others less; in some more numerous and in others less so. The final determination as to whether these achievements were sufficient or worthwhile cannot be an objective one; it depends on one's values and expectations.

Research in this area is clearly problematic but is sorely needed. Many research questions may be identified with regard to each and every one of the dimensions discussed previously as well as with regard to the relationships between them.

Among the issues that have arisen from the experience with citizen participation in neighborhood rehabilitation programs are the following five:

1. Does mandated government-inspired participation necessarily lead to co-optation and prevent radical change? Can citizens obtain power in such a situation?
2. Does one need to personally participate in order to benefit from citizen participation? Can anyone represent anyone else?
3. Should all aspects of planning or design involve citizen participation?
4. Is the environment that results from a process of citizen par-

ticipation a better one than would have resulted without their participation?

5. Which is more important—the process of participation or the "product" that results?

These are, of course, not unrelated issues, and they are relevant also to other instances of citizen participation. Because citizen participation is such a value-laden concept, the answers to many of the questions that arise are often based upon values and ideological positions. It is therefore extremely important that attempts be made to learn more about the factors that affect the manner in which citizen participation functions. This will enable a more reasoned and systematic evaluation of the principle.

In conclusion, through the comparative perspective we have seen that it is possible to discuss programs from different countries within a common framework. Despite great differences in the context and specific details of the programs and the involvement processes, there are similarities in the general trends as well as in the broad issues that arise. Variability in the involvement process exists within countries, as it does between countries. But the phenomenon of resident involvement and participation in neighborhood rehabilitation seems to have a basic structure, which is expressed in different elaborations and emphases while still retaining its essential core.

REFERENCES

Ahlbrandt, R., & Cunningham, J. (1979). *A new public policy for neighborhood preservation.* New York: Praeger.

Alterman, R. (1982). Planning for public participation: The design of implementable strategies. *Environment and Planning B, 9,* 295–313.

Alterman, R., Churchman, A., & Law-Yone, H. (1981). *A handbook for public participation in planning.* Haifa: Technion—Israel Institute of Technology, Center for Urban & Regional Studies (in Hebrew).

Alterman, R., & Frenkel, A. (1985). Implementation of project outputs: Services provided and their beneficiaries. In R. Alterman, N. Carmon, & M. Hill (Eds.), *Comprehensive evaluation of Israel's Project Renewal* (Vol. 3). Haifa: Technion–Israel Institute of Technology, Samuel Neaman Institute for Advanced Studies in Science and Technology.

Appleyard, D. (1983). Case studies of citizen action and citizen participation in Brussels, Covent Garden, Delft and Camden. In L. Susskind & M. Elliott (Eds.), *Paternalism, conflict and coproduction* (pp. 69–118). New York: Plenum Press.

Armistead, J., Fainstein, S., & Fainstein, N. (1980). *Community development block grants: Citizen participation and the representation of interests.* Paper presented at the Annual Meeting of the Neighborhood Organization Research Group, Washington DC, August.

Arnstein, S. (1969). A ladder of citizen participation. *Journal of the American Institute of Planners, 35*(4), 216–244.

Azmon, Y. (1983). *Lower class protest movements in Israel*. Paper presented at the Jerusalem Institute Seminar, "The Welfare State and its Aftermath," Jerusalem, May.

Bachelor, L., & Jones, B. (1981). Managed participation: Detroit's neighborhood opportunity fund. *Journal of Applied and Behavioral Science, 17*(4), 518–536.

Baroni, G. (1983). The neighborhood movement in the United States: From the 1960's to the present. In P. Clay & R. Hollister (Eds.), *Neighborhood policy and planning* (pp. 177–192). Lexington, MA: Lexington Books.

Basel, A., Grieff, R., & Muhlich, E. (1978). *Resident's participation in revitalization of housing areas*. Darmstadt, Germany: Institut Wohnen und Umwelt.

Becker, F. (1977). *User participation, personalization and environmental meaning: Three field studies*. Ithaca: Cornell University, Program in Urban and Regional Studies.

Brager, G., & Specht, H. (1973). *Community organizing*. New York: Columbia University Press.

Bruston, A. (1980). *Citizen participation in planning and programming*. New York: United Nations, Economic Commission for Europe, Committee on Housing, Building and Planning. Doc. HBP/SEM. 26/R.2.

Burke, E. (1968). Citizen participation strategies. *Journal of the American Institute of Planners, 34*(5), 287–294.

Churchman, A. (1985). *Resident involvement and participation in Project Renewal*. In R. Alterman, N. Carmon, & M. Hill (Eds.), *Comprehensive evaluation of Israel's Project Renewal* (Vol. 2). Haifa: Technion–Israel Institute of Technology, Samuel Neaman Institute for Advanced Studies in Science and Technology.

Churchman, A., Alterman, R., & Law-Yone, H. (1979). Public participation in Israel. *On Participation*, Issue 8, 3–5.

Cole, R. (1974). *Citizen participation and the urban policy process*. Lexington, MA: Lexington Books.

Committee on Housing, Building and Planning (1980). *Report of the seminar on citizen participation in the planning, implementation and management of human settlements*. New York: United Nations, Economic Commission for Europe, Doc. HBP/SEM, 26/2.

Downs, A. (1981). *Neighborhoods and urban development*. Washington DC: Brookings Institute.

Draisen, M. (1983). Fostering effective citizen participation: Lessons from three urban renewal neighborhoods in the Hague. In L. Susskind & M. Elliott (Eds.), *Paternalism, conflict and coproduction* (pp. 239–290). New York: Plenum Press.

Elliott, M. (n.d.) *Evaluating citizen participation: Illustrations from the European experience*. Unpublished document.

Fagence, M. (1977). *Citizen participation in planning*. New York: Pergamon.

Fainstein, N., & Fainstein, S. (1974). *Urban political movements*. Englewood Cliffs, NJ: Prentice-Hall.

Fainstein, N., Fainstein, S., & Armistead, P. J. (1979). *Citizen participation in the Community Development Grant Program: Dimensions of analysis*. Philadelphia: University of Pennsylvania, School of Public and Urban Policy.

Finlayson, K. (1978). The role of community involvement in low income housing. *Man-Environment Systems, 8*(3), 113–125.

Fisher, R. (1984). Neighborhood organizing: Lessons from the past. *Social Policy, 15*(1), 9–16.

Florin, P., & Wandersman, A. (1984). Cognitive social learning variables and participation in community development. *American Journal of Community Psychology, 12*, 689–708.

Frieden, B., & Kaplan, M. (1975). *The politics of neglect: Urban aid from Model Cities to revenue sharing*. Cambridge, MA: M.I.T. Press.

Friedgut, T. (1979). *Political participation in the U.S.S.R.* Princeton, NJ: Princeton University Press.

Glass, J. (1979). Citizen participation in planning: The relationship between objectives and techniques. *APA Journal*, April, 180–189.

Glenn, J. (1978). Social technologies of freedom. In C. Bezold (Ed.), *Anticipatory democracy* (pp. 251–275). New York: Vintage.

Godschalk, D., & Zeisel, J. (1983). Coproducing urban renewal in the Netherlands. In L. Susskind & M. Elliott (Eds.), *Paternalism, conflict and coproduction* (pp. 291–342). New York: Plenum Press.

Hallman, H. (1973). The neighborhood as an organizational unit: A historical perspective. In G. Frederickson (Ed.), *Neighborhood control in the 1970s* (pp. 123–128). New York: Chandler.

Harloe, M. (1982). Housing and the market. In G. Hellstin, F. Spreer, & H. Wollman (Eds.), *Applied Urban Research*. Bonn: Federal Research Institute for Regional Geography and Regional Planning.

Harris, I. (1984). The citizens' coalition in Milwaukee. *Social Policy, 15*(1), 27–31.

Haskell, C. (1980). *Public funding of neighborhood organizations: A preliminary exploration.* Paper prepared for the International Conference on Neighborhoods, Florence, Italy, March.

Hawkins, R. (1983). Neighborhood policy: An alternative to the dominant conception of neighborhoods. In P. Clay & R. Hollister (Eds.), *Neighborhood policy and planning.* Lexington, MA: Lexington Books.

Jajszczyk, R., & Hlebowicz, J. (1980). *Citizen participation in the management of settlements.* New York: United Nations, Economic Commission for Europe, Committee on Housing, Building & Planning. Doc. HBP/Sem. 26/R.7.

James, R. (1973). National strategies for neighborhood control and citizen participation. In G. Frederickson (Ed.), *Neighborhood control in the 1970s* (pp. 179–194). New York: Chandler.

Johnson, L., & Associates. (1978). *Citizen participation in local development: A catalog of local approaches.* Washington DC: Dept. of Housing & Development, Office of Policy Development & Research.

Kasperson, R. (1977). Participation through centrally planned social change: Lessons from the American experience on the urban scene. In W. R. Sewell & J. T. Coppock (Eds.), *Public policy in planning* (pp. 173–190). London: Wiley.

Kasperson, R., & Breitbart, M. (1974). *Participation, decentralization and advocacy planning* (Association of American Geographers Resource Paper No. 25). Washington DC: Commission on College Geography.

Kweit, M., & Kweit, R. (1981). *Implementing citizen participation in a bureaucratic society.* New York: Praeger.

Landsberger, H. (1980). The trend toward citizens' participation in the welfare state: Countervailing power to the professions. In C. Foster (Ed.), *Comparative public policy and citizen participation. Energy, education, health and urban issues in the United States and Germany* (pp. 228–243). New York: Pergamon.

Langton, S. (1978). Citizen participation in America: Current reflections on the state of the art. In S. Langton (Ed.), *Citizen participation in America* (pp. 1–12). Lexington, MA: Lexington Books.

Mamalis, M. (1983). Housing 'the Co-op' way. *Architectural Psychology Newsletter, 13*(2 & 3), 22–25.

May, J. (1973). Two Model Cities: Negotiations in Oakland. In G. Frederickson (Ed.), *Neighborhood control in the 1970s* (pp. 217–246). New York: Chandler.

Mulvihill, R. (1980). *Citizen participation in the management of human settlements.* New York: United Nations, Economic Commission for Europe, Committee on Housing, Building & Planning. Doc. HBP/Sem. 26/R.6.

Nilsson, N. (1985). Citizen participation, via tenants associations, in Swedish housing rehabilitation. *Participation Network,* Issue 3, March 6–7.

Paris, C. (1975). Birmingham: Participatory urban renewal. *The Planner, 61,* 93–95.

Perlman, J. (1983). Citizen action and participation in Madrid. In L. Susskind & M. Elliott (Eds.), *Paternalism, conflict and coproduction* (pp. 207–238). New York: Plenum Press.

Perlman, J., & Spiegel, H. (1983). Copenhagen's Black Quadrant: The facade and reality of participation. In L. Susskind & M. Elliott (Eds.), *Paternalism, conflict and coproduction* (pp. 35–68). New York: Plenum Press.

Pitkin, H. (1967). *The concept of representation.* Berkeley: University of California Press.

Pressman, J. (1973). Foreign aid and urban aid. In G. Frederickson (Ed.), *Neighborhood control in the 1970s* (pp. 139–164). New York: Chandler.

Rakodi, C. (1983). The World Bank experience: Mass community participation in the Lusaka squatter upgrading project. In C. Moser (Ed.), *Evaluating community participation in urban development projects* (pp. 18–33). London: Bartlett School of Architecture & Planning Development Planning Unit.

Rosener, J. (1978a). Citizen participation: Can we measure its effectiveness? *Public Administration Review, 38,* 457–463.

Rosener, J. (1978b). Matching method to purpose: The challenge of planning citizen participation activities. In S. Langton (Ed.), *Citizen participation in America* (pp. 109–122). Lexington, MA: Lexington Books.

Schmandt, H. (1973). Decentralization: A structural imperative. In G. Frederickson (Ed.), *Neighborhood control in the 1970s* (pp. 17–36). New York: Chandler.

Sharpe, L. J. (1979). Decentralist trends in Western democracies, a first appraisal. In L. J. Sharpe (Ed.), *Decentralist trends in Western democracies* (pp. 9–80). London: Sage.

Shimshoni, D. (1983). *Renewal and the management of innovation.* Preliminary summary submitted to the International Evaluation Committee, unpublished document, Herzliya.

Spiegel, H., & Perlman, J. (1983). Docklands and Coventry. Two citizen action groups in Britain's economically declining areas. In L. Susskind & M. Elliott (Eds.), *Paternalism, conflict and coproduction* (pp. 125–156). New York: Plenum Press.

Stegman, M. (1979). Neighborhood classification and the role of the planner in seriously distressed communities, *APA Journal,* October, 495–505.

Susskind, L., & Elliott, M. (1983). Paternalism, conflict and coproduction. In L. Susskind & M. Elliott (Eds.), *Paternalism, conflict and coproduction* (pp. 3–34). New York: Plenum Press.

Trapero, J. (1980). *Citizen participation in implementation.* New York: United Nations, Economic Commission for Europe, Committee on Housing, Building & Planning, HBP/Sem. 26/R.5.

Unger, D., & Wandersman, A. (1983). Neighboring and its role in block organizations: An exploratory report. *American Journal of Community Psychology, 11*(3), 291–300.

Verba, S., & Nie, N. (1972). Participation in America. *Political participation and social equality.* New York: Harper & Row.

Vonk, F. (1983). Citizen participation in the Netherlands: Some comments. In L. Susskind & M. Elliott (Eds.), *Paternalism, conflict and coproduction* (pp. 343–350). New York: Plenum Press.

Wandersman, A. (1978, August). *Participation: A strategy of human-environment optimization.* Paper presented at the meeting of the American Psychological Association, Toronto.

Wandersman, A. (1979). User participation in planning environments: A conceptual framework. *Environment and Behavior, 11*(4), 465–482.

Wandersman, A. (1984). Citizen participation. In K. Heller, R. Price, S. Reinharz, S. Riger, & A. Wandersman (Eds.), *Psychology and community change: Challenges of the future* (2nd ed., pp. 337–379) Homewood, IL: Dorsey Press.

Wandersman, A., Jakubs, J., & Giamartino, G. (1981). Participation in block organizations. *Journal of Community Action, 1* (September/October) 40–47.

Warren, R., & Warren, D. (1977). *The neighborhood organizer's handbook.* Notre Dame: University of Notre Dame Press.

Wooley, T. (1985). Community architecture: An assessment of the case for user participation in design. In S. Klein, R. Wener, & S. Lehman (Eds.), *EDRA 16/1985* (pp. 150–156). Washington, DC: EDRA.

Zawadzki, S. (1974). Basic trends of international studies on public participation in local power. In F. Bruhns, F. Cazzola, & J. Wiatr (Eds.), *Local politics, development and participation.* Pittsburgh: University Center for International Studies.

5

Islands in the Stream

NEIGHBORHOODS AND THE POLITICAL ECONOMY OF THE
CITY

DAVID BARTELT, DAVID ELESH, IRA GOLDSTEIN, GEORGE LEON, AND WILLIAM YANCEY

INTRODUCTION

The focus of this chapter is on understanding the persistence and change of neighborhoods in terms of the environment of which they are a part. We will argue that neighborhoods are best analyzed within an environment conceptualized as a political economy. Within that political economy, the stream of capital that flows within and among cities is taken as a primary force shaping communities.

Neighborhoods are elements of the environment and at the same time are directly affected by the organization of that environment. Just as the geological structure of landforms helps determine the flow of water from source to outlet, so too does the nature of neighborhoods affect the flow of capital. Just as the best understanding of the shifts and persistence of islands and streams is gained by reference to both landform and water, the understanding of neighborhoods and the changing political economy of cities is improved by awareness of their interdependence.

DAVID BARTELT, DAVID ELESH, IRA GOLDSTEIN, GEORGE LEON, and WILLIAM YANCEY • Institute for Public Policy Studies, Temple University, Philadelphia, PA 19122.

The roots of our approach to urban neighborhoods trace through existing theories of urban structure. The largely ecological paradigm of the first half of this century has been challenged by alternatives that stress historical specificity, class conflict, distributional inequities of income, jobs, and fiscal soundness. Moreover, recent research has increasingly documented the empirical inadequacies of the paradigm and provided support for the alternatives.

We begin with a review and critique of classical urban ecology. The classical ecological paradigm ignored the historical context of urban development and left its economic assumptions unexamined. One recent reaction to this approach, which we term *historical ecology*, provides an important corrective to the ahistorical character of the classical view. Other efforts to develop an alternative view have focused upon the relationship of urban structure to class conflict and modes of production. The alternative that we explore here, political economy, treats the spatial organization of the urban environment as a major factor of production parallel to land, labor, and capital. The major propositions of the three perspectives are summarized in Table 1.

THE CLASSICAL ECOLOGICAL PERSPECTIVE

The roots of the classical ecological paradigm of "the city" can be traced to the works of Park (1925) and Burgess (1925, 1928). Burgess's ideal-typical description of the city was that it became arranged in concentric rings of homogeneous land use and human activity:

> Every community as it grows expands outward from its center. This radical extension from the downtown business district toward the outskirts of the city is due partly to business and industrial pressure and partly to residential pull. Business and light manufacturing, as they develop, push out from the center of the city and encroach upon residences. At the same time, families are always responding to the appeal of more attractive residential districts, further and ever further removed from the center of the city. (1928, p. 106)

According to this view, land has value in relation to its accessibility to transportation networks and the local center of these networks and the markets that they feed—the central business district (CBD). Other things being equal, accessibility (measured in terms of transport costs, time, etc.—often termed the *friction of distance*) and therefore competition for land decreases with distance from the CBD. This results in a concomitant decline in economic activity, population density, and land values (Burgess, 1925; Haig, 1927; McKenzie, 1921; Park, 1936a,b).

TABLE 1. THE MAJOR PROPOSITIONS OF THREE PERSPECTIVES ON URBAN
DEVELOPMENT

Classical ecology	Historical ecology	Political economy
1. City is organized around a single commercial and (light) industrial core from which growth radiates.	1. City is organized around multiple centers that arise from historical developments in production and transportation technology, population movements, and the city's position in the larger economy.	1. City is organized around multiple centers that arise from historical patterns of investment both in the larger and local economies and the constraints imposed by governmental actions at various levels.
2. Land has value relative to transportation networks and the market that they feed, the central business district (CBD)—thus economic activity, population density, and land values decline with distance from the CBD.	2. Internal structure of the city is largely determined by the historical development of the types of economic activities within it with nuclei emerging from the specialized needs for specific resources such as water, transportation, or amenities.	2. Internal structure of the city is characterized by uneven historical development that occurs in response to shifts in the emphasis and growth of the local and larger economies and the extent of capital flow and inertia.
3. Neighborhoods are primarily created by economic competition for land and, secondarily, the occupational, racial, or ethnic character of incumbents.	3. The development and stability of neighborhoods result from the location of work opportunities, economics of the journey to work, and available housing that are, in turn, dependent upon the aforementioned technologies of production and distribution and population movements.	3. Neighborhoods are the result of investments in economic activities and housing, conditioned by governmental action. Their stability depends upon the stability of employment centers, the availability of mortgage capital, and the development of localized sentiments.

The theory is not as structural and reductionist as it appears on the
surface. Although it is certainly true that classical ecologists argue that
the engine of urban growth is fueled by the expansion of the commercial
sector, "if radial extension were the only factor affecting the growth of
American cities, every city in this country would exhibit a perfect ex-

emplification of these five urban zones" (Burgess, 1928, p. 108). The city in the words of Park

> is a state of mind, a body of customs and traditions, and of organized attitudes and sentiments that inhere in those customs and are transmitted with this tradition. The city is not merely a physical mechanism and an artificial construction . . . it is a product of nature, and particularly of human nature. (1925, p. 13)

Park sees human nature as competitive, and it is this competition that gives rise to a particular division of labor and a complementary spatial structure.

Although Park opens *The City* with these thoughts, they were not developed later in his work or the work of his followers. What is traditionally stressed is the expansion of the commercial core. The typical assessment of "the neighborhood" from a classical ecological perspective is to treat it as a residual phenomena.

In his early work, Park argued that each area of the city comes to take on the character of those who inhabit it. "Each separate part of the city is inevitably stained with the peculiar sentiments of its populations" (1925, p. 17). It is this "staining" of the geographical space that Park argued converts it from space to neighborhood. Neighborhoods are more or less stable; although individuals may move through a given neighborhood, its character tends to remain.

> The past imposes itself upon the present, and the life of every locality moves on with a certain momentum of its own, more or less independent of the larger circle of life and interests about it. (1925, p. 17)

Burgess similarly notes the "survival of an earlier use of a district" as a force perpetuating the stability of neighborhoods (1928, p. 108). This stability results from the more general sorting of populations along economic parameters.

Neighborhood life is contingent upon the competitive nature of the species producing a division of labor reproduced in the segregation of land uses. This segregation will follow principally along economic lines (producing concentric zones), and secondarily, the occupational, racial, or ethnic character of the incumbents of neighborhoods.

> Segregation offers the group, and thereby the individuals who compose the group, a place and a role in the total organization of city life. Segregation limits development in certain directions, but releases it in others. These areas tend to accentuate certain traits, to attract and develop their kind of individuals, and so to become further differentiated. (Burgess, 1925, p. 56)

Therefore, to understand the spatial arrangement of the city and its component neighborhoods, the classical ecologists take economic competition as the principal force underlying the separation of land uses at the grossest level and cultural, occupational, racial, or class differences segregating neighborhoods within a particular zone.

It was argued earlier that neighborhoods in the classical ecological paradigm were generally treated as an addendum to or residual of the more general economic process sorting populations across the city. This treatment has led to a series of criticisms by researchers whose work stems directly from classical ecology. For example, Hawley (1944, 1950, p. 211) asserted that as communities grow, their increasing divisions of labor dominate and channel individual spatial competition, producing clusters of use dependent upon similarity of function. Hoyt (1939) found evidence that Burgess's concentric rings were divided into radially organized sectors that developed their character because of the nature of the local topography and the desires of households with varying resources to separate themselves from their economic inferiors. Once established, land uses affected future development possibilities. Gettys questioned the classical assumption that spatial sorting arises simply from the competitive nature of the human species, arguing that it ignores the influences of choice, taste, and customary and institutional controls (1940, p. 471). And Firey (1945), based upon his historical study of Boston's Beacon Hill area, asserted that cultural sentiments and values could enable neighborhoods to successfully resist redevelopment pressures created by economic competition.

Other researchers, whose work shows a more marked departure from classical ecology (but whose theoretical approach remains fundamentally ecological), have underscored the role of culture, sentiment, tradition, and history in the entire process of neighborhood formation. They assert that there are basic differences in the processes underlying immigration and settlement in this country as well as the economic conditions that existed at the time of settlement in American neighborhoods (cf. Ericksen & Yancey, 1979; Lieberson, 1963, 1980; Yancey, Ericksen, & Juliani, 1976). To summarize, classical ecology has to be criticized, if not for its underlying theoretical dynamic then for failing to systematically integrate a theory of neighborhoods into the more general theory of urban form.

A more general critique of classical ecology concerns its view of the city as a monocentric entity. Harris and Ullman (1945) argued that needs for specialized facilities, agglomeration economies, agglomeration diseconomies, incompatible uses, and economic resources combine to produce an urban landscape with multiple nuclei. Hoover and Vernon (1959) similarly rejected monocentricity, the increase in socioeconomic status with distance, and the outward expansion of neighborhoods.

Their analysis of the New York Metropolitan Region led them to a view of the city as having multiple nuclei in which neighborhoods have a five-stage life cycle in which status rises upon initial development, peaks, gradually declines, and is renewed for households of varying socioeconomic levels.

Finally, there is little evidence to support the centrifugal growth hypothesis. Researchers in several disciplines have criticized this postulate of classical ecology for ignoring the role of history and the flow of capital (cf. Bowden, 1971; Guest, 1971; Scott, 1982; Ward, 1968, 1969, 1971).

Support for the proposition that socioeconomic status increases with distance from the CBD is mixed and appears to vary with the age and region of the city and other factors such as the location of industry (Alihan, 1938; Davie, 1937; Duncan, 1964; Guest, 1971; Haggerty, 1971; Schnore, 1963; Voss, 1941). Moreover, predictions for the location of racial, ethnic, and other residential groups based on their socioeconomic status have met with very limited success (Goldstein, 1985; Lieberson, 1963; Taeuber & Taeuber, 1965).

Although the classical model posits that neighborhood status characteristics evolve with outward movements of population, empirical analyses of suburban communities have resulted in controversy surrounding the degree to which a community's status characteristics persist or evolve over time. On the one hand, Farley (1964) found that educational and occupational characteristics across a sample of metropolitan areas persisted from 1920 to 1960 and that suburbs had on average higher status than central urban areas. Farley therefore concluded that his findings generally supported the Burgess model. On the other hand, Guest (1974, 1978) attacked the ahistorical aspects of the classical model, arguing that from 1920 to 1950 suburban status was evolving and population growth was an important determinant of community status. But from 1950 to 1970, persistence patterns emerged, and population growth was less important in determining status characteristics. Similarly, Choldin and Hanson (1982) and Choldin, Hanson, and Bohrer (1980) found that the persistence of status characteristics varied between cohorts of communities that were established before and after 1940, respectively.

Several studies have attempted to link the status characteristics of suburban communities to the presence of jobs. "Employing" communities are those with more jobs than local workers, and "residential" communities have more workers than jobs. Employing suburbs were older, larger, farther from the central city, had lower rents than residential suburbs, and were more concentrated in the Northeast and North Central regions (Schnore, 1956). Employing suburbs had a higher proportion of foreign born, nonwhite, and elderly residents and were more likely to be losing population than residential suburbs, which had growing, higher status populations (Schnore, 1963). Between 1960 and 1970 residential suburbs became more employment-oriented, whereas employment centers became more residential (Stahura, 1979a, 1979b). Despite these changes, 1960 status differences among suburbs persisted through 1970.

Logan (1976) added historical specificity to this argument by showing that although employing suburbs established before 1950 had lower family incomes and rents than their residential counterparts, newer employing suburbs had the highest incomes. He also argued that communities' political strategies with respect to fiscal policies help to manage industrial development and play a role in determining functional composition. Logan and Schneider (1981) asserted that although the status ranking of suburban communities may remain relatively constant, the degree of stratification may increase as the result of the cumulative advantages of high-status places.

In line with Logan's political expectations, Shlay and Rossi (1981) found that zoning practices influence housing type and density, owner occupancy, and nonresidential land uses in suburban communities. Although a relationship was found between zoning practices and median family income, racial composition was not found to be influenced by zoning.

Another assumption of the classical model—that commercial and manufacturing activities are concentrated in the CBD—is also challenged by empirical research. The density of employment, rather than being smoothly continuous across concentric rings, concentrates depending on industry-specific agglomeration and external economies, transportation requirements, and other factors (Davie, 1937; Hoover & Vernon, 1959). In studies of Philadelphia at two points in time, Ericksen and Yancey (1979), Leon (1985), and Goldstein (1985) found that employment density was affected by both industrial type and historical period. In 1928, final market, labor-intensive, and small manufacturing jobs and firms were close to the CBD, but by 1972, their distribution had become far more complex and often bore little relation to distance. Similar findings are reflected in other research that has shown more manufacturing workers have been employed in the suburban ring than in central cities (Kain, 1970; Sacks, 1977; U.S. Bureau of the Census, 1981). Examination of the location of other economic activities showed similarly mixed results. Whether employment or employment density is highest in the CBD varies by industry, and the relationship of these factors to distance from the CBD differs as well (Berry & Kasarda, 1977; Hawley, 1950, p. 279; 1981, p. 181; Hoover & Vernon, 1959).

In summary, patterns of neighborhood change are not just the result of the simple market forces of the classical paradigm but are also heavily influenced by historical periods (Choldin & Hanson, 1982; Choldin *et al.*, 1980; Farley, 1964; Guest, 1978, 1979), regional variations (Schnore, 1956, 1963), and political and planning policies (Logan, 1978; Logan & Schneider, 1981; Shlay & Rossi, 1981). In addition, there is little evidence for the concept of a monocentric city.

THE HISTORICAL ECOLOGICAL PARADIGM

The historical ecological perspective has emerged in response to the ahistorical character of classical ecology and its derivatives. Although the internal structure of the city is viewed by the classical ecologists as the result of competition for urban space, the historical ecologists emphasize historical developments in production and transport technology, regional migration patterns, and a city's position in the larger economy. The historical ecologists also object to the implicit assumption of the classical paradigm that any one model of urban form is universally applicable across time and space. They argue that the concentric zone or sector models may be appropriate to certain cities during certain periods of history but fail as generic models of the internal structure of the city. The historical ecologists do not attempt to present an alternative generic model of urban form but rather to identify the factors that account for particular spatial configurations during specific historical periods.

Two important dimensions of historical ecology can be traced to the work of Harris and Ullman (1959), who presented a model of urban form that departs from the classical paradigm. First, they argued that the city is an open system, in that the economic activities found within the city are the result of its relationship to its hinterland, which includes other cities. Second, they suggested that the internal structure of the city is determined by the types of economic activity within the city. This allows for a variety of internal forms, and "multiple nuclei" are expected to emerge in large cities, reflecting the variety of economic activities. Separate nuclei emerge because of the specialized needs of certain activities for resources such as water, transportation, or the presence or absence of other types of activities. Although the multiple nuclei model contrasts with the classical ecology model of a generic, monocentered city that is shaped by internal competition for urban space, Harris and Ullman did not stress historical specificity. Furthermore, they addressed the forces that shape the internal structure of the city only in the most general terms.

THE INTERNAL STRUCTURE OF THE CITY

More recent works have attempted a greater degree of specificity on both accounts. The major determinants of residential patterns, according to the historical ecologists, are the locations of work opportunities, the economics of the journey to work, and the available housing supply. These factors are in turn determined by historically specific developments in production and transportation technology and regional migration patterns (Johnston, 1970; Ward, 1971).

On the purely descriptive level, the model of the early 20th-century city presented by the historical ecologists is similar to that of classical ecology: a commercial and manufacturing core, heavy industry near the center, nearby immigrant neighborhoods, and exclusively residential, higher status neighborhoods at a greater distance from the center. But the historical ecologists contend that the descriptive accuracy of a model, with respect to the spatial layout of the city, is not sufficient evidence of the causal factors assumed to give rise to those spatial patterns. Ericksen and Yancey (1979), for example, argued that historically specific conditions may have given rise to a pattern of social organization that approximated the concentric pattern, but the pattern alone does not constitute evidence of Burgess's economic assumptions. Rather, the specialized needs of various production technologies and the state of the transportation system during particular historical periods, not competition for central space *per se*, were the major organizing factors of the urban ecology.

Several empirical findings directly challenge the assumptions of the classical model. Job access was a better predictor of the age of housing than was distance from the center, particularly at greater removes from the downtown. Furthermore, distance from the center only weakly predicted housing value for the city as a whole and was not significant in peripheral areas. However, proximity to the center strongly predicted both population density and owner occupancy. The central neighborhoods were the residential location of central city workers who lacked flexibility in the work trip. With increasing distance from the center, although more land was devoted to residential uses, peripheral job locations were more important organizing factors of the neighborhood in which they were located (Ericksen & Yancey, 1979).

Ericksen and Yancey concluded that the degree to which the postindustrial city of the late 20th century continues to exhibit a zonal pattern illustrates the "rigidity of past investments" and the "persistence of historical constraints rather than the general applicability of the Burgess model" (p. 151). In summary, the historical ecologists consider the internal structure of the city to be an expression of historically specific developments in production and transportation technology as well as the constraints placed upon residential patterns by these technological developments, migration patterns, and the economics of the journey to work.

SETTLEMENT PATTERNS AND OPPORTUNITY STRUCTURE

Much of the work of the historical ecologists is composed of empirical studies of the city's "opportunity structure"—the historical relationships among the location of employment opportunities, the journey to work, the growth of the housing supply, and the consequent emergence of ethnic neighborhoods. The historical ecologists have emphasized the industrial expansion of the 19th century, and most of these studies focus upon old, industrial cities. The transition from the 19th-century "industrializing city" to the "industrial city" at the turn of the century and finally the "postindustrial city" after World War II accounts for the settlement patterns and movements of populations (Thernstrom, 1973; Warner, 1968; Yancey & Ericksen, 1979; Yancey, Erickson, & Juliani, 1976). Hershberg, Burstein, Ericksen, Greenberg, and Yancey (1979) argued that the

> "ecological structure," or the distribution in space of people, housing, jobs, transportation, and other urban elements is understood as the material expression of the opportunity structure. A city's ecological structure can thus be considered as a major determinant of differential "access"—to jobs, housing, transportation and services. (p. 57)

Although these studies have focused primarily on Philadelphia, other studies have shown the same processes at work among other old, industrial cities (Ward, 1971; Warner, 1962, 1968).

THE EMERGENCE OF NEIGHBORHOODS

In explaining the development of neighborhoods, the historical ecologists have taken the early 19th century as their point of departure.

During that period, they argue, the small scale of most urban economic activity and the lack of transportation discouraged the formation of exclusively residential or commercial districts (Warner, 1968). Levels of ethnic segregation were low because of the high density of settlement, the central location of manufacturing jobs, and the necessity of walking to work. Immigrant "ghettos" did not appear until later in the century, with the growth of large centers of manufacturing employment and concentrations of older, inexpensive available housing (Greenberg, 1981; Pratt, 1911).

Workers in the downtown industries lived near the center, whereas those working in less centralized industries were more dispersed. Except for the black population, industry was more important than ethnicity in organizing residential patterns. For example, despite their residential proximity to manufacturing jobs, few blacks worked in manufacturing (Ericksen & Yancey, 1979).

With advances in the development of steam technology in the latter half of the 19th century, industrial production increased in scale, and distinct manufacturing centers emerged. Neighborhoods grew around these decentralized industrial sites while the expansion of the streetcar lines resulted in the growth of exclusively residential "streetcar suburbs" populated by white-collar workers and manufacturing workers who could afford the higher commuting costs (Ericksen & Yancey, 1979; Warner, 1968).

Around the turn of the century, the development of outlying tracts resulted in the availability of inexpensive, old housing concentrated near manufacturing jobs. Ethnic communities of recently arrived Southern and Eastern European immigrants developed near concentrations of decentralized manufacturing jobs (Greenberg, 1981).

NEIGHBORHOOD CHANGE IN THE TWENTIETH CENTURY

Several events took place throughout the middle of the twentieth century that set the stage for subsequent citywide patterns of neighborhood change. First, although large-scale immigration from Europe was effectively cut off in 1924, a large number of southern black migrants were attracted to industrial job opportunities that temporarily expanded during each of the two world wars. These migration patterns, together with the cessation of residential construction during the Depression and war years resulted in a midcentury housing shortage (Clark & Clark, 1982; Tinkcom, 1982).

Second, the development of the internal combustion engine and the highway system as well as electrical power and electronic communications freed industries from locating on expensive land in urban centers or near railroads and rivers. Third, the development of the more distant "automobile suburbs" after World War II continued a trend of declining urban population density that began in the nineteenth century.

This decentralization of jobs and population did not have the same effect on all urban neighborhoods. Although some neighborhoods remained relatively stable, others experienced rapid racial transition, and in some cases lost population and experienced abandonment.

The stability observed for some ethnic communities is linked to the city's industrial economy. Ethnic neighborhoods that were characterized by high levels of industrial employment in 1930 were likely to be the location of the same national origin groups in 1970. The stability of these communities reflected the stability of nearby industrial employment as well as the "entrapment" of industrial workers whose housing values had not kept up with inflation. The higher status populations not tied to nearby manufacturing employment abandoned these communities following World War II (Ericksen & Yancey, 1979). The success of Philadelphia's ethnic communities in maintaining strong working-class neighborhoods has been used as a testament of their value system and/or ethnic solidarity. Yet a focus on community resources and ties to the larger industrial economy points to the structural basis for their persistence.

Patterns of black movement in the city between 1930 and 1980 reflect the investment and disinvestment in the city's neighborhoods. The growing black population was unable to move into the stable working-class white communities. Instead, the black population became concentrated in the "streetcar suburbs" that were vacated by white residents who moved to the postwar automobile suburbs on the edge of the city (Ericksen & Yancey 1979).

Leon (1985) has shown how housing abandonment is also rooted in the process of urban growth and the development of neighborhoods in the changing urban economy. Using data for Philadelphia, neighborhoods' positions in the economic organization of the city were portrayed and analyzed in terms of their relationship to industrial capital, the era of transportation technology in which they developed and whether they were redlined by the Home Owners' Loan Corporation (HOLC) for residential investment in 1936.

He found that population movements and patterns of abandonment observed in the 1970s were shaped by the economic organization of the 1930 city, changes in the location of job opportunities, and differential access to residential capital among neighborhoods (Leon, 1985). White population density declined in areas of the city that were redlined and increased in newer neighborhoods, near postindustrial job opportunities and where conventional mortgage credit was available. Areas vacated by whites were occupied by the growing black population and became crowded, impoverished neighborhoods after 1950. After 1970, population declined in most of the older, central neighborhoods except the redeveloping downtown area. These population movements and their consequences varied with a neighborhood's position in the economic organization of the city. Abandonment was highest in the old, centralized "walking industrial" neighborhoods that had been losing population throughout the 1930 to 1980 study period. Some of those neighborhoods that were adjacent to the downtown were eventually "recycled" for industrial uses, whereas those within the downtown were more likely to undergo residential "gentrification." The less centralized, slightly younger "streetcar industrial" neighborhoods remained stable until after World War II, after which the population declined with the loss of local manufacturing jobs. With the cessation of black in-migration and the continued outward movement of population, the impoverished streetcar suburbs were again abandoned with the exodus of the black population after 1970.

This analysis challenges the traditional neighborhood life cycle (Hoover & Vernon, 1959), filtering (Alonso, 1971; Lowry, 1960) and "white flight" (Frey, 1979; Salins, 1980) approaches to neighborhood decline and abandonment. Mainstream urban sociology has not adequately addressed housing abandonment because the economic assumptions of the classical model are inappropriate for the analysis of a declining, industrial metropolis. If, as the classical model posits, urban growth is driven by a constant state of competition for space in an expanding central business district, then large, long term concentrations of abandonment should not exist. Instead, abandonment is best understood as part of a historical process of investment, disinvestment, and reinvestment in urban land markets by sources of industrial and residential capital.

Goldstein's (1985) research on residential segregation in Philadelphia draws summary links between the position of neighborhoods in the city's political economy and the settlement patterns of whites and nonwhites within those neighborhoods. In this study, a measure, the Index of Neighborhood Segregation, was developed to assess the level of residential integration *within* neighborhoods. The substance of the measure can be best described with a simple example. Suppose there are two neighborhoods, each with 50% nonwhite. In one neighborhood, every block has 50% nonwhite, and in the other, 50% of the blocks are all white, and the remaining blocks are all nonwhite. The first neighborhood is, according to this conceptualization, integrated; the second is segregated. A *processual* explanation of these neighborhood differences was sought in a political economic framework: a perspective that views the social organization of space (in this case segregation) as reflective of relations among social classes.

The basic tenet of this perspective, as applied to residential segregation, is that the character of social space is engendered by the factionalization of the labor force resulting from the process of capital accumulation. Assuming that profit results from the ability of capital to extract surplus value from labor, the segmentation of the labor force along color lines facilitates this process by weakening the bargaining position of labor as a whole (i.e., the creation of a surplus labor pool). Historically, blacks have been used by capital to undermine the unified strength of labor to capture a greater share of profit (cf. Baron, 1971; Hill, 1980). Other "actors" in the housing market (e.g., realtors, mortgage-lending institutions) support the separation of white and nonwhite labor through several mechanisms. It has been argued that realtors "steer" potential home buyers into neighborhoods occupied by persons of similar racial and ethnic background (cf. Bartelt, 1979a; Pearce, 1979). Similarly, studies of several cities across the United States indicate the existence of bank policies promotive of disinvestment within city neighborhoods. Such practices are inevitably conducive of crises at several levels (e.g., periods when capital accumulation is threatened because of ineffectual demand among consumers, riots as a results of racial antagonisms, etc.). At the onset of these crises, state action is triggered as a mediator of both intra- and interclass conflict. Depending upon the nature of the particular crisis, the nature of the state response may be to favor either labor or capital.

This analysis of segregation takes the industrial profile of an area, characterized by the size and number of manufacturing firms in 1928 and the degree to which those firms were reliant on other local firms to supply them with their raw materials, as the principal causal factor. In an attempt to discern the relationship between the local organization of production and the flow of housing capital, these characteristics of the neighborhood's production profile were related to the assessment of a neighborhood's 1936 HOLC rating of credit worthiness. Neighborhoods with many manufacturing firms and where the preponderance of firms was small (i.e., less than 10 employees) were more likely to have received a poor rating. In Philadelphia, HOLC redlined most of the nonwhite and industrial neighborhoods. However, many white and nonindustrial communities also received poor ratings by HOLC. Areas that were both redlined and industrial were more likely to have larger nonwhite population settlements in 1940. The industrial areas that saw nonwhite settlement were those areas that experienced the greatest manufacturing job loss since the turn of the century. Nonwhites had particularly good access to manufacturing employment, but the social organization of production, partially supported by racism, rarely provided jobs (Ericksen & Yancey, 1979).

Patterns of segregation within racially mixed neighborhoods responded to not only racial composition but also HOLC assessment and neighborhood industrial profiles. The segregated areas were those in which there was a larger nonwhite population and in areas that were industrial and redlined by HOLC. The loss of manufacturing jobs eroded neighborhood stability and allowed the expanding nonwhite population to enter. However, neither HOLC nor the manufacturing firms themselves promoted the mixing of the races within the neighborhood or in the factory. The effect of HOLC suggests that the state participated in the residential separation of the races.

Analysis of a later period examined the consequences of state action in the form of public housing on the settlement pattern across the city's neighborhoods. Goldstein and Yancey (1986) found that public housing did not influence the trajectory of neighborhood racial change once the relevant historical ecological characteristics were controlled. Consistent with a structural theory of the state (i.e., state actions are constrained by the dictates of capital and will therefore be complementary to the needs of capital), public housing projects promoted segregation within neighborhoods as did HOLC and the local organization of production; however, scattered site public housing during the 1970s exerted no independent effect.

This series of studies of Philadelphia demonstrate how the changing character of the urban neighborhoods is rooted in the process of urban growth. The expansion of the industrial economy in the late nineteenth century gave rise to an urban structure in the early twentieth century that provided a framework for subsequent population shifts. The movements of industrial and residential capital during the transition of the industrial city of the early twentieth century to the postindustrial city of the late twentieth century had differential effects on neighborhoods depending on their position in the changing political economy. The broader economic and institutional developments that were concomitant with technological change are critical determinants of the location of capital investments (and disinvestments). Although demonstrating the impact of capital (as indicated by the location of employment and differential access of residential capital) on local neighborhoods, these studies have failed to examine the underlying factors determining the flow of capital across the city.

THE POLITICAL ECONOMY OF CITIES

Recent work in the political economy of urban structure has provided a historically sensitive framework for research on urban structure and neighborhoods. Cities were not of much concern to early theorists of the political economy of capitalism (Saunders, 1981). Indeed, early theorists, ranging from Smith to Mill through Marx and Engels, simply treated the city as a production site. Except for a few scattered comments about life in the city—largely in a polemical context aimed at theorists who assumed that urbanism, rather than class relations, was the source of social conflict—scant attention is paid to the city. For example, Engels's Manchester is little but a backdrop for his analysis of class conflict (Engels, 1958).

Recently more attention has been paid to the problem of urban structure by analysts who adopt a political economic perspective. A careful reading of these analyses reveals a significant degree of complementarity, sufficient to specify the rudiments of an alternative model of urban structure.

Three themes emerge in recent analyses of the political economy of the city. The first approach views urban structure as a mirror of class economic and political interests (Gordon, 1978; Logan 1978; Molotch 1976, 1979). Urban structure is the outcome of investment decisions made across the urban landscape, and cities develop according to decisions and policies developed and enforced by a ruling class or controlling elite, led by the business community but with strong political support. For instance, Molotch refers to city land use maps as "mosaics of financial interests" (1976). Gordon points to the emergence of suburbs as an outgrowth of class control of the labor process, and Logan points to the protections privileged suburbs develop by their use of zoning controls and development disincentives.

The second approach emphasizes the differential consumption of land by different groups of people (Castells, 1978, 1979). Segregation of class and race groups reflects the inequality of wages. Social divisions between communities and the social cohesion of any one community are largely a function of the underlying economic order. To the extent that labor is divided into relatively distinct categories—by such factors as industry, occupation, income, race, and gender—it divides along consumption patterns as well. The city becomes the social arena within which the conflicts over the consumption of land are played out.

Castells's approach to the political economy of urban areas leads to an understanding of the emergence and resolution of issues confronting urban neighborhoods. It gauges the interests involved, the coalitions that are possible, the expenditures necessary to implement any given program for change, and the relative commitment to a given program by interested parties. However, Castells's analysis ignores history as it replaces historical patterns with an analysis of the current state of conflict between contending consuming classes.

The third approach to political economy begins by pointing to the centrality of spatial relations in the productive process. This approach strongly suggests that the traditional approach of economics, rooted in the concepts of land, labor, and capital, is not sufficient. Understanding the development of an economy in a social context must also include the organization of the economy across space.

Although modern economics implicitly uses these concepts in the form of transport costs and agglomeration advantages (i.e., advantages accruing to firms from their proximity to similar or complementary firms), their implications for the structure of urban neighborhoods have only recently been articulated (Harvey 1973, 1982). Put in its most elemental form, location becomes meaningful only by reference to the organization of the larger economy. The development of space into production sites, market sites, transport use, residential areas, cultural amenities, and the like represents a use of capital with a rate of return deteriorating over time. That deterioration is dependent upon three major factors: the rate of direct financial return and the risk involved with the investment, the extent to which state guarantees or supports are involved, and the expansion of the economy as a whole.

In slightly different terms, capital is confronted by the dilemma of requiring a fixed location in order to generate a return and simultaneously requiring liquidity in order to expand that return. What some analysts have termed *uneven development* is rooted in this dilemma. As one area matures as an investment location, it generates the liquidity necessary to develop other locations. These locations, in turn, being less constrained by past production processes and wage rates, become increasingly competitive and drive out their original capital sources from the market. As Harvey stated:

> Under capitalism there is, then, a perpetual struggle in which capital builds a physical landscape appropriate to its own condition at a particular moment in time, only to have to destroy it, usually in the course of a crisis, at a subsequent point in time. (1977, p. 124)

Historically, this has meant that older industrial cities generated the capital used to develop the national system of cities. However, newer production sites in the South and West successfully compete with these older centers of development in the Northeast and Midwest. Within a metropolitan area, the same principle obtains, with suburban development financed by central city capital sources.

Harvey has applied this approach to housing, finance capital, and neighborhood class structure. As an instrument of finance capital, the mortgage is an investment instrument that is remarkably unwieldy given the nature of the tension noted above. The long-term nature of the investment means that banks tie up capital for extensive periods of time at a marginal return. This is adjusted to by the terms of repayment as amortization yields front-end returns, by differential availability by income and ethnicity (Bartelt, 1979b; Harvey & Chatterjee, 1974) and by development of state guarantees and limits to risk (Bartelt, 1985; Bradford & Marino 1977).

The political economy of cities is more than a mixed bag of three different approaches. Although these approaches are not perfectly consistent with each other, they do contain the necessary elements of a synthesis. The most basic element of the political economic approach to urban structure is the general assertion that cities are what the larger economic order makes them. This simple assertion is not unique to political economists. What the political economists add is that it is possible to understand the structure of the economy, its developmental dynamics (including its spatial features), its links to state structure and behaviors, and the place of cities within the economy without asserting the causal primacy of the market and supply–demand relationships.

The political economists insist that the marketplace is characterized by a high degree of social organization beneath its atomistic, temporary, and calculative exchanges. The appropriate model for understanding an economy is thus not a concatenation of many markets but a set of structured relationships surrounding the production and distribution of goods and services. As an example, the housing market can be understood in terms of the social relationships that bring housing to the point of a transaction, including (but not limited to) the construction industry, the organization and distribution of mortgage capital, specific urban redevelopment plans, the organization of the real estate industry, labor and general population flows, state policies and programs, and the historical specification and labeling of neighborhoods in the city.

Among the organizing principles of the economic system that are of direct relevance for an understanding of neighborhoods in cities are four major elements. These can be termed the *larger economic order, capital flow, capital inertia,* and *uneven development.*

The political economy of urban areas rests, we would argue, on the assertion that cities are settlements that emerged largely because of production and distribution requirements of geographically extensive economic and political orders. Further, they did not emerge in isolation but in active relationships with other urban areas, and minimally with a hinterland supplying materials for its economic system. To speak of the political economy of cities, then, is to consider the economy as a whole as having major nodal points of trade and production. In a slightly different light, the spatial problem of an economy consists of coordinating trade, production, and information across the settlements constituting the economy. Cities emerge, grow, shrink, and even disappear in response to shifts in the emphasis and growth of the entire economy.

The internal structure of the city—that is, neighborhoods linked to each other—is thus dependent upon the larger political economy. The internal development of a city and the movements of populations through historically shifting neighborhoods do not occur by chance, or by some naturalistic progression from center to periphery, or because of some common psychological trait distributed differentially among population subgroups. Instead, the central assertion of ecological theory—that populations move through an urban structure—is elaborated by the addition of a more inclusive view of the economic order, that is, one that incorporates the state, the labor market, and the money market.

The second major element of the political economic perspective is the concept of capital flow. Industrial capitalism requires capital to flow or circulate if the market system is to "work," that is, if the market is to generate a financial return that will induce further production. Capital circulation has two aspects to it that are of primary significance for urban areas—the expansion of capital flow and the velocity of capital flow.

A capitalist economy must expand to remain viable. This expansionist dynamic has consequences for individual firms and for the spatial distribution of the economy as well. If firms expand and if the economy as a whole does well, existing production sites and distribution networks will become inadequate. It is not surprising, then, to see urban structure as being decentralized, with centers of production and distribution emerging in new locations. The decentralization of production and distribution leads to population movements as well.

One dimension of capital flow that is often overlooked is its velocity. All other things being equal, the velocity with which money is invested and yields a return is a significant factor in the generation of new capital. That is, the return to capital is maximized under liquid conditions. A city, among its many characteristics, is a built environment—a place of businesses, residences, industrial plants, and transportation and communication arteries. There is a tension that exists between the investment in fixed sites and the tendency toward a maximized velocity of capital generation.

This leads directly toward a third aspect of capital—its inertia. Capital fixed to a location may well generate a return but its lack of liquidity creates a historical inertia of the developed city. Put simply, it is easier to expand the economic order (given appropriate levels of communications and control mechanisms) by expanding to previously undeveloped land than it is to alter capital fixed in space. Several reasons seem to account for this. First, there is the factor of the costs involved in simply building versus destruction and rebuilding or alteration. More capital is fixed in space by reworking the original investment than in starting from scratch.

Second, as an entire urban economy grows, it sets not just building sites but transportation routes, public amenities, and centers of coordination into specific locations. The expanding and/or changing business has a powerful incentive to stay (given agglomeration economies, for instance) but eventually must confront the inadequacy of a given infrastructure.

Third, the purchase of residences by individuals and families creates its own inertia through ties to nearby places of employment and the development of localized sentiments and loyalties. And, over time, even significant job losses in the area may contribute to the inertia of capital because of the depressing effects of such losses on the market for neighborhood homes. Finally, the overlay of property interest that development creates makes redevelopment problematic.

Related to both the concepts of *capital inertia* and *capital flow* is the concept of *uneven development*. Within an economy, not all industries or regions develop at the same rate or along the same path. This is implied by the sense of expansion and inertia coexisting in the same economy. A second, more dynamic meaning emerges. Essentially, uneven development indicates that newer areas emerge because economic activities face limits to expansion in existing sites.

The location of expansion is contingent upon the costs associated with new locations, that is, labor, coordination, and distribution. Neighborhoods, as Molotch has noted, are investment sites (1979); they are commodities sold along with the house, office building, manufacturing plant, or retail store. The type of investment that takes place, its amount, and its extent all depend on the place of that neighborhood in the overall city economy.

Thus far the emphasis has been placed on political economy as a theoretical framework. There is empirical research that supports this framework as well. Logan's recent work (Logan, 1978; Logan and Schneider, 1981; Logan and Schneider, 1982) has focused on the emergence of suburban areas and variations between suburban communities as the outgrowth of their interaction with the developmental dynamics of their central city. Not only does this perspective link the fact of individual communities to a larger economy, it emphasizes the ways in which political forces may be mobilized to advance economic interests within the constraints of the overall developmental dynamic.

Goldstein (1985) has linked the flow of housing capital to neighborhood segregation, noting the complementary effect of state policy. Goldstein and Yancey (1986) similarly demonstrated the role of the private market and state policy in the citing of public housing and the racial transition of neighborhoods.

These works are complemented by Leon's (1985) analysis of housing abandonment, which he linked to the developmental dynamics of an industrial economy in transition to service sector dominance. In this work, Leon specified how the positions of neighborhoods within the older industrial economy conditions their positions within the newer economic order. One example of the ways in which these positions affect the future of neighborhoods lies in the availability of mortgage capital, the "lifeblood" of housing, to them. Research addressing this issue has demonstrated that mortgage-lending patterns influence the movement of populations across urban areas (Bartelt, 1984; Bradford, 1979; Bradford & Marino, 1977; Goldstein, 1985; Leon, 1985). But to raise this question is also to ask whether neighborhood population characteristics affect lending patterns. It is clear that neighborhoods' racial and ethnic compositions do affect the availability of mortgage capital to them (Bradford, 1979; Goldstein, 1986; Shlay, 1985; Taggart & Smith, 1981; Tomer, 1980).

In sum, although this research does not address all of the issues suggested by the application of the political economic framework to urban structure, it is clear that it raises important theoretical and empirical issues warranting additional research. It is, in fact, the developmental focus of this approach that has led us to the metaphor *islands in the stream* to characterize the place of neighborhoods in the urban structure over time. The political economy of urban areas resembles a river— a force with a tendency to expand beyond its boundaries. Neighborhoods are islands of settlement in the flow of capital, constantly being pushed, pulled, eroded, or built up by the differential flows of the river. As with any metaphor, the imagery has limits. But it is a useful starting point for understanding the relationship of neighborhoods to the political economy of the city, and it helps to reorient theoretical discussions of urban structure and the place of neighborhoods within it.

Activists working on a neighborhood agenda are well aware of the forces of development and their impact on neighborhoods. On the one hand, forgotten neighborhoods are fought for, to be reintroduced to the life-generating flow of capital. On the other hand, neighborhoods being rediscovered by a new flow of people introduced to the city by a changed economic system fight to retain their character against a flood of new capital and gentrifying reinvestment. Small towns fight against suburbanization if wealthy and try to attract it if in need of resources. In short, the backdrop against which neighborhoods live out their current existence and are transformed is the operation of the political economy of urban space.

DIRECTIONS FOR THE FUTURE

We have developed the metaphor of neighborhoods as islands in a stream of capital. The political economy that shapes interurban systems of cities also imposes a historical, developmental pattern on those cities, thereby affecting the intraurban environment of neighborhoods. Pivotal is the conceptualization of immobilized capital—capital fixed in the built environment of the city and thereby establishing an inertial quality of older economic orders on contemporary patterns of capital investment.

The emphasis on immobilized capital—essentially the built environment as a developmental template for urban communities—is not intended to eliminate or supplant analyses on neighborhoods that are based on the political economy of production. Indeed, as we have noted, one of the factors we suspect as key to understanding neighborhood persistence and change is the relationship of job location and job access to a labor force. What has not been developed but is clearly a logical next step is the conceptualization of the relationship between residential capital and capital formation taking place within the industrial, service, and commercial segments of urban economies. It is necessary that this work be extended, tested, and revised by results from many urban areas.

Similarly, the arguments offered here are linked to a developmental process in a historically specific context. It does matter, we argue, when a city is formed (in terms of the larger national economy), when it gets a developmental "push," what kinds of industry and neighborhood structures emerge, and what the nature of the underlying economic changes are. Thus far, our work has focused on the processes of urban neighborhood structure in the post-Depression world of a diversified industrial city. A sound test of the perspective will be its ability to (a) be applied to earlier time periods; and (b) be extended into practical discussions of neighborhood revitalization and change in a postindustrial/service economy.

The implications of our arguments are that neighborhoods have different stakes in the future of a city and that power/money alone is an insufficiently specific organizing goal. Essentially the issue facing neighborhood advocates (inside or outside of governmental positions) is understanding the future prospects for an area, the resources at hand, and the desires of the neighborhood residents, while developing a plan for its future. All of this must be clearly and unambiguously outlined within the economic and political realities of a neighborhood in a city with a specific economic history and a place within the developing political economy.

With these general guidelines in mind, the perspective developed here seems to indicate the following:

1. Neighborhood stability demands an economic base, specifically access to jobs that fit the skill levels of the residents.
2. Revitalizing neighborhoods occurs within a potential, often overt, form of class conflict.
3. Old, industrial cities decline because of economic shifts, not political malice; successful revitalization means economic change.
4. As cities change their economic base in adaptation to national shifts, many neighborhoods become "forgotten"; the task facing those neighborhoods is at once economic and political—to develop a new economic base and the political presence to implement and facilitate it.
5. Overall economic improvement of a city does not guarantee a full or even distribution of benefits for neighborhoods. Neighborhoods excluded from the benefits of economic change have no alternative but to organize and obtain any such benefits.

REFERENCES

Alihan, M. A. (1938). *Social ecology: A critical analysis*. New York: Columbia University Press.

Alonso, W. (1971). A theory of the urban land market. In L. Bourne (Ed.), *The internal structure of the city* (pp. 239–252). New York: Oxford University Press.

Baron, H. (1971). The demand for black labor: Historical notes on the political economy of racism. *Radical America*, 5, 1–45.

Bartelt, D. W. (1979a). Institutional racism and the rental housing market. *Housing and Society*, 6, 48–60.

Bartelt, D. W. (1979b). *Redlining in Philadelphia*. Philadelphia: Institute for the Study of Civic Values.

Bartelt, D. W. (1984). *Redlines and breadlines: Depression and the structure of urban space*. Unpublished paper. Philadelphia: Department of Urban Studies, Temple University.

Bartelt, D. W. (1985). *Economic change, systems of cities, and the "life-cycle" of housing*. Report to the Department of Housing and Urban Development, Washington, DC.

Berry, B., & Kasarda, J. (1977). *Contemporary urban ecology*. New York: Macmillan.

Bowden, M. J. (1971). Downtown through time: Delimitation, expansion, and internal growth. *Economic Geography, 47*, 121–135.

Bradford, C. (1979). Financing homeownership: The federal role in neighborhood decline. *Urban Affairs Quarterly, 14*, 313–335.

Bradford, C., & Marino, D. (1977). *Redlining and disinvestment as a discriminatory practice in residential mortgage loans.* Washington, DC.: United States Department of Housing and Urban Development.

Burgess, E. W. (1925). The growth of the city. In R. E. Park, E. W. Burgess, & R. D. McKenzie (Eds.), *The city* (pp. 47–63). Chicago: University of Chicago Press.

Burgess, E. W. (1928). Residential segregation in American cities. *The Annals of the American Academy of Political and Social Science, 140*, 105–115.

Castells, M. (1978). *City, class, and power.* New York: St. Martin's Press.

Castells, M. (1979). *The urban question.* Cambridge: M.I.T. Press.

Choldin, H. M., & Hanson, C. (1982). Status shifts within the city. *American Sociological Review, 47*, 129–140.

Choldin, H. M., Hanson, C., & Bohrer, R. (1980). Suburban status instability. *American Sociological Review, 45*, 972–983.

Clark, J. F., Jr., & Clark, D. J. (1982). Rally and relapse, 1945–1968. In R. F. Weigley (Ed.), *Philadelphia: A 300-year history* (pp. 649–703). New York: W. W. Norton.

Davie, M. R. (1937). The pattern of urban growth. In G. P. Murdock (Ed.), *Studies in the science of society* (pp. 133–161). New Haven: Yale University Press.

Duncan, B. (1964). Variables in urban morphology. In E. W. Burgess & D. J. Bogue (Eds.), *Urban sociology* (pp. 17–30). Chicago: University of Chicago Press.

Engels, F. (1958). *The condition of the working class in England.* Palo Alto: Stanford University Press.

Ericksen, E. P., & Yancey, W. L. (1979). Work and residence in industrial Philadelphia. *Journal of Urban History, 5*, 147–182.

Farley, R. (1964). Suburban persistence. *American Sociological Review, 29*, 38–47.

Firey, W. (1945). Sentiment and symbolism as ecological variables. *American Sociological Review, 10*, 140–148.

Frey, W. H. (1979). Central city white flight: Racial and nonracial causes. *American Sociological Review, 44*, 425–448.

Gettys, W. (1940). Human ecology and social theory. *Social Forces, 18*, 469–476.

Goldstein, I. J. (1985). *The wrong side of the tracts: A study of residential segregation in Philadelphia, 1930–1980.* Unpublished doctoral dissertation, Temple University, Philadelphia, PA.

Goldstein, I. J. (1986). *The flow of housing capital in the Philadelphia metropolitan area: 1980– 1984.* Unpublished manuscript, Temple University, Institute for Public Policy Studies, Social Science Data Library, Philadelphia, PA.

Goldstein, I. J., & Yancey, W. L. (1986). Projects, blacks, and public policy: The historical ecology of public housing. In J. Goering (Ed.), *Racial integration and housing policy* (pp. 262–289). Chapel Hill: University of North Carolina Press.

Gordon, D. M. (1978). Capitalist development and the history of American cities. In W. Tabb & L. Sawers (Eds.), *Marxism and the metropolis* (pp. 25–63). New York: Oxford University Press.

Greenberg, S. (1981). Industrial location and ethnic residential patterns in an industrializing city: Philadelphia 1880. In T. Hershberg (Ed.), *Philadelphia: Work, space, family, and group experience in the 19th century* (pp. 204–232). New York: Oxford University Press.

Guest, A. M. (1971). Retesting the Burgess zonal hypothesis: The location of white collar workers. *American Journal of Sociology, 76*, 1094–1108.

Guest, A. M. (1974). Neighborhood life-cycles and social status. *Economic Geography, 50,* 228–243.

Guest, A. M. (1978). Suburban social status: Persistence or evolution? *American Sociological Review, 43,* 251–264.

Guest, A. M. (1979). Patterns of suburban population growth, 1920-1975. *Demography, 16,* 401–413.

Haggerty, L. V. (1971). Another look at the Burgess hypothesis: Time as an important variable. *American Journal of Sociology, 76,* 1084–1093.

Haig, R. M. (1927). *Major economic factors in metropolitan growth and arrangement.* New York: Committee on Regional Plan of New York and Its Environs.

Harris, C. D., & Ullman, E. L. (1945). The nature of cities. *Annals of the American Academy of Political and Social Science, 242,* 7–17.

Harvey, D. M. (1973). *Social justice and the city.* Baltimore: Johns Hopkins University Press.

Harvey, D. M. (1977). Government policies, financial institutions, and neighborhood change in United States cities. In M. Harloe (Ed.), *Captive Cities* (pp. 123–140). New York: Wiley.

Harvey, D. M. (1982). *The limits to capital.* Oxford: Blackwell.

Harvey, D. M., & Chatterjee, L. (1974). Government and financial institutions and the structuring of urban space. *Antipode, 6,* 64–86.

Hawley, A. (1944). Ecology and human ecology. *Social Forces, 22,* 398–405.

Hawley, A. (1950). *Human ecology.* New York: Ronald Press.

Hawley, A. (1981). *Urban society.* New York: Ronald Press.

Hershberg, T., Burstein, A., Ericksen, E. P., Greenberg, S., & Yancey, W. L. (1979). A tale of three cities: Blacks and immigrants in Philadelphia: 1850–1880, 1930 and 1970. *Annals of American Academy of Political and Social Science, 441,* 55–81.

Hill, R. C. (1980). Race, class, and the state: The metropolitan enclave system in the United States. *The Insurgent Sociologist, 10,* 45–59.

Hoover, E. M., & Vernon, R. (1959). *Anatomy of a metropolis.* Cambridge: Harvard University Press.

Hoyt, H. (1939). *The structure and growth of residential neighborhoods in American cities.* Washington, DC: Federal Housing Administration.

Johnston, R. J. (1970). *Urban residential patterns.* London: Bell.

Kain, J. F. (1970). The distribution and movement of jobs and industry. In J. Q. Wilson (Ed.), *The metropolitan enigma* (pp. 1–43). New York: Anchor Books.

Leon, G. (1985). *Ghost towns, ghettoes and gold coasts: A sociological analysis of housing abandonment.* Unpublished doctoral dissertation, Temple University, Philadelphia, PA.

Lieberson, S. F. (1963). *Ethnic patterns in American cities.* New York: Free Press.

Lieberson, S. F. (1980). *A piece of the pie.* Berkeley: University of California Press.

Logan, J. R. (1976). Industrialization and stratification of cities in suburban regions. *American Journal of Sociology, 82,* 333–348.

Logan, J. R. (1978). Growth politics and the stratification of places. *American Journal of Sociology, 84,* 404–416.

Logan, J. R., & Schneider, M. (1981). The stratification of metropolitan suburbs, 1960–1970. *American Sociological Review, 46,* 175–186.

Logan, J. R., & Schneider, M. (1982). *Racial segregation and racial change in American suburbs.* Paper presented at the annual meeting of the American Sociological Association, San Francisco, CA.

Lowry, I. S. (1960). Filtering and housing standards. *Land Economics, 36,* 363–370.

McKenzie, R. F. (1921). The neighborhood: A study of local life in the city of Columbus. *American Journal of Sociology, 27,* 145–168.

Molotch, H. (1976). The city as a growth machine: Toward a political economy of place. *American Journal of Sociology, 82,* 309–332.

Molotch, H. (1979). Capital and neighborhood in the United States. *Urban Affairs Quarterly, 14,* 289–312.

Park, R. E. (1925). The city. In R. E. Park, E. W. Burgess, & R. D. McKenzie (Eds.), *The city* (pp. 1–46). Chicago: University of Chicago Press.

Park, R. E. (1936a). Human ecology. *American Journal of Sociology, 42,* 1–15.

Park, R. E. (1936b). Succession: An ecological concept. *American Sociological Review, 1,* 171–179.

Pearce, D. (1979). Gatekeepers and homeseekers: Institutional patterns in racial steering. *Social Problems, 26,* 325–342.

Pratt, E. E. (1911). *Industrial causes of congestion of population in New York City.* New York: Columbia University Press.

Sacks, S. (1977). *Trends in metropolitan America.* Washington, DC: Advisory Commission on Intergovernmental Relations.

Salins, P. D. (1980). *The ecology of housing destruction.* New York: New York University Press.

Saunders, P. (1981). *Social theory and the urban question.* New York: Holmes & Meier.

Schnore, L. F. (1956). The functions of metropolitan suburbs. *American Journal of Sociology, 61,* 453–458.

Schnore, L. F. (1963). The social and economic characteristics of American suburbs. *Sociological Quarterly, 4,* 122–134.

Scott, A. J. (1982). Locational patterns and dynamics of industrial activity in the modern metropolis. *Urban Studies, 19,* 111–142.

Shlay, A. B. (1985). *Where the money flows: Lending patterns in the Washington, DC-Maryland-Virginia SMSA.* Chicago: Woodstock Institute.

Shlay, A. B., & Rossi, P. H. (1981). Keeping up the neighborhood. *American Sociological Review, 46,* 703–719.

Stahura, J. M. (1979a). Suburban status evolution/persistence: A structural model. *American Sociological Review, 44,* 937–947.

Stahura, J. M. (1979b). Structural determinants of suburban socioeconomic compositions. *Sociology and Social Research, 6,* 328–345.

Taeuber, K. E., & Taeuber, A. F. (1965). *Negroes in cities: Residential segregation and neighborhood change.* Chicago: Aldine.

Taggart, H. T., & Smith, K. W. (1981). Redlining: An assessment of the evidence of disinvestment in metropolitan Boston. *Urban Affairs Quarterly, 17,* 91–107.

Thernstrom, S. (1973). *The other Bostonians.* Boston: Harvard University Press.

Tinkcom, M. B. (1982). Depression and war, 1929–1946. In R. F. Weigley (Ed.), *Philadelphia: A 300-year history* (pp. 601–648). New York: W. W. Norton.

Tomer, J. (1980). The mounting evidence on mortgage redlining. *Urban Affairs Quarterly, 15,* 488–501.

U.S. Bureau of the Census. (1981). *Standard metropolitan areas and standard consolidated areas* (supplementary report). Washington, DC: U.S. Government Printing Office.

Voss, J. E. (1941). *Ocean City: An ecological analysis of a satellite community.* Philadelphia: University of Pennsylvania Press.

Ward, D. (1968). The emergence of central immigrant ghettoes in American cities: 1840–1920. *Annals of the Association of American Geographers, 58,* 343–359.

Ward, D. (1969). The internal spatial structure of immigrant residential districts in the late nineteenth century. *Geographical Analysis, 1,* 337–353.

Ward, D. (1971). *Cities and immigrants: A geography of change in nineteenth century America.* New York: Oxford University Press.

Warner, S. B., Jr. (1962). *Streetcar suburbs: The process of growth in Boston.* Cambridge: Harvard University Press.

Warner, S. B., Jr. (1968). *The private city.* Philadelphia: University of Pennsylvania Press.

Yancey, W. L., & Ericksen, E. P. (1979). The antecedents of community: The economic and institutional structure of urban neighborhoods. *American Sociological Review, 44,* 253–262.

Yancey, W. L., Ericksen, E. P., & Juliani, R. N. (1976). Emergent ethnicity: A review and reformulation. *American Sociological Review, 41,* 391–403.

6

The Symbolic Ecology of Suburbia

ALBERT HUNTER

INTRODUCTION

Where we live is a statement of who we are. In the exploding modern metropolis fewer and fewer people live in central cities, but people continue to live and find meaning for their lives in local communities. As metropolitan areas continue to grow in size and numbers, the communities people increasingly come to live in lie beyond the bounds of the central city in the fissionable fragments of countless surrounding suburban communities. For the most part, these suburban communities are far removed from the small towns and villages, the pastoral settings of a bygone era depicted in nostalgic Norman Rockwell paintings. The shopping mall has replaced Main Street, the regional high school the two-room schoolhouse, and the suburban split-level the frame farmhouse. The melding of urban and rural, for better or worse, that was attempted in the idealized utopian setting of suburbia has generated a long list of both apologists and critics. Only within the past few decades, however, has the more neutral eye of the analytical social scientist begun to elicit the crystallized pattern of social and spatial order and the patterns of change apparent in this metropolitan puzzle. No longer is it sufficient to

ALBERT HUNTER • Department of Sociology, Northwestern University, Evanston, IL 60201.

denigrate the conformity and complacency of suburbanites who fled the teeming freedom and anonymity of the cultured city left behind nor to wax bucolic about the spacious greenlands of innocent euphoric child-hood on the city's rim to which people migrated. Rather, the questions have more prosaically come to center upon the realities of how it is people go about the routine business of constructing their everyday lives—of getting a living, making a home, raising a family, and finding meaning to lives lived on the fringe of the modern metropolis.

In the following analysis, we will recast some of these enduring questions about suburbia by drawing on recent sociological research over the past few decades. In doing so, we will introduce a somewhat new way of combining or synthesizing previous research and theories into a new perspective that I call "symbolic ecology." It is a perspective that simultaneously combines four dimensions—the physical and the social and the collective and the individual. We will begin first with the early considerations of classical human ecology focused on the physical and spatial order and structure of cities and suburbs and then consider its evolution into social ecology that includes the major dimensions of social stratification by which groups of people and institutions sort themselves by choice and constraint among the myriad varieties of com-munities within the metropolis. We will then more explicitly address collective and individual questions of identity, captured in the idea of "symbolic communities" (Hunter, 1974), by looking at collective (cultur-al) and individual (psychological) processes by which people attempt to construct meaningful communities as settings for their lives. In doing this, we will look briefly at two related though distinct pieces of research that I have conducted recently with students in the suburban ring of Chicago. The selection of Chicago is not a mere happenstance, a proxi-mate research site, for it is significant as the generic home of urban studies (Hunter, 1979), and the Chicago School was the fountainhead of the two divergent theoretical prespectives of human ecology and sym-bolic interation that I am attempting to synthesize into the single stream of "symbolic ecology."

FROM SPATIAL TO SOCIAL TO SYMBOLIC ECOLOGY

Classical Human Ecology

Suburbs are nothing new. Even in the nineteenth century Adna Weber (1899) was documenting the emergence of outlying communities around the cities of the eastern seaboard of the United States that had appeared as a new unmistakable urban phenomenon. Later, urban historians such as Sam Bass Warner (1962) traced the emergence of these suburban communities to the early extension of rail lines and the creation of the first streetcar suburbs. These early manifestations of suburbia contained a dual component, one that is still present today—the construction of new communities beyond the city's political legal boundaries and the incorporation of preexisting, relatively autonomous communities into the metropolitan fabric of the expanding urban core. In short, metropolitan communities "grow" both by construction of new communities and by incorporation of older ones. As well, the growing population that inhabits these communities of the suburban ring arrive in two basic streams, those moving outward from the central city into the suburbs and those coming to the metropolitan area from other areas (this is not to discount a large internal migration of residents from one suburban community to another, though these do not constitute net population gains).

The classical models of urban spatial structure and change, Burgess's (1925) "concentric zones," Hoyt's (1939) pie-shaped "sectors," and Harris and Ullman's (1945) "multiple nucleii" all captured the rise of suburbs as a function of urban growth and concommitant changes in land values and relative locational advantage. Each of the three spatial models has its underlying rationale that are, respectively, "central place theory," "radial lines of transport," and "strategic location by dominant institutions." Based as they were upon classical human ecology, these theories viewed different populations and institutions as actors within a metropolitan "web of life" competing for scarce resources from the environment, chief among them being the competition for relative locational advantage. The sifting and sorting of populations and institutions would result in a dynamic equilibrium, meaning the physical map of the city might undergo changes, but the ecological processes that generated them would be relatively stable. Dramatic shifts or changes in these processes could be introduced by a number of external factors, primarily shifts in modes of transportation and communication. For example, the earlier shift from pedestrian to rail transport and the later shift from fixed rail to internal combustion engines and auto and truck transport dramatically altered the physical map of metropolitan areas. Perhaps the most famous of these ecological processes of community change was the cycle of "invasion, competition, and succession" developed by Burgess. As the city grew, competition for location at the city center would force populations and institutions located in inner rings to expand into adjacent outer rings, and the resulting competition for land and location would result in local neighborhood change (succession), a process that would be repeated in a wavelike pattern outward across the concentric rings. Hoyt's processes were similar, and to these Harris and Ullman added factors of "attraction and repulsion" as residential populations sought to locate either near benign institutions (universities) or far from noxious ones (stockyards and steel mills). Because human ecology viewed itself as a nonnormative, asocial, underlying substructure, the arbitrary divisions of the resulting metropolitan area into central city and distinct suburbs was seen as but a derivative and arbitrary political overlay on the underlying reality of a single metropolitan ecological community.

The view that city and suburb were intimately linked into a single reality was advanced in the early work of the economist N. S. B. Gras (1922) who developed the concept of a "metropolitan economy," an idea later elaborated in the work of Donald Bogue (1949) as the "metropolitan ecological community." Bogue's work was particularly noteworthy for introducing the idea of a "metropolitan dominance hierarchy." In his research, Bogue described a structure to the metropolitan community wherein a *dominant* central city was surrounded by a series of large but *subdominant* satellite cities, which were in turn surrounded by a larger number of *subinfluent* smaller residential communities and rural areas. Interdependencies among the distinct or separate communities in the "horizontal" spatial structure was clearly evidenced in their "vertical" integration into a power or dominance hierarchy. This idea was later expanded upon by Roland Warren (1973) who emphasized that local communities were inevitably and to varying degrees penetrated by institutions from the larger society (be they business concerns, voluntary associations such as churches or even governments) and that this constituted the "vertical dimension" of community.

The ecological picture of suburbia, then, was one in which suburbs constituted simply the latest addition of local communities to the expanding urban core, now writ large as a metropolitan area. Each local community (suburbs included) was seen to occupy a distinct "functional niche" in the complex "web of life" of the metropolis. The basic processes of ecological interaction, namely competition for strategic location and symbiotic interdependencies among different niches, would result in different local communities occupying relatively stable positions within the metropolitan dominance hierarchy. Suburbs, in particular, were seen to be a residential niche for the location of middle-class populations of families that had spilled over the boundary line of the expanding central city and had come to occupy newer, expensive single-family homes on the city's rim. The resulting stereotype, therefore, was of white, middle-class suburban families living in their single-family homes on large lots with plenty of room for the kids to play in the yard, and with the squalor, density, noise, and dirt of the city left far behind. From the purely ecological perspective, therefore, one could easily conclude that suburbs represented nothing new; they were simply the newest form assumed by the continuing play of these "natural" ecological forces of urban expansion.

THE SOCIAL ECOLOGY OF SUBURBIA

Several historical factors joined at the end of World War II to cause a reevaluation of this seemingly simple picture of suburbia, and this reassessment came from new research that was itself generated by the explosive growth of suburbs in metropolitan areas throughout the nation during this period. The overarching demographic factors included the pent-up demand for new housing at the end of the war and the entry of "baby boom families" into the housing market. Much of the earlier ecological research on urban expansion tended to support one of the central tenets of this theory, namely that the suburbs were populated by middle-class, white families in search of single-family homes and the space and amenities in which to raise children. As Taeuber and Taeuber (1965) remind us, the search for new and better housing has always been led by those who could best afford it (the middle class), and Rossi's (1955) answer to the question of why families move emphasized the desire of families to match their stage in the life cycle and shifting family size to housing needs. Given the baby boom families of the 1950s, the growth of residential suburbs was simply seen to be a response to this growing demand. However, a number of studies began to emerge out of this research that refined and revised this seemingly simple picture. These new studies pointed to important social variations in the composition and growth of these new suburban communities. This new line of research, which has continued to the present, emphasizes the important role of social structure in affecting the composition and dynamics of suburban communities (Popenoe, 1977). Hence, I have labeled research from this perspective, *social ecology*. Social structure is seen as important in two interrelated ways: first, in terms of the variation in social class composition of suburban residents, and second, in the role of political and economic institutions in affecting the distribution of people and jobs in different suburban communities.

Two of the more important early studies of suburban communities that spoke to social class variation were Herbert Gans's (1967) study, *The Levittowners,* and Bennett Berger's (1960) *Working Class Suburb.* Gans's research described the emergence of community among the upper working-class and lower middle-class residents moving into the newly built suburban development of Levittown. For some of the older residents, their new suburban home constituted the fulfillment of a lifelong dream; it was their point of arrival, their final resting place. But, for younger couples with young kids it was the point of departure, a springboard. Therefore, though housing prices defined a limited range of income, social class variation existed as it related to variation in stage of the life cycle. A more significant statement of suburban class heterogeneity was Berger's study of a working-class community that emerged around a newly located industrial plant within a suburb in California. As did Gans, Berger emphasized the degree to which working-class norms and behaviors persisted in this suburban setting, calling into question the stereotype of homogeneous life-styles in middle-class suburban communities. Both researchers made the strategic point that suburbia did not, in and of itself, constitute a new life-style. Rather, the social class and family composition of residents were more likely to determine the nature and quality of life, the definition of who people are, and how they live than was a magical move across a municipal boundary from city to suburb.

Berger's book was also significant for first noting one of the major shifts that would increasingly come to characterize suburbia to the present day—the movement of jobs and industry out of central cities into the suburbs. As the economist John Kain (1968) would later point out, industry and jobs were moving to the suburbs as early as, and at a rate comparable to, the movement of people into the suburbs. This shift in the location of jobs within the metropolitan area clearly began to challenge the older ecological theory that suburbs merely represented the spillover of urban residential populations beyond the city's rim. Something much more dramatic was restructuring the ecological makeup of metropolitan areas. Though economists, geographers, and ecologists would still point to the technological changes in transportation (expressways and truck versus rail) and the nature of industry itself (assembly line processes) and to the shifting demand for less expensive but more expansive land located in the suburbs, an additional component had to be added to these—the competitive politics of economic location. It was clear that decision making by major economic and political institutions, the political economy of suburbia, had to be taken into account in any attempt to explain the emerging structure of suburban communities.

The most extensive work on this emerging political economy of suburbia is to be found in the work of the sociologist John Logan (1978, 1981). Logan has described a complex picture of different types of suburbs, some of which are growing (newer, high-tech, and commercial-office centers), some of which are declining (many of the older industrial suburbs), and some of which are maintaining a steady-state residential character (older, relatively high-status residential suburbs). The new multinucleated metropolitan structure of satellite suburbs now means that suburbs as a whole have surpassed central cities in overall population, and as well, as centers of employment. This was dramatically illustrated by the 1970 census that showed for the first time that most commuting trips from home to work occurred within the suburban ring, not between suburb and central city. Suburbs are now beginning to reflect almost as much variation in their family, social class, and racial composition as did the urban neighborhoods of an earlier era. However, as Logan strongly argues, this variation and increasing inequality from suburb to suburb is not simply the workings of "natural ecological forces" nor the "invisible hand" of the market, but rather, a conscious and calculating set of strategic decisions made by local suburban governments and corporations with respect to tax incentives, zoning revisions, and other public services. These processes reflect at the metropolitan scale the same forces that are at work in interregional competition within the nation as a whole, such as the rise of the Sun Belt and the decline of the Frost Belt and even internationally as multinational corporations and nation-states compete within the world economy (Portes & Walton, 1981).

The much more complex picture of suburbia that begins to emerge is one in which suburban communities not only differ in their ecological position, social-class composition, and rate of growth or decline, but perhaps more importantly they begin to develop specific reputations, have distinct "images," that further feed into these competitive processes. The mystique of "Silicon Valley," for example, may be as significant for its competitive advantage in attracting new jobs and industries as is any cost/benefit market analysis of efficient location. Such localized centers of single industries, to be sure, benefit from economies of scale and the spawning and multiplication of new, similar organizations within a given industry (Wiewel & Hunter, 1986). Furthermore, given the relatively small size of many of these new firms and the fluidity and geographical mobility of both capital and the professional–technical workforce associated with them means such centers will develop national "images" acting as magnets in attracting still additional resources and personnel. These new growth industries are of course related to the dramatic shift in the industrial structure of American society as a whole from smokestack to high tech. The new industries are often closely associated with and identified with centralized growth areas—for in addition to Silicon Valley, one may point to the "Research Triangle" in North Carolina and the "corridor" around Boston. There are already indications that the high growth in these areas is being counterproductive. In Silicon Valley, for example, the demand for land and housing has raised prices beyond the levels that many would-be new firms and residents can readily afford. In addition, the expected gains in tax revenues and high-level employment are not necessarily matching the initial economic forecasts. Many of the jobs require low-skill assembly work, and governments have often given up their tax advantages in special dispensations in the attempt to lure firms to their locale to begin with (Walton, 1982).

The processes by which suburban communities develop such reputations, images, or collective identities cannot be explained solely by these political and economic considerations. It requires additional concepts and propositions that focus on the symbolic construction of community identities, concepts, and propositions that lie waiting to be tapped in the theory of symbolic interaction. By merging these with economic and political propositions, we may emerge with a new theoretical understanding of the symbolic ecology of suburbia.

Symbolic Ecology

In his seminal work, "Sentiment and Symbolism as Ecological Variables," Walter Firey (1945) advanced one of the early and more powerful critiques of the more purely ecological approach of the Chicago School of urban sociologists. By its very title, this work clearly expressed the types of variables and the perspective needed to develop a symbolic ecology of urban communities. Though it was a pathbreaking work, until recently it remained a direction of research that few followed. Firey convincingly argued that "natural ecological forces" could not lead to a satisfactory understanding of urban form unless the "meanings" of urban spaces to residents were incorporated into the analysis. In his most critical example, The Boston Commons, he noted that according to ecological theories of location, it simply should not be there. How could this most "valuable" piece of real estate in central Boston be allowed, in effect, to lie fallow? His answer, of course, was that the historical symbolism and the sentiment attached to this piece of land by Bostonians hallowed it beyond the secular competition for strategic economic location. Firey's work, however, did not lead to a fuller exposition of this pespective. For decades, it was simply treated as a final statement punctuated by a large exclamation mark, not a question mark.

From disciplines other than sociology, similar analyses of urban structure were beginning to converge on the same set of problems. The urban planner Kevin Lynch, in a small but significant book, *The Image of the City* (1960), attempted to categorize the physical form of the city as it is perceived and understood by people as they move about and use it. His categories of urban "edges," "paths," "nodes," and "areas" attempted to link these variable perceptions to the variable activities of people as they journeyed through urban space. In a later work, *What Time is This Place?* (1972), he extends his analysis to an interrelated "space-time" continuum of meanings by which people utilize and understand their physical environment. Urban geographers also began to explore the "cognitive maps" that people construct of their urban environments, noting "distortions" and "selectivity" that led these "mental maps" to depart from two-dimensional Cartesian coordinates. And psychologists, such as Proshansky and his colleagues (1983), initially operating from an interest in "perception," began to explore the ways in which people variably perceived and reacted to their physical environment. As these studies moved out of the laboratory into "field settings," the new area of "environmental psychology" emerged.

As significant as the previously mentioned perspectives were in either challenging older theories or elaborating new ones, they did not directly address the larger social processes by which such symbolic meanings of the urban environment were developed, nor did they directly relate the processes they were uncovering in their research to the earlier ecological theories of urban land use and the dynamics of urban communities. A perspective for doing so, however, was readily at hand and ironically had been from the beginning of the development of the Chicago School's ecological perspective because it came from the same city, the same institution, and the same department—the theory of symbolic interaction developed by George Herbert Mead (1934). Though Mead's corpus of work is slight, the breadth of his interests were not. For the purposes at hand we will focus on one component of that work—the process of identity formation as an outcome of symbolic interaction.

We may begin from Mead's distinction between an "I" and a "me"; the former is a preexisting physical organism, the latter a sense of self as an object, a self-conception. The emergence of the "me" was seen to grow out of or be constructed through interaction with others and the reading of others' reactions to the self as an object. Through an empathetic "taking the role of the other," one could perceive the self as other's perceived one, and those perceptions would lead to the emergence of the self as a clearly identified object. This was of course parallel to Cooley's (1920) earlier idea of "the looking glass self." This process was not simply one of cognitive labeling for it included as well evaluations of the behaviors of the self in interaction. Both self-awareness and self-assessment were the products of social interaction. This social-psychological process of identity formation was itself possible because of the shared meanings that people could place on one another's behaviors, primarily, but not restricted to, interaction through the shared symbol system of language. Coupled with John Dewey's pragmatism, Meads's teleology centers upon the seemingly mundane purpose of collective action and the symbolic communication necessary to accomplish collective ends. Both the self and society were constructed and continuously reconstructed in the very act of interaction itself.

A direct extension of Mead's theory is found in the landmark work of Berger and Luckman (1966), *The Social Construction of Reality*. Not simply selves but all of reality, they suggest, is socially constructed through symbolic interaction. And lest this seem an infinite regress, they, too, provide a pragmatic but not unproblematic solution to exiting this spiral, the degree to which the conception of reality is sufficient for the accomplishment of collective goals in the "real" world so constructed. Epistemologically, this perspective does not discount nor eschew the central scientific assumption of "physicalism." A real objective world is posited as unproblematic; what is problematic is how that real world becomes defined.

The "social construction" perspective has been more recently applied to the sociology of community. Two examples are Gerald Suttles's (1972) *The Social Construction of Community* and Hunter's (1974) *Symbolic Communities*. In these two works, a direct merger of symbolic interaction and human ecology is accomplished not only at the theoretical level but at the empirical level in accounting for specific processes of community identification, organization, and change. Specifically, the ecological conception of community, which sees distinct communities as differentiated niches operating within an ecological web of interdependency, is paralleled by seeing community identities as arising from these same interactions at the conscious level of symbolic communication as community residents interact with individuals and agencies outside of the local community. Strong issue is taken with those who romantically overemphasize communities as grass-roots entities arising internally or spontaneously from the members of the community themselves. To be sure, the content of a community's identity will depend to some degree upon the local history and culture and the social composition of the community in that this is the reality from which will be molded or constructed the community's "identity" (Rivlin, 1982; Taylor, Gottfredson, & Brower, 1984). However, the process of socially constructing a local community's identity is seen to emerge most critically from the interactions that members of a local territory have with outsiders who serve to define the community. This is because local communities and neighborhoods are enmeshed in larger social structures that critically control their fate. This interactive "definition of the situation" includes the cognitive labeling (names) and bounding of the community (territorial boundaries), and as well, the connotations and evaluations of the community relative to other communities. Some communities may be experiencing threat or challenge from the outer world, the "defended community," whereas others may form alliances with adjacent communities to deal with some still-larger external adversary, "hierarchical communities."

These symbolic labels, boundaries, and evaluations of communities are seen on the one hand to be based in part upon the ecological realities of the local communities. That is, the population composition and the nature of the relationships that members of the community have with specific other external agencies and actors are ecological realities of the community that are taken into account in the symbolic construction of local identities. In short, the population composition and the patterns of these interactions are often ecologically shaped or determined. However, these symbolic constructions may also impact upon the ecological composition and interactions that a local community has with the external world. For example, the current process of "gentrification" of selected older, often rundown, urban neighborhoods may be considered a process that is in part determined by the ecological composition of these communities. But also, the symbolic label placed upon these neighborhoods may in turn affect the future ecological composition of the community (Laska & Spain, 1980). These neighborhoods of older, aesthetically pleasing but cheap housing are attractive to young professionals who are either unmarried or childless and therefore seemingly oblivious to the current general condition of the neighborhood. However, once an initial investment is made by these "urban pioneers," they attempt to increase the value of their investment by "advertising" their neighborhood, to use Erving Goffman's (1967) phrase, as the "in" place "where the action is." In short, they wish to change the connotation of the neighborhood in the hope of attracting more middle-class residents. They are, in one sense, acting as rational economic actors attempting to "buy low and sell high"; but as Simpson (1981) points out in his analysis of New York's SoHo community, ironically these early residents often end up pricing themselves and others like them out of the housing market in their own neighborhood. This is a classic case of ecological succession; however, it is an ecological succession that is critically dependent upon the symbolic interaction that goes on with external others in constructing or reconstructing a new community identity.

More recently this combining of the ecological and symbolic perspectives has been extended in the work of Richard Taub and his associates (1977) and by Jeffrey Davidson (1979) to include the bureaucratic and political construction of local communities by external agencies. Specifically, these authors argued that external agencies often have an interest in seeing that a local community becomes clearly defined as a well-organized and powerful political entity. Politicians, for example, who wish to increase their power by pointing to a strong local community power base, and foundations or granting agencies who wish to see their specific programs successfully implemented within local communities are two examples of actors interested in the political construction of community. To be sure, these political constructions are also dependent upon the ecological composition of existing residents, but again, the political construction of a "powerful" local community may operate in such a way as to alter ecological processes that may be affecting the community. One may view attempts to thwart racial succession in certain neighborhoods as an example of this as well as the numerous examples of local community opposition to the building of new expressways and urban renewal. A synthetic circularity exists in that external ecological changes may bring about a heightened symbolic sense of local community identity that, in turn, activates political mobilization to alter the initial ecological processes.

The preceding studies and examples of a merger of symbolic interaction theory with classical human ecology to produce a new synthetic theory of symbolic ecology have implications beyond the collective level itself and may forcefully come to impact upon individual identities as well. Recent programs in community crime prevention and community mental health stress, for example, the psychological benefits for local community residents ranging from increased feelings of personal safety to political empowerment that may counter pervasive feelings of fatalism, insecurity, and alienation (Hunter & Riger, 1986). To the degree that "community" is a renewed focus of attention for dealing with a variety of psychological and social problems, to that degree a more fully integrated theory of community such as that contained within a synthetic theory of symbolic ecology may prove especially important and useful.

RESEARCH EXAMPLES

The recognition that communities themselves may be the objects of analysis has unfortunately been more systematically explored in the ecological than the symbolic realm in social science research. Therefore, in this section I will present preliminary results from recent research that I have been conducting with a number of graduate students on the relationship between the ecological and symbolic realms, research that explicitly exemplifies the synthetic theory of symbolic ecology applied to suburbia. Where better to explore this theoretical synthesis than in the city that produced the two antipoles of the synthesis, the Chicago School of Sociology that birthed both the human ecology and symbolic interaction research traditions. These studies are, in part, a natural extension of my and others' prior work on local urban communities, but by casting the net more broadly to encompass the entire metropolitan area, a number of new and intriguing issues have had to be confronted. Specifically, I will first address the issue of the comparative processes by which a select group of elite residents of suburban communities perceive their communities in relationship to and with their larger surrounding metropolitan environment; and second, I will explore the underlying processes of fission and fusion that are taking place in suburban regions beyond, but not independent of, the central city of Chicago itself.

THE COMPARATIVE PROCESS

I have argued that the social construction of community identities is a social process that takes place in an inter- not simply intracommunity context. The interactions that exist between the residents of a local community and actors and agents external to the community are as significant processes to the formation of collective identities as individual social relationships are to the development of individual identities. This process itself may be considered a more specific case of "the social construction of reality," and as such, there are two central components to it: first, some reading of a posited reality ("reality testing") that assesses attributes and characteristics of the entity itself, and second, a comparative assessment arising through interaction that fixes the identity in relationship to and with other units. It is the latter process that "places" or identifies a collective unit in its social "position" within a broader social structure. The first of these might be thought of simply as some "objective" reading of the situation, whereas the second is a more comparative "subjective" reading of it.

To explore some of these questions, I became interested in how elites in suburban communities defined their community in relationship to and in comparison with their larger ecological context. For other theoretical reasons, I was interested in restricting the analysis specifically to elites as those most likely to be able to affect the social, political, and economic situation of their communities through their actions. Four suburban communities in the Chicago metropolitan area were strategically selected through "dimensional sampling" (Arnold, 1970) to represent two distinct ecological dimensions of communities: (a) their position within the metropolitan hierarchy as either larger satellite suburbs having a substantial employing economic base versus smaller dormitory suburbs with a primarily residential function; and (b) the socioeconomic status of the suburbs ranging from a wealthy elite through middle class to working class to a poor suburban community (see Figure 1). The first comparison therefore is between two satellite communities (Evanston and Chicago Heights) versus two dormitory suburbs (Glencoe and East Chicago Heights). Taking the same four communities, the other comparison is between the two communities of higher socioeconomic status

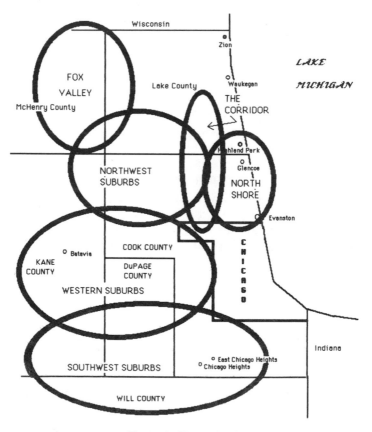

Figure 1. Chicagoland.

(Glencoe and Evanston) versus the two of lower socioeconomic status (Chicago Heights and East Chicago Heights). The positioning of these communities into this two-dimensional space relied upon "objective" ecological census variables such as population size, the labor force ratio of jobs located in the community divided by working adults living in the community, and the income, occupations, education, and housing values of residents of the communities. In short, using these census variables the communities could be fixed in relatively "objective" ecological positions within the Chicago metropolitan area.

A sample of "elites" in each community answered a series of questions about how they viewed their community in relation to its surrounding environment. These questions were both comparative and relational. The first comparative questions asked elites how they would rank their respective suburban communities compared to all other Chicago suburbs. By and large, the elites' subjective readings of their suburbs correspond closely with the objective ecological reality. For example, the respondents in Glencoe unanimously ranked their suburban community higher than all other Chicago suburbs, whereas none of the respondents of the extremely poor suburb of East Chicago Heights ranked their community higher than all other suburbs taken as whole. Likewise, most respondents of middle-class Evanston ranked their suburb higher, whereas less than 10% of elites in Chicago Heights ranked their community higher than other suburbs. Those interviewed were usually forthright in their comparative assessment. The following are typical:

> Glencoe: "This community is a very high income community . . . and it's more a bedroom community than most."
>
> Evanston: "Evanston is a larger and more diverse—half urban, half suburban—type of community. It's a mix."
>
> Chicago Heights: "[It's] an older industrial community. It has provided a good labor market of unskilled, skilled, and middle-class white-collar workers—a mix of population types."
>
> East Chicago Heights: "It's a very poor kind of community."

Recognizing from an interactional perspective that the comparative rankings of a local community might vary depending upon the "points of comparison" or the "reference points," we asked our elites two additional questions: How they would rank their respective communities in comparison to immediately adjacent communities, and to the city of Chicago itself. Differences appear here that reflect these situationally variable comparative assessments. For example, less than a third of respondents from the elite suburb of Glencoe (30%) ranked their community higher than surrounding communities, far less than Evanston's respondents (50%) and even less than the working-class community of Chicago Heights (35%). Glencoe's respondents were in this case comparing themselves to the surrounding elite communities of Chicago's North Shore (Highland Park, Winnetka, Kenilworth, and Wilmette), and as one respondent said, "In any other area we'd be one community instead of five." By contrast, Evanston's respondents were more likely comparing themselves to Skokie, a more middle-class suburb community to its west and to the city of Chicago that lies on its southern border. In short, Evanston, the only suburb of our four immediately adjacent to Chicago, is more likely to be torn betwen the urban and suburban comparison. As one respondent (R) noted in drawing a distinction between North Evanston (closer to the elite suburbs of the North Shore) and South Evanston (closer to the city of Chicago):

> R: I've lived in Southeast Evanston, where most of the people work in Chicago, use Chicago, and tend to identify with Chicago.
> AH: Does this differ in other parts of Evanston?
> R: I think so, yes. Certainly from attitudes with friends who live in Northeast Evanston or Northwest Evanston. . . . I don't think you quite have the urbanity that you have in Southeast Evanston.

It is not surprising therefore, to find that Evanston's elites unanimously ranked their suburb above the city of Chicago as a point of comparison. This unanimity was not shared, surprisingly by one respondent from Glencoe, who ranked that community lower than Chicago, perhaps in comparison to Chicago's elite neighborhood along the Gold Coast. The fact that Chicago is a large and diverse reference point means that different parts of it may be singled out for comparison. This is especially noted by respondents from the very poor, black suburb of East Chicago Heights where 18% of them ranked it higher than the city. Here, however, the point of comparison is likely to be not Chicago's Gold Coast but its large South Side black ghetto. As one respondent said:

> Many of the people that are coming into the community are coming from a hard-core area—the South Side. They are the pople coming from the areas where you have the high crime. So actually, a lot of the parents want to get out of there.

The predominantly working-class community of Chicago Heights, not surprisingly, lies intermediate in its relative perceived rankings to adjacent suburbs (remembering that one of them is the neighboring, poor community of East Chicago Heights), and the modal response of residents sees it ranking the same as the city of Chicago as a whole (43%).

Beyond mere comparative rankings, the interactional perspective of community identity formation suggests that relationships between a community and its environment often delve into the question of local community autonomy (Hunter, 1984). Most dramatically framed in various mass society theories, this issue has been posited as a question of the eclipse of community (Stein, 1960) or the loss of local community control (Altschuler, 1970). Vidich and Bensman's (1958) landmark empirical study of the loss of autonomous action by residents of a small upstate New York town confronted with the forces of mass society perhaps most poignantly captured this thesis.

To explore this issue of local community autonomy versus dependency, respondents from each of the four suburbs were asked questions about the degree to which they saw their suburban community being relatively dependent upon or autonomous from its ecological context. The questions were posed in three substantive or institutional areas— socially, economically, and politically; and in regard to three contexts— surrounding suburbs, the city of Chicago, and the larger national context. We found systematic differences in the expression of autonomy/dependency depending upon both the social-class composition and the metropoitan ecological position of these communities as either dormitories or satellite suburbs.

First, with respect to the institutional sphere of autonomy/dependency, we found that the most dependency (or the least autonomy) was expressed with respect to economic issues, second with respect to social issues, and least with respect to political issues. In short, it appears that elites in these four suburbs clearly recognize an economic dependency upon the larger society but, by contrast, believe that local politics is primarily "parochial politics" and is relatively autonomous from or less dependent upon the larger external environment. When we asked a more specific question about the level of governmental dependency, tapping the important issue of fiscal autonomy/dependency of these suburbs, we found a direct correlation with social class of the community with the highest social-class suburb expressing the least governmental dependency (11%), whereas the poorest expressed the most dependency (57%). However, when we reversed the question by asking the degree to which the elites felt they could influence governmental decisions made at higher levels of government (county, state, and federal), we found that elites from the two larger satellite suburbs expressed the most political efficacy (56% and 53%), whereas elites from the two smaller dormitory suburbs expressed less political efficacy (41% and 34%). We suggest this political efficacy is a direct function of electoral politics and political strength connected with the size, not the social-class composition, of the suburbs.

Second, with respect to level of dependency, we found systematic differences depending upon the social class of the suburbs. The two middle-class communities expressed more dependency upon the city of Chicago, followed by surrounding suburbs, and the least dependency upon the national scene. Just the opposite was true of respondents from the two working-class suburbs who expressed most dependency upon the national scene, followed by surrounding suburbs, with least dependency upon the city of Chicago. We suggest that in the former case, this reflects the dominance of a residential, commuting population in the two middle-class suburbs and a more locally oriented industrial work force in the two working-class communities. These results are supported by an additional question that asked elites to rank the importance of different local interests in the life of their respective communities. Respondents from the two middle-class communities said local residential interests dominated over commercial and indurstrial interests, whereas in the working-class communities, industrial interests were as important if not more important than the concerns of local residents.

In short, the issue of autonomy/dependency of suburban communities in relationships with their larger environment is clearly perceived to vary in systematic ways and is not a simple linear or uniform phenomenon. Rather, it depends upon the specific institutional sphere and upon the relative social-class composition and ecological position or "niche" as satellite or dormitory that the suburb occupies within the overall metropolitan structure. The symbolic, collective identities of these suburbs is clearly dependent upon how they are viewed in relationships with their external environment. Both social-class composition and ecological position of the suburbs affect the nature of these comparative relationships and serve to define their symbolic space.

Symbolic Fission and Fusion

The interactive, comparative process of identity formation suggests, as with individual identities, that they are fluid rather than fixed. Over time, new contents and connotations will be constructed and reconstructed in an ongoing process. An important characteristic of collective identities, however, is that new collective wholes can be constructed, social boundaries can be redrawn, now contracting, now expanding, now exclusive, now inclusive. New wholes may form from previously separate units, and new social units may form from the fragmentation of previously larger wholes. One may apply this fission and fusion in the social construction of collective identities to a wide variety of social units ranging from small groups to families to social classes and racial and ethnic groupings. When translated onto the territorial landscape of symbolic communities, these processes of fission and fusion often result in the emergence of new territorial communities, communities with initially vague names and boundaries that may become crystallized over time into more formal social, economic, and political or governmental structures.

For a good half-century, social analysts have recognized the emergence of metropolitan areas as singular interdependent economic and ecological units. However, the suburban political fragmentation that has accompanied this metropolitan ecological integration has been decried for almost as long. For example, the political scientist, Charles Merriam and colleagues, as early as 1933 called for the creation of an independent Chicago metropolitan "statehood," and Robert Wood (1964) devoted an entire analysis to the more than 1,400 governments that carve up the New York metropolitan area. In more recent decades, this discrepancy between ecological and political realities often took the form of establishing metropolitan governments of various sorts, ranging from comprehensive governmental reorganization on a metropolitan scale as with Metro Toronto, Indianapolis, Indiana, and Miami/Dade County, Florida. It has also included a variety of "special districts" that have been created on a metropolitan scale, districts that are taxing bodies providing singular services or functions, the most common being regional transportation authorities. As partial, halting, and sporadic as this political integration has been, few if any analysts have explored the question of the degree to which symbolic and cultural integration at the metropolitan level is occurring as well.

As suburban rings surrounding central cities continue to expand and begin to equal if not surpass their central cities in area, population, and economic activity, and as nascent forms of governmental integration emerge, an increasing awareness has developed of the need to symbolically define the entire area by a name that incorporates the collective identity of the metropolitan area as a whole. At the same time that this larger process of symbolic fusion of the metropolitan area as a whole is occurring, one is finding a combined fusion and fissioning of clusters of suburbs into distinct submetropolitan suburban regions. I will briefly describe the results of some current research in the Chicago metropolitan area that address these issues of symbolic fusion and fission and then offer an explanation that sees parallels between this process and the process described by analyses of the problem of state building in new nations. In the words of Clifford Geertz (1963), it is the problem of constructing new governments or states on top of preexisting relatively autonomous communities, or as he titled his collection of essays, *Old Societies and New States*. By equating government to state and community to nation, the parallel problem is primarily one of generating symbolic identifications of and with new larger collective wholes that transcend smaller more parochial, "primordial solidarities."

I first became intrigued by this problem when I took the time to notice a "word" that I had heard for a good decade or more and that has found increasing currency within the Chicago metropolitan area, namely *Chicagoland*. This is not a Disney-type amusement park, but rather an expression that one hears and sees increasingly in the media to refer to the entire Chicago metropolitan area. For example, the second section of the *Chicago Tribune* that deals with local matters carries on its masthead "Chicagoland" (the first section being focused on more national and international news). I then began to think about similar "labels" that exist in other metropolitan areas throughout the country, such as Bay Area (San Francisco/Oakland) and "Capitalland" (Albany, NY); the latter was contained in a newspaper clipping recently sent to me by a colleague.

This attempt at symbolic unity is but the latest phase and a new order of integration that lags behind both the earlier economic and ecological integration that prompted subsequent and varied attempts at political integration. These symbolic labels for metropolitan areas represent a classic case of William Ogburn's (1957) "cultural lag," the idea that cultural realities adjust and adapt to preceding ecological, technological, and structural changes in society. Furthermore, it is noteworthy that the time ordering of these levels of integration is paralleled in the processes described for state building in new nations. For example, the first attempts at political integration on a metropolitan scale usually fall into the technological and ecological realm, such as special districts for transportation, water, sanitation, and related environmental concerns. In short, these are the basic ecological and technological underpinnings of an existing metropolitan economy (the need to move workers to jobs and the need to deal with ecological components of consumption and production). However, as Geertz noted in the case of new nations, the cultural realm is the last to fall to these larger scale forces of fusion, for at the cultural realm central value differences are maintained in more parochial and primordial solidarities. This is perhaps most clearly seen in the realm of education where parents' concerns over the socialization of their children brings out the most heightened passions for maintaining the most parochial institutional levels of social organization. The resistance to court-ordered busing, especially across municipal boundaries, led to the whole-scale retreat from this policy, and it is being paralleled today in the resistance to school consolidation by many suburban municipalities.

However, at the same time that this metropolitan label is emerging in an attempt to recapture the symbolic unity of expanding metropolitan areas, one also finds an increasing fission and fusion occurring among differentiated suburban subregions within the metropolitan area. A long-standing fused identity has existed for decades among elite suburbs in many metropolitan areas, for example, the North Shore in Chicago, Marin County in San Francisco, and the Main Line in Philadelphia. However, this early fusion of smaller suburbs located at the apex of the stratification pyramid of suburban communities is now being more broadly generalized as suburban subregions surrounding central cities become more differentiated on a scale larger than the parochial municipal boundaries of a single preexisting smaller suburb. It is simultaneously a process of fusion and fission, fusion of a number of proximate separate suburbs into a single subregional entity and a fission of the metropolitan area as a whole into differentiated, and often competing subregions.

Regional shopping malls, strategically located at the intersection of several suburbs, were perhaps the first signs of this economic fusion of clusters of suburbs in the realm of retailing and consumption (see Steinnes, 1982, work, "Suburbanization and the 'Malling of America'"; and Jacobs, 1984, recent "community case study," *The Mall*). This submetropolitan regional differentiation and fusion of preexisting suburbs is now extending, however, into other economic areas, into organizations and associations, and even the beginnings of more formal political and governmental federations. For example, within the Chicago metropolitan area, in addition to the North Shore, we have been able to identify major subregions, currently designated by compass directions but labels that speak to distinct clusters of suburbs having distinct connotative meanings—the Northwest Suburbs, the Western Suburbs, and Southwest Suburbs. In addition, more distinct "names" for some clusters of suburbs are also begnning to appear such as Fox Valley and the Woodfield Corridor (See Figure 1).

Again, as with the emergence of Chicagoland as a label for the metropolitan whole, at the governmental level many of these subregional federations are focused on basic ecological issues such as the Northwest Municipal Conference comprised of north and northwest suburban communities that are attempting to work out a joint solution for disposing of garbage. The Regional Transportation Authority is divided into distinct north, northwest, and south transit districts, and two of the more specialized governmental subregional "special districts" uncovered are the North Shore Mosquito Abatement District and the Northwest Mosquito Abatement District. This suburban fusion into subregions also shows much economic-centered activity geared to competitive economic development among the different suburban subregions. For example, each of these subregions has its own federated chambers of commerce and boards of realtors. Furthermore, this ecological and economic differentation of metropolitan subregions is often associated with specific types of industries that may differentially affect the health and wealth of their respective communities in terms of economic development and decline. For example, the south suburban area of Chicago has historically been the site of older, heavy industries such as steel, auto, and petrochemicals, and is an area hit hard by plant closings and moves that have left many of these working-class suburban communities facing their own "fiscal crisis" comparable to the Frost Belt cities of the entire northeast. However, only 20 miles to the north, the Woodfield Corridor is an expanding suburban Sun Belt of new office buildings and "high-tech" laboratories focused on the "health industry," a development similar to that of Silicon Valley in the Bay Area.

In short, the national issue of a shifting industrial base and regional differences in economic growth and decline, of Frost Belt cities versus Sun Belt cities, is being played out on the metropolitan stage itself, and this heightened differentition of submetropolitan suburban regions is leading to a social fission and fusion now being picked up in symbolic terms. These symbolic labels, however, are not merely denotatively netural "names"; rather, they are connotatively important for capturing the underlying economic dynamics that in an earlier era were referred to as "boosterism." These symbolic connotations help to create the very reality they are attempting to describe, and as such, they are but the latest phase in the "social construction of community" played out on a newly emerging ecological reality.

The rationale for fusion is undoubtedly linked to economies of scale but economies in the politial, social, and symbolic realms as well as the more purely economic. New development is occurring along expressways and on vacant land often on the borders of existing suburbs, and relatively seamless threads of development (corridors, valleys, etc.) fuse and confuse what were previously somewhat jealously heralded distinct parochial identities. The economies of scale and the related issue of externalities, both positive and negative, that spill over from one adjacent suburban municipality to another generate common subregional "fates." Whether these fates are disasters or daydreams, they provide the basis for mutual identification. One of the clearest examples of economies of scale that submetropolitan regions may realize from this social and symbolic fusion was demonstrated in the Round Lake region in Chicago's northwest suburbs. In a recent referendum, residents of four separate, small suburban municipalities voted to incorporate into a single new suburban government incorporating all four towns.

Are the emergence of both symbolic submetropolitan regions and symbolic labels for entire metropolitan areas interrelated? I have suggested before that they are in fact the outcome of the same ecological and economic processes of differentiation and competition played out on two distinct levels. What is happening at the submetropolitan regional level as suburbs compete among one another for new industries and office developments (Logan, 1981) is also being played out on the national level by competing metropolitan areas (Kasarda, 1980). Just as the smaller scale competition is aided by social and symbolic economies of scale, the designation of Chicagoland serves to symbolically incorporate the entire expanding "assets" of the metropolitan area as a whole, many of which lie beyond the official boundary of the city of Chicago itself. As a result, Chicagoland may more successfully compete with other cities— for example, San Francisco, and other metropolitan areas, the Bay Area. For example, in competition for plant and office locations with other metropolitan areas throughout the nation, Chicagoland can point to major universities throughout the metropolitan area, to research centers such as Fermi Lab located in the far western suburb of Batavia, and to abundant resources of electrical energy generated by nuclear power plants located throughout the metropolian area. In short, at both the metropolitan and the submetropolitan levels, the competitive interactions and comparisons among comparable units are creating newly emerging collective identities. These newly formed collective identities provide new bases of identification among residents, collective identities that permit residents to see that theirs is a shared fate tied to those similarly situated in both an ecological and a symbolic order. The economic competition among metropolitan identities is no less symbolically real than when the "New York" Giants leave the Meadowlands of New Jersey to play the "Los Angeles" Rams in Anaheim, California.

SEARCHING FOR A SYNTHESIS IN FUTURE RESEARCH

A synthesis of the classical sociological theories of human ecology and symbolic interaction is only sketched by broad brush and exemplary details in the preceding pages. In this concluding section, I would like to suggest some directions a fuller elaboration of this synthesis might pursue in future research. I divide this continuing search for a synthesis into four broad questions about critical linkages that should be attempted. First, what are the specific processes by which symbolic and ecological realities become linked? Second, what are the tensions and contradictions in the relationships among specific economic, political, and social institutions brought about by the disjuncture or the "broken links" between these ecological and symbolic realities? Third, how do these ecological and symbolic realities link together in the construction of both collective and individual identities up and down a vertical scale running from the individual through local communities to metropolitan areas and national regions? And fourth, how might researchers creatively construct studies employing multimethod research to link different styles of research together to explore simultaneously these ecological and symbolic realities?

Processes Linking Ecological and Symbolic Realities

Questions about processes linking ecological and symbolic realities are perhaps most appropriately framed as subsets of the more general question of "consciousness," as in the concepts of "false consciousness" and "consciousness raising." We have seen that human ecologists have traditionally eschewed "motives" and conscious human attitudes, beliefs, and values as operating variables in accounting for the patterning and processes of human communities. They relegate these to a black box of assumptions that too often remain unexplored, or they treat them at best as derivative epiphenomena of underlying ecological realities. Similarly, symbolic interactionists would seemingly posit, in the extreme forms of "the social construction of reality," that reality is what people define it to be, and therefore mental constructions of attitudes, beliefs, and values are the central operating reality. It is as if other realities were but random Rorschachs of little or any significance in their own right. However, a synthetic theory of symbolic ecology suggests to both camps that they consider more seriously in their research and theory the variables, concepts, and propositions of the other.

Human ecologists might explore the ways in which symbol systems may impact upon ecological structures and processes, a perspective that was early suggested by Walter Firey, but that few researchers have systematically developed. For example, to what degree do the symbolic rankings (evaluations) of human communities along various dimensions of stratification (values) impact the competitive ecological processes of location that variously distribute people and institutions throughout a metropolitan area? Alternatively, symbolists might more seriously consider the ways in which symbolic variation in local cultures, as reflected in attitudes, beliefs, and values, is a product of a local community's specific ecological niche and of ecological interactions with other communities that local residents may not even be fully aware or "conscious" of.

But beyond the need to see these two realities as mutually influencing one another is the need to spell out the mechanisms or processes by which these linkages are made in the real world of everyday life. One broad category of linking processes, which I have suggested in the preceding analysis, is the media. Especially important are the citywide or metropolitan media of newspapers, magazines, radio, and television as critical communicators of not only of one's own physical and symbolic location but of one's relative location with respect to other people and institutions. From a human ecological perspective, this role of the media may simply be viewed as expressing the underlying ecological structure, whereas from a symbolic interactionist perspective it may be seen as more critically involved in constructing the reality by which people define their local and metropolitan existence. On a third level, which combines the preceding two perspectives, the media are themselves a set of institutional actors that are part of and subject to processes operating in both the ecological and symbolic worlds.

A second major linking mechanism between the ecological and symbolic realities of the metropolis is physical mobility. And here, I am specifically referring to spatial mobility, but I am using it in its full and variable time range from the diurnal mobility of people to more longer term and relatively permanent shifts in residence and location. These are exemplified in the difference between "commuting" and "moving." Whereas the media may portray unknown worlds, what Kevin Lynch (1960) would call the blank spaces in people's "cognitive maps" of a metropolitan area, through physical mobility people come to experience directly these differing worlds of the "urban mosaic." The different paths they traverse and the people from different communities they see and interact with may come to constitute selective social worlds that give people a highly particularistic view of their own physical and social locations. Though particularistic, the challenge is to discover the patterns of mobility that may shift from social group to social group and throughout the life span and that result in people having selectively patterned ways of constructing their symbolic ecology. The patterns of mobility are themselves, of course, a function of the existing urban ecology, and the cognitive maps that become constructed may serve to reinforce and maintain that very structure. In sum, both the media and mobility are distinct processes by which people come "to know about" and "to know" their ecological reality.

Broken Links between Symbolic and Ecological Realities

Much of the preceding discussion, and indeed our analysis of elites' perceptions of their local communities' relative position within a metropolitan structure, suggests that the symbolic and ecological realities are but mirror images of one another. (Though which is defined as the "virtual" and which the "real" image will differ between the two perspectives.) However, an important and fruitful line for future research is to discover and highlight the contradictions and conflicts that may exist between these two realities. These contradictions are important because a large number of existing "urban problems," such as lawsuits over "open housing" in the suburbs, or issues of school consolidation, may be seen as distortions or myopic readings of these ecological and symbolic realities. For example, we have suggested before that the "ecological reality" of a single metropolitan community is only slowly coming to consciousness and often conflicts directly with a prevailing "symbolic reality" of local community autonomy that stresses differentiation and competition rather than unification and cooperation.

One way of exploring these contradictions would be to elaborate more fully Ogburn's (1957) older theory of "cultural lag." However, this theory contains the explicit assumption that technology or "material culture" (read ecological reality) changes more rapidly than "symbolic culture" (symbolic reality), and, as a result, the latter is always in conflict with or lagging behind the former. By opening up this assumption to empirical test, one might be able to distinguish under what conditions specific "contents" or "types" of symbolic reality may actually change first, thereby bringing about contradictions that might be called "ecological lag." Furthermore, symbolic realities, such as local community autonomy, may actually impede or distort technological and ecological change, such as the building of expressways. (To invoke the older notion of symbolic culture as "the cake of custom," this process might be called "cultural drag".)

An additional way to look for possible sources of these contradictions between ecological and symbolic realities is to follow the lead of political scientists such as Robert Dahl (1961) and take an "issues approach." By looking at social conflicts and more specifically emerging political issues, one could see to what degree these are manifestations not simply of conflicting values held by different social groups within a local community but constitute different views of what a community should be in comparison with the ecological realities that currently exist or might exist. Should a community attempt to attract industry, or should it attempt to retain a residential character; should it grow or not grow? These questions of linkage between a symbolic conception of what a community is or should be and the ecological reality it confronts are often the basis of rancorous local community conflicts.

These contradictions are also likely to show up with respect to political conflicts between a local community and its environment that may get expressed in terms of "insiders" versus "outsiders." Issues of open housing, or busing, or the location of expressways may lead to a mentality of "suburbs under siege" (Fritz, 1986), wherein the ecological reality of a single metropolitan area is jealously opposed under the banner of local community control. Lacking political solutions, many of these controversies end up in the courts, resulting in a legally enforced fusion of fates.

LINKING INDIVIDUAL AND COLLECTIVE IDENTITIES

The application of symbolic interaction to human ecology is more than mere metaphor—and nowhere is this more apparent than in searching for the linkage between individual and collective identities. By living in this or that local community, one does not merely acquire the benefits nor bear the costs of collective goods and services; one also makes a statement to the larger world of the kind of person one is. Suburban community status in a symbolic metropolitan structure becomes a reflected or "secondary status" acquired by individuals by virtue (positive or negative) of residing in a given community. The symbolic status of the community may be more widely known than the status of any given individual and is therefore readily used to place people both spatially and socially. One's social class, life-style, or ethnicity (to use the dimensions of Shevky and Bell's [1955] *Social Area Analysis*) are readily communicated by one's place of residence. This may have significant implications not only for influencing or altering individual identities (especially of children in their early developmental stages) but may also be important in affecting the degree of identification *with* a given community on the part of residents. As Bell and Boat (1957) found, the convergence or divergence of individual social class with the social-class composition of the community may significantly affect attitudes and behaviors of individuals. The degree to which people identify with neighbors and become involved in local collective activities from routine acts of neighboring to local community organizations may depend on this linkage of identification between the indvidual and collective levels. As people search, by choice and constraint, to maximize their values (Bell, 1972), where they end up living, in a literal territorial sense, may have broad repercussions for both how they think of themselves and what they do.

Furthermore, individuals may attempt to assert or claim an individual identity that requires some alteration of the collective identity of the community they live in. On the one hand, this might be most easily facilitated by a move to a new community that brings about a better match between individual and collective characteristics. On the other hand, it might bring about an attempt to assert a redefinition of the identity of their current local community. Much organized community action may be interpreted as an attempt to alter the "image" of a local community thereby altering the identities of local community residents to the larger world as well as to themselves. The conditions under which communities "exit" or "voice" is chosen may depend upon this central link of "loyalty" between individual and collective identities (Hirschman, 1974).

LINKING MULTIMETHODS OF RESEARCH

It has become a truism within the behavioral sciences that the theories we develop and test are often method-bound. Therefore, any attempt at theoretical synthesis between the diverse concepts and propositions from both symbolic interaction theory and human ecology requires a rethinking of traditional research methods. Traditionally, for example, human ecologists have often relied upon more macrosociological data such as official census statistics, whereas symbolic interactionists have relied upon more microlevel data of interpersonal encounters either through experiments in the lab or participant observation. To bring about an empirical as well as theoretical synthesis of symbolic ecology may therefore require a creative merger of different research styles within the same piece of research. The use of census data, archives, in-depth interviews, and observation might be necessary for a multiple operationalizing of the "objective" concepts of the ecologists with the *verstehen* understanding sought by symbolic interactionists. For example, the social-class variation in a suburban community might be "objectively" assessed through census data, whereas the variable perception of that social class variation by residents might be assessed through interviews. The convergence or divergence between the two could be treated not simply as a "validity check of the methods" but as significant data for an analysis of the social construction processes of those perceptual realities.

Finally, a multimethod approach to the study of symbolic ecology might contribute a broader social, not simply sociological, synthesis. An understanding of the emerging ecological structure of metropolitan areas and the symbolic place of suburbs within that structure might bring about a conscious convergence of the symbolic and ecological realities in the everyday lives of residents. C. Wright Mills (1959) reminded us that the sociological imagination requires an understanding of the intersection of history and biography. On a more limited scale, if the objective ecological forces of history can be linked to the symbolic meanings of local community residents, then symbolic ecology may contribute to a more understandable and more meaningful social life.

Acknowledgments

I would like to thank Richard Fritz and Nancy Wagner for their assistance in the research reported in this chapter, and Abe Wandersman for his editorial suggestions.

REFERENCES

Altschuler, A. (1970). *Community control*. New York: Pegasus.

Arnold, D. (1970). Dimensional sampling. *American Sociologist*, 5, 147 150.

Bell, W. (1972). The city, the suburb, and a theory of social choice. In S. Greer & D. Miner (Eds.), *The new urbanization* (pp. 132–168). Chicago: Aldine.

Bell, W., & Boat, M. D. (1957). Urban neighborhoods and informal social relations. *American Journal of Sociology*, 62, 391–398.

Berger, B. (1960). *Working class suburb*. Berkeley: University of California Press.

Berger, P., & Luckman, T. (1966). *The social construction of reality*. Garden City, NY: Doubleday.

Bogue, D. J. (1949). *The structure of the metropolitan community*. Ann Arbor: University of Michigan Press.

Burgess, E. W. (1925). The growth of the city. In R. E. Park & E. W. Burgess (Eds.), *The city* (pp. 47–62). Chicago: University of Chicago Press.

Cooley, C. W. (1920). *Social process*. New York: Scribner.

Dahl, R. (1961). *Who governs?* New Haven: Yale University Press.

Davidson, J. (1979). *Political partnerships*. Beverly Hills, CA: Sage.

Firey, W. (1945). Sentiment and symbolism as ecological variables. *American Sociological Review*, 10, 140–148.

Fritz, R. (1986). *Suburb under seige*. Unpublished doctoral dissertation, Northwestern University, Evanston, IL.

Gans, H. J. (1967). *The Levittowners*. New York: Random House.

Geertz, C. (1963). *Old societies and new states.* New York: Free Press.

Goffman, E. (1967). *Interaction ritual.* New York: Doubleday.

Gras, N. S. B. (1922). *Introduction to economic history.* New York: Harper.

Harris, C. D., & Ullman, E. L. (1945). The nature of cities. *Annals of the American Academy of Political and Social Science, 242,* 7–17.

Hirschman, A. (1974). *Exit, voice, and loyalty.* Cambridge, MA: Harvard University Press.

Hoyt, H. (1939). *The structure and growth of residential neighborhoods in American cities.* Washington, DC: U.S. Federal Housing Administration.

Hunter, A. (1974). *Symbolic communities.* Chicago: University of Chicago Press.

Hunter, A. (1979). Why Chicago? The rise of the Chicago School of urban social science. *American Behavioral Scientist, 18,* 44–56.

Hunter, A. (1984). Local community autonomy/dependency: Elite perceptions. *Social Science Quarterly, 65,* 181–189.

Hunter, A., & Riger, S. (1986). The meaning of community in community mental health. *Journal of Community Psychology, 14,* 55–71.

Jacobs, J. (1984). *The mall.* Prospect Heights, IL: Waveland Press.

Kain, J. (1968). The distribution and movement of jobs and industry. In J. Q. Wilson (Ed.), *The metropolitan enigma* (pp. 1–43) Garden City, NY: Doubleday.

Kasarda, J. D. (1980). The implications of contemporary redistribution trends for national urban policy. *Social Science Quarterly, 61,* 373–400.

Laska, S., & Spain, D. (Eds.). (1980). *Back to the city.* New York: Pergamon.

Logan, J. R. (1978). Growth, politics, and the stratification of places. *American Journal of Sociology, 84,* 404–416.

Logan, J. R. (1981). The stratification of metropolitan suburbs: 1960–1970. *American Sociological Review, 46,* 175–186.

Lynch, K. (1960). *The image of the city.* Cambridge, MA: M.I.T. Press.

Lynch, K. (1972). *What time is this place?* Cambridge, MA: M.I.T. Press.

Mead, G. H. (1934). *Mind, self, and society.* Chicago: University of Chicago Press.

Merriam, C., Parratt, S. D., & Lepawsky, A. (1933). *The government of the metropolitan region of Chicago.* Chicago: University of Chicago Press.

Mills, C. W. (1959). *The sociological imagination.* New York: Oxford.

Ogburn, W. F. (1957). Cultural lag as theory. *Sociology and Social Research, 41,* 167–173.

Popenoe, D. (1977). *The suburban environment.* Chicago: University of Chicago Press.

Portes, A., & Walton, J. (1981). *Labor, class, and the international system.* New York: Academic Press.

Proshansky, H. M., Fabian, A. K., & Kaminoff, R. (1983). Place-identity: Physical world socialization of the self. *Journal of Environmental Psychology, 3,* 57–83.

Rivlin, L. G. (1982). Group membership and place meanings in an urban neighborhood. *Journal of Social Issues, 38,* 75–93.

Rossi, P. H. (1955). *Why families move.* Glencoe, IL: Free Press.

Shevky, E., & Bell, W. (1955). *Social area analysis.* Stanford, CA: Stanford University Press.

Simpson, C. A. (1981). *SoHo: The artist in the city.* Chicago: University of Chicago Press.

Stein, M. (1960). *The eclipse of community.* Princeton: Princeton University Press.

Steinnes, D. N. (1982). Suburbanization and the "malling of America." *Urban Affairs Quarterly, 17,* 401–418.

Suttles, G. D. (1972). *The social construction of communities.* Chicago: University of Chicago Press.

Taeuber, C., & Taeuber, I. (1965). *Negroes in cities: Residential segregation and neighborhood change.* Chicago: Aldine.

Taub, R. P., Surgeon, G. P., Lindholm, S., Otti, P. B., & Bridges, A. (1977). Urban voluntary association, locality based and externally induced. *American Journal of Sociology, 83,* 425–442.

Taylor, R., Gottfredson, S., & Brower, S. (1984). Neighborhood naming as an index of attachment to place. *Population and Environment, 7,* 103–125.

Vidich, A., & Bensman, J. (1958). *Small town in mass society.* New York: Doubleday.

Walton, J. (1982). Cities and jobs and politics. *Urban Affairs Quarterly, 18,* 19–30.

Warner, S. B. (1962). *Streetcar suburbs: The process of growth in Boston, 1870-1900.* Cambridge: Harvard University Press.

Warren, R. L. (1973). *Perspectives on the American community* (2nd ed.). Skokie, Il: Rand McNally.

Weber, A. (1899). *The growth of cities in the nineteenth century: A study in statistics.* New York: Macmillan.

Wiewel, W., & Hunter, A. (1986) The interorganizational network as a resource: A comparative case study of organizational genesis. *Administrative Science Quarterly, 30,* 482–496.

Wood, R. (1964). *1400 governments.* New York: Doubleday.

7

Neighborhood Preservation and Community Values in Historical Perspective

DAVID R. GOLDFIELD

INTRODUCTION

The scene could be suburbia anywhere: the neat, ranch-style homes surrounded by white picket fences, doors bedecked in wreaths heralding the Christmas season, the toys of summer—a boat, a bicycle, a grill—huddled in corners of back yards. If the scene is familiar, however, the location is not. This is the South Bronx, one of the most notorious physical and human wastelands in the nation, an obligatory station for politicians taking a pilgrimage to discover and expose poverty and urban decay. To casual observers, the scene in this ninety-home development known as Charlotte Gardens is bizarre; to residents it is the fulfillment of their American dream of a single-family home even if Times Square is only a short, twenty-minute subway ride away. The three-bedroom homes that sell for a modest $52,000 have a long waiting list of hopeful buyers. Fortunate residents enthused about their new environment. "I always dreamed of having my own private house," Deloris Deleston confessed. Her neighbor, Julio Cruz remarked that "It's not like living in an apartment where you don't know your next-door neighbor." And

DAVID R. GOLDFIELD • Department of History, The University of North Carolina at Charlotte, Charlotte, NC 28223.

twelve-year old Melody Sellers noted that "In the summertime, it's like the country." ("Community of Delight," 1984, p. 3)

The development, organized by the nonprofit South Bronx Development Organization and financed by a consortium of banks, foundations, businesses, and local and federal agencies, represents the latest in a century-long effort to blend resident needs and public policy in the creation of a positive neighborhood environment. In a broad sense, Charlotte Gardens is also an experiment in neighborhood preservation because it seeks to maintain through re-creation a neighborhood ethic lost as a result of public policy blunders, landlord neglect, tenant abuse, financial disinvestment, and the irresistible workings of a changing metropolitan economy and demography. The ethic and its physical manifestation is essential, many believe, to our local and national well-being. Early in this century, housing reformer Robert A. Wood argued that "the neighborhood is large enough to include in essence all the problems of the city, the State, and the Nation. . . . On the other hand, it is small enough to be a comprehensible and manageable community unit" (Wood, 1970, pp. 148–149). Urban sociologist Charles Horton Cooley, a contemporary of Wood's, noted on a more personal level that "the fact that the family and neighborhood groups are ascendant in the open and plastic time of childhood makes them even now incomparably more influential than all the rest." For Cooley, the neighborhood fostered and inculcated "loyalty, truth, service, and kindness" (Cooley, 1909, p. 26). More recently, presidential candidate Jimmy Carter in 1976 acknowledged the importance of family and neighborhood as character builders and added: "If we are to save our cities we must revitalize our neighborhoods first" (quoted in Fisher, 1984, p. xviii).

Although Americans generally agreed on the importance of the neighborhood, there has been significant divergence of perceptions between policymakers and residents and within each group as well. Neighborhoods differed widely in socioeconomic status and hence in interests and internal resources; cities possessed economic bases and political systems that facilitated or inhibited various policy treatments; and policies affected individual residents within the same neighborhood in different ways. The complexities are not surprising given a standard definition of neighborhood offered by sociologist Suzanne Keller:

> A neighborhood is a locality with physical boundaries, social networks, concentrated use of area facilities, and special emotional and symbolic connotations for its inhabitants. (Keller, 1968, p. 128)

Thus a neighborhood possesses physical, social, institutional, and psychological characteristics. Rare are the policies that can contemplate such an array of factors; rare are the residents who can perceive the distinctions; and rarer still are the neighborhoods whose boundaries coincide with all of these elements. It is understandable that neighborhood-based policies and citizens' organizations have had such checkered records over the past century. What is more surprising, perhaps, are the modest victories achieved by planners, reformers, politicians, and residents in securing their residential havens.

The suburban neighborhood amid the rubble of the South Bronx represents, to date at least, one of those victories—the happy coincidence of public policy and resident desires, even though the visual aspect may jar the senses. Charlotte Gardens does not, of course, stand for the neighborhood panacea of the future—the diversity of neighborhoods and the perceptions of them preclude a magic-bullet approach to neighborhood planning and preservation. But the community does indicate a movement away from stereotyping city and suburb, the dichotomy between them, and the respective neighborhoods and residents within each environment. Perhaps policymakers and residents alike, after seeking the ingredients of the "good life" in the far-flung periphery, have come to realize that those ingredients are replicable in an urban setting as well and offer different advantages besides. This perception has come, in part, because as in the late nineteenth century, the dominant form of what is urban is changing rapidly today to a less dense, more sprawling spatial entity and that is especially so in the vast metropolitan catchment areas of the South and Southwest. Different city types imply different neighborhoods.

Considering the purported importance of neighborhoods in our national culture, it is not surprising that for the past century, policymakers and residents alike have responded to threats to neighborhood integrity by evincing a strong preservation instinct. Whether this instinct has manifested itself in the creation of new neighborhoods or in the rehabilitation of old districts, our policies, whether emanating from planners, politicians, or residents, reflect the strong desire to preserve what the neighborhood represents, even if that means destroying its present form to create a place more in tune with our values.

Neighborhood preservation policy has gone through four stages of development since the late 19th century, each stage reflecting the changing perceptions of the urban environment. The first stage emerged during a period of intense concern that the new urban environment of the late nineteenth century endangered American ideals. The major policy objectives were protection and enrichment, with residents advocating the former and new professional groups the latter. The second stage appeared as fears subsided and urban professionals—planners and theorists—advanced physically oriented solutions for neighborhoods, though still complementary to the village ideal. The federal government adopted some of these solutions in its housing policies from the 1930s to the 1960s.

Even before the end of this period, a third stage of neighborhood preservation policy became evident: a widespread reaction against public policy combined with another change in urban theory that downplayed the neighborhood's physical role in the metropolis and stressed the psychic and social attributes perceived by residents. One result was the recasting of public policies during the 1970s. At that time, the fourth stage emerged: neighborhood self-government—an emphasis on process rather than on public planning. The tension between public policy and private needs persisted, however. Continued evolution of perceptions and theories about urban and neighborhood development ensured an unstable relationship between plan and process—a merger that had looked promising in the early 1970s. New perceptions about the nature of the modern metropolis and its neighborhoods as well as the relative inattention to aesthetic and design principles in contemporary process-oriented neighborhood preservation may lead back to a more comprehensive vision of the neighborhood environment. What follows is a historical explication of the four stages of neighborhood preservation policy and the ideas and values that helped to shape these policies.

THE INDUSTRIAL CITY AND NEIGHBORHOOD PRESERVATION

The nature of American urbanization changed dramatically in the late nineteenth century precipitating the first in a long series of policies designed to defend the neighborhood idea. The combination of industrialization and massive overseas migration produced large, dense, and disorderly agglomerations of structures and people. By this time also, the neighborhood had become or was perceived as being the last vestige of village life in the new city, a vestige threatened by inundation from the new forces. Americans, befitting their English culture, had generally been uncomfortable in cities to begin with, and as early as the 1840s when they possessed both the means and the excuse for leaving the city, they did so. But these early suburban environments were merely less dense versions of the city and soon their residents were clamoring for the services and amenities enjoyed by their urban counterparts. The idea of these early suburbanites and later reformers was not to excise the city from American life but rather to sanitize and order it: to preserve it in their own image (Goldfield & Brownell, 1979; Jackson, 1985). As discrete neighborhoods emerged in expanding cities following the Civil

War, they provided both the model and the efficacy of scale for the amelioration and preservation of urban life.

Two identifiable groups of preservation-oriented neighborhood residents emerged at this time—those seeking to fortify neighborhood boundaries against the incursion of alien residents and land uses and those clamoring for improved services. These remain today as the primary motivating factors for neighborhood organization, resulting in two distinctive yet occasionally overlapping organizational types. Beginning in the 1880s, middle-class neighborhoods in several northeastern cities organized to ensure resident homogeneity—protective associations, as residents called them. Through informal agreements or through more formal devices such as restrictive covenants, property owners vowed to maintain the racial, religious, and/or class integrity of their community. Such groups were especially prominent in the campaign for zoning regulations during the years immediately preceding our entrance into World War I. Though courts would strike down overt attempts to utilize zoning for discriminatory purposes, indirect language stressing lot sizes, maintenance requirements, and permitted use were effective surrogates. In fact, such an association was instrumental in pushing through the nation's first comprehensive zoning ordinance in New York City in 1916, a code evolving out of concern about the invasion of garment district factories and their immigrant workforces into the fashionable Fifth Avenue neighborhood. Occasionally, these protective groups resorted to force in ultimately futile attempts to discourage prospective residents of different racial or ethnic backgrounds. During the summer of 1919 in Chicago, the violence of white neighborhood groups against black households eventually precipitated a major race riot (Goldfield & Brownell, 1979; Tuttle, 1970).

Early improvement associations generally eschewed protective tactics, more from the fact that pressures toward heterogeneity in these neighborhoods were not evident. Neighborhood improvement groups instead concentrated on service delivery. A technological and bureaucratic revolution occurred in the late nineteenth-century city that at once widened the gap between those areas serviced by the latest innovations—sewer and water, electricity, public transit—and those without such benefits, while throwing up a political labyrinth that pushed government further away from the average citizen. The neighborhood improvement association was an attempt to solve the bureaucracy and secure necessary services. The failure to procure these services invariably signified neighborhood disinvestment. Thus, the West Baltimore Improvement Association blamed its neighborhood decline in the 1890s on being "greatly neglected" by the city (Arnold, 1979).

Working-class or immigrant neighborhoods held different agendas. Protection was less an objective as numerous residents hoped eventually to leave for better surroundings, and improvement, although obviously desirable, was unlikely because they lacked the financial and political strength to essay more than cosmetic changes in their environment. Moreover, immigrant neighborhoods especially were rarely neighborhoods in the typical sense: a relatively homogeneous, spatially and cognitively defined area. In the more crowded immigrant cities, ethnicity varied block by block and distinctive subnational groups existed within blocks and even within buildings. Such organizations as existed in these areas were more ethnic than spatial. This accounts for their persistence long after most households left for other districts. Here, preservation implied culture rather than structure.

These neighborhoods, for all their diversity, became, rather, targets for reform, some of which threatened their cultural integrity. Government surveys, foundation reports, and individual studies such as Jacob Riis's shocking *How the Other Half Lives* (1891) and Upton Sinclair's *The Jungle* (1906) aroused both sympathy and fear. Although some urban reformers and policymakers preferred to improve these districts through legislation, the establishment of housing and health codes, for examples, others adopted a more direct approach. The settlement house movement had its origins in London's working-class East End during the 1880s; as similar neighborhoods emerged in American cities, the idea of an oasis in the midst of chaos, poverty, and despair to provide moral guidance, language instruction, cultural reinforcement, the values of citizenship, and a place to play took root in this country as well. Stanton Coit, an Amherst graduate with a German PhD opened up the Neighborhood Guild in New York City in 1886 predicting that this initial American settlement house would be "the foundation of a civic renaissance in America." Though the movement proceeded slowly—by the time Jane Addams founded the famed Hull House in Chicago in 1889, there were only a half-dozen settlement houses in the United States—a decade later there were more than 100 such operations (Davis, 1967; Lubove, 1962).

Today, the settlement house approach would be called "ghetto enrichment"—a strategy not so much to alter the physical structure of the poor neighborhood as to enlighten and improve the residents therein. The strategy ran counter to the prevailing early twentieth-century wisdom that emphasized environmental determinism; that is, good houses make good people. Also, the ideals of enlightenment and improvement intimated an elitist aspect to settlement reform—that professional social workers were the only individuals qualified to set neighborhood priorities. But such an interpretation may be viewing our reformer predecessors through the prism of the activist 1960s and 1970s rather than perceiving the selflessness of settlement house workers. They possessed an avid desire to introduce newcomers to a new culture and to ensure or at least to facilitate the passage of immigrants through the maze of a pre-government-welfare America, even if most neighborhood residents rarely availed themselves of these services and even looked askance at the earnest, mostly young men and women with college degrees and decided ideas on doing it right.

The settlement house and the community center movement that transformed the neighborhood school into a multipurpose activity center were not aimed at transforming the neighborhood in any case. They were individual-specific programs that were meant to preserve old values in a "new" neighborhood, that perceived citizenship and education as higher priorities than service delivery or structural rehabilitation. But these reform efforts also clearly implied that program initiative came from the professional, the social worker. Occasionally, social workers would plunge into the political arena and actively organize neighborhood residents to obtain benefits and services from a recalcitrant political system. Settlement worker Mary Follett urged in 1918 that

> the people should organize themselves into neighborhood groups to express their daily life, to bring to the surface the needs, desires, and aspirations of that life, that these needs should become the substance of politics, and that neighborhood groups should become the recognized political unit. (Follett, 1918, pp. 189–192)

But this early call for neighborhood self-government should not obscure the fact that social workers would exercise the leadership and priority-setting roles in such organizations. Even so, these early neighborhood groups were virtually irrelevant additions to the body politic. The machines, with their own ward-based organizations distrusted these upstart groups, and political reformers avoided neighborhood, especially immigrant neighborhood interests as too reminiscent of the evils of ward-heeler politics. And the ethnic fragmentation apparent in immigrant neighborhoods precluded cohesive action in most instances.

The social worker's conception of "neighborhood" was imprecise—not surprising given the complexities of the concept and the individual emphasis of settlement strategy. A more spatially oriented neighborhood preservation policy emerged with the growth of another new professional community, city planners. Though planners did not possess their own professional group until 1917, there was an expanding coterie of architects, landscape architects, and engineers who devoted increasing amounts of their professional time to the physical manipulation of urban spaces. The City Beautiful movement spawned by the Columbian Exposition of 1893 in Chicago emphasized aesthetic applications to the urban environment. Though its policies were not neighborhood-specific, City Beautiful programs attempted to develop civic consciousness by encouraging neighborhood groups to spruce up and preserve their districts through plantings and landscaping, to hold aesthetic competitions, and to lobby city fathers for funds and policies directed toward beautifying public places. The campaign was mostly fluff and detracted attention away from pressing urban problems, the roots of which went considerably beyond cosmetic remedies. Nevertheless, the movement raised civic and neighborhood consciousness and identified urban services as a crucial element in neighborhood preservation and improvement (Burg, 1976; Wilson, 1964).

By 1910, City Beautiful had demonstrated its superficiality and given way to City Efficient—an overall physical strategy designed to probe deeper into the urban environment in order to make the city a more effective economic engine, relieve congestion, protect residential property values, and, ultimately, to inject greater certainty and order into the urban environment. Again, this was not a neighborhood-specific program, but its implications affected neighborhoods by providing a planning prop for the tendency toward preservation through exclusivity. Daniel H. Burnham's 1909 *Plan of Chicago* was the signal event for this movement, emphasizing an expansive circulatory system, numerous monumental public buildings, and copious buffers of parks and open spaces on the periphery, protecting newer residential areas. Essentially, the Chicago plan was City Beautiful with a road system, but colleagues in the field seized upon the transportation circulation pattern as the innovative feature of the plan and road building joined landscaping as a major activity of the rising profession of city planning. By 1916, the formal segregation of land use in the form of zoning completed the planner's repertoire for ordering the city and preserving residential neighborhoods. One year later, the professional planning organization appeared (Burnham & Bennett, 1909; Hines, 1974).

By that time, there were relatively few planners concerned with the social potential of city planning, though their European colleagues had recognized and acted upon that potential by using zoning to mix social groups and evolving a housing policy to upgrade or create residential neighborhoods. The clients of most of the early American planners, after all, were not governments, much less the poor, but, rather business groups that were primarily concerned with the protective aspect of neighborhood policy. Then, too, once immigration slackened and the economy boomed, the perception of incipient class warfare or at least

unrest in the tenement neighborhoods subsided, and the housing surveys by the teens indicated an improvement in living conditions. Yet
there remained a cadre on the fringe of the protoplanning profession
that believed in the physical manipulation of the neighborhood to attain
social objectives. And Clarence Perry became this group's leading
spokesman from 1910 through the 1930s.

THE NEIGHBORHOOD UNIT PLAN

Perry had been involved in the community center movement and
had witnessed the efficacy of the school as the focal point for neighborhood life. Accordingly, by the 1920s, he proposed an ideal neighborhood that preserved the qualities of life that neighborhoods had
traditionally fostered but that the industrial city had jeopardized or destroyed altogether. The neighborhood unit plan, as he called it, utilized
the school as the organizing point for a "superblock," defined by the
distance a child could walk to school. The separation of pedestrian from
vehicular traffic was a major feature of the unit plan. He understood that

> the automobile has been . . . a destroyer of neighborhood life . . . [by] cut-
> ting up residential areas into small islands separated from each other by
> raging streams of traffic. (Perry, 1924, pp. 415–421)

Yet Perry also recognized that planners could not ignore the automobile
and sought a compromise to provide residents access to their neighborhood without impeding pedestrian flow in the interior of the superblock. In addition, Perry defined significant areas for open spaces,
clustering homes to maximize recreational activities. Finally, the superblock contained convenience stores, religious institutions, and outposts
of civic service agencies. Perry believed that the modern city rather than
becoming atomized as some social scientists argued had actually become
overcentralized and that contemporary neighborhoods were places
where "men cease to be persons" (Perry, 1929, p. 127). Perry's was a
village ideal: The superblock would provide the nurture, space, and
security that were lacking in the city at large; they would be island
communities against the urban maelstrom. Lewis Mumford, a colleague
and supporter, explained that Perry

> show[s] how, through deliberate design, it [the neighborhood] could be
> transformed into . . . a neighborhood . . . a unit that would now exist, not
> merely on a spontaneous or instinctual basis, but through the deliberate
> decentralization of institutions that had, in their over-centralization, ceased
> to serve efficiently the city as a whole. (Mumford, 1954, p. 261)

Diverging from the mainstream of American city planning at the time, Perry hoped to utilize physical planning to achieve social ends, admitting that he "maintained a constant interest in investing physical planning with expansive social purposes." (Gillette, 1983, p. 426). A reconstituted neighborhood would be the vehicle to achieve this objective.

If Perry was relatively isolated from the nascent planning profession, he was well within a European tradition of blending physical and social goals and, in fact, had received inspiration from some early experiments in this methodology, especially the garden city communities designed by English accountant Ebenezer Howard. Howard shared Perry's concerns about the increasing dehumanization of urban life and, particularly, the disintegration of the neighborhood. In *Garden Cities of Tomorrow*, Howard expounded his philosophy and proffered a solution that went considerably beyond merely restructuring the neighborhood, though in a sense, the garden city he proposed was a neighborhood writ large, a village setting much like the superblock with clustered cottages, open spaces, convenience shops, pedestrian paths, and, most notably, places of work: these garden cities were eventually to be self-contained communities, independent of the major city, beyond its normal commuting distance. The hope was that sufficient numbers of these garden cities could be constructed to relieve London of its perceived congestion and provide the working class with a salubrious environment and hence a salubrious life. The design features—the single-family cottages and careful landscaping—were to appeal directly to English sensibilities (similar to American ideals, of course) (Howard, 1965).

Howard's vision attained fruition first in Letchworth in 1904 and then in Welwyn in 1915, and he inspired English new-town development for the next half century. The vision became clouded in the American rendition of garden city as planners concentrated on the garden and dropped the city. Moreover, the social objectives and the goal of merging residence and workplace received little attention. The Russell Sage Foundation supported the construction of two American garden city prototypes—Sunnyside Gardens and Forest Hills Gardens—both in the New York City borough of Queens in 1910. The planning was of high quality, but the result was nothing more than another well-planned middle-class suburb. As historian Roy Lubove summarized the experience, Forest Hills "proved nothing except the obvious—that attractive suburban communities could be created for those able to afford them" (Lubove, 1962, p. 227).

Despite the shortcomings of these suburbs, Perry remained convinced that, ultimately, planned suburban neighborhood development could perform the vital social function of reducing the burdens of poverty and providing a positive environment for the urban working classes. With colleagues Henry Wright, Clarence Stein, and Lewis Mumford, Perry helped to organize the Regional Planning Association of America (RPAA) in 1922 (Lubove, 1963). The garden city or suburban neighborhood unit approach implied a regional perspective on urban problems. Burnham, of course, had also made this point in his Chicago plan but that focused narrowly on road systems. The RPAA had broader objectives in mind and put its ideals into reality by developing Radburn in 1927 in New Jersey, literally 45 minutes from Broadway via commuter train. Perry's neighborhood unit plan formed the physical foundation of the community, but, regrettably, the Depression interrupted a fair test of his planning principles. Nevertheless, the road differentiation, clustered housing, open spaces, and localized institutions worked in their brief trial. A promotional film depicted a child bouncing a ball all the way from home to school without encountering a motor vehicle. Radburn was clearly the most sophisticated community in terms of planning at that time and served as a prototype for the 1960s' generation of new towns, particularly Columbia, Maryland, and Reston, Virginia. But again, it was another middle-class enclave, however innovative its physical form (Schaffer, 1982).

By the late 1920s, it was obvious that the creation of suburban neighborhoods merely provided another residential alternative for the increasingly mobile urban middle class. It was a method, in a sense, to preserve the urban neighborhood or at least to utilize its ideal, without the threat and disorder of the new urban environment; it was preservation through creation. This is not to say that Perry ignored the city milieu entirely. His posited urban setting for the neighborhood was one that involved re-creation of the neighborhood, instead of beginning anew in a suburban environment. Though critics charged Perry with village nostalgia or even with antiurban biases, he maintained that the neighborhood unit would work in the city as well. To demonstrate the versatility of the unit plan in the city, Perry proposed the Five Block Plan that included residential space for 1,000 families, recreational facilities, convenience stores, and the separation of vehicular from pedestrian traffic. Because a vacant five-block area in the central city, especially in neighborhoods where poorer residents lived, was difficult if not impossible to find, Perry recommended clearance of existing structures. As with the suburban rendition of the plan, these would be island communities, "self-contained," as he put it, protected from the deleterious influences of surrounding urban life (Perry, 1929, pp. 108–111).

Perry was realistic enough to recognize that, initially at least, the

Five Block Plan must be a middle-class solution and in fact would strengthen and preserve the middle-class presence in the city, a presence threatened by the rapid expansion of suburbia. The urban version of the neighborhood unit plan would, according to Perry, "provide a barrier against the encroachment by deteriorated neighborhoods" (Perry, 1929, p. 128). Not that those "deteriorated neighborhoods" were beyond salvation; for the time being, the example of middle-class neighborhood units would "give object lessons in improved housing environment and community organization which will of themselves ultimately aid the reform of slum areas" (Perry, 1929, p. 128). Unlike his European counterparts, including Howard, Perry believed that the social homogeneity of neighborhoods was essential to their preservation; heterogeneity prompted decline in civic participation that ultimately would lower neighborhood defenses. Of course, by the 1920s, there were very few examples of socially heterogeneous neighborhoods in the United States (Perry, 1929, p. 128).

By the 1930s, Perry's planning ideals began to influence the planning profession at large. The publicity surrounding Radburn and the New Deal nostalgia for the simpler life of village America added currency to the unit concept. In 1933, Harland Bartholomew, one of the most respected professional city planners of that time, addressed the National Conference on City Planning and noted the value of the Five Block Plan for urban redevelopment. As the federal government turned to formulating an urban policy for the first time, the neighborhood unit seemed to be an acceptable foundation for the housing program just then emerging. When the U.S. National Resources Committee (USNRC) issued the first-ever federal report on cities in 1937, the Perry plan appeared front and center. Urban living would be advanced

> by the organization of the urban area as a whole into neighborhoods and satellite communities each of which provides for a maximum of opportunity for the daily activities and needs of its inhabitants, each of which possesses a social and political coherence which can arouse and hold community loyalty and participation, inspire reasonable civic leadership, and can perform effectively its specialized function in the metropolitan region. (USNRC, 1937, p. 85)

The RPAA and especially members Lewis Mumford and Catherine Bauer had become effective lobbyists for the neighborhood concept at the federal level, and the report on cities was one manifestation of this influence. Another more concrete example of Perry's neighborhood unit plan at the policy level appeared in a Public Works Administration (PWA) low-income housing project in Philadelphia, the Carl Mackley Houses, though a dangerous variation of the concept was already creeping into the federal bureaucracy that assumed that high-rise dwellings and increased densities would still leave the unit concept intact (Gillette, 1983, p. 429). This was not a disingeneous hope because by then, the ideas of Swiss architect Charles-Edouard Jeanneret, better known as Le Corbusier, were attaining widespread approbation in the planning and architecture communities. Le Corbusier favored slender white skyscrapers randomly sited in parklike settings to maximize open space in the dense city. So the residential high-rise became an acceptable architectural form, but in the American rendition, the parklike setting received considerably less attention and more important, less land. But the concept remained compatible with the prevailing notion that the fragile neighborhood required fortresslike physical qualities in order to ensure its preservation.

The illogical conclusion of the blend of Perry and Le Corbusier was most evident in a plan devised by New York's Robert Moses and his Urban Redevelopment Corporation and financed by the Metropolitan Life Insurance Company in 1943. The project, called Stuyvesant Town, sprawled over 18 city blocks on the site of a former slum area and had the capacity to house 25,000 residents. *Fortune* magazine called it "a self-contained new community, a virtual suburb within the city" (Gillette, 1983, p. 437). The development was a conscious attempt to attract and maintain the white middle class already demonstrating a wanderlust for suburbia. Planner Joseph McGoldrick warned that without such new neighborhoods, the planned postwar highway construction program would "lead people right out of cities and greatly aggravate financial difficulties already chronic" (Gillette, 1983, p. 437). As for the radical surgery on existing neighborhoods required to erect those new middle-class fortresses, McGoldrick rationalized that blighted neighborhoods in an organic version of Gresham's law would infect and consume stable and sound neighborhoods: "We must cut out the whole cancer and not leave any diseased tissue" (Gillette, 1983, p. 437). When the federal government launched its major postwar housing construction program, codified in the 1949 Housing Act, this philosophy of urban renewal prevailed. The result was a national series of high-rise ghetto neighborhoods that resembled Perry's neighborhood unit plan and its governing village ideal only in the superblock itself and in the social and racial segregation it promoted. The design aspect of Perry's plan was completely submerged. After viewing Stuyvesant Town and subsequent iterations of similar plans, veteran settlement house reformer and Perry follower Mary Simkhovitch sighed,

> Many of my city planner friends think it foolish to engage in housing unless it is on an impressive scale. I suppose a woman looks at it differently. . . . My

life at Greenwich House has taught me not to despise small things. . . .
Neighborhood planning should be developed in accord with a city plan, but
the reverse is true also. (Simkhovitch, 1938, p. 293)

Apparently, the threats to neighborhoods and the values they fostered
loomed so large to policymakers that solutions to preserve these values
in new neighborhood forms took on oversized proportions as well.

THE REVOLT AGAINST NEIGHBORHOOD PLANNING AND THEORY

Perhaps because policymakers and planners could so readily distort
the form and function of the neighborhood unit plan and because the
expanding metropolis of the post-Depression era differed from the city
of a generation earlier that had generated the neighborhood planning
movement, critics of the neighborhood concept in general and of Perry's
unit plan in particular were emerging by the 1940s. In fact, as early as
1929, Jesse Steiner, an erstwhile friend of the neighborhood concept and
president of the National Community Center Association, reached the
conclusion that modern communications technology and the professionalization and specialization of work rendered the neighborhood obsolete as a primary planning unit. Moreover, lengthy experience in immigrant districts convinced colleague Niles Carpenter that ethnic
districts "are far too numerously populated to present anything re-
motely resembling the close-knit primary group community life characteristic of the generic neighborhood" (Gillette, 1983, pp. 429–430). Consequently, any policy or physical planning implementation that seeks to
create a homogeneous neighborhood becomes instead a "pseudo-neigh-
borhood," an environment alien and irrelevant to its residents (Gillette,
1983, pp. 429–430). In 1933, sociologist Louis Wirth added his authoritative voice to the growing chorus of skeptics about neighborhood
planning, chiding the nostalgia of the unit planners and reminding them
of the momentous technological changes in urban life since the turn of
the century:

Some believe that the hope of our social order lies in the return to the local
ties of neighborhood. The trend of our civilization . . . lead[s] in the opposite
direction. There can be no return to the local self-contained neighborhoodly
community except by giving up the technological and cultural advantages of
this shifting . . . community life, which few would be willing to do. (Wirth,
1933, p. 179)

For Wirth, the modern city and the island neighborhood posited by
Perry and others were mutually exclusive. For better or worse, technology had integrated the neighborhood with the city and with the

region. The neighborhood had become an artificial construct, and planners and academics would do better to concentrate on policies of an urban or a regional scale. Instead of planning upward and outward from the neighborhood level, planning should begin at the regional level and move downward to the block or even the household unit. Although Wirth shared with the RPAA the bias toward regional planning, he utilized that perspective as a starting point, whereas for the RPAA, the successfully planned region was the result of effective neighborhood planning. Indeed, by the early 1930s, the 10-volume Regional Plan of New York (RPNY) had replaced Burnham's Chicago plan as the latest and most sophisticated word on regional planning, and the plan perceived every major land use, transportation, and housing problem from a regional base. Wirth doubtless had this planning extravaganza in mind when he extolled the virtues of region-based planning. Although the authors of the New York plan acknowledged the neighborhood planning unit as a possible strategy for developing suburban communities, it represented a minor element in the overall regional plan. If the plan possessed a major focus other than the region, it was the island of Manhattan, the heart of the city, and how to ensure its continued economic vitality over the next generation. Neighborhood preservation was merely an adjunct to preserving the dominant economic role of the island in the region. The authors scarcely mentioned the role of the city's neighborhoods or even of its people for that matter (Duffus, 1930). Robert Moses took up the plan's recommendations with a vengeance and implemented the roads, bridges, and parks—all designed to decongest the city, which in one sense they did, but, especially after World War II, they merely facilitated the suburban exodus much as Burnham's Chicago plan had misfired in its intent to retain the supremacy of the central city.

The attack on neighborhood planning persisted and intensified in the two decades after World War II. The reaction again was less against Perry's neighborhood unit plan as against its interpretation through the federal urban renewal policy. In addition, the social sciences, especially sociologists, began to demur from the facile environmental determinism that marked their early professionalism and also began to question the notion of homogeneity as a positive undergird for neighborhood integrity. Reginald R. Isaacs, a Chicago planner, issued a harsh indictment of the neighborhood on several counts in 1948:

> aspirations to produce the social relationships of the unplanned countryside by utilizing the neighborhood as a planning formula in the city not only illustrates a sense of morbid sentimentality, but would result in failure. (Isaacs, 1948, p. 19)

Having accused neighborhood planners of irrelevant nostalgia, Isaacs next attacked their elitism, accusing them of using their concept as "an instrumentation for the segregation of ethnic and economic groups" and saying that "fear of minority group infiltration is substituted for a common denominator of neighborhood consciousness to exclude inharmonious groups" (Isaacs, 1948, p. 21). As for the argument of neighborhood planners that, at the least, the well-planned neighborhood would stimulate civic consciousness and political participation among residents supported by their collective and concentrated environment, Isaacs scoffed,

> It is quite apparent that the efforts to develop neighborhood cells within the city structure results, psychologically, only in causing people to look and think introvertedly within the narrow confines of their neighborhood. (Isaacs, 1948, pp. 19, 21)

Too much preservation was a bad thing.

It is important to keep in mind, though, that Isaacs's attack was not against the neighborhood *per se* but rather an assault against both its emphasis as a planning mode and what the neighborhood planners hoped to accomplish through their unit plans. Indeed, in subsequent years, strong defenders of neighborhood preservation appeared who were equally strident in their criticism of neighborhood planners and their plans. By the 1960s, it was apparent, as it was only dimly so in the late 1940s, that the irony warned against by earlier critics of neighborhood planning was coming to pass in cities across the nation: Urban neighborhoods were being destroyed in the name of neighborhood preservation, and the group allegedly to be redeemed and uplifted by this environmental transformation—the urban poor—were being hurt the most in terms of torn social fabric, dislocation, and heightened insecurity.

Jane Jacobs's *Death and Life of Great American Cities* (1961) was a searing rebuke of planners in general and of the neighborhood unit concept in particular. She relished the disorder, heterogeneity, and spontaneity of urban life—the very characteristics neighborhood planners sought to exorcise; where they saw the problem, Jacobs perceived the solution. In addition, she excoriated, as did Isaacs, the elitist pretentions of the planners and urged neighborhood organization and planning by the residents and neighborhood-based government, an idea advanced by Mary Follett nearly a half-century earlier but one that remained in the realm of the ideal. The nascent trend of middle-class inner-city rehabilitation also impressed Jacobs as she viewed this movement as confirmation of the vitality of heterogeneity, though subsequent events were to demonstrate that her enthusiasm in this regard was premature.

Perhaps the most sensitive and in many ways most sensible critique emanated from sociologist Herbert Gans's *Urban Villagers* (1962) because it severely undermined the physical and design orientation of planners. His study recalled the feelings of the early social workers that the life of the mind was often more crucial to immigrant success than the age of the building or the repair of the street, that preservation of a neighborhood image was more important than structural preservation. Although he disagreed with Jacobs's interpretation of the neighborhood as a heterogeneous, cosmopolitan entity—such districts were rare in American cities—Gans shared her distrust of neighborhood planners. His analysis of Boston's dowdy and decaying West End revealed a rich mosaic of cultural and psychological attachments despite the relative poverty of the physical environment, a series of neighborhoods consisting of "relatively homogeneous groups, with social and cultural moorings that shielded it fairly effectively from the suggested consequences of number, density, and heterogeneity" (quoted in Silver, 1985, p. 25). In fact, he concluded in a statement that was utmost heresy to Perry's generation of neighborhood planners: "People's lives are not significantly influenced by the physical environment" (quoted in Silver, 1985, p. 25). Here was a relatively fresh view of neighborhood preservation. The applications of design innovations are irrelevant in these districts, Gans contended:

> To a poverty-stricken family, the separation of car and pedestrian traffic or the availability of park and playground within walking distance are not very crucial; their needs are much more basic. (quoted in Silver, 1985, p. 171)

Gans did not dismiss the idea of neighborhood planning; indeed, he expressed considerably more faith in the neighborhood idea than earlier critics of Perry who questioned the relevance of the neighborhood in the schema of the modern metropolis. Gans, rather, and Jacobs as well, directed their criticism more to the nature and character of neighborhood planning than to the importance of the neighborhood itself, which both felt remained a vital unit in urban life. "Neighborhood planning is necessary, of course," Gans allowed, "but of a social and political type which supports community, state, and federal programs for elimination of poverty" (quoted in Silver, 1985, p. 171).

Gans wrote in the context of a major urban crisis, amid cities strewn with the carcasses of neighborhoods gutted by urban renewal, civil disturbance, redlining, and neglect. It was a time of federal programs groping desperately for solutions and of neighborhood residents themselves, mostly voiceless and powerless heretofore, coming together and demanding participation in their own future. Given this background, it is not surprising that Gans and others rejected the physical determinism of the planners, that he challenged them to go into the neighborhoods and listen to the residents and allow them to set the agenda and priorities. Eventually, planners and politicians would follow this advice, though neighborhood organizations in the form of improvement and protective associations had been around longer than the neighborhood policymakers. It was not until the late 1960s that planning and resident participation began to merge to evolve a new neighborhood planning preservation policy.

NEIGHBORHOOD SELF-GOVERNMENT

By that time, lower income neighborhoods had joined middle-class districts in clamoring for a voice in the decision-making process. Actually, the broadening of the base of neighborhood self-government efforts dated back to the settlement house era but concerted organizing efforts in the poorer districts did not occur until just prior to the Depression years. The earliest major participatory experiment was the Cincinnati Social Unit Organization (CSUO) in that city's Mohawk–Brighton neighborhood, an immigrant district, though not a slum, covering 31 blocks. The social unit plan was the brainchild of Wilbur and Elsie Phillips. The idea was to focus on one community service, in this case health care—a vital concern in the congested district whose residents generated a high birth rate and little disposable income for quality health services. Residents in each of the 31 blocks (comprising approximately 500 people) formed a block council and elected one representative to a citizens' council. The Phillipses formed an occupational council parallel to the citizens' committee, consisting of physicians, nurses, and social workers—the relevant personnel in the health delivery system. A general council composed of representatives from the citizens' and occupational councils acted as the governing body. Historian Robert Fisher (1984) who studied the Mohawk–Brighton organization commented that within 2 years, "the Cincinnati Social Unit Organization had established one of the most comprehensive, effective, and cooperative public health programs in the nation" (Fisher, 1984, p. 25). Unfortunately, the very success of the organization led to harrassment from City Hall. Mayor John Galvin charged that the organization was but "one step away from

Bolshevism . . . , a government within a government" (Fisher, 1984, p. 25).

The CSUO experience indicated both that organized neighborhood residents could have a significant impact on the quality of their lives quite apart from any physical or design alterations and apart from the political system. Indeed, most subsequent neighborhood self-government groups rarely defined preservation in structural terms. The latter point avoided the snare of an unresponsive bureaucracy encumbered with red tape, but it also roused suspicions if not fear of competition. These themes would resurface frequently during the next half-century. The confrontational aspects of such groups were especially evident during the 1930s when individuals or organizations linked to larger labor movements turned their efforts to neighborhood organizing as a vehicle to further union or political objectives. The Communist party, for example, sought to build the national Unemployed Council through neighborhood cells that would demand relief funds and adequate housing. Despite some initial success, especially in black neighborhoods, the rigid hierarchy of party governance and its "translocal" interests inhibited sustained neighborhood self-government. By the mid-1930s, the party was emphasizing union organizing activities that leaders believed had only a tangential neighborhood base (Fisher, 1984, pp. 36–44).

But the Depression spawned a more permanent neighborhood organizing ideology in that of Saul Alinsky. New Deal legislation, particularly the Wagner Act, offered a significant boost to union organizing activities and Alinsky, an organizer for the new, militant Congress of Industrial Organizations (CIO), entered Chicago's Back-of-the-Yards neighborhood, a district of second-generation immigrant families, many of whom worked in the adjacent stockyards. The neighborhood was already notorious in the annals of American urban life, having been the scene for Upton Sinclair's gruesome depiction of the meat-packing industry, *The Jungle* (1906). In 1970, Alinsky, reminiscing about the neighborhood, depicted it as he found it in 1938:

> It was the nadir of all the slums of America, worse than Harlem is today. You had this dingy gray mile-by-two-miles of track, south of the big slaughterhouses. Clapboard frame houses, one behind the other. Many of them with outhouses. The neighborhood was practically all Catholic. You never saw so many churches. It made Rome look like a Protestant Gothic town. (quoted in Fisher, 1984, pp. 51–52).

Alinsky came into this inauspicious environment to organize a neighborhood council as a pressure group to persuade the meat packers to bargain with the packers' union, raise wages, and improve working conditions. With all elements of the neighborhood supporting the union, the management acquiesced to their demands. From this initial success, the Back-of-the-Yards Council moved on to secure improved services for the neighborhood and, by the 1950s, it had become more of a traditional protective association, especially against incursions from blacks. In this sense, Alinsky was almost too successful in helping to build a neighborhood preservation consciousness that heightened the insularity of the community. But Alinsky hoped to use the council as a model for a nationwide network of "people's organizations," as he called them, at the neighborhood level. The model emphasized the use of local leadership, allowing them to set the agenda and using whatever tactics necessary to attain that agenda. The professional organizer would merely act as the catalyst (Fisher, 1984, p. 52).

World War II and the subsequent suspicion of radical-tainted, militant groups postponed Alinsky's dream of a nationwide neighborhood movement. In fact, similar organizations would not emerge again until the 1960s. Instead, the dominant theme of neighborhood organization became protection as urban populations held increasing numbers of minorities and disinvestment threatened the defenses of neighborhoods. There were exceptions to this rule, especially in a handful of Southern communities such as Natchez, New Orleans, Savannah, and Charleston where decades of decay had taken a significant toll on historic neighborhoods. Except for the French Quarter residents in New Orleans, however, most of these groups came from outside the historic district and, in fact, tended to view residents as interlopers or obstacles to neighborhood preservation (Goldfield, 1982a). Nevertheless, the historic preservation movement that gained momentum after the late 1940s provided an important counter to federal policies that concentrated on demolition and the creation of new neighborhoods.

The other exception to the general organizational trend occurred in suburbia. Federal subsidies to new home construction and the interstate highway network begun in 1956 spurred the creation of instant communities. Some developers such as the Levitt Company provided for neighborhood organizations in their suburbs for the purposes of overseeing recreational facilities, maintenance, and the character of new development. Frequently, membership in a neighborhood group accompanied the purchase of a home. Early in a suburb's life, participation rates were high, but after several years and some turnover in the initial group of residents enthusiasm in neighborhood self-government waned. Many residents spent increasing amounts of time commuting, and there was little perceived danger from local government or diverse social groups. Preservation in the protective sense was simply not an issue (Goldfield & Brownell, 1979).

But the combination of urban renewal, the civil rights movement, and urban disorder terminated the relative lull in neighborhood organizing activities by the 1960s. The questioning of authority in many aspects of American life led many to question the validity of planners and politicians making decisions that adversely affected the lives of neighborhood residents without those residents participating in the decisions. In addition, both groups had strikingly different perceptions of neighborhood preservation. Also, civil rights activists, much as union organizers had discovered in an earlier generation, found that the neighborhood was an effective unit for organizing protest groups. The pressures of the 1960s worked to create a significant alteration in federal urban policy that sought not to remake or destroy neighborhoods but to develop strategies to work within the existing physical structure and with existing residents. For the first time since concern about neighborhood preservation surfaced in the 1880s, planners, professionals, policymakers, and residents themselves placed physical and design concerns in the background, if including them at all in the new neighborhood strategy picture. The concern now was with poverty and its amelioration, unemployment, services, and education—people—rather than space-oriented solutions, harking back to Jane Addams's simple confession 80 years earlier: "I do not believe in geographical salvation" (quoted in Silver, 1985, p. 162).

President Lyndon B. Johnson's War on Poverty generated the Community Action Program (CAP) in 1966, which established Community Action agencies (CAAs) to promote neighborhood self-help projects by providing grass-roots organizations with seed money for this purpose, bypassing state and city bureaucracies that had, historically, held suspicions about neighborhood-based government. By 1968, over 1,000 CAAs had received federal funds that they utilized to support child social welfare programs and to press for improved quality and level of public services. The stress on neighborhood organizing incorporated primarily black and poor urban residents into the political process for the first time, and the rise in black officeholding citywide was a direct result of civic lessons learned in the neighborhood groups and their programs. It was also an official acknowledgment that poor neighborhoods contained qualities (and residents) worth preserving. At least one national organization, the National Welfare Rights Organization emerged from local, neighborhood-based welfare associations. Also, the federal program drew neighborhood leaders into the bureaucracy, giving them, in effect, a political education, administrative skills, and decent salaries. Predictably, state and local leaders hacked away at the program and President Richard M. Nixon's "new federalism," represented by revenue sharing, effectively terminated the direct grant-in-aid program to poor neighborhood organizations. Nevertheless, these groups remained a political force in their respective communities through the 1970s and 1980s (Fisher, 1984).

In several instances, the experience with CAAs led unintimidated city officials to institutionalize some of their features on a citywide basis. In New York City, for example, the city administration formed the Office of Neighborhood Government (ONG) in 1970 in order to decentralize city services. The ONG ordered the formation of district service cabinets including residents and members of various city agencies. The city's 62 planning districts (comprising approximately 125,000 inhabitants each) formed the basic units of these cabinets that were responsible for delivering services to constituent neighborhoods. Though considerably larger than a neighborhood unit, the districts proved successful in improving the level and quality of services throughout the city (Mudd, 1976).

The decentralization of urban functions and administrative process accelerated with the passage of the Community Development Act during the last year of the Nixon administration. The Community Development Block Grant (CDBG) mandated citizen participation for any project to which local officials applied the block grant funds. As much as the Wagner Act 40 years earlier had encouraged labor union organizers to launch major recruitment campaigns in American industries and neighborhoods, the block grant provisions accelerated and broadened the neighborhood self-government movement begun during the Johnson administration (Goldfield & Brownell, 1979).

The citizen participation mandate occurred at a time of heightened neighborhood consciousness in any case. The depredations of urban renewal, the emphasis of civic leaders on downtown revitalization, the stretching thin of services as a result of voracious annexation in Southern and Southwestern cities, and the revived interest in urban living had already combined to move neighborhood preservation front and center as a *political* force on the local scene by the early 1970s. In Atlanta, a coalition of predominantly white neighborhoods banded together in 1973 to block the construction of I-485 in the city, a project advocated by downtown businesses and the development community. At roughly the same time, several eastside Atlanta neighborhoods—Inman Park and Ansley Park among them—were being rediscovered by young middle-class urbanites who were demanding an upgrading in urban services, a chronic complaint of the city's black neighborhoods as well. The neighborhood and racial coalition helped to elect, in 1973, the city's first black mayor, Maynard Jackson, thus ending for the time being the domination of urban government by a relatively narrow elite with close ties to the financial-mercantile interests and northside residential areas.

A similar series of events in San Antonio helped to defeat the Good Government League, a group of business leaders that had dominated local politics since the 1950s. Texas law had enabled San Antonio, unlike Atlanta, to satisfy its insatiable land appetite, spreading services thin, especially in the older neighborhoods. The westside, predominantly Mexican-American districts were especially neglected in the land boom, as streets went unpaved or fell into disrepair, parks were poorly maintained and lacked adequate equipment, fire protection was haphazard, and the zoning commission seemed willing to allow commercial incursions on residential neighborhoods in the area. Development in the higher elevated northside area caused periodic flooding on the west side, and the opening up of these new areas threatened the Edwards aquifer and hence the purity of the city's water supply—an issue that expanded the concern to other areas of San Antonio. In the midst of mounting concern over the costs of growth—both financial and environmental, the city underwent a court-ordered shift to a district electoral system. In the first election held under the new system in May 1977, 5 Mexican-Americans and 1 black came onto the 11-member city council and antigrowth advocate Lila Cockrell became the new mayor (Abbott, 1981).

As the San Antonio scenario implied, alterations in electoral procedures, precipitated by the 1965 Voting Rights Act and subsequent court decisions striking down at-large electoral systems as inherently discriminatory in certain parts of the South, enhanced the role of neighborhoods in urban politics, making the neighborhood "interest" an integral part of the local political system, a bulwark against the ill effects of the growth ethic and the withdrawal or diminution of vital urban services. The Community Development Act reinforced these trends and led some city administrations to institutionalize the neighborhood's voice in electoral politics. Perhaps the most noteworthy effort occurred, not surprisingly, in Atlanta where a neighborhood coalition had been so crucial to the political fortunes of Maynard Jackson. The new mayor divided the city into 24 neighborhood planning units and assigned a staff planner to each unit as a facilitator to enable residents to draw up an agenda of neighborhood needs, an agenda that would be especially useful in determining the allocation of block grant funds. The Atlanta process became a model for neighborhood-based government in cities throughout the country and paralleled the neighborhood council movement already underway in several European cities (Silver, 1985).

Indeed, it seemed as if the Western world had awakened in the early

1970s to the fact that neighborhood preservation and self-government were preferable to urban renewal. Within a 3-year period beginning in 1971, West Germany, Sweden, Great Britain, and the United States all passed legislation terminating urban renewal policies and providing incentives for conservation efforts. The shift was not only from renewal to rehabilitation, but more important, from plan to process.

And within this shift there was a growing recognition in the new public policy that neighborhood preservation implied more than housing: it included infrastructure, services, and institutional support. The revelation occurred primarily as a result of citizen agenda setting as well as from the reemphasis on the total neighborhood environment in the theoretical literature.

PLAN AND PROCESS: THE UNEASY ALLIANCE

The merger of neighborhood preservation planning and neighborhood self-government was more a marriage of convenience and necessity rather than of love, and frequently neighborhood groups held the shotgun to effect the union. The merger did not signify a relationship that would endure happily ever after or even in the short run, for there were forces at work in the 1970s and on into the 1980s that threatened neighborhood preservation at the very time when the urban neighborhood was in ascendancy as an important factor in the planning and policymaking elements of city administration.

The 1970s were not particularly prosperous years for the nation's cities, especially for those outside the so-called Sun Belt. New York City's incipient bankruptcy and the near collapse of Cleveland's financial structure merely highlighted the growing economic woes of cities whose population and economic base had fled to the suburbs or out of the region altogether, leaving behind a decaying infrastructure and a poorer citizenry demanding greater services. By the middle of the decade, city administrations focused on at least four strategies designed to reverse or at least halt the downward spiral: upgrading infrastructure; "cutback" planning; downtown revitalization; and neighborhood rehabilitation.

One policy emphasized the use of block grant funds for infrastructure, thereby relieving the city treasury of an onerous burden or of expensive services. Chicago, for example, expended $32 million in block grant funds for snow removal. Though the stated purpose of the Community Development Act was to assist less affluent segments of the urban population and their neighborhoods, loose federal oversight and local financial necessities compromised the original intent of the act

(Peirce, 1984a). City administrations have also engaged in what Cleveland planner Norman Krumholz called "cutback planning"—trimming bloated bureaucracies and budgets and, in some instances, adopting a "triage" concept for neighborhood assistance and services (Krumholz, Cogger, & Linner, 1975). The latter strategy categorizes neighborhoods as medics defined battlefield casualties, that is, terminal, recoverable with appropriate treatment, and stable, directing finite resources into the last two classes while giving up on the first. Sometimes local officials based their assessments on superficial windshield surveys (as in Memphis) that merely catalogued surface physical conditions ignoring nearly two decades of research to the contrary as well as the concrete fact of the distinction between housing market and housing condition. Roger Starr, head of New York City's Housing and Redevelopment Authority, suggested in 1976 that fire and police stations and public schools be shut down in decaying areas to induce more rapid decline and population removal. The "triage" strategy, of course, worked as a self-fulfilling prophecy (Fisher, 1984, p. 124).

It may seem anomalous that at a time when neighborhoods and their residents were expanding their role in city government that very government would be able to foist policies on certain neighborhoods that can only be characterized as creeping demolition. But "triage" and neighborhood power are not at all contradictory given the wide variety of neighborhood types and residents. Neighborhood self-government implies an insularity, even a selfishness, not a unanimity of purpose and interest. Even as civic leaders counted neighborhoods, they were well aware that some were more equal than others.

A more common strategy in effecting an urban revival focused on downtown revitalization. The new urban mayors of the late 1970s and the 1980s are as much pitchmen and recruiters as they are administrators. Economic development is a major objective of city administrations today, and downtown is frequently one of the primary focal points of this effort. Gleaming office towers, spacious pedestrian and shopping malls, trolleys, markets, and even parks are the high-tech paraphernalia of downtown revival. But the boutiques and bank buildings often bear no congruence with the shabby inner city neighborhoods on the periphery and, in fact, the new downtowns have occasionally gobbled up these neighborhoods. Critics charge that these subsidies to real estate developers neglect the interests of nearby residents. As Lewis Mumford asked a half-century ago:

> Does a city exist to promote the life of its citizens? Or do the citizens exist in order to increase the size, the importance, and the commercial turnover of the city? (Mumford, 1925, p. 199)

The question is relevant as well in relation to the fourth urban revival strategy, the upgrading of existing neighborhoods, specifically the encouragement through public-private partnerships of residential rehabilitation. The changing demography of our metropolitan areas— the growing numbers of elderly, singles, and adult-oriented couples— enhanced the possibilities for urban residence. Low-interest loans, urban homesteading programs, and investments in infrastructure subsidized this back-to-the-city movement. Actually, the growing popularity of brownstones, row houses, infill housing (new construction architecturally compatible with but not imitative of existing structures), and adaptive reuse for residential purposes resulted more from new household formation and movement within the city than from households emigrating from suburbia. In any case, these subsidies in addition to private-directed rehabilitation revitalized a number of inner city neighborhoods, most notably Adams-Morgan in Washington, DC, the Victorian District in Savannah, and the Fourth Ward in Charlotte, North Carolina. The results were an increased tax base, reduced service levels (education and welfare, in particular because new residents had fewer children than former inhabitants), and a physical upgrading of previously declining areas. On occasion, the upgrading included displacement of previous, usually poor and black, residents reminiscent of, though not on the same scale as the displacement engendered by urban renewal.

Of course, there are examples of more sensitive rehab-preservation projects, most notably Savannah's Victorian District, a 45 block neighborhood replete with distinctive wood-frame, gingerbread-style houses erected between 1870 and 1900 just south of the city's downtown. Once a fashionable area, the district had fallen into disrepair by the early 1970s, the homes having been subdivided into rental properties. As part of Savannah's renewed interest in its rich history, it was likely that the general rehab fever about in the city would eventually infect even this neighborhood. The residents were predominantly black, poor, and elderly renters who would be unable to withstand a speculative onslaught. In 1977, investment banker Leopold Adler II brought together an interracial group of neighborhood leaders, bankers, architects, and preservation specialists to form a nonprofit development corporation, the Savannah Landmark Rehabilitation Project. The objective of the firm was to rehabilitate roughly one third of the 800-odd homes in the district without displacing their low-income residents. Financed initially by federal subsidies and more recently by private syndicates taking advantage of historic-structure tax benefits, Savannah Landmark attained its goal in 1984 and, in addition, constructed 44 infill units designed to blend in with the Victorian character of the neighborhood (Peirce, 1983).

The strategies of urban revival that have impinged on neighborhood stability indicate the limits of the citizen participation process in neighborhood preservation. The insularity and occasionally conflicting interests of neighborhoods mentioned earlier is one obvious constraint on the citizen role. Another is the subtle co-option that occurs when neighborhood leaders become part of the bureaucratic process, even on the payroll of the city administration. Studies have indicated that neighborhood leaders tend to be of higher status than their constituents and more concerned with land use and zoning issues than with health and human services questions. Further, most neighborhood groups are short-lived, a situation that reduces their long-term political power. Even institutionalized neighborhood government is waning: Atlanta, for example, has reduced the number of professional staffers who attend to neighborhood planning from 24 to 6. City administrators have discovered that interest in participation varies widely between and within neighborhoods (Hutcheson, 1984). Further, with finite resources and heightened neighborhood consciousness, decision making places local officials on a continuous edge of controversy; in some instances, this has slowed or even paralyzed policymaking. This is especially a dilemma in district-based electoral systems that often pit neighborhoods against each other on a citywide basis. Some wonder whether the interests of the city as a whole are thereby undermined (Goering, 1979).

Whatever the shortcomings of neighborhood self-government, it is unlikely that a reversion to a planner-oriented neighborhood preservation policy will occur in the near future. National organizations from the Neighborhood Housing Services to the Association of Community Organizations for Reform Now (ACORN) have proven their effectiveness at local organizing and lobbying for proneighborhood measures at the state and federal levels of government. Further, the political and fiscal role of cities within the nation demands a strong neighborhood self-government component. The political influence of cities is shrinking nationally as their relative share of the population declines. Urban policy was hardly a major issue of debate between candidates Reagan and Mondale during the 1984 presidential election campaign and outside of enterprise zones and a phasing out of revenue sharing, one would be hard pressed to delineate the urban policy of the second Reagan administration. Also, under the president's "new federalism," states and localities must now assume programs, especially in the social services area, once funded mostly or partially through federal expenditures (Peirce, 1984b).

The financial and political difficulties encountered by cities in recent years have one positive effect: They force local authorities to search for creative solutions to local problems. The emergence of the new development-oriented mayor is one example of this adaptation; another is the growing self-help movement within neighborhoods: Tenants assuming control over their public housing projects, homeowners establishing development corporations to rehabilitate neighborhood dwellings, and cooperative day care and health care arrangements are some of the indications that neighborhood residents are looking less to the city hall, the state house, and to Washington, and more to themselves (Peirce, 1984c).

AGENDA FOR FUTURE POLICY AND RESEARCH: DESIGN AND URBAN THEORY

One aspect of neighborhood self-help that has not received sufficient attention, both by residents and policymakers alike, is design. This is understandable given the widespread revulsion from the "good-houses-make-good-people" notion so evident in planning and government policy through the 1960s; it is even more understandable given some of the design choices for the "good houses." The most notorious but by no means the only miscalculation was the Pruitt-Igoe housing project erected in the mid-1950s in St. Louis and purposely destroyed in 1972 by the city. The project won architectural prizes as a model of Corbusian design, but soon after construction elevators failed, plumbing broke down, vandalism skyrocketed: there were too many unprotected areas, the parks between the towers became battlegrounds for gangs, and parents found it impossible (not surprisingly) to supervise children from the upper floors. The design may indeed have been appropriate if located in a different area with apartments scaled to a professional clientele with no children. But as public housing, it was a totally disastrous effort ("The Death," 1972, p. 11).

In European urban neighborhoods, design remains an important component of self-government efforts. In Stockholm, Sweden planners went through a "Pruitt-Igoe phase" of neighborhood building during the late 1960s and early 1970s, constructing high-rise blocks of flats in new suburbs inhabited by disproportionate numbers of immigrants ("guest" workers, mainly). These instant ghettos soon became synonymous with vandalism, service breakdowns, alcoholism, and family stress. Of course, the oppressive design features were only part of a larger problem, but by the mid-1970s, the city's planners reversed their policies and took assiduous care of the design element in subsequent suburban and urban neighborhood projects. From 1975 to the present, residential structures rarely reached heights above three stories; there were considerably more one-story dwellings, and devices such as terracing, landscaping, and the grouping of units in courtyards fostered an intimacy not shared by the preceding generation of neighborhood building or rehabilitation. The residents prefer these arrangements, and social problems are minimal (Goldfield, 1982b).

There are at least two reasons for the Swedish reemphasis on design. First, almost all Swedish planners are architects; hence their training includes considerable work in urban design. In fact, they have been especially proud of their design efforts—both interiors and exteriors— over the years. Swedish planner-architects have pioneered techniques to maximize light, create the sense of interior space, and site interior fixtures and appliances to ensure convenience. This tradition goes at least as far back as the late 1920s when planner-architects adopted the functionalist style to neighborhood building. For the Swedes, design was as much a political and social statement as it was a physical exercise. Swedish planner-architect Uno Åhrèn wrote in 1930 that functionalism "is the only truly grand democratic movement of our time" (Sidenbladh, 1981, p. 68). The equality of each building, its simple lines, its siting within the contours of nature bespoke this democratic purpose. Even during the design-poor era of the late 1960s, planner-architects struggled against politicans who were more interested in quantity than aesthetics and functionality.

A second reason for the importance of design in Swedish neighborhood building is the tradition of citizen involvement in design issues. As early as the 1920s, cooperative groups experimented with designs of building groups to ensure privacy while at the same time offering opportunities for collective activities such as cooking, eating, and entertainment. More recently, women's groups have been involved in designing interiors and the location of external services. Because approximately three out of every four adult women are engaged in the workforce outside the home, they have demanded the siting of rooms, fixtures, children's play areas, and social services to reflect the fact that parents, especially women, currently spend relatively little time in the residential area and that time spent must not be wasted on design elements that inconvenience the users. In 1979, a group of women architects, engineers, journalists, sociologists, and politicians formed the Kvinnors Byggforum (Women's Building Forum) to encourage certain design standards for neighborhood planning, including the decentralization of open space and the incorporation of single-family home qualities in building groups—gardening, workshops, and proximity to nature in particular (Kvinnors Byggforum, 1982).

In fact, it is the single-family home ideal (though not isolated on a half-acre plot) that is coming to occupy more design prominence, not so

much as a building type, but in the amenities such a dwelling can provide even in a dense urban environment. The Swedes, like the Americans, have never been totally comfortable with an urban environment
and have sought to escape it at the first opportunity; and, like the Americans, Swedes prefer single-family home living. With high land prices in
the city, many (40% of Swedish households) Swedes have sought a
compromise by purchasing small single-family homes for summer residences. The Women's Building Forum seeks to modify this practice by
utilizing design to produce some of the attributes of single-family dwellings in existing urban neighborhoods (Goldfield, 1982b).

Which brings us back to the South Bronx and Charlotte Gardens.
The corrective to our environmental determinism offered by Jane Jacobs
and Herbert Gans in the 1960s was necessary, but the Charlotte Gardens
experiment as well as the experience with traditional public housing
demonstrate that design does matter. The training of planners in this
country, to say nothing of city administrators, concentrates on social,
technical, and communication skills. Design is usually an afterthought
in professional education. In addition, design considerations have generally come under the rubric of neighborhood improvement—more of a
concern for affluent districts. Yet recent experiments in Charleston, for
example, where city administrators have adapted the famed Charleston
single house to public housing neighborhoods, have indicated that
lower income residents relish innovative design features as much as
other citizens.

Regrettably, the historiography of neighborhood development and
preservation in the United States has not emphasized the relationship
between design and resident satisfaction and behavior modification.
Historians still operate under the reaction to the excessive environmental determinism during the years prior to the 1960s. To be sure, planning
historians have paid close attention to the design details of such neighborhood planners as Perry, Mumford, and Bartholomew, but the architectural aspect of structures receives less scrutiny; this is not surprising
because most planners concentrated on layout rather than on architecture, a major exception being George Pullman's plan for his industrial
community, Pullman, Illinois, in the 1880s, and post-World War II public housing projects, both of which had disastrous results. The division
of architecture from planning has resulted in a history that replicates this
dichotomy.

Perhaps, as Frank Lloyd Wright observed a half-century ago, we
have no "esthetics comparable to [our] great political idea of democracy" (cited in Wilson, 1983, p. 115), no American democratic version of
functionalism, whose repetitiveness and simplicity suited the tenets of

democratic socialism. But this is not entirely so: we do possess a design ideal that reflects our individualistic democracy. Catherine Bauer, a housing reformer and colleague of Clarence Perry, iterated this American design ethic in the late 1930s:

> a home where children can be reared in decency and health where they may develop the mental-moral vigor and pride in community that will make them first class citizens. . . . This means better housing and not merely "minimal standards" that sacrifice space and privacy to better plumbing, a private garden for every family that wants one and not at the expense of hours of travel. (quoted in Bauman, 1980–1981, p. 4)

Of course, the trick is to make this design ideal accessible to all who desire it. The Charlotte Gardens experiment indicates its possibility, though on a small scale to be sure. Suburbia, an intellectual and design anathema to many social scientists, may yet hold the design model for urban neighborhoods of the future.

That this may come as a surprise to historians of neighborhood planning is not unusual considering the fact that many of us remain bound, consciously or otherwise, to the Wirthian conception of the city as a distinctive entity, as different from suburbia as from the rural countryside. In fact, we may be embarking on a posturban era, a prospect recognized by geographers but not yet by historians: cities of lower densities, altered functions, and transitory populations depending on urban residence because of the stage-in-life cycle, poverty, or preference—the first two encompassing significantly greater households than the last. So we have the space and diversity to experiment with design; indeed, the trends toward infill and adaptive reuse are examples of such experimentation. In other words, the era may be past when we can discuss a distinctly urban design and design context, but rather we must advance design possibilities on the basis of residents' perceptions and ideals.

There is still no merger in the historical literature between neighborhood planning and neighborhood self-government. Historians of neighborhood movements rarely discuss neighborhood plans and vice versa. This is to be expected because there was little formal relationship between the two until the 1970s. Yet the fact that these two elements of American history occurred simultaneously and parallel to each other affords the historian the opportunity to discover why the estrangement was not resolved until recently. And, more especially, how the two may maintain a working agreement. For, increasingly, cities and their neighborhoods are on their own, and creative planning solutions demand input from a wide spectrum of citizens, especially the neighborhood residents themselves.

Our perceptions of neighborhood preservation, and hence our plans, have been influenced by stereotypes of city and suburb, design, density, and decay. We have either been too physical in our planning orientation or too unmindful of the specific design needs of groups regardless of background or location; we have been too project-oriented or paid too much attention to process; and we have planned too much or not at all. Neighborhood preservation—both in the creation of new areas and the traditional ideals such creations reflect and in the maintenance of existing districts for the very same reasons—has reflected these stereotypes. As our urban and planning theory improves, so will our practice; as distinctions between city and suburb blur, as citizen and plan attain a more intimate partnership, and as aesthetics regain greater respectability, neighborhood preservation efforts—in new forms and old—will more closely approach the harmony of people and planning sought by Lewis Mumford in *The City in History*. It is the value of history to cover the chartered territory so that we need not retrace our steps amid the old, worn ideas unless we want to pluck something new and fresh from them as we continue to move forward.

REFERENCES

Abbott, C. (1981). *The new urban America: Growth and politics in sunbelt cities.* Chapel Hill: The University of North Carolina Press.

Arnold, J. L. (1979). *The neighborhood and city hall: The origin of neighborhood associations in Baltimore, 1880–1911. Journal of Urban History, 6,* 3–30.

Bauman, J. F. (1980–1981). Visions of a post-war city: A perspective on urban planning in Philadelphia and the nation, 1942–45. *Urbanism Past and Present, 6,* 1–11.

Burg, D. F. (1976). *Chicago's white city of 1893.* Lexington: University Press of Kentucky.

Burnham, D. H., & Bennett, E. H. (1909). In C. Moore (Ed.), *Plan of Chicago.* Chicago: The Commercial Club.

Community of delight rises from rubble of South Bronx ghetto. (1984, December 22). *Los Angeles Times,* p. 3.

Cooley, C. H. (1909). *Social organization.* New York: Harper & Bros.

Davis, A. F. (1967). *Spearheads for reform: The social settlements and the Progressive movement, 1890–1914.* New York: Oxford University Press.

The death of Pruitt-Igoe. (1972, March 19). *The New York Times,* p. 11.

Duffus, R. L. (1930). *Mastering a metropolis.* New York: Harper & Bros.

Fisher, R. (1984). *Let the people decide: Neighborhood organizing in America.* Boston: Twayne.

Follett, M. (1918). *The new state: Group organization, the solution of popular government.* New York: Longmans, Green.

Gans, H. (1962). *The urban villagers.* New York: Free Press.

Gillette, H. J. (1983). The evolution of neighborhood planning: From the progressive era to the 1949 housing act. *Journal of Urban History, 9,* 421–44.

Goering, J. M. (1979). The national neighborhood movement: A preliminary analysis and critique. *American Planning Association Journal, 45,* 506–14.

Goldfield, D. R. (1982a). *Cotton fields and skyscrapers: Southern city and region.* Baton Rouge: Louisiana State University Press.

Goldfield, D. R. (1982b). National urban policy in Sweden. *American Planning Association Journal, 48*, 24–38.

Goldfield, D. R., & Brownell, B. A. (1979). *Urban America: From downtown to no town.* Boston: Houghton Mifflin.

Hines, T. S. (1974). *Burnham of Chicago: Architect and planner.* New York: Oxford University Press.

Howard, E. (1965). *Garden cities of tomorrow* (rev. ed.). Cambridge, MA: M.I.T. Press.

Hutcheson, J. D., Jr. (1984). Citizen representation in neighborhood planning. *American Planning Association Journal, 50*, 183–93.

Isaacs, R. R. (1948). The neighborhood theory: An analysis of its adequacy. *Journal of the American Institute of Planners, 14*, 15–23.

Jackson, K. T. (1985). *Crabgrass frontier: The suburbanization of the United States.* New York: Oxford University Press.

Jacobs, J. (1961). *The death and life of great American cities.* New York: Random House.

Keller, S. (1968). *The urban neighborhood.* New York: Random House.

Krumholz, N., Cogger, J. M., & Linner, J. H. (1975). The Cleveland policy planning report. *Journal of The American Institute of Planners, 41*, 298–304.

Kvinnors Byggforum Manifest 82-01-14: Det gäller vårt liv. Mimeograph in author's possession, 1982.

Lubove, R. (1962). *The Progressives and the slums: Tenement house reform in New York City, 1890–1917.* Pittsburgh: University of Pittsburgh Press.

Lubove, R. (1963). *Community planning in the 1920s: The contribution of the Regional Planning Association of America.* Pittsburgh: University of Pittsburgh Press.

Mudd, J. (1976). Beyond community control: A neighborhood strategy for city government. *Publius, 6*, 113–135.

Mumford, L. (1925). Realties versus dreams. *Journal of the American Institute of Architects, 13*(June), 30–39.

Mumford, L. (1954). The neighborhood and the neighborhood unit. *Town Planning Review, 24*, 258–269.

Peirce, N. (1983, December 31). Savannah: A model for revival without gentrification. *Washington Post*, p. 17.

Peirce, N. (1984a, December 29). Community development: an anniversary review. *Washington Post*, p. 21.

Peirce, N. (1984b, October 20). Future budget decisions will key on states. *Washington Post*, p. 21.

Peirce, N. (1984c, September 8). St. Louis housing units became national model. *Washington Post*, p. 20.

Perry, C. A. (1924). Planning a city neighborhood from the social point of view. In *Proceedings of the National Conference of Social Work* (pp. 415–421). Chicago: University of Chicago.

Perry, C. A. (1929). *Neighborhood and community planning* (Vol. 3). New York: Regional Survey of New York and Its Environs.

Schaffer, D. (1982). *Garden cities for America: The Radburn experience.* Philadelphia: Temple University Press.

Sidenbladh, G. (1981). *Planering för Stockholm, 1923–1958.* Stockholm: Liber.

Silver, C. (1985). Neighborhood planning in historical perspective. *American Planning Association Journal, 51*, 161–74.

Simkhovitch, M. K. (1938). *Neighborhood: My story of Greenwich House.* New York: Longmans.

Tuttle, W. (1970). *Race riot: Chicago in the red summer of 1919.* New York: Atheneum.

U.S. National Resources Committee, Committee on Urbanism. (1937). *Our cities: Their role in the national economy.* Washington, DC: U.S. Government Printing Office.

Wilson, W. H. (1964). *The City Beautiful movement in Kansas City.* Columbia: University of Missouri Press.

Wilson, W. H. (1983). Moles and skylarks. In D. A. Krueckeberg (Ed.), *Introduction to planning history in the United States* (pp. 88–121). New Brunswick, NJ: Center for Urban Policy Research.

Wirth, L. (1933). The scope and problems of the community. In L. Wirth (Ed.), *Cities and Social Life* (rev. ed., pp. 3–19). Chicago: University of Chicago Press.

Wood, R. A. (1970). *The neighborhood in nation building* (rev. ed.). New York: Arno Press.

8

Communities in Transition
FROM THE INDUSTRIAL TO THE POSTINDUSTRIAL ERA

WILLEM VAN VLIET-- AND JACK BURGERS

INTRODUCTION

One of the underlying purposes of community planning is the creation of settings that support the activities of households and institutions. In this context, spatial planning aims at the realization and maintenance of a state of congruence between human behavior and the physical environment. The relationships between individual and institutional activities on the one hand and the environment on the other can be analyzed on different spatial levels and for different time spans. Studies range from the scale of "vertical villages" in high-rise buildings (Wekerle, 1976) to "urban villages" (Gans, 1962), to "global villages" (McLuhan, 1968), and from observations on the use of urban parks and playgrounds measuring time in minutes (Gold, 1972; Hole, 1966) to historical research seeking to uncover developments during the course of centuries (Hohenberg & Lees, 1985).

In this chapter, we will adopt a fairly long-range perspective to analyze several societal trends and their implications for the spatial scale of communities. Thus our analysis follows developments from roughly the end of the eighteenth century, when the Industrial Revolution radi-

WILLEM VAN VLIET-- • Pennsylvania State University, University Park, PA 16802. JACK BURGERS • Department of Sociology, Tilburg University, Tilburg, The Netherlands.

cally changed existing patterns of spatial form, up to the present time when economic and technological factors once again are transforming the spatial order of communities. Our approach is catascopic in nature, that is, we examine macrolevel developments as a framework within which smaller scale units such as neighborhoods evolve. Our approach focuses on the direction of changes in the spatial features of communities. We are not concerned with the detailed nature of such changes. Such accounts are already available, and we will refer to them where appropriate.

As an analytical device, we will adopt a classification that distinguishes four basic societal functions: an economic, a social, a cultural, and a political subsystem (cf. Parsons, 1937). Our analyses will examine the "activity space" of these subsystems. More specifically, we will be concerned with the extent to which the geographical space within which the subsystems operate has increased or decreased. An especially important question in this connection, in fact the main problem to be dealt with in this chapter, is whether the spatial scale of the four subsystems has developed in the same direction and at the same pace. In other words, we will address the question of congruence between the economic, social, cultural, and political subsystems in terms of the development of their spatial scales.

A CONCEPTUAL FRAMEWORK OF COMMUNITIES

Before turning to our analysis, it is important to clarify what we mean by community. Community has in common with other social science concepts like intelligence and social class that it often proves a powerful explanatory variable, yet it is hard to find a consensus regarding its precise definition. In his classic review of 94 definitions of community found in the literature, Hillery (1955) distilled as the three most commonly mentioned elements the following: (a) social interaction; (b) common ties in the sense of a shared value system; and (c) a geographical area. A major portion of the community literature has indeed concerned itself with social and cultural aspects of life in local areas (Poplin, 1979). However, Hillery's distillation provided an incomplete indication of the range of functions attributed to communities. Additional community functions include, for example, the production, distribution, and consumption of goods and services, socialization, social control, and mutual support (Warren, 1978). Others have provided similar taxonomies, often at the neighborhood level (Banerjee & Baer, 1984; Hallman, 1984; Wireman, 1984).

We have found it useful to adopt a basic fourfold classification of community functions derived from Parsons's (1937) general action systems theory. As shown in Figure 1, we view communities as consisting of an economic, a social, a cultural, and a political subsystem. The economic subsystem comprises those processes and structures that are concerned with the production, distribution, and consumption of goods and services. As such, it also includes the procurement of resources and their allocation through the market and bureaucratic mechanisms. The social subsystem provides a framework for a community's social integration. It refers to relations of solidarity, formed as people relate to each other individually and in the context of social institutions. The cultural subsystem manifests itself in the value systems of a community as well as in the more material expressions thereof, including the built environment. The political subsystem, finally, embodies the public decision-

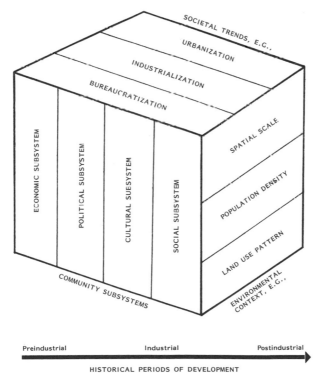

Figure 1. A conceptual framework for the historical analysis of communities and their environmental context.

making function of communities. It involves the formulation of collective goals as well as the selection of means toward their implementation.

It is important to note at the outset that we use community as a theoretical concept and analytical tool that is not tied to a specific spatial level or moment in history. This enables us to examine, at different points in time, to what extent people are part of different communities. For example, the neighborhood unit may once have been the spatial scale for most aspects of all four subsystems, but today it does not necessarily constitute a community in any sense at all (Leighton & Wellman, 1979). Also, people may economically be part of a global system, with political loyalties to a nation-state, whereas socially they are members of a neighborhood. Our perspective makes it possible to examine such multiple layers of community as they have changed since the Industrial Revolution.

Having outlined the four community subsystems, we now want to point out the relations with their environmental contexts. These relations are reciprocal, that is, the subsystems generate particular environmental configurations, and these configurations facilitate or hinder the functioning of the subsystems in certain ways. Some examples will make these patterns of influence less abstract. Meyersohn (1963), for one, suggested that the individualism seen as typical of North America has manifested itself in an abundance of owner-occupied detached houses, each with a private yard. He made the more general point, along with many others, that cultural values mold the physical landscape. Similarly, Willhelm and Sjoberg (1960) demonstrated the role of economic interests in zoning committee decisions about land-use changes, whereas Form (1954) provided an early analysis of the role of political factors in the determination of urban land uses.

In practice, of course, the four subsystems interact with each other and exert a joint influence on the environment. Thus in North America it has been a combination of political lobbying, economic pressures, and cultural climate that has brought about extensive residential development characterized by single-family dwellings built at low densities in outlying areas.

It should be clear that the relationships between the economic, social, cultural, and political subsystems and their environments are mutual; that is, also the functioning of these subsystems is affected by characteristics of the physical environment. For example, the just-mentioned low-density environments hinder the activities of households whose needs and life-styles diverge from the "familism" pattern thought to be congruent with the traditional suburban environment (Van Vliet--, 1985). The segregated land uses and the low population densities do not provide a sufficient critical mass of people to support jobs, day-care centers, medical services, retail outlets, and the like within easy access, making these environments difficult to live in for single-parent households, dual-earner families, and others whose mobility is limited.

Finally, it is important to examine the interactions between the community subsystems and their environmental contexts in a historical perspective because the interrelationships change as they are affected by societal trends like (re)industrialization and (de)urbanization. As we shall see later, such changes may result in incongruities between the spatial scale of the subsystems, thus hampering the functional capabilities of communities.

It is clear that the historical interstices of the various community subsystems and their environmental contexts engender a broad array of questions. Comprehensive coverage of these questions is beyond the scope of this chapter, and we have necessarily had to be selective in our discussion. Accordingly, we have chosen to focus on size or spatial scale as one of a number of potentially relevant environmental variables. Size has been featured prominently in much of the community literature. It is also a relatively unambiguous factor, lending itself well to comparative analysis across community subsystems, across history, and across cultures. However, it should not be confused with size in an organizational sense. For example, the banking industry has greatly expanded its scale of operations, which has expressed itself on a larger spatial scale (e.g., multinational enterprises) but also on a smaller spatial scale (e.g., automatic teller machines on street corners). As much as possible, our discussion will seek to distinguish between organizational and spatial scale and link changes in the former to changes in the latter.

In what follows, we first review the emergence of industrial societies in terms of trends as they have affected the spatial scale of the various community subsystems. The discussion will then turn to the present and examine in some greater detail changes in spatial scale as a function of recent developments. Where appropriate and possible, we will augment the historical analysis with cross-cultural observations. The conclusion considers future directions of research.

THE ERA OF INDUSTRIALIZATION

There exist various detailed accounts of cities in ancient (Fustel de Coulanges, 1864/1956; Hammond, 1972), preindustrial (Sjoberg, 1960), and medieval (Pirenne, 1956/1925; Platt, 1976) times. The industrial city, although itself by no means a homogeneous category, is commonly regarded as a very distinctly different type of settlement, emerging around 1770 and maturing in the late nineteenth and early twentieth centuries. There is general agreement that the most outstanding characteristic of the industrial city has been the substitution of mechanical operations for manual activities in the production process.[1]

The various strands in the literature differ in the interpretation and relative weighting of such factors as culture, technology, and class relations in the development of the industrial city (Saunders, 1981). There is much less ambiguity, however, as to what these relevant factors and trends are. Next, we identify some of these trends and examine them regarding their implications for the scale of the economic, political, cultural, and social functions of communities. The discussion is naturally organized around the city because this is the most salient spatial form in the process of urbanization that accompanied industrialization.

TRENDS

The emergence and development of the industrial city are characterized by several important trends. To begin with, there was a specialization of increasingly interdependent activities, while labor shifted from the production of primary products to the production of manufacturing goods and services. Furthermore, there was an increase in particularly the urban population whose activities stimulated the further development of transportation and communications networks and required greater coordination of actions by central authorities. Later, we will briefly describe these trends further, before considering their implications for the four community subsystems.

The introduction in the eighteenth century of capital-intensive technology into the production process initially involved the use of water as the source of inanimate power, replacing the exclusive reliance on human labor. By the 1780s, however, the waterwheel had become largely obsolete. The steam engine made possible the siting of factories away from rural riversides in more favorable locations, for example, near raw materials, transportation nodes, or an available labor force (Harris & Ullman, 1945; Mumford, 1938). These locations were often

---

[1]Beyond this agreement, there have been widely divergent viewpoints regarding the nature and classification of preindustrial cities, for example, in connection with their functioning as relatively autonomous entities or dependent subsystems within larger feudal societies. This debate is rather peripheral to our concern that is with a change in the manufacturing process that instigated new forms of human communities, functioning on a new spatial scale.

existing towns. As the factories multiplied, the towns expanded.[2] A reorganization of land in the countryside (the "enclosures") and the enactment of poor laws added further to the movement of rural migrants attracted by urban jobs. The process of industrialization, therefore, went hand in hand with the process of urbanization. However, urbanization is more than the simple growth of urban populations. More appropriate seems a broader conceptualization of urbanization as the spatial expression of the urban process (Popenoe, 1965). This process refers to the increasingly specialized division of labor among organizational units in a community context. The greater interdependence of such highly differentiated units requires a process of rationalized coordination expressed in bureaucratization.

Several additional trends were important during the early industrial period. There were, for example, major demographic changes besides the important migration from rural to urban areas (Matras, 1977, p. 38 ff.). These changes included a sharp reduction in the death rate and an increase in the birth rate, resulting in a significant expansion of domestic economic markets (Deane, 1969). At the same time, an agricultural revolution was taking place. Farmers adopted new production techniques and new entrepreneurial attitudes, leading to more large-scale and more efficient output. Furthermore, international trade provided the industrializing areas both with access to raw materials and markets for their products. The institutionalization of this global commerce formed an important impetus for investments in further technological innovation and industrial growth (Deane, 1969).

These developments in the economic realm could not have occurred without requisite changes in transportation technology. The improvements in this connection were physical as well as organizational in nature. Authorities used, for example, enhanced road surfacing materials and constructed new roads, while they also upgraded the procedures for road maintenance. Particularly important were the construction of canals, often creating a last strategic link in a network of navigable waterways, and the expansion of dock facilities. Later on, steamships, railways, streetcars, and automobiles greatly increased the speed and regularity of the transportation of goods and people, with significant effects on urban spatial structure (Deane, 1969; Warner, 1962).

---

[2]Not all towns prospered though. Some established urban centers like Bristol and Newcastle in England had strong and well-entrenched guilds whose inflexible organization was incompatible with the emerging technology of industrial production. Consequently, these towns declined, whereas more hospitable smaller ones like Liverpool, Manchester, and Birmingham were favored by factory investors and grew rapidly (Choldin, 1985).

What, one may ask, was the significance of the trends, briefly summarized here, for the functions of communities? In this chapter, we emphasize changes that have occurred in more recent history in the spatial scale of community functions. However, the contemporary developments find their origins in the earlier period just sketched. It is, therefore, important to cover, however briefly, various facets of community scale in the 1770 to 1920 period. This review will then be extended and elaborated in our discussion of recent developments.

IMPLICATIONS FOR SCALE

The Economic Subsystem

It is quite clear that the trends identified in the preceding section expressed themselves in a greatly enlarged scale of the economic functions of communities. The family as a unit of production was increasingly replaced by private corporations and public enterprises. The providers of commercial goods and services became more oriented toward supralocal markets on a regional and national level and were indeed increasingly international in scope. Travel time on Britain's main trade routes was in 1830 only one third to one fifth of what it had been in 1750 (Deane, 1969). The growing economic surpluses helped strengthen cities as financial centers, promoting further industrial expansion. Thompson (1965) argued that such a critical aggregation of people and business creates a "ratchet effect," ensuring steady growth because of economic diversification, local capital investments, and other factors.

As employers engaged in mass production and operated on a larger scale, workers organized themselves in trade unions whose actions crossed national boundaries. The provision of welfare services and housing for the poor also became a less parochial matter and more strongly anchored in national legislation that guaranteed people a minimum subsistence level. Examples in this connection are Britain's Shaftsbury Law of 1851 that enabled municipalities to use public funds to build houses for the working population, the Torrens Law of 1816 that dealt with the demolition and renovation of dilapidated housing, and further legislation in 1875 that laid down the first minimum standards for buildings, sites, ventilation, and sewage (Barnes, 1923).

From this brief sketch, it is clear that the scale of the economic functions of communities underwent considerable change with the advent of the Industrial Revolution. This change had clear implications for spatial scale. Foremost was the greatly expanded geographical range that characterized the accessing of resources, and the production, distribution, and consumption of goods and services. Related spatial changes include the increased concentration of population in urban centers, the centralization of manufacturing jobs, higher density of housing that became a profitable commodity, expanded intra- and interurban transportation networks, and major infrastructural developments. Of course, these changes in the economic realm did not occur in a vacuum. They were closely intertwined with changes in the other sectors that we review next.

The Social Subsystem

Also in regard to the social subsystem of communities, there has been an increase in scale during the period of industrialization. The changes in this respect are apparent in manifold ways, and here we can only briefly point to some of them. One important change was the emergence of new occupational and social classes as production technologies became more capital-intensive and more specialized. The literature contains numerous discussions of the implications of this development for the integration of and conflict in communities. We do not want to add to these discussions. The point here is rather the broadening of the geographical range of solidary associations concurrent with the shift in the production process. Formerly, people were bound to a local feudal estate or used to take oaths regarding the duties and privileges of burghership of a particular town. Now they found themselves more strongly embedded in supralocal allegiances at the regional or national level. The emergence of trade unions, mentioned earlier, is relevant in this context. The local community declined in significance as a frame of reference guiding people's actions.

Thus norms governing bonds of human association came to be shared across much larger geographical areas. In conjunction with this, the scale of people's social interactions expanded also. This is most evident in altered patterns of sociospatial differentiation. Although residential segregation did exist already in the preindustrial (Sjoberg, 1960) and medieval (Pirenne, 1956/1925) city—especially according to occupational groupings—there was littte separation between people with unequal positions in the social hierarchy. This situation is still characteristic for many of the developing countries. Apprentice and master, servant and boss would often live in the same house. Public space was hardly specialized and was the stage for a mixture of activities—trade, play, political meetings, education, punishment, and execution. There were, however, rigid and clearly defined social norms regulating interaction. The social order was based especially on recognition of outer appearances, for example, clothes, skin color, speech, tattoos. Location of one's residence was generally a rather unreliable indicator of one's class position. During the Industrial Revolution, the rapid and massive influx of highly heterogeneous migrant populations into existing urban centers disrupted an established and stable situation. Spatial separation of the diverse groups into relatively homogeneous neighborhoods seemed a good way to bring some order to the apparent chaos. Processes of self-selection combined with economic and political constraints to produce new patterns of residential segregation and integration (Van Vliet--, 1980). Extending an *a posteriori* interpretation by Shevky and Bell (1955), Timms (1971) suggested that prevailing residential patterns reflect the level of a society's development. Specifically, Timms argued that the major dimensions along which people are separated from each other in space (social rank, family status, ethnicity, and migrant status) exist independently of each other only in modern cities. In the preindustrial city, there would have been a close linkage between social rank and family status on the one hand and between ethnicity and migrant status on the other. In the industrializing city, the last two dimensions were no longer as strongly interrelated, whereas only cities in advanced industrialized societies would show the full pattern of residential differentiation. Recent factorial ecological studies appear to support this hypothesis (Berry & Kasarda, 1977).

The changes in the scale of the social subsystem are closely intertwined with changes in its spatial scale, and the two types of change are sometimes hard to disentangle. For example, the emerging labor unions provided an enlarged and much more complex organizational context for the relations between employees and employers. This larger organizational arena was mirrored in a larger spatial scale of operations. For example, it was chiefly on the basis of support given by workers in larger geographical areas that collective bargaining agreements could be concluded. Other spatial aspects of the changing social system included residential segregation with neighborhoods that became more homogeneous in ethnic background and social class and increased salience of the dwelling as a private domain. There were also large-scale transformations of urban landscapes, of which the one in Paris engineered by Haussmann is perhaps best known (Hohenberg & Lees, 1985), with the consequence (intended or otherwise) of increased isolation of the working classes. Furthermore, a separation of home and workplace began to emerge. Initially, commuting distances were quite short. In New York, as late as 1899, the average commuting distance was only about one quarter of a mile (Pred, 1966, p. 209). Long hours of work and difficulties of getting about on foot still narrowly circumscribed the ambit of daily life for most people. The spatial structure of the early industrial city was very much cellular (Hawley, 1981). The typical pattern was a congeries of more or less self-contained districts, each with its own industries, market, shops, cafes, and other institutions. The average radius of these districts was generally less than 3 miles. It was not until the spread of improved public and private transportation, in the latter part of the 19th century and in the early decades of this century, that the spatial scale of people's daily social interactions expanded significantly.

The Cultural Subsystem

According to one view, culture can be seen as the product, man-ifestation, or reflection of the values, norms, preferences, and beliefs in a community (cf. Altman & Chemers, 1980). In this view, the built environment of communities forms part of the cultural subsystem. Important changes in the production of the built environment are de-scribed well by Alexander's (1964) distinction between unself-conscious and self-conscious processes as two fundamentally different ways of environmental form making.[3] The direct, unself-conscious form-making process of indigenous cultures is guided by certain fairly complex and rigidly maintained "unspoken rules." These covert "rules" produced physical settings integrally linked to explicit sociocultural conditions on the one hand and physical and technological constraints on the other. The resultant spatial arrangements and physical structures exhibited little variation. Both the building norms and their products evolved over an extended time frame. The builders were close to their materials and techniques of construction. They usually inhabited the shelters they produced and subsequently altered them as required by unanticipated events and emerging dysfunctions. In short, the unself-conscious form-making process was one of direct, iterative responses to slowly evolving sociophysical requirements. Detailed accounts depicting examples of re-sultant environments are found in Altman and Chemers (1980), Tuan (1974), and Rapoport (1969, 1977).

A fundamentally different situation emerged when communities experienced a transformation from unself-conscious to self-conscious

[3]The following paragraphs are based on a more extended discussion provided elsewhere (Studer & Van Vliet--, 1987).

form-making processes. New developments in, for example, trade, manufacturing, and government required new types of buildings. Their design and construction became increasingly the responsibility of specialists who replaced resident builders. The process of incremental, element-by-element, component-by-component adaptive change—the continuous process of construction-testing alteration—was replaced by one in which all parts of the system were in flux and required simultaneous comprehension and conceptual organization. Sociophysical accommodation was no longer slow, incremental, and adaptive but rapid, synoptic, and willful. The increasingly complex functions of conceptualizing, organizing, and producing built environments led to more specialized professionals, technicians, entrepreneurs, organizations, and processes (Rapoport, 1969). Moreover, new construction technologies and building materials vastly relaxed the physical constraints, thus elaborating and complicating the range of possible design solutions. (An example would be the introduction of steel-reinforced concrete, opening up new possibilities for high-rise construction.) A side effect was that it made structures less alterable, rendering incremental adjustments to emerging sociophysical incongruities less practicable. The production of built environments responsive to user needs was also hindered by the increase in social and administrative distance between community residents and architects, builders, and planners who often originated from different class-cultural backgrounds and operated according to standardized criteria and bureaucratic procedures in more large-scale firms (Lipman, 1969).

Another important aspect of cultural change relates to the differential use of space according to gender. With the increased separation of public and private domains came a new division of labor. It articulated gender-based role repertoires that restricted women's activities mainly to household work and child care. This social construction of the physical environment has had important effects for urban spatial form. It is only since fairly recently that ensuing incongruities have been documented (Franck, 1987).

Culture may also have immaterial referents and connote the values, norms, customs, and life-styles shared by the members of a community. In this sense, the period of industrialization has shown a geographical expansion of the cultural component of communities. Improved communication techniques facilitated a general diffusion of values. Better transportation networks brought previously inaccessible market commodities similarly within reach of formerly isolated regions. The adoption of more universal standards was also apparent in the codification of law and further strengthened by institutional linkages between communities.

The Political Subsystem

As cities became industrialized, there were significant political transformations. The nation-state, which had had limited functions before the industrial period, greatly expanded its role as a central government. This process was paralleled by a loss of autonomy on the part of cities, first observed by Weber (1921/1958). Engels's (1845/1958) description of the condition of the working class in Manchester, England, left little doubt about the virtual absence of municipal capabilities to deal with fundamental infrastructural problems like the provision of sewers, clean water, and fire protection. Initial philanthropic efforts in the private sector were increasingly supplemented by programs administered by professionals in state bureaucracies. These programs covered various fields, for example, social welfare, housing, and town planning. They were typically mandated by national legislatures that formulated goals and developed uniform criteria for the redistribution of nationally collected tax revenues. This development was pivotal in the creation of industrial cities.

It is important to note that local communities, defaulting on their collective responsibilities, helped to create a de facto intervention role for central authorities, but they nevertheless retained de jure autonomy in many aspects of local decision making. This incongruity is a potential source for problems, most likely to become manifest under conditions of fiscal austerity. At the same time that national government began to expand its role, political parties attempted to increase their power base. These efforts also found expression in the built environment as party- or union-affiliated associations built housing for their members. As a result, blocks and entire neighborhoods emerged that were colored by a particular denomination or political conviction.

In concluding our thumbnail sketch of changes in the scale of community functions during the period of industrialization, we want to emphasize that we have presented a highly simplified picture. A number of important developments were only briefly discussed or mentioned in passing. Our aim is to develop a conceptual framework to synthesize the scale development of the community subsystems, illustrating the various trends but not offering detailed portrayals that are available already. We recognize various historical patterns, but we see these for the purpose of the present analysis merely as variations of a basic trend, namely the increase in spatial scale of the economic, social, cultural, and political functions of industrializing communities. The following, more detailed discussion examines for each of these four community functions how recent and contemporary developments have accelerated, arrested, or reversed this trend.

THE POSTINDUSTRIAL ERA

The *postindustrial* label is both ambiguous and misleading. Originally used by Bell (1974) to describe a marked growth in the tertiary employment sector, the term has never been clearly defined. It commonly refers to a change from the production and consumption of goods to services, the greater significance of scientific knowledge, and the increasing importance of social planning by a technocratic elite. In most advanced industrialized nations, the share of the service sector indeed continues to increase, whereas the industrial and agricultural sectors continue to lose jobs. For example, in the United States, the share of the service sector increased from 63.4% in 1973 to 69.5% in 1983. During the same period, other countries showed similar increases: West Germany, 52.4% (up by 7.2%); France, 58% (up by 8.6%); Great Britain, 63.7% (up by 9.2%); and The Netherlands, 67.1% (up by 9.5%). This growth in the service sector has been accompanied by a decline of the industrial sector that in the United States employed 28% of the workforce in 1983, down by 5.2% from 10 years earlier, with other countries often showing still greater decreases. The agricultural sector, too, is experiencing steady decline, holding in most industrialized countries between 5% and 10% of the national labor force. However, as Gershuny (1978) noted, specific operational definitions of "postindustrial" and "service occupations" have not been advanced. The trends have not been examined in a systematic fashion, although some such work is beginning to appear (Simmie, 1983).

Even with a more precise referent, the term postindustrial remains a dubious descriptor because industrial activity is bound to stay with us for a long time to come. It is true that many corporations are engaged in disinvestment, contributing to a decline in heavy industries such as steel production (Bluestone & Harrison, 1982). However, a considerable restructuring of regional economies is taking place, and *reindustrialization* might be a more appropriate term to denote postindustrial processes. Nevertheless, here we will conform to the common terminology and use postindustrial to refer to the era following the maturation of industrial cities.

Dissynchronous Scale Developments

During the time that cities were industrializing, the economic, social, cultural, and political subsystems all increased in scale. In more recent decades, these four subsystems have shown more differential scale developments. The economic subsystem has continued to expand, whereas the social subsystem is more strongly characterized by a bipolar development. The cultural subsystem has generally further increased its spatial range, whereas in the political subsystem there has been a tendency to revert certain state responsibilities to lower levels of government. In short, what we have seen are dyssychronous scale dynamics. That is, the direction and pace of scale development of one subsystem have not necessarily been in harmony with those of other subsystems. An implication of such uneven development may be a greater potential for friction as the four subsystems interface with each other. This situation creates challenges that increase the significance of community planning.

The later discussion will not offer a comprehensive and detailed analysis of any given single subsystem. Rather, we will examine broad patterns of the four subsystems as they interface with each other. In doing so, we will follow the same sequence as in the first part of the chapter, starting with the economic subsystem.

The Economic Subsystem

Castells (1983, p. 210) suggested that for multinational corporations space and distance have been dissolved by transportation technology, the mobility of capital, and the permeability of political boundaries. The American soft-drink companies battling each other in their quest for the Chinese market were only a more visible instance of the expansion of economic markets in an increasingly interdependent world system. Small enterprises have been appreciated by some as being beautiful (Schumacher, 1973), and they are certainly still bountiful (Granovetter, 1984), but large multinational corporations have greatly increased their market share. Large-scale operations now dominate the economic functions of communities, as illustrated by the following statistics. In 1980, the number of corporations with direct investments outside the countries in which their headquarters were based was well over 10,000 (Stopford & Dunning, 1983). Together, they had de facto control over decision making in at least 90,000 foreign affiliates. About 43% of the multinational enterprises (MNEs) derived 25% or more of their sales from their foreign activities. Furthermore, the value of the stock of foreign investments by MNEs in 1980 was $512 billion, some 89% higher than in 1975 (Stopford & Dunning, 1983). In 1978, multinational production was estimated to be 30% of the gross national product (GNP) of nonsocialist countries and predicted to become 41% in 1988 and 43% in 1998 (Carlo, 1983).

The formation of larger corporations was propelled by the internationalization of capital. Three interrelated conditions are closely intertwined with this increase in capital mobility (Bradbury, 1985). First, there have been further improvements in transportation and communication technologies, reducing the friction of distance. Containerization, air cargo, satellite telecommunications, and advanced data-processing systems have made the location and control of production less and less dependent on geographic constraints. Second, automated manufacturing techniques and modern division of labor now permit a decomposition of production processes in such a manner that a finished product can often be assembled by unskilled labor in any of a number of locations remote from the decision-making center in the corporation's headquarters. The chief limitations are the perishability and weight of the products. Third, there now exists a global reservoir of workers. Earlier, we described how in the industrializing city, capital attracted labor, particularly from rural areas. Extensive movements of migrant workers—still observed in the late 1960s, for example, from Mediterranean countries to Western and Northern Europe—have now been halted or reversed and are being replaced by the movement of capital attracted by labor that is cheap, pliant, and willing to be trained for limited jobs. Such labor is typically found in places much in need of capital investment. Consequently, it is not uncommon that corporations are in a position to extract additional benefits—for example, tax abatements or infrastructural provisions—that are offered as incentives by communities in distress. The recent location decision by General Motors concerning its Saturn plant is a case in point. It has been shown, however, that under given conditions also the new forms of capital mobility induce labor migrations (Sassen-Koob, 1985). In either case, the vulnerability of the receiving or sending community is evident.

The manifestations of capital mobility are many. They include the employment of Brazilian workers in the manufacture of U.S. cars; the tripling of Dutch investments in the United States between 1977 and 1983 (Centraal Bureau Voor de Statistiek, 1984, p. 253); and the disinvestment in and lateral diversification of the U.S. steel industry, a euphemism for diverting capital into a different, more profitable line of business. The outcome tends to be the same: high unemployment and havoc in the communities left behind. A rapidly growing literature is documenting the adverse effects on the wealth (Flaim & Sehgal, 1985) and health (Fleming, Baum, Reddy, & Gatchel, 1984) of displaced workers; implications for the community fabric (Feagin, 1983, pp. 20–37); and efforts of communities to restructure their economic base (Bendick, 1983; Redburn & Buss, 1984). Nor have the so-called boomtowns necessarily fared well. The benefits bestowed upon them were often distributed unevenly, and social disruption and a decline in services have not been uncommon (England & Albrecht, 1984; Feagin & Shelton, 1985; Freudenburg, 1981).

A different externality of many large-scale production processes is the emission of pollutants with effects that may extend themselves across regional and indeed international boundaries and that may take decades to be undone. Such environmental degradation includes acid rain produced by coal-burning plants and toxic waste generated by chemical and nuclear facilities. There exist extensive reviews of these issues, and here it suffices to direct attention to them as important supralocal problems associated with supralocal economic systems.

Also within metropolitan areas, jobs have moved as employment decentralized, affecting blue- as well as white-collar workers (Quante, 1976; Schwartz, 1976). Reasons offered for the changed patterns include lower taxes, lower land costs, better accessibility, and bucolic residential environments intended to entice top personnel. There is an extensive literature on the problems that have ensued, particularly for inner cities, and on the programs and policies that have been proposed to deal with them (e.g., Bradbury, Downs, & Small, 1982; Gale, 1984). For our purpose, the main point is that these developments represent additional facets of the continuing scale increase in the economic system.

The service sector in the economy is more constrained by space in that the interactions between the suppliers and the consumers of the service more often require face-to-face contact. Obvious examples are restaurants, cafes, and discos for which such contacts are the raisons d'être. Also medical care and education fall into this category. However, even here, a growing number of transactions that formerly required personal contact can now be conducted by the consumer in relative isolation: pharmacies and drug stores now sell do-it-yourself kits for a variety of routine medical tests; correspondence courses have proliferated, and television has greatly expanded its educational programming (U.S. Bureau of the Census, 1985). The emancipation from spatial constraints is greater still in retail trade. Mail-order sales in the United States have tripled since 1968 (U.S. Bureau of the Census, 1985). More households than ever before own refrigerators and freezers for storing perishable items that are increasingly bought in bulk from large chain stores in more distant locations than the corner grocery store. Numerous other statistics could be cited to illustrate the growing spatial and temporal separation of producers and users of services, for example, drive-in arrangements for theatres, banks, and fast-food outlets; banking by phone or automated teller machines; telephone answering machines; video recorder sales, and so forth. We will return to this point in our discussion of the social subsystem of contemporary communities.

The just-noted trends notwithstanding, proximity will remain especially important for many elderly people, single-parent households, dual-earner families, and other population groups whose mobility is limited and whose economic and social well-being and daily life are more bound up with their local environment. Also in the corporate sector, decentralization has its limits. For example, when inducements by the West German government to relocate industrial headquarters failed, a decentralization policy was not enforced. The government was allegedly convinced that such decentralization would isolate the companies from essential supporting services, thus endangering their international competetiveness (Olbrich, 1984).

Summing up the major spatial aspects of recent developments of the economic subsystem, the principal change is the greatly increased mobility of capital. This change has had profound ramifications for the growth and decline of local communities and regional inequities. Spatial form has been heavily affected by urban fringe development, the increase in private automobile ownership, major highway construction. the movement of jobs and people from central city areas to the suburbs and, more recently, to nonmetropolitan areas. Gentrification is often seen as a "back-to-the-city" movement by a relatively more affluent population. However, research shows that gentrification is a rather limited phenomenon, found only in neighborhoods combining the advantages of historic location, attractive architecture, and access to amenities. Also, about 80% of the gentrifiers are already city dwellers (Palen, in press).

The Social Subsystem

The age of industrialization was also the era of nationalism. Earlier we noted that the development of mature industrial cities was, in large part, predicated on the emergence of nation-states, capable of mobilizing and exploiting collective resources. Two genocidal world wars eradicated the last vestiges of the legitimacy of nation-states as frameworks for social solidarity and economic development, while accentuating people's integration in more encompassing, global configurations with international jurisdictions. The formation of large geopolitical blocks, the supranational implications of environmental pollution, the increased mobility of capital, and the growth of multinational corporations, discussed earlier, are but a few of the factors that have made nationalism a, by and large, atavistic principle of solidarity in postindustrial societies.

In conjunction with this development, perhaps somewhat paradoxically, the expanding welfare state has taken over many functions formerly performed by the extended family, the church and other traditional institutions, or the private sector (e.g., philanthropy). Thus, in a way, the state has increased its significance. However, analysts have shown that the welfare state, with its mixture of socialist and liberal principles, is an ideological hybrid that fails to command a strong moral commitment of its subjects (Van Heek, 1973). People's orientation to the state appears to have become highly instrumental in character. Moreover, as we will show later, policies of the welfare state are now increasingly being abandoned in favor of a process of privatization.

On an individual level, some research suggests that personal communities have been "transformed" thanks to efficient and cheap communication and transportation that have liberated people from spatial constraints (Lee, Oropesa, Metch, & Guest, 1984; Tsai & Sigelman, 1982; Wellman, 1979). More than before, people are now embedded in social support systems that extend themselves across entire metropolitan areas and beyond (Fischer et al., 1977).[4]

Although the tenor of this discussion has emphasized an increase in scale, it is important to note that at the same time a decrease of scale occurred as the process of individualization continued. The extended family made way for the nuclear family, and demographic trends show steady rises in the number of single-parent families and one-person households. The latter result from both a greater incidence of divorce and the younger age at which children leave the parental home. In addition, there seems to have been a greater valuation of privacy or, perhaps more precisely, a desire and ability to create private spaces, providing children, for example, with their own rooms (Wolfe, 1978). Environmentally, these developments have manifested themselves in lower dwelling occupancy rates and a general inflation of land uses. For

---

[4]This is not to say that neighborhoods no longer form communities in the sense of a solidary social unit. Numerous studies indicate that "urban villages" (Gans, 1962) continue to exist, and many people still show attachment to their local environment (Fried, 1982; Riger & Lavrakas, 1981; Rivlin, 1982; Unger & Wandersman, 1985). The neighborhood appears to remain particularly important to those population groups who cannot or choose not to share in the spatial emancipation, for example, certain ethnic groups, the elderly, children. and others whose mobility is limited.

example, figures provided by the Regional Plan Association (1975, pp. 32 33) show that, whereas in 1950 each resident in the United States used, on the average, 0.2 acres of urban land, every new resident added between 1950 and 1960 took up an additional 0.35 acres, which increased further to 0.4 acres in the 1960 to 1970 period.

The two processes of the expanding welfare state versus continuing individualization tend to give postindustrial communities a dual structure: On the one hand, there is the public sphere of macrolevel institutions characterized by instrumental rationality and systemic features (Berger, Berger, & Kellner, 1977; Dreitzel, 1977; Habermas 1981); on the other hand is the private world of individuals and small households, oriented toward the meaningful experience of everyday life (Karp, Stone, & Yoels, 1977). Castells (1983), who has taken a similar view, suggested that space be conceptually divided between organizational and experiental space. More recent analyses of the disparate private and public realms can be found in Popenoe (1985) and Bellah, Madsen, Sullivan, Swidler, and Tipton (1985).

To sum up, major aspects of spatial change in the social subsystem are twofold. On the one hand, there have been scale increases as seen in a decline of the nation-state as a framework for solidary attachments and a greater personal mobility allowing more people to have friendships evolving around common interests and less constrained by space. On the other hand, there has been a continuing trend of individualization with various demographic aspects that has found expression in, for example, lower occupancy rates for dwellings and more space use per capita.

The Cultural Subsystem

The increases in the scale of economic activities and social bonds find a parallel in a general diffusion of culture. Expanding markets and increasingly interlocking and interdependent economic and social units require a common, shared value system, sufficiently general to provide coherence to highly differentiated socioeconomic structures. Cultural diffusion has been aided greatly by the introduction of various technological innovations and infrastructural changes that have reshaped regional and national settlement patterns. Private car ownership has greatly increased. In the United States, in 1981 there were 537 cars per 1,000 population, a rise of 17% over 1973. During the same period, private car owners increased in Great Britain by 16%, in France by 26%, in West Germany by 40%, in The Netherlands by 43%, and in Japan by 79%. This vast increase in personal mobility was accompanied by greater exposure to mass media, particularly television. In the United States, between 1973 and 1980, ownership of TV sets went up by 34% to 635 per 1,000 population. Other industrialized countries show similar increases. Furthermore, there has been a growing usage of modern communication techniques, reflected in, for example, the possession of private telephones that in the United States increased between 1973 and 1981 by 21% to 788 per 1,000 population, whereas France experienced a rise of 122%. These trends have transformed the world, in McLuhan's (1968) words, to a "global village." The construction of roads, airports, and the like have further reinforced the institutional connections (e.g., unions, churches, political parties) that link communities in a hierarchical pattern (Firey, Loomis, & Beegle, 1957). It is now commonly accepted that the traditional contrast between rural and urban communities is historically important but increasingly unreal, as all types of settlements have become enmeshed in large "urban fields" (Friedman & Miller 1965).

These combined trends put pressure on local culture. One notable development has been the diminished significance of the public sphere that has to a large extent become "aspatial." Television broadcasts, newspapers, and magazines transmit one-way information, consumed in private homes, replacing public exchanges formerly taking place in parks, coffee houses, and literary salons. Political debates are often watched on television and conducted in special columns in newspapers and magazines. It is now possible to enjoy literature, art, music, and plays in one's home, without having to go to a library, museum, concert hall, or theatre. One could argue that these developments have merely broadened access to a cultural heritage that was previously a privilege of a small elite and, further, that the "at-home experience" is only a surrogate that cannot replace genuine and direct exposure to culture. Although this may be true, visits to cinemas, for example, have dropped at the same time that television ownership has gone up. Of course, these few statistics do not necessarily prove this point that is an empirical question requiring further study.

The cultural diffusion trend, noted before, appears to be mitigated by two factors. First, the original creation of culture is closely intertwined with the local availability of (typically urban) resources. Examples include conservatories, film and sound-track studios, art galleries and ateliers, publishing firms as well as an atmosphere conducive to cultural creativity (compare Berlin and Paris in the interbellum period). Urban centers also have a greater "critical mass" of artists, musicians, scientists, entrepreneurs, and talent generally. Proximity to these sources of creativity promotes and diversifies cultural expressions (Fischer, 1984). Data illustrating this point come from research in progress showing that in the United States leading musicians and poets come significantly more often from large cities than would be expected on the basis of the distribution of the general population (Van Vliet-- & Ritti, in preparation). For example, in 1910, 53.7% of the U.S. population lived in communities smaller than 2,500, but only 16.1% of nationally recognized poets born in the 1905 to 1914 decade came from such small places. On the other hand, in 1910, 9.2% of the U.S. population lived in cities of 1 million or larger, but 32.2% of the poets born at this time originated from places that size. A similar rural deficit is evident for musicians, also for social and physical scientists, Fortune 500 executives, political representatives, and even major league baseball players. Furthermore, rural underrepresentation has become significantly more pronounced in more recent decades. There are various reasons for this pattern, but important in this context is the continued and even increased significance of spatial proximity in career development.

Cultural diffusion is counterbalanced by a second factor, namely the revival of regional and local authenticity. The search for roots and attempts at preservation of local identity are a prevalent theme in, for example, modern film and literature as well as the built environment (Appleyard, 1981). Simon and Wekerle (1987) have recently studied the "miniaturization" of a Toronto neighborhood. They report how planners, caught between pressures to model a new neighborhood in a traditional form and a scarcity of resources, reduced backyards, porches, open space, and so forth to minimal dimensions. The apparent result was that the very features that would normally make this type of neighborhood environment attractive became nonfunctional. For example, outside space was designed such that it discouraged comfortable and spontaneous contact and socializing among neighbors. Also, technologies such as cable television that have diffused culture may promote countervailing trends, for example, by providing local news and facilitating local input in community planning (Catanese, 1984).

The trend of cultural diffusion, attenuated by a renewed interest in local character, is also noticeable with respect to the built environment. In response to severe housing shortages following World War II, countries in Western capitalist nations as well as collectivist economies in East Bloc countries embarked on massive housing production programs, utilizing industrially standardized and prefabricated building components (e.g., Fish, 1979; Misztal & Misztal, 1987; Morton, in press; Sillince, in press; Wollmann, in press). The resultant housing environments have often been criticized for their monotony and lack of human scale. Another relevant trend has been the professionalization of planning and design. Practitioners united themselves in international associations and stipulated conditions of formal training, often based on a general adherence to principles of functionalist design. These principles, embodied in the 1933 Athens charter of the Congres International d'Architects Modernes (CIAM), stipulated a strict separation of land uses, which found widespread acceptance and also contributed to the uniformity of many postwar urban areas.

Recently, actors in the provision of housing, such as construction companies, development corporations, architectural bureaus, housing associations, mortgage lending institutions, landlords, and real estate firms have shown steady increases in the scale of their operations. The implications of this trend are not fully clear. In a study of architectural firms, Blau and Lieben (1983) found, contrary to artistic stereotypes, that firms that won awards for high quality and creative designs were characterized by larger size. The large firms employed more consultants, made more use of sophisticated computer techniques, and operated on a lower profit margin. However, bearing in mind that the now infamous and demolished Pruitt-Igoe public housing project in St. Louis was an award-winning design, it remains to be demonstrated that larger bureaucratic organizations do indeed provide built environments that are more responsive to user needs.

In part as a response to these developments, we have seen demands for local citizen participation (Genovese, 1983), the introduction of more flexible design techniques (Habraken, 1972), an orientation to more small-scale design (Simon & Wekerle, 1987), a reversal of high-rise building (Michelson, 1976b), a policy emphasis on renovation and rehabilitation (Den Draak, 1985), and a concern more generally with the requirements of special population groups like women and children. These shifts, and the extent to which they substantially alter the production and quality of housing, await further systematic assessment.

The Political Subsystem

In recent decades, a major development in the political functions of communities has been the democratization of decision-making procedures. On the one hand, this trend has manifested itself in a greater plurality of stakeholder parties, often operating at a subcommunity level in regard to a given issue. On the other hand, the state has set itself up as an arbitrator and provider of what is in the public interest, similarly bypassing the local community level. Of course, this neutral function, attributed to the welfare state by those with liberal political leanings, has been hotly disputed by conservatives who deny that the state serves anybody's interests and radical critics who argue that the state serves only the interests of the ruling class (Gordon, 1977).

Whatever the merits of these alternative viewpoints, economic downturns have made it increasingly difficult for the state to continue to perform the functions that it had assumed in more prosperous times. The inability of the state to deliver what people had come to expect eroded popular support, exactly when it was needed most (Habermas, 1979). This legitimacy crisis, coupled with recent fiscal imperatives, has resulted in a significant turnabout in policies of the welfare state. This realignment goes by different names, for example, privatization in the United Kingdom (Forrest & Murie, 1987) and New Federalism in the United States (Benton, 1985). The manifestations are multifold, but the outcome is essentially the same: a shifting of responsibilities from the state to lower levels of government and to the private sector (Clarke, 1984; Hill, 1983). In the United States, the move away from categorical grants to the emphasis on the Community Development Block Grant Program first signaled this shift (Liebschutz, 1984). In the United Kingdom, the massive sale of public housing to deliver cash receipts to the treasury is perhaps the most salient expression of this policy change.[5]

Policy analysts have recently begun to provide wide-ranging studies of the implications of these developments (Van Vliet--, 1987). For our purpose, the most significant aspect is the increased political responsibility that local communities are forced to assume in the face of a reality of problems with solutions that clearly transcend local levels. Particularly hard hit in the United States are communities in which local spending levels were heavily dependent on intergovernmental aid (Johnson, 1985). Writing in the 1960s about the "postcity age," Webber (1968, p. 1093) noted that "we cannot expect territorially defined governments to deal effectively with problems whose causes are unrelated to territory and geography." This observation applies not only to fragmented metropolitan government but holds true more generally.

Findings from another study indicate that a sense of community is positively related to levels of participation in local politics (Steinberger, 1984). And indeed at the neighborhood level, there are ample examples of active participation by local residents in issues that concern them. Tenants have successfully organized rent strikes when absentee landlords defaulted on their basic responsibilities for maintenance and the provision of basic services like hot water and electricity. In some places, squatters, assisted by organizations like the Association of Community Organizations for Reform Now (ACORN) or the Urban Homesteading Assistance Board, have been able to become legal owners of abandoned

---

[5]It is ironic that the veil of democratization and decentralization is a convenient cover for these changes that are, by and large, forced onto communities unable to resist them. For a more positive view of the French case, see Meny (1983).

housing that they subsequently renovated. In other instances, residents in gentrifying neighborhoods have been able to organize effectively to resist eviction by real estate speculators. Also blockwatches and tenant patrols have sometimes been able to reduce vandalism and crime rates. These examples are positive signs of the vitality of local communities; they also point to the limited scope of successful action. Consider the following case. Poletown was, until recently, a thriving neighborhood in Detroit. It was a stable, well-integrated community, mostly middle class, with people from a variety of ethnic backgrounds and age groups harmoniously living together. When General Motors (GM) selected the area for a new plant, the residents appealed to their elected officials for help. The politicians, however, joined by the United Automobile Workers (UAW) and the Detroit Archdiocese, colluded with GM. In spite of unified local opposition, 1,500 homes were torn down, along with 16 churches, 144 businesses, 2 schools, and a hospital.[6]

The example just described, although not a daily occurrence, is not an uncommon situation (Feagin, 1983; Molotch, 1976). It illustrates the great difficulties faced by local communities that wish to affect "higher order" issues impacting on them. Earlier, we discussed the scale of economic activities and the greatly increased mobility of capital as well as related issues such as environmental degradation, global resource interdependencies, unemployment, and housing construction. All these policy domains constitute problem areas for which the local community does not form an effective framework for political decision making; nor does it possess the requisite capabilities for coping with them. Indeed, in many instances individual countries are not in a position to address the extant problems, and international cooperation is required. Obvious examples are U.S.-caused acid rain in Canada, the pollution of the river Rhine in Europe, and the influence of International Monetary Fund (IMF) policies and oil prices on housing construction in the Third World.

FUTURE DIRECTIONS OF RESEARCH

The preceding discussion indicates that historically the economic, social, cultural, and political subsystems of communities have developed differentially along dimensions of scale. Throughout the Industrial Revolution, scale generally increased in all four subsystems. Gradually,

---

[6]A full account of this episode is provided by an award-winning documentary entitled "Poletown Lives," available from Information Factory, 3512 Courville, Detroit, MI 48224. Phone: (313) 885-4685.

however, incongruities have begun to emerge. The economic, social, and cultural functions do still display small-scale features to be sure, but the dominant pattern has been one of continued scale increases. Trends in the political subsystem appear to be at odds with these developments. Currently prevailing national policies of privatization, decentralization, and deregulation all contribute to a shifting of responsibilities from the state to the private sector and to lower levels of government. However, local communities do not form an effective framework for addressing supralocal problems. Although the pace of these developments and various aspects of it may vary between North America and Europe, the basic pattern seems to be the same. Where does this leave us? What are some possible implications for studies needed next?

To begin with, several important areas of inquiry concern the implications of the changing role of the state for local communities. First, we observe the impotence of nation-states vis-à-vis a number of environmental, economic, and demographic issues. The diminished authority of the nation-state is perhaps most clearly illustrated by very common tax evasion practices engaged in by multinational enterprises. They routinely conduct international transfer pricing by which, for example, the profit of an American MNE in France is attributed, through fictitious buying–selling games, to a holding company with a branch in some tax haven. The failure of national governments to tax as much as one third of their wealth represents an unprecedented undermining of their authority (Carlo, 1983). The present political systems are inadequate in dealing with the newly emerged economic forms. What is needed are studies to propose and evaluate alternative international formats that are more effective.

The policies of the New Federalism also entail a reduced role for national government. The responses of local communities to the privatization and devolution of functions require careful study. What are, for example, the implications for neighborhood revitalization? One noted observer of the American scene expects that the role of neighborhood organizations in this context will increase, given the severe cutbacks in federal aid to cities (Downs, 1983). However, as public officials have fewer funds to distribute, political organization becomes less significant for neighborhood groups. Clarke (1984) cited evidence that these groups are adopting new organizational structures, agendas, and skills in order to work effectively as partners in joint ventures with private-sector actors. Early evaluations are not encouraging, and research is needed to assess the efficacy of alternative management styles and decision-making processes under the new circumstances.

A third focus of inquiry related to the diminished role of national government concerns ramifications for regional inequities and community growth. Obviously, the drastically reduced national tax base, referred to in our discussion of MNEs, leaves national government with fewer resources to redress extant inequalities. In addition, the United States has, if anything, an urban policy that stipulates that general economic growth is the most effective way of ameliorating the problems of distressed communities. Given also the aversion to planned intervention and the reliance on market forces to achieve this objective, present regional inequities are not likely to be removed. These developments have led one critic to comment that communities have disappeared from the national urban policy (Logan, 1983). Research needs to examine not only the nature and extent of disparities between communities but also how communities respond. For example, how can communities induce growth of small service firms that provide a large majority of new jobs in cities (Clark, 1985). What factors explain the rise and decline of such firms?

Another direction for future research concerns innovations in decision-making procedures. Community planning involves the bringing to bear of knowledge on the decision making regarding an array of community problems. Built environment researchers, in particular, have generally been bent on generating a functional understanding of environment–behavior relationships, that is, how people and the environment mutually affect each other. However, even if we had nomological knowledge of environment–behavior relationships or community systems more generally—permitting precise if-then statements regarding the consequences of particular spatial configurations—the problem of achieving or maintaining congruence would not necessarily be solved (Studer & Van Vliet--, 1987). Remaining normative issues cannot be addressed in such a technical and neutral fashion. Needed are new modes of collective decision making to formulate community goals and to select means toward their implementation. The current political framework, we concluded, is inadequate for conducting effective public discourse on the relevant issues. Planners are now proposing procedures for rational argumentation, across different levels and between different sectors of communities, potentially bringing the political function of communities more in line with their economic, social, and cultural functions (Goldstein, 1984). Researchers have only just begun to test these proposals in experimental work, and numerous empirical questions remain (e.g., Mitroff & Emshoff, 1979). In the context of housing policy, for example, problems can be seen as ill-structured. They are ill-structured problems because they are characterized by, among other things, ambiguous or unknown policy goals (e.g., the "decent home and suitable living environment" promised to all American families by the 1949 National Housing Act) and ambiguous or unspecified policy instruments (Harmon & King, 1985). Fundamental to getting a better grasp on these problems is a delineation of the entire field of policy options. An attempt in this direction is a variation of Kelly's repertory grid method developed by Dunn (1985) at the Graduate School of Public and International Affairs of the University of Pittsburgh.

Another exciting research area would appear to be the interface of spatial and temporal planning. We have seen that many functions in modern communities have become much less bound by geographical constraints. Considering the greatly increased mobility of people, goods, services, and information, temporal coordination may gain in significance. Thus the issue of congruence between people and the built environment should be seen in a broader, diachronic perspective and at the same time situated in a broader societal context (Michelson, 1977, 1987). For example, residential satisfaction should be understood within a broader time perspective accounting for anticipated opportunities for improvement in a given housing market. Satisfaction of apartment dwellers with their housing has been found to be, at least in part, a function of perceived prospects for future mobility. Respondents expecting to move expressed considerably greater satisfaction with their present conditions than did those who did not see any chances for such improvement (Michelson, 1980).

The time dimension is explicitly considered in the work of time geographers (e.g., Carlstein, Parkes, & Thrift, 1978; Michelson, 1985; Parkes & Thrift, 1980). Their research has examined, for example, the coordination of the activity schedules of households with the opening hours of community services and facilities such as schools, day-care centers, medical centers, and shops. Issues of space–time planning will become more pressing as the proportion of dual-earner households continues to rise and as investment costs in production hardware and services become higher. These developments encourage arrangements such as "shared tenancy" whereby firms make joint use of, for example, computer and telephone systems leased by a developer (Schwanke, 1985). Such facilities may involve continuous day and night schedules. In a provocative article, Melbin (1978) explored the night as a new frontier of community life and noted remarkable similarities with life in the frontier communities of a century or more ago. His analysis raises many points meriting further study.

Finally, it is likely that employment activities, particularly in the office sector, will lose their 9-to-5 character and will become more home-based as well. Such decentralization, facilitated by technological advances, has already been documented for the banking sector in Great Britain (Marshall & Bachtler, 1984). Such developments would generate a range of questions regarding, for example, the provision of public transit and the significance of the local residential environment. Also the increased leisure time and its growing orientation to the local and home environment may spark renewed interest in community affairs, now found sorely lacking by some observers (Bellah *et al.*, 1985; Popenoe, 1985). Clearly, these thoughts are highly speculative, and research is needed to formulate and test specific hypotheses derived from further systematic reflection on the emerging developments.

REFERENCES

Alexander, C. (1964). *Notes on the synthesis of form.* Cambridge: Harvard University Press.

Altman, I., & Chemers, M. M. (1980). *Culture and environment.* Monterey, CA: Brooks/Cole.

Appleyard, D. (1981). Place and non-place; The new search for roots. In Judith I. De Neufville (Ed.), *The land use policy debate in the United States.* New York, London: Plenum Press.

Banerjee, T., & Baer, W. C. (1984). *Beyond the neighborhood unit: Residential environments and public policy.* New York: Plenum Press.

Barnes, H. (1923). Housing: The facts and the futures. London: Ernest Benn, Ltd.. (Cited by N. Carmon in Housing policy in western countries: Toward broader social responsibility. *Social Praxes*, 8(3/4), 53–71, 1981.)

Bell, D. (1974). *The coming of post-industrial society.* London: Heinemann.

Bellah, R. N., Madsen, R., Sullivan, W. M., Swidler, A., & Tipton, S. M. (1985). *Habits of the heart: Individualism and commitment in American life.* Berkeley: University of California Press.

Bendick, M. (1983). The role of public programs and private markets in reemploying workers dislocated by economic change. *Policy Studies Review*, 2(4), May, 715–733.

Benton, J. E. (1985). American federalism's first principles and Reagan's new federalism policies. *Policy Studies Journal*, 13(3), 568–575.

Berger, P., Berger, B., & Kellner, H. (1977). *The homeless mind.* New York: Random House.

Berry, B. J. L., & Kasarda, J. D. (1977). *Contemporary urban ecology.* New York: Macmillan.

Blau, J. R., & Lieben, K. L. (1983). Growth, decline, and death: A panel study of architectural firms. In J. R. Blau, M. La Gory, & J. S. Pipkin (Eds.), *Professionals and urban form* (pp. 224–251). Albany: State University of New York Press.

Bluestone, B., & Harrison, B. (1982). *The deindustrialization of America.* New York: Basic Books.

Bradbury, J. H. (1985). Regional and industrial restructuring processes in the new international division of labour. *Progress in Human Geography*, 9(1), 38–63.

Bradbury, K. L., Downs, A., & Small, K. A. (1982). *Urban decline and the future of American cities.* Washington, DC: The Brookings Institute.

Carlo, A. (1983). Multinational enterprises and national state: An incurable conflict. *International Journal of the Sociology of Law*, 11, 105–121.

Carlstein, T., Parkes, D., & Thrift, N. (Eds.). (1978). *Human activity and time geography* (Vol. 2). London: Edward Arnold.

Castells, M. (1983). Crisis, planning, and the quality of life: Managing the new historical relationships between space and society. *Environment and Planning D: Society and Space, 1,* 3–21.

Catanese, A. J. (1984). *The politics of planning and development.* Beverly Hills, CA: Sage Publications.

Centraal Bureau voor de Statistiek (1984). *Statistisch zakboek.* Gravenhage: Staatsuitgevery.

Choldin, H. M. (1985). *Cities and suburbs: An introduction to urban sociology.* New York: McGraw-Hill.

Clark, T. N. (1985). Urban policy analysis. *Annual Review of Sociology, 11,* 437–455.

Clarke, S. E. (1984). Neighborhood policy options. *American Planning Association Journal,* Autumn, 493–502.

Deane, P. (1969). *The first industrial revolution.* Cambridge: Cambridge University Press.

Den Draak, J. (1985). Housing in the context of revitalization policies. In W. Van Vliet--, E. Huttman, & S. Fava (Eds.) *Housing needs and policy approaches* (pp. 305–312). Durham, NC: Duke University Press.

Downs, A. (1983). Some changing aspects of neighborhoods in the United States. *Urban Law and Policy, 6,* 65–74.

Dreitzel, H. (1977). On the political meaning of culture. In N. Birnbaum (Ed.), *Beyond the crisis* (pp. 83–132). New York: Oxford University Press.

Dunn, W. N. (1985). *Methods of the second type: On coping with the wilderness of public policy analysis.* Paper prepared for presentation at the Annual Research Conference, Association for Public Policy and Management, Washington, DC, October 26.

Engels, F. (1958). *The condition of the working class in England in 1844.* Oxford: Basil Blackwell. (Original work published 1845)

England, J. L., & Albrecht, S. L. (1984). Boomtowns and social disruption. *Rural Sociology, 49*(2), 230–246.

Feagin, J. R. (1983). *The urban real estate game: Playing monopoly with real money.* Englewood Cliffs, NJ: Prentice-Hall.

Feagin, J. R., & Shelton, B. A. (1985). Community organizing in Houston: Social problems and community response. *Community Development Journal, 20*(2), 99–105.

Firey, W., Loomis, C. P., & Beegle, J. A. (1957). The fusion of urban and rural. In P. Hatt & A. J. Reiss, Jr. (Eds.), *Cities and society* (pp. 214–222). New York. Free Press.

Fischer, C. S. (1984). *The urban experience* (2nd ed.). New York: Harcourt, Brace, Jovanovich,

Fischer, C. S., Jackson, R. M., Stueve, C. A., Gerson, K., Jones, L. M., & Baldassare, M. (1977). *Networks and places: Social relations in the urban setting.* New York: Free Press.

Fish, G. S. (Ed.). (1979). *The story of housing.* New York: Macmillan.

Flaim, P. O., & Sehgal, E. (1985). Displaced workers of 1979-83: How well have they fared? *Monthly Labor Review,* June, 3–16.

Fleming, R., Baum, A., Reddy, D., & Gatchel, R. J. (1984). Behavioral and biochemical effects of job loss and unemployment stress. *Journal of Human Stress, 10,* Spring, 12–17.

Form, W. H. (1954). The place of social structure in the determination of land use: Some implications for a theory of urban ecology. *Social Forces, 32*(4), 17–23.

Forrest, R., & Murie, A. (1987). The privatization of British public housing. In W. Van Vliet-- (Ed.), *Housing markets and policies under conditions of fiscal austerity.* Westport, CT: Greenwood Press.

Franck, K. (1987). Women's housing and neighborhood needs. In E. Huttman & W. Van Vliet-- (Eds.), *Handbook of housing and the built environment in the U.S.* Westport, CT: Greenwood Press.

Freudenburg, W. (1981). Women and men in an energy boomtown: Adjustment, aliena-tion, and adaptation. *Rural Sociology, 46*(2), 220–244.

Fried, M. (1982). Residential attachment: Sources of residential and community satisfac-tion. *Journal of Social Issues, 38*(3), 107–119.

Friedman, J., & Miller, J. (1965). The urban field. *Journal of the American Institute of Planners, 31,* 312–320.

Fustel de Coulanges, N. D. (1956). *The ancient city: A study on the religion, laws, and institu-tions of Greece and Rome* (W. Small, Trans.). New York: Doubleday Anchor. (original work published 1864)

Gale, D. E. (1984). *Neighborhood revitalization and the postindustrial city.* Lexington, MA: D. C. Heath.

Gans, H. J. (1962). *The urban villagers.* New York: Free Press.

Genovese, R. G. (1983). Dilemmas in introducing activism and advocacy into urban plan-ning. In J. R. Blau, M. LaGory, & J. S. Pipkin (Eds.), *Professionals and urban form* (pp. 320–339). Albany: State University of New York Press.

Gershuny, J. (1978). *After industrial society?* Atlantic Highlands, NJ: Humanities Press.

Gold, S. M. (1972). The non-use of neighbourhood parks. *Journal of the American Planning Institute, 38,* 369–378.

Goldstein, H. A. (1984). Planning as argumentation. *Environment and Planning B: Planning and Design, 11,* 297–312.

Gordon, D. M. (1977). *Problems in political economy* (2nd ed.). Lexington, MA: D. C. Heath.

Granovetter, M. (1984). Small is bountiful: Labor markets and establishment size. *American Sociological Review, 49,* 323–334.

Habermas, J. (1979). *Legitimationsprobleme in Spatkapitalismus.* Frankfurt am Main, West Germany.

Habermas, J. (1981). *Theorie des kommunikativen Handelns.* Frankfurt am Main, West Germany.

Habraken. (1972). *Supports: An alternative to mass housing.* New York: Praeger.

Hallman, H. W. (1984). *Neighborhoods: Their place in urban life.* Beverly Hills, CA: Sage Publications.

Hammond, M. (1972). *The city in the ancient world.* Cambridge, MA: Harvard University Press.

Harmon, P., & King, D. (1985). *Expert systems: Artificial intelligence in business.* New York: Wiley.

Harris, C. D., & Ullman, E. L. (1945). The nature of cities. *Annals of the American Academy of Political and Social Science, 424,* 7–17.

Hawley, A. H. (1981). *Urban society; an ecological approach.* New York: Wiley.

Hill, R. C. (1983). Markets, state, and community: National urban policy in the 1980s. *Urban Affairs Quarterly, 19,*(1), 5–20.

Hillery, G. A. (1955). Definitions of community: Areas of agreement. *Rural Sociology, 20,* 111–123.

Hohenberg, P. M., & Lees, L. H. (1985). *The making of urban Europe 1000–1950.* Cambridge: Harvard University Press.

Hole, V. (1966). *Children's play on housing estates* (Ministry of Technology, National Building Series Research Paper 3g). London: Her Majesty's Stationery Office.

Johnson, M. S. (1985). Metropolitan dependence on intergovernmental aid. *Social Science Quarterly, 66,* 713–723.

Karp, D. A., Stone, G. P., & Yoels, W. C. (1977). *Being urban: A social psychological view of city life.* Lexington, MA: D. C. Heath.

Lee, B. A., Oropesa, R. S., Metch, B. J., & Guest, A. M. (1984). Testing the decline-of-community thesis: Neighborhood organizations in Seattle 1929 and 1979. *American Journal of Sociology, 89*(5), 1161–1188.

Leighton, B., & Wellman, B. (1979, March). Networks, neighborhoods, and communities: Approaches to the study of the community question. *Urban Affairs Quarterly, 14*(3), 363–390.

Liebschutz, S. F. (1984). Community development dynamics: National goals and local priorities. *Environment and Planning C: Government and Policy, 2,* 295–305.

Lipman, A. (1969). The architectural belief system and social behaviour. *British Journal of Sociology, 20*(2), 190–204.

Logan, J. R. (1983). The disappearance of communities from national urban policy. *Urban Affairs Quarterly, 19*(1), 75–90.

Marshall, J. N. & Bachtler, J. F. (1984). Spatial perspectives on technological changes in the banking sector in the U.K. *Environment and Planning A, 16,* 437–450.

Matras, J. (1977). *Introduction to population: A sociological approach.* Englewood Cliffs, NJ: Prentice-Hall.

McLuhan, H. M. (1968). *War and peace in the global village.* New York: McGraw-Hill.

Melbin, M. (1978). Night as frontier. *American Sociological Review, 43,* 3–22.

Meny, Y. (1983). Permanence and change: The relations between central government and local authorities in France. *Environment and Planning C: Government and Policy, 1,* 17–28.

Meyersohn, M. (1963). National character and urban development. *Urban Policy, 12,* 78–96.

Michelson, W. (1976a). *Man and his urban environment.* Reading, MA: Addison-Wesley.

Michelson, W. (1976b). *Reversing the "inevitable" trend: High-rise housing in Sweden and Denmark* (Research Paper No. 79). Toronto: Centre for Urban and Community Studies, University of Toronto.

Michelson, W. (1977). From congruence to antecedent conditions: A search for the basis of environmental improvement. In D. Stokols (Ed.), *Perspectives on Environment and Behavior* (pp. 205–219). New York: Plenum Press.

Michelson W. (1980). Long and short range criteria for housing choice and environmental behavior. *Journal of Social Issues, 36*(3), 135–149.

Michelson, W. (1985). *From sun to sun: Daily obligations and community structure in the lives of employed women and their families.* Totowa, NJ: Rowman & Allanheld.

Michelson, W. (1987). Congruence: The evolution of a concept. In W. Van Vliet--, H. Choldin, W. Michelson, & D. Popenoe (Eds.), *Housing and neighborhoods: Theoretical and empirical contributions.* Westport, CT: Greenwood Press.

Misztal, B., & Misztal, B. (1987). Scarce state resources and unrestrained processes in the socialist city: The case of housing. In W. Van Vliet-- (Ed.), *Housing markets and policy under fiscal austerity.* Westport, CT: Greenwood Press.

Mitroff, I., & Emshoff, J. (1979). On strategic assumption making: A dialectical approach to policy and planning. *Academy of Management Review, 4*(1), 1–12.

Molotch, H. (1976). The city as a growth machine: Toward a political economy of place. *American Journal of Sociology, 82,* 309–332.

Morton, H. (in press). Housing in the Soviet Union. In W. Van Vliet-- (Ed.), *The international handbook of housing policies and practices.* Westport, CT: Greenwood Press.

Mumford, L. (1938). *The culture of cities.* New York: Harcourt Brace.

Olbrich, J. (1984). Regional policy and management jobs: The locational behaviour of corporate headquarters in West Germany. *Environment and Planning C: Government and Policy, 2,* 219–238.

Palen, J. J. (in press). Patterns of neighborhood change. In E. Huttman & W. Van Vliet--

(Ed.), *Handbook of housing and the built environment in the U.S.* Westport, CT: Greenwood Press.

Parkes, D. N., & Thrift, N. J. (1980). *Times, spaces, and places; a chronogeographic perspective.* New York: Wiley.

Parsons, T. (1937). *The structure of social action.* New York: McGraw-Hill.

Pirenne, H. (1956). *Medieval cities.* Garden City, NY: Doubleday Anchor. (Original publication in 1925)

Platt, C. (1976). *The English medieval town.* New York: David McKay.

Popenoe, D. (1965). On the meaning of "urban" in urban studies. *Urban Affairs Quarterly,* *1*(1), 65–82.

Popenoe, D. (1985). *Private pleasure, public plight; American metropolitan community life in comparative perspective.* New Brunswick, NJ: Transaction Books.

Poplin, D. E. (1979). *Communities: A survey of theories and methods research* (2nd ed.). New York: Macmillan.

Pred, A. R. (1966). *The spatial dynamics of urban-industrial growth: 1800-1914.* Cambridge: M.I.T. Press.

Quante, W. (1976). *The exodus of corporate headquarters from New York City.* New York: Praeger.

Rapoport, A. (1969). *House form and culture.* Englewood Cliffs, NJ: Prentice-Hall.

Rapoport, A. (1977). *Human aspects of urban form: Towards a man-environment approach to urban form and design.* New York: Pergamon Press.

Redburn, F. S., & Buss, T. F. (Eds.). (1984). Introduction. In *Public Policies for Distressed Communities* (pp. ix–xii). Lexington, MA: D. C. Heath.

Regional Plan Association. (1975). *Growth and settlement in the U.S.: Past trends and future issues* (RPA Bulletin #125). New York: RPA.

Riger, S., & Lavrakas, P. J. (1981). Community ties: Patterns of attachment and social interaction in urban neighborhoods. *American Journal of Community Psychology, 9*(1), 55–66.

Rivlin, L. G. (1982). Group membership and place meanings in an urban neighborhood. *Journal of Social Issues, 38*(3), 75–93.

Sassen-Koob, S. (1985). Capital mobility and labor migration: Their expression in core cities. In M. Timberlake (Ed.), *Urbanization in the World-Economy.* Orlando, FL: Academic Press.

Saunders, P. (1981). *Social theory and the urban question.* New York: Holmes & Meier, 1981.

Schumacher, E. F. (1973). *Small is beautiful: Economics as if people mattered.* New York: Perennial Library.

Schwanke, D. (1985). Advanced technology for small tenants. *Urban Land, 44*(1), 16–19.

Schwartz, B. (Ed.). (1976). *The changing face of the suburbs.* Chicago: University of Chicago Press.

Shevky, E., & Bell, W. (1955). *Social area analysis.* Stanford: Stanford University Press.

Sillince, J. (in press). Housing in Hungary. In W. Van Vliet-- (Ed.), *The international handbook of housing policies and practices.* Westport, CT: Greenwood Press.

Simmie, J. M. (1983). Beyond the industrial city? *Journal of the American Planning Association,* Winter, 59–76.

Simon, J. C., & Wekerle, G. (1987). The miniaturization of an urban neighborhood: The residents' response. In W. Van Vliet--, H. Choldin, W. Michelson, & D. Popenoe (Eds.), *Housing and Neighborhoods: Theoretical and empirical contributions from North America and Europe.* Westport, CT: Greenwood Press.

Sjoberg, G. (1960). *The preindustrial city.* New York: Free Press.

Steinberger, P. J. (1984). Urban politics and communality. *Urban Affairs Quarterly, 20*(1), 4–21.

Stopford, J. M., & Dunning, J. H. (1983). The scope and pattern of multinational enterprise activity in the early 1980s. In *The World Directory of Multinational Enterprises 1982-1983, Company Performance & Global Trends*. Detroit: Gale Research Co.

Studer, R., & Van Vliet--, W. (1987, March). Sociophysical congruence as a problem of supply and demand. *Architecture and Behaviour, 3*(2).

Thompson, W. R. (1965). *A preface to urban economics*. Baltimore: The John Hopkins Press.

Timms, D. W. G. (1971). *The urban mosaic*. Cambridge, MA: Cambridge University Press.

Tsai, Y., & Sigelman, L. (1982). The community question: A perspective from national survey data—the case of the USA. *The British Journal of Sociology, 33*(4), 579–588.

Tuan, Y. (1974). *Topophilia: A study of environmental perception, attitude, and values*. Englewood Cliffs, NJ: Prentice-Hall.

Unger, D. G., & Wandersman, A. (1985). The importance of neighbors: The social, cognitive and affective components of neighboring. *American Journal of Community Psychology, 13*(2), 139–169.

U.S. Bureau of the Census. (1985). *Statistical abstract of the United States*. Washington, DC: U.S. Government Printing Office.

Van Heek, F. (1973). *Van hoogkapitalisme naar verzorgingsstaat*. Meppel, The Netherlands: Boom.

Van Vliet--, W. (1980). An extended comment on the environment as a social symbol. *Journal of the American Planning Association, 46*(3), 337–340.

Van Vliet--, W. (1983). Families in apartment buildings: Sad storeys for children? *Environment and Behavior, 15*(2), 211–234.

Van Vliet--, W. (1985). Communities and built environments supporting women's changing roles. *Sociological Focus, 18*(2), 73–77.

Van Vliet--, W. (Ed.). (1987). *Housing markets and policies under fiscal austerity*. Westport, CT: Greenwood Press.

Van Vliet--, W., & Ritti, R. R. (in preparation). *Developmental advantage and the social organization of opportunity*.

Warner, S. B. (1962). *Streetcar suburbs: The process of growth in Boston, 1870-1900*. Cambridge, MA: Harvard University Press.

Warren, R. L. (1978). *The community in America* (3rd ed.). Chicago: Rand McNally.

Webber, M. M. (1968). The post-city age. *Daedalus, 67*, 1091–1110.

Weber, M. (1958). *The city* (D. Martindale & G. Neuwirth, Trans.). New York: Free Press. (Original work published 1921)

Wekerle, G. R. (1976). Vertical village: Social contacts in a singles high-rise complex. *Sociological Focus, 9*(3), 299–315.

Wellman, B. (1979, March). The community question. *American Journal of Sociology, 84*, 1201–1231.

Willhelm, S., & Sjoberg, G. (1960). Economic vs. protection values in urban land use change. *Journal of Ecology and Sociology, 19*, 151–160.

Wireman, P. (1984). *Urban neighborhoods, networks, and families: New forms for old values*. Lexington, MA: D. C. Heath.

Wolfe, M. (1978). Childhood and privacy. In I. Altman & J. Wohlwill (Eds.), *Children and the Environment* (pp. 175–222). New York: Plenum Press.

Wollmann, H. (in press). Housing in West Germany. In W. Van Vliet-- (Ed.), *The international handbook of housing policies and practices*. Westport, CT: Greenwood Press.

Index